"There is only one book you need to read for a comprehensi[ve] [overview of]
the field of political marketing – the third edition of *Political [Marketing:
Principles and] Applications*. The book not only details the latest academic stu[dies but]
real-world examples, case studies and applications for practitioners. And, of course, no
one knows the field of political marketing better than Jennifer Lees-Marshment."

*Professor Travis N. Ridout, Thomas S. Foley Distinguished
Professor of Government and Public Policy,
Washington State University, US*

"Political marketing is going through fundamental transitions as we move further into the
world of instant news and grassroots activism fuelled by social media. In this new world,
misinformation and misdirection have been upsetting social and political norms. Jennifer
Lees-Marshment's new edition comes at a critical time, giving us highly relevant case
studies and sharp, perceptive analyses of today's politics and political marketing. This is
an excellent addition to the literature and is highly recommended."

*Emeritus Professor Dennis Johnson, George
Washington University, US*

"The strategies, tools, and tactics offered by the practice of political marketing continue
to influence and shape both election campaigns and approaches to governing. This book
is essential reading for anyone interested in understanding how political marketing works
and why it matters."

*Associate Professor Anna Esselment, University
of Waterloo, Canada*

"Led by a pre-eminent scholar – who has personally developed more than her fair share
of the concepts – this book covers the key ideas that anyone studying the field of political
marketing needs to know. The examples are numerous and fascinating, helping the book
do a great job of illustrating the importance of political marketing. I'd wholeheartedly
recommend this book."

*Associate Professor Neil Bendle,
Ivey Business School, Canada*

"It is almost impossible to imagine modern politics without political marketing, even
though many people in politics and many people who study it are still reluctant to recognise that marketing is what they are doing. This updated edition of an indispensable
textbook will help students explore all aspects of an activity that is central to the way the
world works these days – and, perhaps, to understand it better than many of the politicians
who are involved in it!"

*Professor Roger Mortimore, Professor of Public Opinion &
Political Analysis, Kings College London, UK*

"A comprehensive and accessible book which covers both theory and practice, providing
students with academic knowledge but directing them to apply it, and discussing the skills
to acquire to enter professions related to political marketing."

Dr Chris Rudd, University of Otago, New Zealand

Political Marketing

Substantially revised throughout, the third edition of *Political Marketing* continues to offer students the most comprehensive introduction to this rapidly growing field. It provides an accessible but in-depth guide to what political marketing is and how it is used in practice and encourages reflection on how it should be used in the future.

New features and benefits of the third edition:

- Fully updated throughout with new research on emerging practices in the field and ethical implications such as the use of big data, authenticity and the limitations of voters as consumers in light of Brexit;
- A new employability section on political marketing in the workplace;
- Extensive pedagogical features including new peer-reviewed case studies, democratic debates, and fully updated practitioner perspectives, best practice guides, and class discussion points and assessments.

Led by a leading expert in the field and including contributions from other key academics in the field, this textbook is essential reading for all students of political marketing, parties and elections, and of comparative politics.

Jennifer Lees-Marshment is an Associate Professor at the University of Auckland, New Zealand. She is a world expert in political marketing, having authored the highly cited 'Market-Oriented Party Model', and is editor of the book series *Palgrave Studies in Political Marketing and Management*.

Brian Conley is an Associate Professor in the Government Department at Suffolk University in Boston, US. His research and teaching interests are in the areas of political parties, the US electoral politics and political marketing. With Jennifer Lees-Marshment and Kenneth Cosgrove he co-edited *Political Marketing in the United States* (2014).

Edward Elder's research focuses on political marketing and communication in New Zealand and the United States. He published the book *Marketing Leadership in Government* (2016) and worked as an analyst for *Vote Compass* leading into the 2017 New Zealand general election.

Robin Pettitt is a Senior Lecturer at Kingston University, London, UK, who specialises in the internal life of political parties and is currently writing a book on how parties recruit and retain their activists.

Vincent Raynauld is an Assistant Professor in the Department of Communication Studies at Emerson College, Boston, US. His areas of research interest and publication include political communication, political marketing, social media, research methods, e-politics, elections, and journalism.

André Turcotte is an Associate Professor in the Riddell Graduate Program in Political Management and the School of Journalism and Communication at Carleton University in Ottawa, Canada. His research focuses on elections, market intelligence and opinion research, and he has advised politicians at all levels of government in Canada.

Political Marketing

Principles and Applications

Third edition

Jennifer Lees-Marshment, Brian Conley, Edward Elder, Robin Pettitt, Vincent Raynauld and André Turcotte

Routledge
Taylor & Francis Group

LONDON AND NEW YORK

Third edition published 2019
by Routledge
2 Park Square, Milton Park, Abingdon, Oxon OX14 4RN

and by Routledge
52 Vanderbilt Avenue, New York, NY 10017

Routledge is an imprint of the Taylor & Francis Group, an informa business

First edition published by Routledge 2009
Second edition published by Routledge 2014

British Library Cataloguing in Publication Data
A catalogue record for this book is available from the British Library

Library of Congress Cataloging in Publication Data
Names: Lees-Marshment, Jennifer, author.
Title: Political marketing : principles and applications / Jennifer Lees-
    Marshment, Brian Conley, Edward Elder, Robin Pettitt, Vincent
    Raynauld and Andrâe Turcotte.
Description: Third edition, Revised edition. | New York : Routledge, 2019. |
    "Second edition published by Routledge 2014"—T.p. verso. | Includes
    bibliographical references and index.
Identifiers: LCCN 2018058618| ISBN 9780815353201 (hardback) | ISBN
    9780815353225 (paperback) | ISBN 9781351136907 (master ebook) |
    ISBN 9781351136891 (web pdf) | ISBN 9781351136884 (ePub) | ISBN
    9781351136877 (mobipocket/kindle)
Subjects: LCSH: Campaign management. | Political campaigns. |
    Marketing—Political aspects.
Classification: LCC JF2112.C3 L44 2019 | DDC 324.7/3—dc23
LC record available at https://lccn.loc.gov/2018058618

ISBN: 978-0-8153-5320-1 (hbk)
ISBN: 978-0-8153-5322-5 (pbk)
ISBN: 978-1-351-13690-7 (ebk)

Typeset in Times New Roman
by Swales & Willis Ltd, Exeter, Devon, UK

Printed and bound in Great Britain by
TJ International Ltd, Padstow, Cornwall

Contents

3   Political market research   **53**

ANDRÉ TURCOTTE AND JENNIFER LEES-MARSHMENT

Figures

Tables

Boxes

About the authors

Brian Conley is the Director of Graduate Studies and an Associate Professor in the Government Department at Suffolk University in Boston. His principal research and teaching interests are in the areas of political parties, US electoral politics, and political marketing and communication. His research and writing have appeared in *Studies in American Political Development, American Review of Politics, Journal of American Studies* and *Political Science Quarterly*, as well as in numerous political anthologies on US politics. In 2014, he edited, with Kenneth Cosgrove and Jennifer Lees-Marshment, *Political Marketing in the United States* for Routledge. Current research projects include a book with Routledge examining the rise of the conservative Right within the Republican Party between Goldwater and Trump. He received his PhD in Political Science from the New School for Social Research in New York City.

Edward Elder is a PhD graduate from the University of Auckland whose research focuses on political marketing and communication in New Zealand and the US. His work can be found in books such as *Marketing Leadership in Government, Political Marketing in the 2016 U.S. Presidential Election* and *Political Marketing and Management in the 2017 New Zealand Election*. He also worked as an analyst for *Vote Compass* leading into the 2017 New Zealand general election.

Jennifer Lees-Marshment is an Associate Professor at the University of Auckland, New Zealand. She is a world expert in political marketing, having authored the highly cited 'Market-Oriented Party Model' and founded the UK PSA Political Marketing Group early in her career, and having organised many events and edited special issues and books since. She is an author/editor of fifteen books, including *Political Marketing and Management in the 2017 New Zealand Election* (Palgrave 2018), *The Political Marketing Game* (Palgrave Macmillan 2011) and *The Routledge Handbook of Political Marketing* (2012). Jennifer has interviewed over 200 political practitioners including advisors to Prime Ministers and Presidents. She has given keynotes and held visiting professorships around the world and is also editor of the book series *Palgrave Studies in Political Marketing and Management*. Her most recent work, *The Ministry of Public Input* (Palgrave 2015), won the IAP2 Australasia Research Award and she is currently working on a new book, *Political Management*. See www.lees-marshment.org for further details.

Robin Pettitt is a Senior Lecturer at Kingston University – London. He specialises in the internal life of political parties and is currently writing a book on how parties recruit and retain their activists. His main area of expertise is the role of members in the internal life of political parties, including policy making and campaigning. He has published on party conferences, internal political marketing and the rhetoric of party leaders. Robin teaches on British politics, with an emphasis on 'authentic assessment' that replicates 'real life' tasks in politics, and research methods.

Vincent Raynauld is an Assistant Professor in the Department of Communication Studies at Emerson College (Boston, US) and Affiliate Professor in the Département de lettres et communication sociale at Université du Québec à Trois-Rivières. He is also serving as a Member of the Université Paris-Est Créteil-based research network Réseau Démocratie Électronique (Paris, France), as Research Associate in the Groupe de Recherche en Communication Politique (GRCP) (Canada), as Academic Advisor for the non-profit research organisation Samara (Canada), as a Member of the North American Digital Diplomacy Initiative (NACDI), and as International Vice-Chair of the PSA Political Marketing Group. His areas of research interest and publication include political communication, political marketing, social media, research methods, e-politics, elections and journalism.

André Turcotte is Associate Professor at Carleton University's School of Journalism and Communication as well as in the Riddell Graduate Program in Political Management. His research focuses on elections, market intelligence and opinion research. He has also advised politicians at all levels of government in Canada and provided opinion research advice to many of Canada's leading private sector firms and government organisations.

Acknowledgements

For the third edition, I was grateful to share the burden of updating this book with colleagues from Canada, the US, the UK and New Zealand. I very much appreciate André, Brian, Edward, Robin and Vincent being willing to share the load of reading new literature, updating examples, assessments and case studies, and completing work on time. Vincent, Brian and Edward also provided valuable review of my chapters. As well as lightening the load, it made the process so much more enjoyable and added valuable fresh perspectives.

I would also like to acknowledge the University of Auckland's School of Social Sciences for providing funding for a research assistant to help me complete the branding chapter and PhD student Joyce Manyo for completing that work. Summer scholar Alexa Frost also undertook identifying and collecting political marketing literature published since 2014, which all chapters draw on.

Routledge had the foresight back in 2008 to see the potential for a textbook in this field, and it's work to facilitate the book's success has enabled us to be in the position to produce a third edition. Making market demand line up with pioneering research in new fields is not an easy task and I very much appreciate the publisher's ability to get this right. They have significantly contributed to supporting scholarship and learning in the field of political marketing.

Furthermore, I wish to thank Ken Cosgrove, Phil Harris, Dennis Johnson, Michael Mintrom, Jenny Lloyd, André Turcotte, Andrew Hughes and Gordica Karanfilovska, who have provided significant support to me in the past few years in particular.

This book is dedicated to my current and former students in New Zealand – some of whom are now practicing political marketing – who have helped to sustain my faith in the importance of researching and teaching political marketing.

Jennifer Lees-Marshment, University of Auckland,
New Zealand, 1 October 2018
www.lees-marshment.org

This book is supported by an online resource site which is annually updated with new academic literature, audio-visual links and websites, which provide further reading and links to clips to use in teaching political marketing: www.political-marketing.org.

1 Introduction to political marketing

by Jennifer Lees-Marshment

Political marketing is a fundamental part of political life. A large number of political players, including presidents and prime ministers, politicians and parties, as well as government departments and councils turn to marketing in their pursuit of political goals. Market research is used when deciding on their policies and service design, to help them understand what the people they serve and seek votes from want and need; voter profiling helps create new segments to target; strategy guides the creation of the political brand to develop an attractive vision; internal marketing guides the provision of volunteer involvement; analytics and experimental research test and refine communication messages; and delivery management sets expectations and helps to convey progress once a politician is elected or a programme has begun. Political marketing is complex, broad and constantly evolving, as this third edition is testament to. No longer confined to advertising or campaigns, marketing influences policy development and leadership decisions. In government, significant resources are devoted to policy research, marketing and branding whole nations. Politicians use communication to build long-term relationships with voters rather than just sell their product.

Just as the practical impact of political marketing on governing, policymaking, party politics and electioneering is deep, wide and ongoing, so is its potential democratic impact. Once very much a hidden activity, uses of marketing in politics have now moved onto the agenda since the impact of big data forms of market research on online advertising during the US 2016 Election and the 2016 Brexit Referendum in the UK became public. Political marketing raises many ethical questions, but its democratic impact is multifaceted, varied and depends on how political practitioners choose to use the tools and concepts that marketing offers. The world depicted in movies such as *Game Change, Wag the Dog, The Iron Lady, The Ides of March* and *No* and television series such as *House of Cards, The West Wing, VEEP* and *Scandal* may portray more extreme practices, but there is no doubt that modern politics cannot function without marketing. Mainstream media increasingly feature discussions about political marketing, whether they relate to political branding or uses of big data.

As an area of academic research, practice and teaching, political marketing is a modern and dynamic field seeking to understand, learn from, comment on and even influence practitioner behaviour. Not bound by positivist methods or grand philosophies, political marketing explores a range of political behaviours from a strategic perspective that is both analytical and applied. It considers what works, not just what has happened in the past, and what organisations and practitioners should do as well as what they might have been successful at or done wrong. It is continually updated with passing elections, governments, policies and technologies.

Applicable to the real world, political marketing attracts students who want to explore a subject they can use after graduation. It offers fresh perspectives on old questions; taking the normally profit-oriented marketing analysis into an arena where values are still important, and contributing applied research to classic issues of leadership, citizenship, ethics, ideology, beliefs, policy and principles.

This book provides an accessible synthesis of academic research on political marketing, featuring diverse theories and global empirical examples. It seeks to explain what political marketing is and how it is used in practice, and to encourage reflection on how it should be used in future.

The book is organised into seven core chapters covering strategy (Chapter 2 on political strategy and Chapter 4 on political branding), researching (Chapter 3 on political market research), organising (Chapter 5 on internal political marketing) and communicating (Chapter 6 on broadcast political marketing communication, Chapter 7 on relational political marketing communication and Chapter 8 on political delivery marketing), with a concluding chapter which summarises the effectiveness of political marketing and debates the ethical implications. This introductory chapter explains:

- The basic components of political marketing, including overall definition, goals, market, product, tools and approaches.
- Why marketing, communication and politics students should study political marketing.
- Researching and teaching political marketing, including the relationship to political science and marketing, the pragmatist research philosophy, and barriers to researching and teaching the field.

The basic components of political marketing

Political marketing is about how political organisations and practitioners – including candidates, politicians, leaders, parties, governments and NGOs – use marketing tools and concepts to build understanding of and develop products in response to the market, and to involve as well as to communicate and interact with their political markets in order to achieve their goals.

Political marketing offers a range of tools and approaches, and how these are used varies depending on the nature of the organisation or practitioner's goals, market and product.

Political goals

Political goals are wide-ranging. Political marketing is not just focused on winning an election; political goals are more intangible, normative and values-based than that. Elections are just the means to a bigger, nobler end of wanting to make the world a better place. For some, getting into power is a step on the way to achieving such an end. Others may never stand a chance of getting into government but can nevertheless exert significant influence on debate and policy. Political practitioners hold a range of ambitions:

1. Create policy change, including putting issues on the agenda, attracting public support, communicating the vision and passing legislation.
2. Improve representation of minorities such as disabled persons or an ethnic group.
3. Change behaviour in society such as reducing drink driving.
4. Gain support from new segments in the market such as the healthy pensioners.

5   Create a long-term positive relationship with voters in a district, constituency, electorate or riding.
6   Increase the number and activity levels of volunteers in a campaign, party or movement.
7   Win control of government or become a coalition partner in government.
8   Manage expectations of leaders.
9   Get credit for delivery.
10 Attract more support or votes.

The relative importance of such goals varies, of course, depending on the party, candidate, electoral environment and the rules of the marketplace. For major parties, the goal is to win enough votes in general elections to win control of government and to do whatever is necessary to achieve this. Minor parties tend to be more interested in advancing a particular cause or influencing debate. Individual candidates are more interested in their particular seats than the overall party's success. Furthermore, once a party or candidate gets into power, the priority of goals can change again.

The political market

The political market is also more complex than just voters. Mortimore and Gill (2010, 257) argue that 'a wise party will not confine its opinion research to the voting public. Political parties, like companies, are dependent on various stakeholders and suppliers.' Political stakeholders include all those interested and with an investment in the party or candidate, such as members or volunteers within a political party or campaign, other politicians, lobbyists, interest groups, donors, the media, professional associations or unions, electoral commissions, and party or government staff (see Figure 1.1).

   The importance of different stakeholders differs from one organisation to another – and for politicians and parties, between opposition and government. From an ethical perspective, as Hughes and Dann (2009, 252) argue, once in government politicians need to meet 'the broader stakeholder needs of society,' not just their own target markets. Pragmatically, all stakeholders could potentially impact the ability of a political organisation or actor to achieve their goals. Once in government, politicians need to consult with key groups affected by each proposed policy and will get lobbied by interest groups regarding their proposed legislation – otherwise delivery will be impaired.

   One other aspect of the political market is culture. Kiss (2013, 71) notes that cultural factors also influence political marketing activities, as leaders adopt certain messages, gestures and deeds to respond to social, sports and cultural aspects of the country they are campaigning in. This can include traditional cultural activities such as baseball in the US, hockey in Canada, football in the UK and rugby in New Zealand. It can be targeted at sub-national ethnic groups, with politicians appearing at religious festivals and events or sampling traditional food. Understanding both who their stakeholders are and what the culture is can help political elites be seen to understand, represent and connect with their different publics.

The political product

The political product is not just policies but the entire behaviour of a political organisation or practitioner, including political figures and volunteers, not all of which are

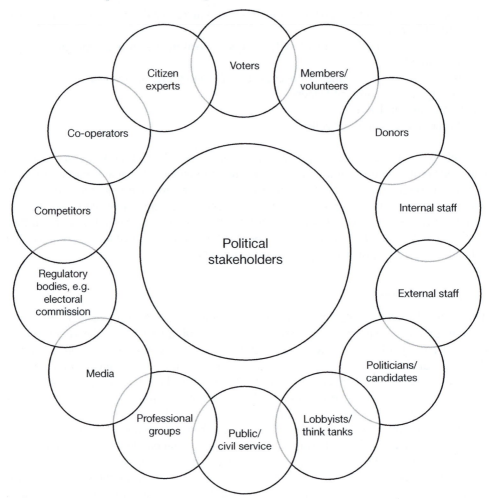

Figure 1.1 The different stakeholders in politics

controllable or tangible. The political product is also constantly evolving and is never complete – it isn't like an iPhone that is manufactured and can be picked up from a shop. It thus includes:

1   Leadership/the candidate – their powers, image, character, support/appeal, relationship with the rest of the party organisation (advisors, cabinet, members, MPs), relationship with the media.
2   Members of the legislature (senators, MPs)/candidates for election – e.g. their nature, activity, how representative of society they are.
3   Membership or official supporters – their powers, recruitment, nature (ideological character, activity, loyalty, behaviour, relationship to leader).
4   Staff (researchers, professionals, advisors, etc.) – their role, influence, office powers, relationship with other parts of the party organisation.
5   Symbols – name, logo, anthem.

6   Constitution/rules.
7   Activities – meetings, conferences, rallies.
8   Policies – proposed, current and those implemented in power.

Political marketing functional tools

Marketing techniques which are ubiquitous in business are increasingly common in politics. They offer politicians new ways of engaging with and responding to an increasingly demanding electorate. Political marketing offers political elites a range of functional tools they can use to achieve their goals of obtaining support from their market for their product (see Figure 1.2).

First, there are a range of political market research tools that enable political actors to identify and understand the public and other markets. Market research includes the usual quantitative and qualitative techniques, such as polls and focus groups, but also role play and deliberation and, more recently, big data and market surveillance. Segmentation and voter profiling helps politicians understand voters and volunteers at an individual level to then connect them into new groups that they can target. Strategies include: positioning, which suggests that parties and candidates need to take account of the competition and ensure they occupy a distinctive, superior position from which they can attract support; adopting a sales- or market-orientation towards electioneering, which involves either focusing on using research to create effective communication to sell the product to the voter or utilising the results of research to create a product that the voter will desire because it meets their needs and wants; and political branding to create a long-term sustainable relationship with voters, which includes developing positive brand personalities for leaders, superior brand equity over competing parties and nation branding.

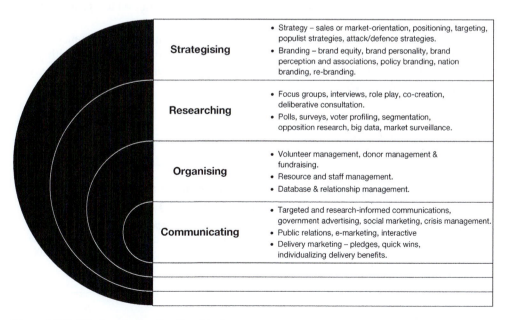

Figure 1.2 Political marketing functional tools

Political marketing offers tools for organising effectively, such as for internal party marketing and volunteer management. Communication includes selling but also strategies to build up long-term relationships with voters, including targeted communication, market-oriented political advertising, e-marketing, public relations, governing leadership communication and relational communications. Delivery marketing includes using pledges, communicating delivery challenges, managing problems in delivery, and communicating progress and success, including delivering quick wins and individualizing delivery.

Each element of political marketing – from the four areas of researching, strategising, organising and communicating – connects with and influences each other. While segmentation might take place under market research, it is then used to inform communication, strategic product development and voter profiling in GOTV campaigns. To be most effective, political marketing is not just about cherry-picking one or two tools from marketing; it is about an overall framework of interrelated activities that politicians can use to achieve a range of goals in a way they are comfortable with.

Political marketing approaches

Political marketing is also about a way of thinking about, relating to or approaching the public. Political marketing approaches can have a profound impact on the effectiveness of political marketing tools.

Political marketing as selling

Political marketing is commonly seen as equalling selling, placing the emphasis on using market research to test the effectiveness of both the message and the medium in persuading key voters to switch their support for a policy, politician or party. It does not affect the political product on offer but rather how it is sold. This is referred to as sales-oriented (Lees-Marshment 2001).

How politics is sold varies: while persuasive forms of communication remain common, communication can also be used to create a long-term positive relationship with voters that can be sustained even when voters do not agree, and cannot be made to agree, with the decisions of political elites.

Political marketing as a product-based transaction strategy

Practitioner Perspective 1.1 on the importance of strategy in political marketing

Strategy is the most important thing for winning and losing elections by any measure.
The Late Lord Philip Gould, advisor to UK PM Tony Blair,
interviewed in 2007

Source: Lees-Marshment (2011)

Some academics and practitioners argue that strategy is more important in determining the effectiveness of political marketing than any other aspect or tool (see Practitioner Perspective 1.1). Elites use market research before designing and developing a product or brand to identify voter demands and then tailor their product to suit those demands. This is referred to as market-oriented (Lees-Marshment 2001). The focus is on elites changing what they do to suit voters instead of the other way round. Market-oriented approaches are transactional in focus: they say *let us know what you want, and we will offer it to you, and then you can vote for it.*

The concept of a market-orientation in politics has attracted a lot of discussion because it changes the status of political elites in relation to the public; on one hand requiring politicians to listen to voters more, and on the other resulting in elected officials having less room to show leadership and make the 'right' decisions for the country.

Relational political marketing

Political marketing practice also includes a more relational strategy, using marketing to create long-term positive relationships between voters and political elites that help sustain politicians in times of crisis or failure and enable them to enact transformational leadership decisions. Voters are still listened to, but as Jackson (2013, 252) notes, the approach is to build 'relationships centred on dialogue, which leads to trust and empathy'.

In 2010, Anita Dunn, who was President Obama's first White House Communications Director and Senior Strategic Advisor for the 2008 Obama campaign, delivered a keynote at the APSA (American Political Science Association) Political Marketing Workshop. Dunn argued that political marketing is changing from being transaction based – *'this is the product I offer to you'* – to transformational – *'work with me to create change'.* Voters want to be engaged and get involved rather than be seen as consumers of a political product.

Research in the *Routledge Handbook of Political Marketing* (Lees-Marshment 2012) suggested a movement towards seeing internal stakeholders as integral to successful political marketing and to long-term, mutual and interactive communication, and towards using marketing to help create room for leadership. Practitioners can therefore choose more dialogical and transformational approaches to achieve and maintain relationships with political consumers over the long term.

Experiential or co-creation political marketing

An alternative concept is experiential marketing, suggested by Jackson (2013), which is focused on involving the consumer in an active experience with the brand. Voters are not just spectators but feel part of the event. Work in the *Routledge Handbook of Political Marketing* also suggested that political market research was increasingly used to involve the political consumer in answering the question of how to meet voter demands, with the public asked to step into the decision makers' shoes and help to solve the problems (Lees-Marshment 2012, 373). Figure 1.3 integrates all of these approaches to show a potential pathway from sales-oriented political marketing to one that is more about co-production.

Political marketing is therefore complex and diverse. This book will outline a wide range of ways in which it is used in government, politics and elections.

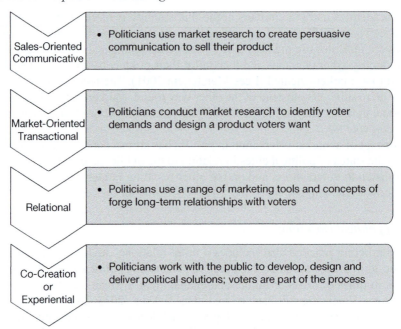

Figure 1.3 The development of political marketing approaches

Why marketing, communication and politics students should study political marketing

The importance of political marketing to political science, marketing and communication has been documented extensively by academics. Political scientists Savigny and Temple (2010, 1049) observe how 'contemporary politics has become dominated by the use of marketing strategies, techniques and principles' and 'political marketing has become an important sub-field in the discipline of politics'. Similarly, Harris and Lock (2010, 43) note that political marketing is now 'a significant area of international research in contemporary marketing'. Finally, a review of recent works focusing on different aspects of political marketing, such as branding, has shown high levels of intertwinement between the fields of strategic communication as well as in marketing and political science (e.g. Lilleker 2015; Serazio 2017).

Studying political marketing not only makes students aware of a profound area of political, communications and marketing practice; it also helps them gain important employability skills and prepares them for working in a wide range of jobs (see Table 1.1). At the end of each core chapter is a section on political marketing in the workplace which discusses the range of employment opportunities.

The cross-disciplinary nature of political marketing helps students develop learning agility – the ability to take on new ideas – which employers all value in the fast-changing work landscape. For political science and communication students, it opens the door to a range of jobs enabling them to leverage the knowledge and skills acquired throughout their studies. For marketing students, it ensures they reflect on responsible business ethics and understand the nature of political as well as corporate organisations, which a pure business-school education will not prepare them for. It also helps them

Table 1.1 Benefits of studying political marketing: Employability skills and jobs in political marketing

Employability skills from studying political marketing	Jobs in political marketing
1 *Political skills* – understanding of current issues through discussing current political situations and behaviour 2 *Advisory skills* – such as impartial analysis and producing high-quality reports by evaluating contemporary political behaviour using academic theory rather than personal opinion 3 *Analytical skills* – projecting future issues/scenarios through discussions and case study/report assignments 4 *Interpersonal skills* – peer learning through small group work in seminars 5 *Leadership/Teaching skills* – for those who become discussion leaders 6 *Writing skills* – through report writing 7 *Professional workplace attributes* – such as reliability, learning agility, ability to learn new ideas, ability to work independently and ability to respond well to feedback	• **Strategy** e.g. Prime Minister's Director of Strategy, Strategy Consultant, Policy Strategist • **Market research** e.g. Data Analyst, coders, pollsters • **Branding** e.g. Branding Director, trade and enterprise • **Internal marketing** including organisational roles such as Campaign Manager, Engagement Officer, Outreach Officer, Local Organiser, Field Director, Fundraising Manager, Community Organiser • **Communication** e.g. Communications Advisor, Press Secretary, Head of PR, Marketing Director, Digital Marketer, Social Media Coordinator, Relationship Manager, Media Advisor, government relations • **Delivery** including government roles such as Head of the Delivery Unit and more traditional titles such Deputy Secretary (Results and Delivery), Executive Director and Chief of Staff

understand the political environment, which impacts on business. As Baines (2012) argues in *The Financial Times*:

> Political marketing, when it is good, has an uncanny ability to market ideology. Business schools should take note. After all, their students, many of whom will in time become managers and chief executives, will have to develop and market ideology internally, usually in the form of missions, visions and values, to gee up their constituent employees, supply-chain partners and shareholders.

Marketing, communication and political science students will gain a range of benefits from studying political marketing. This book will enable students to:

- Understand that political marketing is not just about spin or selling but is a complex and diverse activity affecting policy, leadership decisions, government and resource allocation as well as campaign management.
- Realising that principles of strategic communication are central to political marketing as they can inform strategies for reaching out to as well as sharing content and interacting with a mass public.
- Appreciate how marketing may be used within the political environment but that there are differences between marketing business and marketing politics.
- Engage in applied discussion and assessment, relating studying to practice.
- Reflect on the ethical implications of the use of marketing in politics, policy and government.
- Understand the potential roles in the workplace related to political marketing.

Box 1.1 reports what students themselves have found valuable about studying political marketing.

Box 1.1 Student comments on the value of studying political marketing

Political marketing is relevant to politics, communication and marketing today

- Political marketing you see every day in the news, everyone talks about it.
- It's about understanding what goes on in the world today.
- It is important we study political marketing because marketing ideas and concepts have penetrated much of civil society. NGOs, charities, activist groups and faith organisations use various marketing techniques to promote their cause and messages to contemporary audiences.

Political marketing has a direct career/practice link

- It's useful for future career . . . the research is something you can apply in politics.
- It opens doors . . . it's opened a lot of doors for me.
- It's a skill in demand.
- With political marketing you get out there and talk to people.
- It's a contribution . . . not just theoretical; can recommend how to improve things.
- In political marketing you can take the things you study and learn and put them into practice.
- It has practical applications – not only in elections but also in internal party/political matters as well.
- It makes you think as though you are in the workplace of politics. You are able to learn and grasp ideas that would have normally been considered as 'learn on the job' skills.

As a new field, there are more opportunities to make an impact

- Political marketing is not a dinosaur field.
- You can contribute to a field you are working on . . . so many areas where there's a gap.

Source: Graduate students' comments during a presentation to undergraduates about studying political marketing at postgraduate level, 2011, Auckland University; and comments on the Political Marketing Group Facebook page in 2014 and Political Marketing and Management Network Facebook group in 2018

The key argument is employability. Students go from studying political marketing to working in government, parties, NGOs, campaigns and consultancy companies with a clear understanding of how political marketing can work. Political marketing it is not just about knowledge for its own sake; it is applicable to the real world and useful after graduation.

Researching and teaching political marketing

Practitioner Perspective 1.2
Politics and business 'are parallel universes with their own solar systems, time zones and laws of gravity'.
Businessman and political advisor Maurice Saatchi (2008)

Despite the value of political marketing, researching and teaching the subject is not always easy in the tradition-bound, hierarchical, ivory tower profession of academia. Like all cross-disciplinary fields, or even just new areas of research, political marketing has been affected by its parent disciplines and pressure to conform to prevailing – and arguably ill-fitting – methodological approaches.

Political marketing and the disciplines of political science, communication and marketing

The basic notion that an area such as politics could use marketing was first suggested in the 1960s by Kotler and Levy. They argued that marketing, previously confined to commercial and business organisations, could be used by all organisations, including non-profit, state, public sector and charitable ones:

> The [marketing] concept of sensitively serving and satisfying human needs . . . provides a useful concept for all organisations. All organisations are formed to serve the interest of particular groups: hospitals serve the sick, governments serve the citizens, and labour unions serve the members . . . Marketing is that function of the organisation that can keep in constant touch with the organisation's consumers, read their needs, develop 'products' that meet these needs, and build a program of communications to express the organisation's purposes.
>
> (Kotler and Levy 1969, 15)

What makes politics – and the more recent field of communication – amenable to a marketing perspective is their direct or indirect interest in the relationship between elites and the market: electorate and candidates; volunteers and campaigns; audience and media. All these disciplines aim to understand how an organisation or elite acts in relation to their market and vice versa. However, it should be noted that politics is very different to business for several reasons such as:

1   Politics is not about making money, and it isn't even just about getting votes.
2   Politics is about principles, ideals and ideology, and what the world should be like, not just what works.
3   The political product has symbolic value, is intangible as well as tangible and is continually evolving.
4   There is only a limited range of political products available to 'buy', and political consumers often support one political product simply to avoid another.

5   Volunteers make up the producers' labour force, and the product is difficult to deliver.
6   Political parties exist to provide representation and to aggregate interests by reconciling a variety of conflicting individual demands.
7   Politicians are duty bound to show political leadership and judgment rather than just offer voters what they want.

The apparent ethos and even just the language of business can therefore appear at odds with politics (see Practitioner Perspective 1.2).

Business marketing concepts and techniques therefore need to be adapted to reflect political behaviour. Political marketing is created by applying marketing concepts from business to politics but not by simply imposing one upon the other. Lees-Marshment (2001) calls this process of combining the two disciplines a 'marriage' because political marketing literature needs to draw on both disciplines. Or, as an anonymous reviewer of the 1st edition of this textbook suggested, political science and marketing are the parents, and political marketing is the child of that marriage which has some of its parents' traits but is its own separate entity. As a field, it is still developing but has its own models of branding, strategy, market research, communications and delivery which are derived from, yet distinct from, pure commercial marketing models or pure political science theories. The field has its own journal, handbooks, this textbook, a book series (*Palgrave Studies in Political Marketing and Management*) and online resource (www.political-marketing. org). It is increasingly taught all around the world in political science, marketing and communication departments, and in applied politics or political management programmes in the US and Canada.

Political marketing research philosophy: Pragmatism

As a younger field of research, political marketing has not yet engaged in substantial debate on methodology. Informal discussions have often lamented the challenges of trying to make a complex field that captures interactive and related activities fit the positivist, causality-focused nature of standard political science research on elections and voting behaviour. Having reviewed new work in political marketing since 2014 for this textbook, it is heartening to see increasingly advanced methodologies and attempts to fit the quantitative, causal mode that political scientists often advocate for. However, we should also take the time to pause and consider what is the best methodological approach for our field, not for parent disciplines.

Political marketing scholars and students love their field because it captures the reality of political practice, because it is connected to what is happening in the real world and offers concepts and analysis that can be applied. Building on this basic driver in our work, I argue that the best philosophy for our field is pragmatism. Pragmatism chooses the methodology dependent on the research question, and it aims to have a potential practical application by identifying what works. One of the earliest writers on pragmatism, James (1907, 46), explains that 'the term is derived from the same Greek word πρᾶγμα, meaning action, from which our words "practice" and "practical" come.' Pragmatism is more about applied than abstract research (O'Leary 2007) and focuses on 'helping individuals solve practical problems' (Vogt 2005, 244).

Such flexibility on methodology is appropriate for a rapidly expanding field and area of practice. It also allows those who wish to pursue quantitative, positivist and causal research to do so without hindering more nuanced, interpretist, qualitative forms of research through a foolish emphasis on numbers at the expense of understanding. But above all, our end goal should be to stand independent of our 'parents', political science and marketing, and retain our interest in producing research which is useful for practice. Furthermore, in terms of ontology, pragmatists believe that reality is constantly renegotiated, debated, interpreted – that there isn't one truth – and this appeals to a field that understands the incredibly complex reality of political practice.

Pragmatism also calls for putting everything back up for questioning and rethinking. There is a revolutionary nature to pragmatism that particularly suits research on political marketing, which is ground breaking and highly original research and does not – or cannot – fit into existing modes or models. As Scammell's review of the field observes, the four Ps (product, pricing, promotion and place) 'need considerable stretching to make much sense in politics' (1999, footnote 50). James (1907, 54) emphasises that pragmatism 'stands for no particular results. It has no dogmas, and no doctrines.' Pragmatism is less different to existing theories, literatures and paradigms, and is quite prepared to challenge existing thinking or academic conventions. James (1907, 79–80) explains that:

> Pragmatism [is] a mediator and reconciler and said, borrowing the word from Papini, that she 'unstiffens' our theories. She has in fact no prejudices whatever, no obstructive dogmas, no rigid canons of what shall count as proof. She is completely genial. She will entertain any hypothesis, she will consider any evidence . . . she widens the field of search . . . Pragmatism is willing to take anything, to follow either logic or the senses and to count the humblest and most personal experiences. She will count mystical experiences if they have practical consequences . . . you see already how democratic she is. Her manners are as various and flexible, her resources as rich and endless, and her conclusions as friendly as those of mother nature.

I encourage colleagues who publish in my edited books and book series to add recommendations for practice at the end of their research. I also task students with creating advice for practitioners in their assignments. I respect the value of critiquing political behaviour, but such critiques should be utilised to facilitate better understanding of the limitations of current practice and to improve future practice. The great strength of political marketing research is its applied potential – it is useful to practice. While it is somewhat ironic to argue that as modern a field as political marketing select its home in a philosophy rooted in century-old thinking, pragmatism is a valuable methodology to adopt in our field.

Barriers to researching and teaching political marketing

As already noted, conducting cross-disciplinary research is not easy. Part of the problem is practical – political marketing requires scholars and students to learn and understand two disciplines, not just one. There are also battles to be fought against those who like to defend traditional – or siloed – academic territory, with more traditional academics claiming that political marketing is not acceptable, that it is not 'what we do' in political science or marketing.

While it is harder to dismiss political marketing the more it grows, the more students it has, and the more books it produces and sells, it remains the case that political marketing scholars face challenges in having their work recognized by internal and external performance management systems that are dominated by single-discipline, inward looking, rigid professionals and processes. Universities are not well equipped for cross-disciplinary teaching as academic departments are still very much operating in an insular way and are not well integrated with each other. It should be the case that political marketing programmes and supervision at the UG, MA and PhD level can be taught by either a political scientist or marketing scholar yet be open to students from both those disciplines and faculties; but this rarely happens. The hierarchical and siloed nature of universities sadly puts up many barriers to cutting-edge and innovative teaching.

Moreover, the very appeal of political marketing – that it is applicable to the real world – can be at odds with the more established *modus operandi* of academia, which is to create knowledge for its own sake and not to understand and improve practice. In centres and programmes of applied politics in the US, political marketing is more likely to be taught by practitioners than academics. Practitioner-focused teaching in public sector management which trains government staff is often found in business schools instead of political science departments. Political marketing and management may well end up following the same trend, which would be a shame for political science. Institutions which are prepared to be more open and buck this trend will, however, be able to be ahead of the game in capturing student interest in political marketing and enjoy significant success as a result, as shown by the programmes on political management at George Washington University in the United States and Carleton University in Canada.

As Scammell (2014, 179) concluded, 'Political marketing . . . has flourished over the past fifteen or so years . . . It has become a vibrant, sometimes anarchic, mix of analysis and advocacy, welcoming input from practitioners as well as academics from business, political and communications fields.' While concerns about the ethical and democratic implications of political marketing are both legitimate and worth respecting, this hardly calls for less attention to the field. Rather, it is an argument for putting more resources into studying an area of practice that can have so much impact on the world, as the 2016 presidential election indicates. If political marketing is a problem for democracy, then that is all the more reason for universities to research and teach students about it so they can be well informed about both the effectiveness and the ethics of political marketing before they begin to practice it themselves. The last chapter of this book will discuss the ethical implications of marketing politics so that readers can make their own choices about what to think and do about political marketing.

Summary

Political marketing is a substantial aspect of modern politics; politicians, advisors, parties, movements, NGOs, governments and even whole nations use strategy, research, branding, communication and delivery to help them achieve goals ranging from winning elections to achieving policy change. It attracts significant attention from politicians, academics, journalists and the public. Political marketing also has profound impact on the way the political world operates. The rest of this book will enable readers to better understand the concepts and techniques of political marketing, and the final chapter will summarise how to practice it effectively but also debate its ethical implications. Further resources, including links to audio-video examples of political marketing, are available on the following website: www.political-marketing.org.

Whether readers are students, scholars or practitioners, they become properly informed about scholarly research and the pragmatic application and principled implications of political marketing so they can make appropriate choices as to what to think, study, research and practice when marketing politics.

"

Discussion points

1   In your own words, describe what political marketing is about. What tools do political marketers use, and what do you think is the best approach they should take – sales-oriented communicative, market-oriented transactional, relational or co-creation/experiential?

2   List the differences and similitudes between the fields of political science, communication and marketing.

3   What are the most important goals for world leaders and the parties in your country?

4   Identify the potential stakeholders for a party or candidate, and then debate which are most important and why.

5   Describe and evaluate the product for the governing party or a local candidate in your country.

6   Identify and discuss the careers that studying political marketing might be useful preparation for.

Assessment questions

Essay/exam

1   Define political marketing, and explain what it involves in terms of tools and approaches.

2   Discuss what factors make up the political product, considering both theoretical concepts and empirical examples.

3   Explore and evaluate the nature and varying importance of the different stakeholders a political party, candidate or government needs to consider.

4   What are the differences between business and politics?

Applied

1   Assess the extent to which a political organisation or practitioner has used the different political marketing approaches – sales-oriented communicative, market-oriented transactional, relational or co-creation/experiential – and how effective each has been, making recommendations for future action.

2   Analyse the behaviour of a political organisation or figure in a recent period (such as the last election or last year), and critique how well they responded to their stakeholders, designed their political product and achieved their goals.

References

Arndt, Johan (1978). 'How broad should the marketing concept be?' *Journal of Marketing*, 42(1) (January): 101–3.

Baines, Paul (2012). 'Political marketing has lessons for business schools'. *The Financial Times*, 12 November 2012. www.ft.com/content/e58afb24-2755-11e2-abcb-00144feabdc0 (accessed 7 June 2013).

Harris, Phil and Andrew Lock (2010). 'Editorial: "Mind the gap": The rise of political marketing and a perspective on its future agenda'. *European Journal of Marketing*, 44(3/4): 297–307.

Hughes, Andrew and Stephen Dann (2009). 'Political marketing and stakeholder engagement'. *Marketing Theory*, 9(2): 243–56.

Jackson, Nigel (2013). 'General election marketing – selling a can of beans, building a favours bank or managing an event?' *Journal of Public Affairs*, 13(3): 251–9.

James, William (1907). 'Lecture II: What pragmatism means'. In *Pragmatism: A new name for some old ways of thinking*. New York: Longmans, Green and Co.

Kiss, Balázs (2013). 'Cultural paradigm contra political marketing, or two answers to the same question'. In Kōstas Gouliamos, Antonis Theocharous and Bruce Newman (eds) *Political Marketing Strategic 'Campaign Culture'*. London: Routledge, 57–73.

Kotler, Philip and Sidney J. Levy (1969). 'Broadening the concept of marketing'. *Journal of Marketing*, 33(1): 10–15.

Lees-Marshment, Jennifer (2001). 'The marriage of politics and marketing'. *Political Studies*, 49(4): 692–713.

Lees-Marshment, Jennifer (2003). 'Political marketing: How to reach that pot of gold'. *Journal of Political Marketing*, 2(1): 1–32.

Lees-Marshment, Jennifer (2011). *The Political Marketing Game*. Houndmills, UK and New York: Palgrave Macmillan.

Lees-Marshment, Jennifer (ed.) (2012). *The Routledge Handbook of Political Marketing*. London and New York: Routledge.

Lilleker, Darren G. (2015). 'Interactivity and branding: Public political communication as a marketing tool'. *Journal of Political Marketing*, 14(1–2): 111–28.

Mortimore, Roger and Mark Gill (2010). 'Implementing and interpreting market orientation in practice: lessons from the UK'. In Jennifer Lees-Marshment, Jesper Strömbäck and Chris Rudd (eds) *Global Political Marketing*. London: Routledge, 249–62.

O'Leary, Z. (2007). *'Pragmatism'. In The Social Science Jargon Buster*. London: SAGE Publications Ltd, 207–9.

Saatchi, Maurice (2008). 'Business and politics are worlds apart'. *The Financial Times*, 24 March 2008. www.ft.com/content/724f9f4c-f9a7-11dc-9b7c-000077b07658 (accessed 15 May 2008).

Savigny, Heather and Mick Temple (2010). 'Political marketing models: the curious incident of the dog that doesn't bark'. *Political Studies*, 58(5): 1049–64.

Scammell, Margaret (1999). 'Political marketing: lessons for political science'. *Political Studies*, 47(4): 718–39.

Scammell, Margaret. (2014). *Consumer Democracy: The Marketing of Politics*. New York: Cambridge University Press.

Serazio, M. (2017). 'Branding politics: Emotion, authenticity, and the marketing culture of American political communication'. *Journal of Consumer Culture*, 17(2): 225–41.

Vogt, W. Paul (ed.) (2005). 'Pragmatism'. In *Dictionary of Statistics & Methodology* (3rd ed). Thousand Oaks, CA: SAGE Publications, 244.

2 Political strategy

by Brian Conley and Jennifer Lees-Marshment

Practitioner Perspective 2.1 on the importance and complexity of strategy

Strategy is the most important thing for winning and losing elections by any measure. Unless you've got a strategy that is robust, long-term and linked to serious political projects, you're not going to win elections.
> Philip Gould, Strategy and Policy Advisor for the UK Labour Party from
> 1987 to 2005 (Lees-Marshment 2011).

Without a clear strategy, you have to jump from stump to stump. A strategy helps you to prioritise between the important and the insignificant.
> Claus Hjort Frederiksen, a minister in the Danish government led
> by Fogh (Lindholm and Prehn 2007, 20)

The first thing that you need to identify about the process of formulating strategy is that there is no one model and no one process.
> Murray McCully, New Zealand National strategist & MP/Foreign Minister,
> interviewed in 2007 (Lees-Marshment 2011)

We live in a world where we know more than we've ever known, data-predictive modeling getting better and better, and yet we get surprised in politics every week. I love that . . . You can have all the data and all the models and you get surprised.
> David Plouffe, Campaign Manager, Barack Obama 2008,
> interviewed in 2016 (Mathesian 2016)

Political marketing strategy is about how parties, candidates and governments think and plan in order to achieve their goals. It requires consideration of many different factors, including: the nature of the market, its history and culture; structure of government; and the interests of internal and external stakeholders and competitors, as well as existing resources and goals. As Barber (2005, 212) contends, political strategy is about 'the forming of objectives and implementing the tasks necessary to achieve those objectives with a pattern of consistency over time given the limitations of available resources'. Strategy is not just used to win power. It is also key, as Fischer *et al.* (2007) argue, to providing effective leadership and delivery in government. However, as Practitioner

Perspective 2.1 indicates, strategy is not something that is easy to model. Political strategy is 'often an iterative process', writes Winther Nielsen (2012, 301); 'whenever new information is obtained, it might change the strategy outlook'. Nonetheless, political marketing has developed a number of concepts and frameworks to help us understand strategy. This chapter will discuss:

- Targeting.
- Positioning.
- Market- and sales-oriented strategies.
- Populist strategies.
- Strategy and the environment.
- Measuring political strategy.
- Implementing political strategy, especially in government.
- Political strategy in the workplace.

Targeting

Targeting is about strategic resource allocation and focusing products where there is a market for them and where they will likely win the support necessary to achieve stated goals. Targeting ensures that resources go where they will be most useful and effective.

Practitioners firstly need to decide who to target. As researchers note, there are a number of ways to do this. At the most basic level, targeting involves dividing the electorate into voter groups or segments based on past voting behaviour, beginning with whether or not they were traditional supporters of a party and, if they vote, how likely they are to continue supporting a particular candidate/party. As part of its targeting strategy, campaigns or parties also have to determine whether they are going to primarily focus on their existing base or on voters they will need to either motivate or persuade to vote for them. It is also now conventional for campaigns and parties to segment 'voters by geographic . . . demographic and psychographic characteristics,' notes Conley (2018, 32), 'with more and more refined and specific classifications created within these groupings, based on both the quality of the data gathered and the campaign's technical ability to analyze the data'.

Indeed, political marketers are increasingly engaging in more and more sophisticated and data-driven approaches that allow for highly refined targeting strategies. In the 2012 US presidential election, for example, both Barack Obama and Mitt Romney targeted women voters in the styling and messages of their advertisements.[1] In one ad, Michelle Obama encouraged the public to join 'Women for Obama' to help the campaign.[2] The campaigns also divided the women further to identify single women voters – swinglers – because their vote was more unpredictable. Rosin (2012) argues that single women, who make up a fast-growing voting bloc of over 55 million voters in the US, are more likely to 'switch alliances, hold out for the best deal, express their outrage by suddenly going cold on a candidate who has irritated them and then warm up quickly to a new one who makes a better offer'. But there was a long-term strategy at play here: Obama may have wanted their vote in 2012, but the Democratic Party also wanted to turn them into more loyal voters over the long term.

Similarly, in the 2015 UK general election, with the aid of Jim Messina (Obama's 2012 Campaign Manager), the Conservatives developed a data-driven targeting programme that enabled the party and its leader, David Cameron, to strategically reach selected voters with a unique message on an individual-to-individual basis anywhere in the country (Mullen 2016). In one instance, explain Ashcroft and Oakeshott (2015, 511), 'letters and leaflets delivered to voters were so specific that a piece of direct mail might have up to 4,000 variations'.

Davidson and Binstock (2012, 25) note how parties and candidates have targeted seniors in the US since John F. Kennedy's campaign for the presidency in 1960. They have done so by, among other things, holding events in places such as nursing homes, senior centres, congregate meal sites, and retirement and assisted living communities. Some states, including larger and critically important swing states, have a high proportion of seniors, and it is thus quite worthwhile for political marketers to target them. In 2008, Florida, for example, had 27 electoral votes and 25 per cent of its voting-age population was aged 65 and older. Pennsylvania had 21 electoral votes and 23 per cent of its voting-age population was in this age range. At the same time, research has also shown that the interests and needs of senior voters are far from monolithic, and therefore it is possible to identify diverging policy needs within the senior target group. Davidson and Binstock (2012, 26) note that 'poor and wealthy older Americans have substantially different stakes in issues concerning Social Security' because those who are least well off will rely more on Social Security, and this needs to be taken into account when planning a communication strategy (see Box 2.1).

Box 2.1 Advice for practitioners on how to reach senior voters

1   Pay serious attention to the greying electorate, especially given that older voters are more likely to pay attention to campaigns, get involved, donate and actually vote.
2   Utilise online forms of communication to reach senior voters.
3   Research actual needs and behaviours of seniors, instead of relying on myths and stereotypes.
4   Segment deeply, as there are varying needs within the senior group, with some fit and able to work and fully engage in society and others badly affected by low income and ill health.
5   Be open to new ways of viewing seniors – engage in 'a process of ongoing discovery'.
6   Be aware that retirement is changing, and it is not just about old-age benefit and concessions on public transport.

Source: Adapted from Davidson and Binstock (2012, 29)

Targeting is arguably even more important for smaller parties as it helps conserve precious resources and deploy them more effectively. In the UK, the Liberal Democrats increased their seats in government by focusing their targeting efforts on regions where they had a chance of winning instead of spreading their resources evenly throughout the country. They built up geographical clusters, which, as Russell and Fieldhouse (2005, 210) note, enabled grass-roots supporters to work across seats if needed and helped to build up 'shared credibility from having a historical and realistic chance of winning seats in the region'. The Liberals in Canada, under the leadership of Justin Trudeau, relied on a similar strategy prior to the 2015 federal election to help move the party from a minority, third-place position to the majority in Parliament by picking up a record 184 seats.

They did so, in large part, by fine-tuning their segmentation and targeting efforts. Rather than depend on 'simply "winnable" and "unwinnable",' writes Delacourt (2016, 299), 'Trudeau's Liberals divided the nation's 388 electoral districts into six types, named for metals and compounds.' They varied from 'platinum ridings', which were regarded as 'sure bets,' to 'gold' and 'silver' districts, where the party had a real chance of picking up seats, to 'bronze' districts that would likely make the party the majority if they made any gains, to 'steel' and 'wood' districts where the party was essentially non-competitive.

Targeting is an effective strategy when communication and product targeting are linked. Tony Blair, for instance, succeeded by displaying his policy promises to reduce class sizes on glossy billboards throughout traditionally Tory middle England (Lees-Marshment 2001). Kiss (2009) observed how the Hungarian Socialist Party (HSP) targeted the country's youth through a variety of communication strategies. In 2004, a new prime minister, Ferenc Gyurcsány, was elected and the party chose a new president, István Hiller. Each worked to respond to the youth segment through both product development and communication. Gyurcsány's youth, his passion for youthful pastimes such as partying and sports, and his frequent jogging were communicated through the media or directly on the internet and via direct mail. He was regularly seen and photographed at universities, pubs and rock festivals. The party also abolished policies unpopular with the youth, such as compulsory military service, and created programmes to help young people with housing problems and to publicly support Hungarian pop music. This helped rejuvenate the party's image. It was seen as more modern and dynamic. To support his effort, the party also began using new colours and slogans, emphasising the youth of the party by seating young people – particularly young women – on the stage behind the speakers and using a picture of a condom on the youth organisation's website. This targeting strategy was successful: the HSP achieved a larger majority, in part due to increased support from the youth voter segment, in the 2006 election and thus remained in government.

In addition to creating large target groups, parties and candidates also try to divide the electorate up into micro- and nano-target groups using increasingly complex data analysis and analytics techniques. In the 2005 UK election, for example, all of the three main parties identified key target groups (see Table 2.1), and such groups were then targeted with direct mail and telemarketing (Savigny 2005). Obama's successful use of a range of micro-targeting strategies in the 2008 and 2012 US presidential elections, an approach that has come to be known as the 'Obama Model', demonstrated for the first time the transformative potential of skillfully integrating data and analytics into a voter targeting regime (Newman 2016; Mullen 2016). The campaigns used 'micro-targeting methods and customer analytics that relied on data-mining techniques used to analyze very large databases . . . to determine all facets of strategy,' writes Newman (2016, 781), 'including where direct mail, e-mail, and other voter contact is targeted, along with the messages that are used'. In particular, the Obama team sought to harness the power of social media to not only communicate with targeted segments but also to engage with and learn from them on an ongoing basis (Newman 2016, 786).

Positioning strategies

Positioning refers to the strategies used by parties and candidates to place themselves within the marketplace (Bigi *et al.* 2015). 'It is a process of establishing and managing the images, perceptions, and associations that the consumer applies to a product,' Cwalina and Falkowski (2015, 158) assert, 'based on the values and beliefs associated

Table 2.1 Examples of target groups identified by UK parties in the 2005 election

Labour	Conservative	Liberal Democrats
Upscaling new owners Don't believe in consumption as means of expression. Busy people, so convenience is the watchword.	**Corporate chieftains** Senior business people living in large detached houses in outer metropolitan suburbia. Tend to have four-bedroom homes surrounded by trees and protected from view by laurels and rhododendrons. Drive Lexus or BMW cars.	**Golden empty nesters** Wealthy older people living in provincial regions in 1930s houses. Lib Dems have strong challenge to Tories in this sort of neighbourhood. Support the National Trust. They are not concerned about the economy but rather with value for money.
Coronation St Found in northern maritime and industrial regions. Represent good market for mass brands.		
Rustbelt resilience Found in traditional mining communities, gardens well tended with newly painted house exteriors. Few read books or travel to offbeat holiday locations. They eat fish and chips. Solidly Labour.	**Burdened optimists** Modest qualifications. Many have built up debts. Made the Thatcher revolution. No belief in collective social responsibility. Place high value on personal freedom. Indulgence and immediate gratification sets the trend for everything.	**University challengers** Mostly aged 18 to 24, in areas of provincial cities which contain halls of residence. Much less ideologically driven than previous generations.

Source: Excerpts from Patrick Wintour, (2005). 'Postcode data could decide next election'. *The Guardian*, http://www.spinwatch.org/content/view/613/9/ (accessed May 8 2008)

with it.' The goal, they explain, is to craft the 'optimal location in the minds of existing and potential customers so that they think of the brand in the "right way".' Such associations, Baines *et al.* (2014, 174) noted, can take place and be facilitated in a variety of different ways:

1 **Rational:** linked to specific policies or proposals.
2 **Affective:** related to the image of a party or a leader or are tied directly to certain emotions.
3 **Cognative:** linked to actions taken by leaders or parties or to outside events.

What is clear, however, is that positioning invariably takes place in contrast to or in competition with other parties, policies, personalities or products. Positioning involves forging 'coherent and consistent images,' Baines *et al.* (2014, 173) explain, 'despite attempts by adversaries to undermine their credibility and consistency'. As such, a key challenge for parties and political organisations is not only determining how to position themselves in relation to a targeted group, and, if necessary, how to counter competing narratives, but actually discerning how effective they have been in conveying the intended message. An organisation must craft a message that is not only credible and will resonate with the targeted segment but one that can withstand outside scrutiny and the inevitable distortion that comes from being interpreted and reinterpreted in the press and social media. It is understood, Baines *et al.* contend (2014, 175), that positioning is subject to at least 'four descending levels of abstraction based on decreasing control over the message'.

At the first level is what a campaign or parties 'wish to convey'. But this has to contend with the reality of what is reliably and clearly articulated by the candidate or party, how it is interpreted by 'journalists and other commentators', and finally what the 'general public thinks about the messages they receive'. And, again, we can add to this the impact of political opponents intent on publicly challenging any and all positioning efforts.

To confront these and other challenges, Bannon (2004) has proposed five principles for successful positioning (see Box 2.2).

Box 2.2 Bannon's five principles for successful political positioning

1   **Clarity of the position:** know what the competitive advantage is and what voters think of this.
2   **Consistency of position:** a voter needs to know where they are; the organisation needs to offer a consistent and sustained approach.
3   **Credibility of positioning:** the voters' judgment of the quality of political proposals will always prevail.
4   **Competitiveness:** offer value that competing products do not.
5   **Communicable:** position must be easily communicated to targets.

Source: Bannon (2004)

Devine (2013) discusses how, in 2012, Obama's campaign positioned him as being the best candidate to take the country forward in the *next* four years. The campaign adopted the keyword 'forward' in speeches, ads and at the podium to keep the focus on the future, not the *past* four years. Devine (2013, 145) argues that this positioning worked as it convinced voters that Obama had a better plan for the second term, and even voters who viewed his first term negatively were willing to trust him to move in the right direction going forward. Applying Bannon's principles of successful positioning, Obama's position was seen as credible; it was consistent and clear, easy to communicate and seen as superior to Romney's slogan which was a more vague 'Believe in America'.

Somewhat surprisingly, given his brash and often offensive behaviour, Trump was seen by voters as being more trustworthy than Hillary Clinton in polls conducted during the closing weeks of the 2016 US presidential election for the same reason: his positioning was highly consistent throughout the general election, and it rarely deviated from established themes that connected with his targeted voter segments (Conley 2018). Indeed, the consistency of his position helped minimize the impact of the fact that many voters, including many of his supporters, questioned whether he could or would deliver on some of his key campaign pledges, such as building a wall along the US-Mexican border and the promise that he would compel Mexico to pay for it.

Collins and Butler's (2002) theory of market positioning explains the difference a position can make in terms of the strategic options available (see Table 2.2). They argue that candidates need to be realistic and take this into account – for example, a nicher is unlikely to become a leader in a single electoral period.

Hillary Clinton's bids for the US presidency, first in 2008 and then again in 2016, arguably failed, in part, because she began both elections in a leader position as the

Table 2.2 Collins and Butler's constraints and options for each market position

	Constraints	Options
Market leader	Has to appeal to a broad range of voters, and their interests conflict. Subject to continuous attack.	Defensive strategies to maintain and/or expand market share.
Challenger	Champions new issues which can make challenger appear to be out of step with public opinion; but otherwise has a similar product to leader and needs to convey differentiation or superiority.	Characterises leader negatively (e.g. as corrupt or incompetent). Brand position on new issue early to gain support once the issue becomes more salient.
Follower	Insecure position as follows the leader, but lacks the marketing resources to do so and is subject to losing their market support to challengers.	Can use cloning and copy the leader; or imitate them by adapting product aspects so they still differentiate or seek support from distinctive segments. They also need to protect their market share and thus avoid too much radical change.
Nicher	Specialises in serving the needs of a niche better than other competitors.	Can transform through radical strategic change and new product positioning but needs to communicate it effectively.

Source: Adapted from Collins and Butler (2002, 7–13)

most well-known Democratic candidate due to her time as First Lady and Secretary of State. Gorbounova and Lees-Marshment (2009) note how in 2008 the Clinton product was largely informed by market intelligence, promoting the theme of responsiveness and emphasising Clinton's proposals on issues that worried voters most: ending the Iraq war, universal health care and reviving the economy. In terms of Clinton herself, the strategy in both the 2008 and 2016 campaigns focused on characteristics such as her experience and the fact that she had been tested and thoroughly vetted already. However, Hillary Clinton met a surprise challenger in both elections: the largely unknown Senator Barack Obama, who appeared as very fresh and energetic, and then Donald Trump, an unpredictable and unprincipled real estate mogul and reality TV personality. In contrast to both Obama and Trump, who effectively tapped into a deep public desire for change in Washington, Clinton's emphasis on experience turned out to be more of a liability than an asset. Clinton responded by going on the attack, arguing in 2008 that Obama was unelectable, hypocritical and, above all, inexperienced, capable only of inspiring oratory rather than governing, and in 2016 by claiming that Trump was fundamentally unfit for the office. However, both Obama and Trump responded with a counter-attack on her leader position, painting her as part of an elitist, Washington political establishment that had failed to address the concerns of average working people in the country. Each market position has its advantages and disadvantages.

In contrast to broad-based appeals, niche political marketing is about strategically developing your product and communication to suit a small, defined group with relatively homogenous members and interests. Harada and Morris (2012, 93) explored the use of niche marketing by the Canadian and Scottish Green parties. They argue that effective parties will follow niche market-oriented behaviour with four key principles (see Box 2.3).

Box 2.3 Harada and Morris's principles of effective niche market-oriented behaviour

1   Identify a focused area of specialisation.
2   Develop an organisation capable of forging a unique party reputation and fostering long-lasting relationships with supporters.
3   Utilise market research to inform a product that will maintain and expand support.
4   Actively resist niche incursions by other parties by adjusting the product in response to market research.

Source: Adapted from Harada and Morris (2012)

They noted how, in Canada and Scotland, the two parties followed these principles with mixed results. In the 2004 and 2008 federal elections, the Canadian Green Party was successful at being specialised, promoting ecology-based policies with a unique grass-roots approach, but did not use market research to design the product. It showed some signs of forging strong relationships with its volunteers, but this was mitigated by a top-down campaign organisation and a corresponding failure to effectively adjust the product in response to public feedback. The Scottish Green Party was also a classic specialised party, focused on ecology with the same grass-roots approach; but it was more effective in solidifying constituent relations. However, it did not attempt to change or adjust the product in response to market research at all. Harada and Morris concluded that the strong principles of Green parties present a challenge to them seeking to expand their market through adjustment of the product in response to public opinion.

Strategies can also be developed into means of cooperating or competing with other parties. Barber (2009) notes how, in the lead up to the 1997 UK election, the leader of the Liberal Democrats, Paddy Ashdown, asked his party to accept cooperation with Labour in order to defeat the Conservatives. The Lib Dems would go on to double their seats in the House of Commons that year. They then pursued a strategy of *constructive opposition* to the Labour government. Under a new party leader, Charles Kennedy, the party became more opposed to Labour as they moved closer to the centre ground and the Conservatives. They also came out against Blair taking Britain into an unpopular war in Iraq, which gained them more support in the 2001 election. In 2010, they formed a coalition with the Conservatives under David Cameron to get into power to enact some of their policy goals. The party has therefore exhibited a wide range of strategies in response to their own policy goals and ideals, the competition they have faced and their changing position in the political marketplace.

In 2007, the new Australian Labor Party leader, Kevin Rudd, was positioned as a challenger – as someone, as Downer argues (2014), who was both socially progressive and economically conservative with specific points of difference from the Liberal opposition. After Rudd's fall in popularity, however, Julia Gillard took over and was positioned as a forward-looking market leader with clear and differentiating stances on education and health.

Market- and sales-oriented strategies

A broader strategic consideration is whether politicians and parties should adopt a sales or a market-orientation. A market-orientation argues that for politicians and parties to win elections they need to use market research to inform how they design their product and brand, thus creating something voters want to support and reducing the need for communication. A market-orientation involves the politician or party being aware and responsive to ordinary voter concerns and demonstrating this in the way they *behave* – that is, in the political products they design, offer and implement in order to satisfy market demands. This kind of behaviour is distinct from the idea that marketing is simply about selling or promoting something. It is more concerned with understanding, responding to and ultimately developing a relationship with voters. 'Such a move,' write Johns and Brandenburg (2014, 90) 'can . . . be understood as a shift in competitive posture, from *leading* . . . to *following*' the contours of the market. However, a market-orientation is not reducible to just doing what everyone wants, as the market can be segmented and it involves addressing needs as well as wants.

There are several models of market-orientation in politics: Newman's (1994, 1999) model of political marketing based in the US, Lees-Marshment's (2001) Market-Oriented Party (MOP) framework based in the UK and Ormrod's (2005) Political Market-Orientation Model, which is European. Lees-Marshment's (2001) model of a market/sales/product-oriented party framework is one of the most cited and critiqued theories in political marketing. It has been applied empirically to parties around the world (see Lilleker and Lees-Marshment 2005 and Lees-Marshment *et al.* 2010) as well as being applied to and cited in other arenas, such as the European Parliament, and other fields, including economics, law, medicine, urban studies and social work. Working from a political science perspective, this model applied marketing concepts as well as techniques to the overall behaviour of political parties and suggested a stage-by-stage process to show what a party with each one of the three orientations might do from the beginning of an electoral term through to election and delivery in government (see Figure 2.1).

A product-oriented party (POP) is a traditional party, making the case for what it believes in during elections without reflecting on what voters want or how they might react to its product, even if it fails to gain support. It argues for what it stands for, believing its product is of such value that people will vote for it because it is inherently better or right. Smaller parties or single-issue movements may adopt this approach if their goal is to represent a particular section of society or put issues on the agenda, as opposed to winning power.

A sales-oriented party (SOP) is also reluctant to change its product, but it uses market intelligence to identify persuadable voters and design more effective communication strategies to sell the party and its products to them. A SOP does not change its behaviour to suit what people want, but it tries to make people want what it offers. Using market intelligence to understand voters' response to its behaviour, the party employs the latest advertising and communication techniques to persuade voters that it is right (see Figure 2.2).

A classic example of a SOP is the Labour Party in the UK in the early 1990s. Lees-Marshment (2001) explains how the Labour leader, Neil Kinnock, was elected in 1983 to unite the party and appease its left wing but lacked wider electoral appeal. A number of other product weaknesses were apparent, such as unpopular policies in the manifesto,

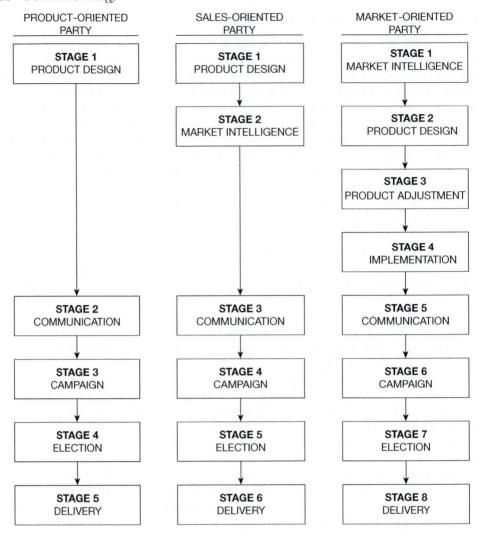

Figure 2.1 Lees-Marshment's (2001) model of the political marketing process for product-, sales- and market-oriented parties

including a unilateralist policy on defence, expansion of state ownership and intervention in the economy. The party also had a poor reputation for economic management and retained strong party links with the unions. However, the party put significant effort into communication. Staff with professional expertise were recruited to reorganise communications; an advertising agency was appointed, and a new symbol was adopted: a red rose. Labour appointed MORI to conduct surveys, polling and a panel study, especially of target groups and marginal seats, to inform campaign design. However, Labour still lost, with polls indicating public dissatisfaction with its product. The party had only used marketing to shape its communication strategies rather than to help design its product.

Researchers have identified other examples of parties following a sales orientation. In their study of German parties, for example, Maier *et al.* (2010) found that while

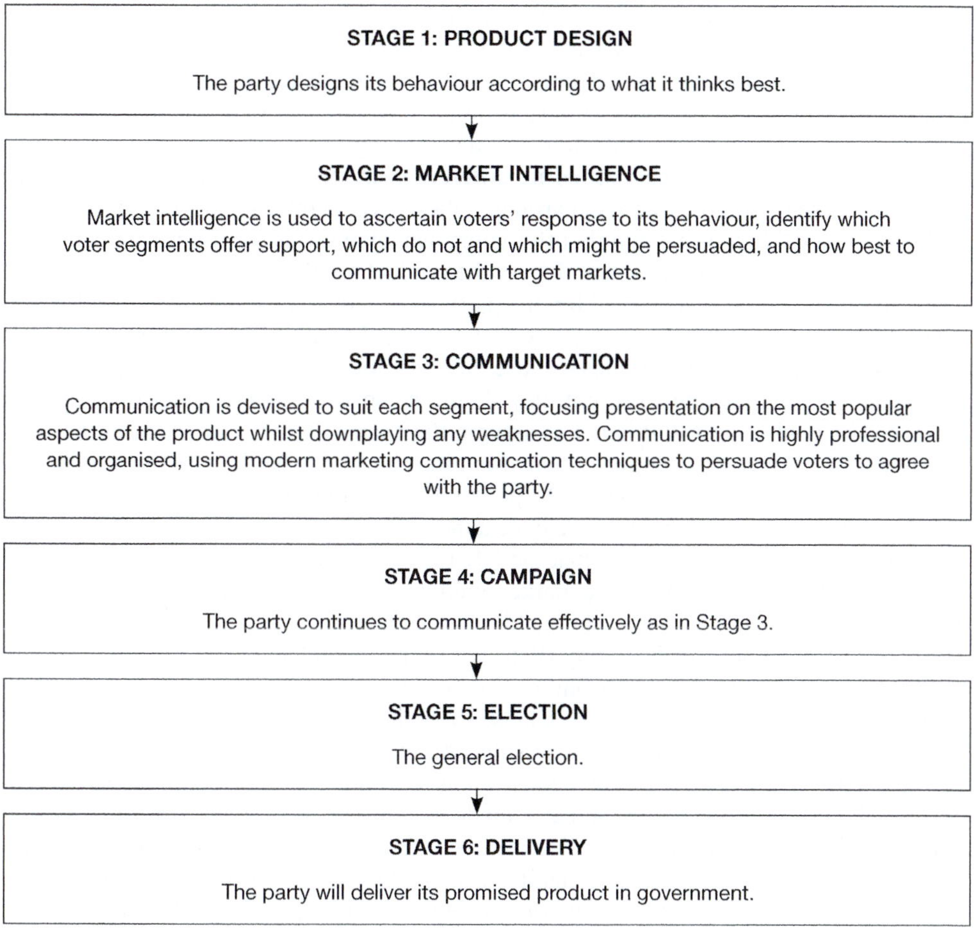

STAGE 1: PRODUCT DESIGN

The party designs its behaviour according to what it thinks best.

▼

STAGE 2: MARKET INTELLIGENCE

Market intelligence is used to ascertain voters' response to its behaviour, identify which voter segments offer support, which do not and which might be persuaded, and how best to communicate with target markets.

▼

STAGE 3: COMMUNICATION

Communication is devised to suit each segment, focusing presentation on the most popular aspects of the product whilst downplaying any weaknesses. Communication is highly professional and organised, using modern marketing communication techniques to persuade voters to agree with the party.

▼

STAGE 4: CAMPAIGN

The party continues to communicate effectively as in Stage 3.

▼

STAGE 5: ELECTION

The general election.

▼

STAGE 6: DELIVERY

The party will deliver its promised product in government.

Figure 2.2 The political marketing process for a sales-oriented party

Source: Lees-Marshment (2001)

some parties in the country did use market research, they do so primarily for the purposes of refining their communication and campaigning strategies. Similarly, Kiss and Mihályffy's (2010) analysis of Hungarian parties in the 2006 elections found that most were sales-oriented with the focus on using sophisticated communication strategies through an 'expanding arsenal and paraphernalia of campaigning techniques . . . strategies and tactics, activists and managers, advisors and counsels' (2010, 155). Additionally, Strömbäck (2010b, 59) concludes that in Sweden, although the New Moderates moved towards a market-orientation, the dominant trend remained sales-based, and no party admitted to using research when developing policies.

By contrast, a MOP designs its behaviour to provide voter satisfaction to reach its goal. It uses market intelligence to identify voter demands, then designs a product that meets their needs and wants, which is supported and implemented by the internal organisation and is deliverable in government. It does not attempt to change what people think but to deliver what they need and want.

This concept is very different from more traditional views of political parties as organisations dedicated to pursuing a particular ideological vision. It also differs from the narrow view that marketing, if used, only impacts how candidates or parties communicate. Instead, the MOP concept places emphasis on the development of a product and market intelligence rather than communication and campaigning.

Understanding that political parties are different from businesses – they have complex products, markets and goals, and, in particular, they have members and a unique ideological history – a MOP does not simply offer voters what they want, or follow opinion polls, because it needs to ensure that it can deliver the product on offer. A MOP needs to ensure that its product will be accepted within the party and needs to take this into consideration when adjusting its offerings, using party views and political judgment to inform how it responds to public concerns. Parties can use their ideologies as a means of creating effective solutions to public demands, but they should do so without trying to reshape public opinion. The goal of an MOP is not to assume the characteristics of a catch-all party or to move to the Downsian centre; rather, it is to ground its behaviour in the market and in voter needs and demands. The MOP political marketing process shows the different activities parties would carry out to achieve a market-orientation: (see Figure 2.3).

Lees-Marshment (2001) argues that the UK Labour Party became a MOP by the 1997 UK election. It conducted extensive market intelligence that informed the development of the product, particularly among traditional Labour supporters who had voted Tory in 1992. The party elected a new leader, Tony Blair, who supported change and was popular with voters. The party distanced itself from trade unions in response to market research telling them this had lost them votes in 1992. Clause IV of the constitution was altered to remove an unpopular commitment to state ownership, and the slogan 'New Labour, New Britain' was adopted. Specific pledges were made in areas most important to voters, such as education and the health service, and the party made a commitment to fiscal prudence as well as to reductions in government spending and income taxes in keeping with voter demands rather than party ideology. A mini-manifesto was launched a year before the election to pre-test policies. Product adjustment was carried out, with specific pledges for delivery kept short and limited, and details about how they would be achieved, such as cutting waiting lists in the NHS by reducing money spent on bureaucracy, were added. Reassurances were made on income taxes and economic management. 'Middle England' voters were targeted, especially in party communications, and a strong leadership style ensured high party unity. The product was skillfully communicated to voters before the campaign even started, and thus the campaign was generally uneventful. Labour won the 1997 election and increased its membership in the process. The party would go on to win elections in 2001 and 2005 (see Lees-Marshment 2001).

The MOP and SOP concepts suggest very different relationships between parties and voters. The SOP's main aim is to persuade and change voters' minds; in contrast, the MOP aims to respond to their views. Lees-Marshment argues that marketing sales techniques cannot make up for the lack of a comprehensive, unified political product that offers a positive, achievable alternative to existing government policies and responds effectively to the concerns and demands of the public. Political marketing is more effective for major parties if it is used to inform how the product on offer is designed.

Comparative political marketing research has uncovered a range of examples of market-oriented party/candidate behaviour around the world (see Lilleker and Lees-Marshment 2005, and Lees-Marshment *et al.* 2010 for further details). For example, Matušková *et al.* (2010) explored how the Czech Social Democratic Party (CSSD) adopted a market-orientation and substantially increased its support, coming close to winning the 2006

STAGE 1: MARKET INTELLIGENCE

The party aims to understand and ascertain market demands. Informally it 'keeps an ear to the ground', talks to party members, creates policy groups and meets with the public. Formally it uses methods such as polls, focus groups and segmentation to understand the views and behaviour of its markets, including the general public, key opinion influences, MPs and members. It uses market intelligence continually and considers short- and long-term demands.

STAGE 2: PRODUCT DESIGN

The party then designs a 'product' according to the findings from its market intelligence before adjusting it to suit several factors explored in Stage 3.

STAGE 3: PRODUCT ADJUSTMENT

The party then develops the product to consider:

Achievability: ensures promises can be delivered in government. In an era of pledges, annual reports, and timetables for action, delivery capability is a big issue. The factors that go into this include the overall leadership team, economic management, capability, party unity and voters perception of the party's ability to deliver their desired outcome.

Internal reaction: ensures changes will attract adequate support from MPs and members to ensure implementation, taking into account a party's ideology and history and retaining certain policies to suit the traditional supporter market where necessary. Changes in policy thus need to be placed within, or with reference to, the party's traditional ideological framework wherever possible. This will be a sometimes delicate, yet essential, balancing act between the demands of external and internal supporters. This is, in effect, about internal marketing – and applying the same concepts for the wider public to those within the party organization.

Competition: identifies the opposition's weaknesses and highlights the party's own corresponding strengths, ensuring a degree of distinctiveness.

Support: segments the markets to identify untapped voters necessary to achieve goals, and then develop targeted aspects of the product to suit them. The party does not adopt the 'catch-all' approach of trying to get everyone on board. It is more 'traditional markets plus'.

STAGE 4: IMPLEMENTATION

Changes are implemented throughout the party, needing careful party management and leadership over an appropriate time frame to obtain adequate acceptance to create party unity and enthusiasm for the new party design.

STAGE 5: COMMUNICATION

Communication is carefully organised to convey the new product so that voters so that voters are clear before the campaign begins. Not just the leader but all MPs and members send a message to the electorate. It involves media management but is not just about spin-doctoring; it should be informative rather than manipulative and built on a clear internal communication structure.

STAGE 6: CAMPAIGN

The party repeats its communication in the official campaign, reminding voters of the key aspects and advantages of its product.

STAGE 7: ELECTION

The party should win not just voters but attract positive perception from voters on all aspects of behavior including policies, leaders, party unity and capability; as well as increasing the quality of its membership.

STAGE 8: DELIVERY

The party then needs to deliver its deliver its product in government.

Figure 2.3 The political marketing process for a market-oriented party

Source: Lees-Marshment (2001)

parliamentary general elections. The party analysed the market and used the results to develop a product and strategy aimed at specific target groups of voters. Lees-Marshment (2009a) argues that the New Zealand National Party became market-oriented beginning in 2005. The new leader, John Key, appealed to ordinary voters across different market segments, being both an extremely successful businessman and the son of an immigrant single mother. The opening address of the campaign showed a group of multicultural children, followed by a range of visuals showing Key amidst varied groups in society. Campaign ads ended with the phrase: 'You've just got to choose it', giving the power to the voter. The National Party appealed to traditionally conservative voters, with promises to lower taxes and to fight crime, but also to the less well off by maintaining Labour's 'Working For Families' benefit scheme and by having Key visit 'struggle street' – or low socio-economic areas in the country. National succeeded in being elected, in 2008 and then again in 2011 and 2014, and generally polled well against a fragmented Labour opposition (Lees-Marshment *et al.* 2015).

Obama's 2008 and 2012 campaigns, as noted above, also provide clear examples of market-oriented strategy, as did David Cameron's and Justin Trudeau's 2015 victories in the UK and Canada, respectively (Newman 2016; Mullen 2016; Delacourt 2016). In an effort to win an outright majority in Parliament, the Conservatives ran a highly disciplined and targeted market-based campaign in the 2015 UK general election that sought to not only identify and exploit key, 'wedge' issues but also the 40 or so vulnerable seats, mostly held by Liberal Democrats, where a Conservative victory was essential to the party's chances of securing a majority. The chief architect of this strategy, explains Mullen (2016, 21), was Lynton Crosby, a renowned Australian political consultant affectionately known as the 'Wizard of Oz'. 'Crosby insisted upon total control over the election strategy,' Mullen writes (2016, 21), and 'demanded unwavering discipline from all sections of the party to ensure that everyone was "on message".' Once in charge, Crosby relied on copious amounts of market research to concentrate the party's time and energy on certain 'salient issues', namely the economy, tax cuts, unemployment and quality public schools, as well as 'key target seats'. It was a strategy that depended not only on the traditional mobilisation of party volunteers across the country but also on a multifaceted social media and digital marketing campaign.

Trudeau and the Liberals in Canada exhibited a similar preoccupation with the strategic potential of data and market research. A former math teacher, who enjoyed doing 'logic puzzles' and other numbers games in his spare time, Trudeau gravitated 'to the mechanics of modern political campaigning,' Delacourt writes (2016, 299). Such an aptitude was on display when, in a clever and unexpected move, the Trudeau campaign revised its 'escalator' ad to position him to the left of both the Conservative Stephen Harper and left-leaning New Democratic Party leader Thomas Mulcair on the issue of deficit spending. It did so after targeted voter research indicated that voters were open to deficit spending, rather than the need to balance the budget – a position that had become sacrosanct in Canadian politics – if the spending would improve the quality of life in the country, according to Delacourt (2016, 314). In the ad, Trudeau was able to differentiate himself and the Liberals from both Harper and Mulcair by declaring that, in contrast to spending cuts, which had hurt the country (the escalator stops), he had a plan to get the economy (and the escalator) going again by 'investing in jobs and growth and lowering taxes for the middle-class'. This, Trudeau explained, is 'real change'.

Market-oriented behaviour can also be seen in newer democracies. Patrón Galindo (2009) explored how the Peruvian centre-left party APRA (People's Revolutionary

American Alliance) adapted a market-oriented strategy to help reorganise and relaunch after losing popularity during the late 1980s. APRA sought to fill the gap left by parties on the left by ideologically positioning itself on the centre-left. However, the party avoided being too left-wing as they were also seeking support from key sectors in the country, such as the private sector, international organisations and corporations. Internally, it created a new division tasked with creating policy as well as a School of Training in Municipal Issues designed to help prepare party members for campaigning and governing. The leader, Alan Garcia, sought to project a new image as a more *mature* and *centrist* politician to counteract negative voter perception from when he was previously in power. The party and Garcia regained power in 2006.

Wakefield (2009) observed how the Japanese Liberal Democratic Party (LDP) adapted elements of the MOP concept. LDP candidates developed and nurtured *koenkai* – private support organisations affiliated with individual candidates rather than the party – to campaign as it was illegal for volunteers to do so for the party. Koenkai Aksi not only provided a source of market research about voter preferences but also a means of engaging with voters in an ongoing way. LDP candidates used their influence in Tokyo to secure lucrative public construction projects which rewarded loyal voters and businesses with jobs and contracts, thus enhancing voter satisfaction. At a national level, meanwhile, the party emphasised the economic gains felt by many, and voters responded positively to the various economic inducements offered by the LDP (see also Asano and Wakefield 2010).

Incomplete and short-lived market-oriented parties

Despite its apparent advantages, few parties follow the market-oriented concept fully, and maintaining it once in government is difficult. Political marketing is often criticised because of its association with Tony Blair's New Labour design in the UK in 1997. Lees-Marshment (2001) argues that New Labour was not a perfect example of a MOP. Blair followed some, but not all, aspects of the MOP model. The main weaknesses were that, in terms of internal reaction analysis, changes Blair made to the party's product to increase its external support created significant dissatisfaction within the party; in particular, the change in Clause IV, a constitutional clause that held considerable ideological and emotive value for many party members. In terms of the competition, Blair accepted the achievements of Thatcherism without saying how Labour would be that different. Similarly, New Zealand National's orientation in 2008 wasn't a perfect example of a MOP as it lacked distinctiveness from Labour, failed to convey delivery management and produced a Commitments Card that had a long, rather than focused, list of promises. There was no clear vision, and expectations were not managed well.

In Peru, the APRA lost support in government because they delivered policies that were different from what they promised (Patrón Galindo 2010). If the major weakness in MOP strategies is delivery, this can cause problems for governing – both pragmatically and normatively. Kotzaivazoglou and Zotos's (2010) analysis of the 2004 elections in Greece identified how the New Democracy (ND) party used market research to design its electoral product on clearly market-oriented lines, focusing on issues that were important to the voters and adopting an issue-focused, highly targeted communication strategy. The ND won the election but once in government failed to deliver on most of its election promises, leading to significant voter discontent. In Australia, although Hughes and Dann (2010, 88) contended that 'the 2007 campaign of Kevin Rudd will likely go down in Australian political marketing history as the turning point in the acceptance and use of marketing strategy at a national level by a major political party', their predictions that internal debates within the Labor Party about the political implications of adopting a market-orientation would make it difficult for the party to remain market-oriented in government proved correct, as the Rudd/Gillard/Rudd government 2007–2013 demonstrated. Other difficulties with market-oriented politics include, as noted by Wakefield (2009), that the Japanese-style use of the MOP concept led to corruption from close working relationships between government and business interests. This eroded public faith in the LDP at the same time that central government lost its ability to 'buy' voter support with economic projects during poor economic times in the 1990s. In 1993, the LDP fell from power.

Critiques of the Lees-Marshment Market-Oriented Party Model

The Lees-Marshment model has been subject to a range of criticisms (see Ormrod 2006). For example, no party ever follows the MOP model completely. What parties often do is employ a hybrid approach, implementing either a sales or market-orientation or aspects of each. Comparative studies of market-orientation have found a mixed pattern of market-oriented behaviour: parties may adopt different orientations at different times, moving back and forth. A 14-nation study of political market-orientation by Lees-Marshment *et al.* (2010) concluded that while political marketing is a global activity and political parties around the world utilise marketing techniques and concepts, the extent to which marketing is used to design the political product varies from one election to the next. The trend in orientation is 'diverse and fluctuating' and does not depend on being an established versus a new democracy, nor is it limited to countries with a particular political system.

Indeed, a growing body of work is examining how different orientations, including product approaches, may interact and inform market-based strategy (Bigi *et al.* 2016; Johns and Brandenburg 2014; Ormrod *et al.* 2015). In particular, scholars have explored the possibility that there are a variety of different ways that parties, campaigns and other political organisations may learn from and engage with voters and the market overall. As Bigi *et al.* (2016, 367) note, 'information [can] flow from customers to innovative offerings not only by means of traditional market research but also through informal knowledge and market observation by managers and others.' At the same time, it is possible that 'there is a flow of information from innovative technology to customers'. Organisations, in other words, whether in business or politics, may be able to do some leading, rather than simply following the market. In fact, some researchers have wondered whether or not 'innovative' or more product-based approaches and strictly market-based strategies are 'mutually exclusive' (Johns and Brandenburg 2014, 90; Bigi *et al.* 2016). In Case Study 2.1, for example, Aditya Tejas examines the UK Labour Party's return to more sales- and ideologically oriented strategies ahead of the 2017 general election.

Other criticisms of the model are normative, echoing those of Kotler and Levy's (1969) early article on broadening the concept of marketing, and are linked to concerns about the democratic consequences of political marketing. As Temple argued, 'the main impact and importance of Lees-Marshment's work may well be the debate it has engendered about the role of political marketing in modern democracies' (2010, 274).

The Market-Oriented Politics Model applied to institutions

The market-oriented concept has been applied to other areas of politics, not just to elections and political parties. Balestrini and Gamble (2011) applied the MOP model to the

European Union (EU) to explore the link between the electorate's needs and wants and EU policymaking, arguing that public discontent with the EU reflects a lack of responsiveness. They argue that the EU needs to adopt a market-orientation to policymaking to address the democratic deficit and propose a new model for doing so (2011, 97). They suggest that the EU should consider the electorate's needs in addition to the ideology and goals of the governing political parties. Specifically, they contend that the EU should employ the following steps in its policymaking process:

Stage 1: Identify the problem.

Stage 2: Build a policy agenda.

Stage 3: Explore policy options and make selections.

Stage 4: Implement the policy.

Stage 5: Evaluate the policy.

The MOP model has also been applied to other countries; for example, Ahmad (2017) also applied and adapted marketing models to the Indonesian parliament.

Populist strategies

Marketing can be linked to populism, and Winder and Tenscher's (2012) analysis of populism argues that parties and candidates can engage in a populist form of market-orientation by going through several distinct phases: market intelligence, product design and communication, and election and post-election strategies (see Figure 2.4). Among the more significant risks here, scholars argue, is that a market-orientation may encourage, or even empower, a party to become a populist one that strives to win at all costs by following public opinion without any principles (Johns and Brandenburg 2014, 90; Ormrod *et al.* 2015).

Winder and Tenscher (2012) explore cases such as Ross Perot's independent candidacy in the 1992 US presidential elections, Venezuelan leader Hugo Chávez and Austrian Freedom Party's (FPÖ) leader Jörg Haider. They note, for example, how Perot's campaign was effective because it showed him to be 'in touch with ordinary people's needs and fears (inclusion) and against the ruling class (exclusion)'; and his communication reflected the growing dissatisfaction among the people (2012, 237).

Similar cleavages have been at work within recent upticks in right-wing populism in Europe and the US. In their study of Marine Le Pen and the National Front (FN, rebranded 'National Rally' or 'RN' in June 2018) in France, for instance, Stockemer and Barisione (2017, 102) contend that 'radical right-wing parties in Europe' are hoping to gain mass popular support by joining 'elements from both a populist "ideology" and a populist communication "style".' Ideologically, they assert, populism is pitched as a form of '"people-centrism and anti-elitism"' that hinges on the 'exclusion of specific population categories from the community of people, considered as a homogeneous body' (2017, 102). In Europe and US, the main targets for exclusion within this resurgent right-wing populism have been immigrants, particularly refugees and Muslims from the Middle East. As a style of communication, on the other hand, populist rhetoric relies on 'simple and strong language', 'emotional language' and constant 'references to the "people"', as well as a 'synergy between the ordinary people and [a] charismatic leader,' they write (2017, 102).

In France, such a 'populist reshaping of the party's message . . . rendered the new FN under Marine Le Pen more attractive to sympathizers, members and potential recruits,' Stockemer and Barisione (2017, 102) contend. But it is also seen as playing a key role in the gains made by the right-wing parties and politicians across Europe over the last several years, from the FPÖ in Austria to the Golden Dawn in Greece to the Alternative for Germany and the Northern League in Italy.

Questions about the strength of this resurgent right-wing populism, and especially how it might be buttressed by market-based strategies, have become particularly relevant in the wake of Donald Trump's unexpected victory in the 2016 US presidential election (Conley 2018). Both organisationally and rhetorically, Trump's campaign closely adhered to Stockemer and Barisione's (2017) model of reactionary populism. Simplified, repetitive and emotionally-charged language; public attacks on liberal elites as well as any perceived outsiders; claims that he alone, as the party leader, would protect the country from the twin threats of economic globalisation and immigration – it was all intended to position Trump with his targeted voter groups as a populist defender of a forgotten Middle American majority. Given his reliance on data-driven positioning, and willingness to merely parrot what he understood his audiences to want, Trump effectively epitomised populism.

Such tactics can have a destabilising effect on a society, especially maturing democracies, as Otto Eibl argues in his analysis of Andrej Babiš and the emergence of market-oriented strategies in the Czech Republic over the last several years. Much like Trump, Babiš is a successful, but not uncontroversial, businessman who claimed he would remake Czech politics by running the country as a business. In practice, however, he has proved to be a highly divisive figure who, owing to his skillful use of market research and targeting strategies, has been able to successfully position himself as an outsider and populist reformer (see Democratic Debate 2.1).

Market intelligence

To identify counter consumers, understand their moods and frustrations, and identify simple solutions

Product design and communication

The leadership drives adjusting the product to suit the internal market creating clear-cut messages through skilled communicators

Election and post election

Maximising the vote, evaluating and then creating stable relationships

---

Figure 2.4 Winder and Tenscher's (2012) populist marketing strategy

Strategy and the environment

Box 2.4 Ideal types of political marketing strategies by Winther Nielsen (2013)

Entrepreneurial	If an organisation adopts an entrepreneurial strategy, it thinks it can control its environment and thus is willing to engage in more innovative strategy even if it might lose resources. An example is how the, then, president for the European Commission Jacques Delors pushed to create the single market in the EU to stimulate economic growth.
Decoupling	The decoupling strategy is where an organisation feels in control but decides to avoid risk.
Defense	Organisations that take a defence strategy feel their lack of control and thus carry on as before, avoiding risk, but also refusing to change and sticking to their old habits (e.g. if a political party continues to ignore low polling numbers and refuses to change its policies and so continues to lose public support).
Conformity	A political organisation that knows it can't control its environment and thus decides to comply with the prevailing culture and norms, and is thus very risk averse (e.g. UK New Labour's decision to change the party to suit public opinion after losing three elections in a row).

Strategy is about responding to the environment, and Winther Nielsen (2013) argues there are four ideal types of political marketing strategies (see Box 2.4). It is vital, Lees-Marshment *et al.* (2015, 101, 102) argue, that parties and politicians remain 'responsive' to the 'policy needs' of the public once in office. In their study of New Zealand's 2014 general election, they found that 'responsiveness to policy needs and . . . the presentation of a likeable and credible leadership brand were central to John Key and the National Party's decisive win over David Cunliffe and the Labour Party' (2015, 102).

Winther Nielsen (2012) argues there are three faces of political marketing strategy: design, emergent and interpretive, which depend on the assumptions of individual political actors, the political environment in which they operate, their strategic political behaviour (varying from forming a clear, long-term plan to being ad hoc or norm/ritual based) and their objectives:

Design political strategies create a clear plan from the start, which appears most logical but, as Winther Nielsen notes, may be unrealistic to apply to politics because it is rarely possible to foresee events and because markets are inherently unstable. Before it was beset by questions about his personal life, for example, Bill Clinton's 1992 campaign was carefully planned to focus on the economy.

Emergent political strategies are 'carried out on the run', so behaviour is more reactive to a wide range of information and intelligence. It is a pragmatic approach to the complexity of politics, but the lack of a clear long-term direction might result in less effective behaviour. Winther Nielsen suggests that UK New Labour's attempts to change policies to suit voters under Tony Blair was an emergent strategy – there is certainly evidence of them using political market research (PMR) extensively.

Interpretive political marketing strategy involves political organisations such as political parties trying to influence and change their environment rather than just responding to it. The example provided is Obama's 2008 campaign's ability to transform the playing field, in the primaries and then in the presidential election, using language, symbols and norms. His advisors decided that the political environment had changed and thus created the possibility that a strategy focused on change might work for a candidate who was, at the start of the race, largely unknown. Of course, changing the environment might be hard – however, it may be where politicians get to showcase their leadership skills.

The tactics adopted with regard to the competition also need to change to suit different circumstances. Sometimes it is about cooperating and sometimes it is about directly opposing a particular candidate, party or policy. There are a range of ways to attack and defend a political organisation or figure. In Winther Nielsen's (2015, 344) analysis, strategy is often shaped by calculations concerning whether a party believes it has more or less 'control over the environment' weighed against the likelihood of 'losing or gaining resources'.

Measuring political strategy

Political strategy is not easily discernable or measurable, and it is rarely public – parties and candidates don't tend to publicise their strategy. This is partly because they don't want the other side to know what they are planning, but mostly it is because political strategy needs to be flexible and adapt to changing circumstances. Given this, market-based strategies can be difficult to measure empirically (Johns and Brandenburg 2014). Nevertheless, scholars have recently tried to develop more rigorous measurements of political marketing, and readers may like to explore the following sources for ideas about question wording and methodology in future research:

- Strömbäck (2010a) created a survey to explore the extent to which parties in different countries both used political marketing techniques and adopted the orientations within the Lees-Marshment model and what affect the system might have on which orientation parties' chose.
- Ormrod and Henneberg (2006) analysed UK party manifestos in the 2005 election, applying Ormrod's concepts through QSR NVivo, to examine the number of occurrences and relationships between concepts, assessing whether they were not developed, somewhat developed or highly developed.
- Johns and Brandenburg (2014) measured voters' perception of parties' market-orientation utilising questions on a public opinion poll.
- Winther Nielsen (2015) ran binary regression tests on data gathered from surveys and elite interviews to discern how likely political strategists were to choose certain hypothesised market-based political strategies in the context of Danish politics following the 2011 general election.
- Lees-Marshment *et al.* (2014) and Lees-Marshment (2018) utilised a Vote Compass survey and post-election survey which asks questions regarding the 2014 and 2017 New Zealand elections about how in touch leaders were with ordinary peoples' concerns and the responsiveness of party policies to voters' wants and needs.
- Bendle *et al.* (2018, 73) conducted a 'frequency-inverse document frequency' analysis of candidate posts on Facebook and Twitter during the 2016 US Republican presidential primary, to measure the frequency of words in a specific text (*e.g.* Jeb

Bush's tweets) compared to texts from other candidates, and ran regression tests on how different Democratic opponents would likely impact strategic assessments of Trump's strength as the party nominee by Republican voters over the course of the primary season.

Implementing political strategy

Politicians and advisors have to ensure they can get enough political support, within and outside of the party, for any proposals, otherwise they have limited chance of being implemented (Glaab 2007, 67; Lindholm and Prehn 2007, 23; Pettitt 2012). Even the best-designed strategies fail because of unanticipated events or internal opposition (Barber 2005), especially within political parties.

Factors that hinder strategy implementation

The effectiveness of any political strategy depends on a range of factors. Lindholm and Prehn's (2007) study of strategy in Denmark concluded that it is harder to develop strategies when public support is high as, during those periods, there seems less need to innovate and reposition. Conversely, it is easier to gain internal support for change when the party has lost several elections, such as after UK Labour lost successive elections from 1979 to 1992 (Barber 2005) and changed to 'New Labour' under Tony Blair and when the Moderate Party in Sweden turned to marketing in 2002 after experiencing its worst election result since 1973.

There are also a number of barriers to effective positioning. Parties can sometimes struggle to simultaneously occupy the centre ground where most voters sit and be differentiated from their core competitors. Strategy is harder in government than in opposition (Lees-Marshment 2008, 2009b) – it is difficult for incumbents to reposition because they are bound by their previous behaviour and record. Fischer *et al.'s* (2007) comparative study of political strategy in government suggests that the power of a government to implement its chosen strategy depends on a number of factors, such as its existing power, the strategic qualities of the leaders, and market conditions such as the state of the economy and approaching elections.

The nature of government also makes strategy, and indeed political marketing as a whole, more complex. First, the pressures of daily government business limit the amount of time officials have to think about electoral considerations. When the 'Promise' report, outlining future party strategy and rebranding ideas, was presented to Tony Blair in 2004, for example, he asked his private secretary, Jonathan Powell, to make sure he had time in his schedule to review it (Promise 2006). Government can end up being driven more by crisis – where it doesn't want to be – and less by strategy – where it wants to go. In the US, for example, delivery in government is often hindered by the federal system of government, which works against cross-unit or inter-state cooperation for long-term benefit.

Research also shows that parties and candidates struggle in particular to maintain a market-orientation once in power. Government is a very distinct environment. It brings a whole host of factors into play – from new resources, information and advice to the civil service or bureaucracy to think tanks and interest groups who hope to influence the policymaking process. This is particularly relevant to the issue of policy delivery in government. 'Government is about power,' Conley (2014) asserts, 'but it is also about constraints, which can be both relatively enduring, such as existing institutional constraints, as well as unexpected, like changing political circumstances and attitudes.' Leaders, in particular, find it hard to remain in touch, as they enjoy power and also want to make a difference while in office. Box 2.5 outlines the range of factors working against maintaining a market-orientation.

Box 2.5 Factors hindering maintenance of a market-orientation in government

1   Loss of objective advisors with that gut feel and ability to offer blunt criticism.
2   Realities and constraints of government.
3   Increasing knowledge and experience among leaders, encouraging feeling of invincibility and superiority.
4   Weak opposition, which encourages and facilitates complacency.
5   Difficulty and slow pace of delivery in government.
6   Lack of time to think about future product development.

Source: Adapted from Lees-Marshment (2008)

Positive influences that aid strategy

The leader plays an important part in the success of political strategy. Fischer *et al.* (2007, 185) note that the advantage with Tony Blair is that he was a prime minister 'who thinks and acts in strategic terms . . . [and] encourages others to do the same', whereas the former German Chancellor Schröder had a more situational leadership style that focused on immediate needs rather than the big picture, which was 'detrimental to the development of a coherent strategy'. Scholars have also found that the attitude of the leader towards a market-orientation is a key factor in its implementation (Lees-Marshment *et al.* 2010; Winther Nielsen 2015; Strömbäck, Grandien and Falasca 2013; Pettitt 2012). As one practitioner – Murray McCully, a New Zealand MP and strategist – said when interviewed:

> At the end of the day this is a process that is about having respect for the views of the public . . . If you thumb your nose at the public and do things to them without seeking their consent then it comes back and bites your backside real quick . . . You should look respectfully about what you can learn about market research and polling and focus groups and so on. Not slavishly follow the detail but understand the substance of it.
>
> (Quoted in Lees-Marshment 2010, 74)

Political strategy also benefits from a specific group driving it. Both Glaab's (2007) study of Germany and Lindholm and Prehn's (2007) analysis of Denmark suggest that strategy tended to become associated with, and carried out by, a small informal group – usually centred around the leader; indeed, strategy worked only if they too were able to think strategically. Boaz and Solesbury (2007, 123, 132), and Glaab (2007, 100) suggest that several factors can help, including effective stakeholder support and management, making sure they have time in the schedule away from daily government business to reflect on strategy, having clear goals, and resisting the temptation to be diverted by short-term issues and problems. They also argue that leadership is crucial – there needs to be support from politicians and senior bureaucrats for staff engagement with strategy.

Government strategy units also encourage new thinking and change the nature of the civil service to reward strategic thinking. In the UK, the Labour government created the Prime Minister's Strategy Unit in 2003 during its second term in office, which examined spending reviews and five-year plans for different departments. The role of the Strategy Unit was to provide advice to the prime minister and to support government departments, including helping them to build their strategic capability and to identify and effectively address emerging policy challenges.

Research also points to a number of ways for politicians to try to avoid losing a market-orientation once in power. Gathering market intelligence on an ongoing basis is crucial. It can help ensure political leaders remain aware of any shifts in public support for their policies. Lilleker and Lees-Marshment (2005, 225–6) suggest strategies a government needs to implement to ensure it finds space and time to think about product design and development for the next election. Studying empirical examples from Blair and Clark, Lees-Marshment (2008) suggest a number of tools that can be used by governments (see Box 2.6).

Box 2.6 Tools to regain a market-orientation in government

1 **Conduct listening or consultation exercises to get back in touch:**
   e.g. UK Labour's 'The Big Conversation' in 2003 and 'Let's Talk' in 2005.

2 **Refresh the overall team:**
   e.g. the UK Labour 2005 campaign conveyed 'Team Labour', showing a range of politicians within the government, not just Blair; and NZ Labour refreshed the cabinet in 2007 and encouraged older MPs to retire, leaving room to promote those more junior.

3 **Use public-friendly, non-political communication:**
   Blair appeared on non-political television, such as the popular daytime programme *Richard and Judy,* and *Ant and Dec's Saturday Night Takeaway,* a mainstream Saturday evening programme, before the 2005 election; and after winning a he third term part in a comedy sketch with comedienne Catherine Tate for the charity television fundraising show *Comic Relief.*

4 **Acknowledge public concern with leaders' difficult, unpopular decisions or issues:**
   UK Labour enacted a 'masochism' strategy, where Blair met the public and listened to, and showed respect for, voters' disagreement with his decision to take the country into the Iraq war, explaining the pressures on a leader to take a decision whether it was popular or not.

5 **Develop new strategy for future terms, ensuring there is the space and time to think about product design/development for the next election:**
   In 2007, Clark implemented new policies such as KiwiSaver, free part-time child care and a new pension scheme and acknowledged the need to reduce income tax in response to market demand and economic conditions; in the UK, the Strategy Unit established in Blair's second term helped provide a means by which new ideas from academia, think tanks, private industry and non-governmental organisations were integrated into government.

Source: Adapted from Lees-Marshment (2008)

Governments need to be open to new information and willing to adapt in order to maintain a market-orientation in power (Lees-Marshment 2009b, 215–16). Many governments have struggled to reinvent themselves and offer a newly developed product after being elected. To ensure effective redevelopment, governments need to proactively question whether existing behaviour and practices actually maximise their performance, and they must be willing to challenge the status quo while being open to new ideas. Parties in government need to ensure that consultation and market research are disseminated so that politicians remain in touch. They need to ensure, in particular, that there are appropriate resources and time to maintain and develop a clear strategy, that there is continual debate as to how to best serve the public and other markets, and to maintain a balance between leadership and following public opinion.

Political strategy in the workplace

Political strategists are employed in government, parties and campaigns. They may be pollsters, advertisers, campaign managers or policy specialists, and may be inside the party or candidate's team or come from outside as a consultant. Once on board, they become part of the key decision making group that influences the overall direction of the organisation or campaign.

For example, Philip Gould was Strategy and Policy Advisor for the UK Labour Party from 1987 to 2005. Gould's job, however, was not formally that of a strategist. Instead, he came to the party from a career in advertising after founding his own polling and strategy company. He was known for his qualitative market research, championing the use of focus groups to identify why voters did not like Labour in 1992 despite their negative feelings towards the Conservative government. He then played a key role in modernising the UK Labour Party, including abandoning Labour's attachment to nationalism and embracing market economics, in the lead up to their successful general election campaign in 1997 – their first in 18 years. Paying tribute to Gould after his death, Prime Minister Tony Blair noted, 'he was my guide and mentor, a wise head, a brilliant mind.'

Another practitioner, Nicholas Reece, assumed a direct strategist position as Director of Strategy in the Australian Prime Minister's Office under Julia Gillard. Indeed, governments often require strategic skills among staff even if they are neutral civil servants or career staff rather than partisan. Boaz and Solesbury (2007, 121) note how the UK civil service provides a list of the core skills of a strategic thinker, which include the ability to:

- Shape and set a long-term vision for the department that takes into account both broader government priorities and delivery systems.
- Make trade-offs between different policy areas and over different time scales.
- Present ministers and colleagues with key choices based on robust evidence and champion the role of strategic thinking in the organisation.

Over the last decade, however, the work and profession of political strategy has been largely redefined by the team of strategists who helped elect Obama in 2008 and 2012, most notably David Axelrod and Jim Messina. Together, over of the course of two presidential elections, Axelrod and Messina built what has become known as the 'Obama model'. Axelrod, who served as Obama's strategic advisor for both campaigns, got his start in the rough-and-tumble world of Chicago politics in the 1980s. From the start, Axelrod played a leading role in Obama's messaging. He was instrumental, for example, in focusing the 2008 campaign on a message of 'change'. He had understood as early 2006, as he outlined in a memo he sent to Obama that assessed the strengths and weaknesses of potential general election opponents, that the need for 'change' in Washington would be the central theme of the 2008 election. To ensure voters recognised that Obama was the vehicle for the political change they desired, in both 2008 and 2012, Axelrod – aided by Messina, who served as Chief of Staff in 2008 and Campaign Manager in 2012 – erected a campaign infrastructure unprecedented in its use of data and market research to design unique targeting and positioning strategies. Messina is an expert in integrating data analytics and computer modelling into political strategy. In 2012, he oversaw a campaign that, as he described it, 'used data to inform almost every major decision' that was made. Doing so allowed the Obama campaign to run a highly targeted campaign that was in a way, 'personalised' for each Obama supporter (Messina 2013). One of the ways they achieved this was by running, every day, for months, tens of thousands of computer simulations on massive polling samples collected each night.

The 'Obama model' has since been exported abroad, but with mixed results. Both Axelrod and Messina worked on the 2015 UK general election, for example, but on opposite sides: Axelrod supporting Miliband and Labour, and Messina working with Lynton Crosby for David Cameron and the Conservatives. In that election, Messina's big data, numbers approach won. A year later, he helped Mariano Rajoy hang on as Prime Minister of Spain. However, Messina has also been involved in a string of defeats, including Cameron's 2016 failed bid to keep Britain in the EU and Theresa May and the Conservatives' inability to sustain a majority in the 2017 UK snap election. Messina also advised Italian Prime Minister Matteo Renzi's unsuccessful 2016 constitutional reform referendum.

Political strategists connect with a range of other areas of political marketing, and they have to be able to understand the minute details but also see the bigger picture. They help to interpret information and data to find a way forward to help political parties, campaigns and governments achieve their goals. Their work is therefore vital in political marketing, even if their jobs are not always directly advertised. To become a strategist, finding work in market research, communication, campaigning or policy will be useful. Lindholm and Prehn offer advice for how to be an effective strategist (see Box 2.7).

Box 2.7 Lindholm and Prehn's advice for political strategists

1 Have the facts at your fingertips and know what you are talking about.
2 Create a simple policy you can explain.
3 Make a plan and write it down.
4 Define your target group and go after this group, not the entire electorate.
5 Absorb knowledge, learning from what you see.
6 Be pragmatic.
7 Be courageous and strong.
8 Reinforce your analytical skills and learn to read the interests of others.
9 Define where you see yourself in five to ten years and work to get there.
10 Be very patient.

Source: Adapted from Lindholm and Prehn (2007, 59–69)

Summary

Political strategy is fundamental to political marketing: it determines how governments, parties and candidates think and behave in relation to the electorate. Strategy informs all other aspects of marketing, which will be explored in subsequent chapters. It includes targeting, positioning, defence/attack strategies and delivery. It is not easy to implement strategy, but the support of leadership, teams and units, and maintaining research and reflection, can all help strategy be implemented and maintained even in power.

Box 2.8 provides a best practice guide for market-based political strategy. Practitioners who have success with political strategy often end up in influential political positions as they are able to offer advice on a number of interconnected areas of political marketing. Before parties, candidates and governments can respond to what the market demands and how it behaves, they need to know what that is.

The next chapter will look at how political organisations use political market research to understand the market.

Box 2.8 Best practice guide to political strategy

1   Devise your strategy first: set achievable goals (not just winning votes) then figure out how to achieve them.

2   Allow time for strategy development: make it a core process with leadership support and internal resources.

3   Ensure the strategy is both clear and flexible: like a ship that adjusts its route in response to changes in the weather but retains the same destination.

4   Consider a range of stakeholders: voters, members/volunteers, donors, internal staff, external staff, politicians and candidates, lobbyists and think tanks, public/civil service, professional groups, media, regulatory bodies, competitors, cooperators and citizen experts.

5   Consider the candidate/organisation's history, beliefs and vision.

6   Create a targeting strategy using a range of data, analytics and predictive software to identify and better understand different segments and potential supporters.

7   Break segments such as seniors and women voters down into smaller groups (micro or nano targeting) where resources will be most effective, and diversify the product to better meet divergent needs within a segment.

8   When targeting, create a strategy for brand development, not just communication, so it will be convincing to new target groups.

9   Choose the right orientation strategy to suit the circumstances. A sales-oriented party might not win against other market-oriented competitors, but if your goal is not to win, or the opposition is sales oriented or product oriented, then you may not need to adopt a market-orientation. However, parties/candidates wishing to win control of government most likely need to become market oriented.

10   Minor parties or outsider candidates can adopt niche market-oriented behaviour and develop a product that responds to research into their specialist market.

11   Make the strategy localised: adapt ideas from global knowledge sharing to create a unique campaign each time.

12 When positioning, make sure the adopted position is consistent, credible, competitive and communicable, and stake your position early to force other parties to react to you.

13 Anticipate attacks and be proactive in response to them.

14 Do the ju-jitsu move: flip opponents' strength over by attacking them on their usual strengths to help undermine voter loyalty and get their traditional supporters to consider switching.

15 Cooperate with the competition if it brings benefits.

16 Make sure the product and positioning are authentic.

" " Discussion points

1 Think of examples where recent political candidates, leaders or parties have targeted certain groups – what were those targets, how did they respond to them and how effective was their targeting strategy overall?

2 Consider the current or recent positioning of particular candidates or parties. To what extent are they following criteria for successful positioning?

3 Which category (product-, sales- or market-oriented party) do current parties/ candidates/ leaders best fit into?

4 Discuss the main differences between the product-, sales- and market-oriented parties in Lees-Marshment's model, and debate which approach is more likely to win an election.

5 Think of candidates, parties or governments that have won elections with significant public support, only to lose touch and, with it, lose votes over time. Identify and discuss any who have succeeded in regaining a market-orientation.

6 What obstacles are there to effective strategy, and what tools can politicians or parties use to maintain effective strategy, especially once in government?

Assessment questions

Essay/exam

1 'Strategy is the most important part of political marketing.' Explain and critique the validity of this statement, illustrating your argument with examples and theory.

2 Discuss and evaluate the effectiveness of party positioning, utilising theories by Bannon, Collins and Butler, Cwalina and Falkowski, Baines *et al.*, and Harada and Morris.

3 To what extent did the parties that won power in the last election follow the Lees-Marshment Market-Oriented Party Model?

4 Discuss the effectiveness and limitations of the model of market-, sales- and product-oriented parties as a means of explaining modern party or candidate behaviour.

5 Discuss the extent to which the Lees-Marshment model of market-oriented parties is followed in detail, comparing examples such as UK Labour/Blair in 1997, Australia Labor/Rudd in 2007, US Democrats/Obama in 2008 and 2012, UK Conservatives/Cameron in 2015, Canadian Liberals/Trudeau in 2015 and US Republicans/Trump in 2016, and noting where the cases do not follow the model as well as where they do.

Applied

1   Apply Baines *et al.*'s analysis of positioning to candidate or party behaviour in a recent election and determine which type of positioning was employed.
2   Assess the extent to which *x* party or candidate(s) met Bannon's (2004) five principles for successful positioning (clarity, consistency, credibility, competitiveness and communication).
3   Identify and justify which position from Collins and Butler's theory you think the parties at the last national election fitted into (market leader, challenger, nicher, follower), and critique how effectively they managed the constraints and options for each market position.
4   Assess a minor party or political movement against the criteria put forward by Harada and Morris, and make recommendations for what they should improve.
5   Apply the Lees-Marshment model of a market-oriented party in detail to Obama's 2008 and 2012 campaigns and his two terms in government, exploring the extent to which he maintained a market-orientation in government as well as campaigning.
6   Identify a range of empirical examples of political organisations or leaders which fit the ideal types of political marketing strategies outlined by Winther Nielsen, and critique their effectiveness.
7   Assess whether the parties in *x* country fall into a product-, sales- or market-oriented party category, and make recommendations as to whether they should retain or change their orientation to achieve their goals in the future.
8   Create a political marketing Strategic Plan: write an original, present-day political marketing plan that assesses how well a party uses marketing research and strategy, and give recommendations for how it can improve its use of marketing to achieve its goals or objectives. Write as if you were a marketing consultant, planning how the party can use marketing in the years leading up to the next election. The plan is not a traditional essay and can therefore be written in report style, although it should include references to academic literature, where relevant, and primary sources.

Case study

Case Study 2.1 The failure of Blairism and the limits of market-orientation

Aditya Tejas (University of Auckland)

This case study will consider the poor reputation that Tony Blair and his market-oriented political style enjoyed in the later years of his administration and after, and contrast it to the resurgent popularity of the UK Labour Party under the more ideologically focused leadership style of Jeremy Corbyn. In considering these, it will address some of the limitations of market-oriented PMR and argue that increasing polarisation among voters in Western countries makes effective sales orientation a better option for opposition parties in the future.

Tony Blair made heavy use of market-oriented and interactive PMR techniques during his campaign and administration. In-depth focus groups were targeted at key 'loyalist' and 'undecided' voter segments to gain a nuanced and qualitative understanding of how they viewed Blair as a leader, and how they related to the overall New Labour brand. Based on these findings, Blair updated his policies and brand by becoming, for example, tougher on security and immigration issues in his second term in the face of uncertainty after the September 11th attacks and economic insecurity (Langmaid 2011).

Initially, Blair enjoyed success with this strategy. In both the 1997 and 2001 elections, Labour won by a landslide and Blair enjoyed approval ratings of over 50 per cent in 1997 (BBC 2007). Kuhn (2007) attributes this in part to the administration's carefully tuned media management, which consisted of both setting the news agenda, by promoting and downplaying certain stories, and pushing the brand of the New Labour party. The three key features of this strategy were centralisation, professionalisation and politicisation. Despite the initial successes of this 'public relations democracy', Kuhn notes that the mood of the press towards New Labour began to sour due to the administration's reputation for 'spin'-based media management, and by the time of the Iraq War Blair's image was already seriously tarnished, with approval ratings barely holding above 40 per cent at that time. By the time he announced his departure in 2006, his approval rating was in the 30s.

Here it is worth contrasting Blair's style with that of current Labour leader Jeremy Corbyn, whose relationship with the media and the electorate have also been quite troubled. According to Nunns (2017), Corbyn set three objectives as leader: to put forward a left policy platform, to democratise the party, and to make it more like a social movement than a traditional political party. This strategy is distinctly different from Blair's, which was highly centralised and undemocratic within the party apparatus and relied on focus groups and polls to determine the overall direction of the party brand. Blair did this in order to appeal to voters who did not traditionally vote for the Labour Party by changing its policies and image to be more appealing to them.

By contrast, Corbyn's distinctly sales-oriented, ideological approach drew in supporters among younger voters, even as the traditional class divide among voters seems to have closed, a strategy which saw Labour's vote share increase by the highest amount since 1945 (*Financial Times* 2017). Notably, age is the primary divider in UK politics now, with voters under 40 and young first-time voters expressing a strong preference for Labour. Notably, in the 2017 general election, Labour picked up voters from a variety of sources, including those who had formerly voted for the UK Independence Party (UKIP), the Liberal Democrats (Lib Dems) and the Greens. This was despite the fact that Corbyn's tone on immigration differed significantly from UKIP's and his stance towards Brexit ran against that of the Lib Dems.

Considering the personal brands of the two leaders, we can see that Blair's attempt to reach out to newer groups of voters and to maintain a professionalised and positive relationship with media stakeholders seems to have backfired, resulting in him becoming unpopular with the general public and among the media. By contrast, Corbyn's strategy seems to have won significant minorities of voters from two parties whose policies ran counter to his own.

Lessons for political marketing scholarship and practice

This example appears to show a shift in public responsiveness away from Blair's market-oriented strategy and towards more ideological leaders who come across as honest, even at the risk of alienating voter groups.

One of the key aspects of building a successful political brand involves creating a sense of solidarity and exclusivity in order to galvanise one's voter base and define the party against its opposition. Corbyn's Labour enthusiastically embraced this strategy, most clearly seen in their slogan for the 2017 general election – 'We are Many, and They are Few' – and Corbyn's declaration that the Labour Party poses a threat to the Conservative Party and the finance sector.

This oppositional branding, which is polarising and potentially alienating to many voter segments, seems to have paid off because of Corbyn's cultivated image as an honest and ideologically principled leader. His victories, not just among core Labour voter segments but also former UKIP and Lib Dem voters, show the power that a leader's rhetoric and branding can have in actively setting the political agenda and discourse of a nation, rather than the market-oriented strategy of seeking to understand the immediate concerns of voters and altering one's policies to suit them.

References

BBC (2007). 'Tony Blair: Highs and lows'. *BBC News*, UK Politics, 10 May 2007. http://news.bbc.co.uk/2/hi/uk_news/politics/4717504.stm (accessed 10 January 2018).

Financial Times (2017). 'Election 2017: how the UK voted in 7 charts'. *Financial Times*, 17 July 2017. www.ft.com/content/dac3a3b2-4ad7-11e7-919a-1e14ce4af89b (accessed 10 January 2018).

Kuhn, R. (2007). 'Media management'. In *Anthony Seldon* (ed.) *Blair's Britain, 1997–2007*. Cambridge: Cambridge University Press, 123–43.

Langmaid, R. (2011). 'Reconnecting the Prime Minister'. Blog post on *The Landmaid Practice*, 31 October 2011. www.langmaidpractice.com/reconnecting-the-prime-minister/ (accessed 29 September 2017).

Nunns, A. (2017). *The Candidate*. S.l.: OR Books.

Democratic Debate 2.1   A divided nation – a consequence of exaggerated marketing? The case of the Czech Republic

Otto Eibl (Masaryk University)

The use of marketing in the political arena is often criticised. Sometimes this criticism is justified, sometimes it is not (Henneberg 2006a). Although the question of whether marketing can undermine democracy may seem straightforward, answering it can be difficult. Marketing itself is a set of neutral tools that can be used for both sublime and subversive reasons. Its impact on democracy is also dependent on our attitudes towards democracy (see Henneberg *et al.* 2009) and is deeply connected with political culture and the general atmosphere in particular countries. In other words, it is the context that matters. If a society places a premium on democratic values, and if the citizens are politically active and ready to deliberate, marketing can be helpful. On the other hand, marketing and its use could be treacherous because voters who are less politically engaged, not so well informed and apathetic might fall prey to political parties and candidates with populist or even extremist views.

Unfortunately, the Czech Republic is a perfect example of the latter. The public image of politics and the relationships between voters and political parties has been heavily damaged over the last 20 years. This process of alienation of citizens and politics started in the time of the Opposition Agreement (1998–2002) between primary political rivals Václav Klaus and Miloš Zeman (see Kopeček 2015). It resulted in the Czech population having very low levels of trust in political institutions and only moderate interest in politics in general.

This and many scandals within traditional politics created a perfect opportunity for a new and potent political actor, Andrej Babiš, a controversial billionaire who bought influential media house MAFRA (which includes two important dailies, one nationwide radio station and various other media platforms) shortly before the 2013 parliamentary election and who now faces several scandals. His political movement, ANO 2011, quickly became popular and ended in second position in the 2013 parliamentary election; four years later, they won the election by a considerable margin – in particular, but not exclusively, due to political marketing.

An entirely new style of politics

The marketing team around Babiš understood that the Czech political market was saturated and that another ideologically-based party would not be successful. Hence, Babiš and his movement were not presented as an ideological alternative to other political parties. The campaign communication stressed Babiš's reputation as a successful and incorruptible entrepreneur with exceptional managerial skills, someone who would be able to put the country on the right track (the main claim was 'YES, it will be better'). What they offered was a completely new political style personalised by Babiš (one of his main catchphrases was 'To run the state as a firm'). Babiš refused to label himself and his fellows as politicians because, according to him, politicians only 'chatter' and don't work for the sake of the country (a position intended to invoke the popular tradition of Václav Havel's antipolitical politics?). All this was seen by many citizens as a breath of fresh air in Czech politics.

When he decided to enter politics, Babiš quickly adopted the strategy of a tactical populist, which is based on a follower mentality (Henneberg 2006b, 31). Simply put, most of the time Babiš does and says what people want him to do and what they like. This, together with Babiš's team's extraordinary sense for targeted, meaningful, comprehensible, permanent and multi-channel communication (with great emphasis on social media platforms) helped ANO gain the dominant position in the Czech political market.

Consequences of Babiš's political marketing

Unfortunately, Babiš's use of political marketing techniques causes significant problems for the Czech political system. It has led to ideological flexibility, politics of permanent conflict and limited coalition potential.

Ideological flexibility

Babiš's publicly- and repeatedly-declared goal is to make the Czech political system more efficient and eliminate corruption. Other policy goals appear to be more flexible. Babiš's position on many issues changes frequently over time because he constantly tries to be in line with the majority of voters. The list of issues about which he has already changed his mind is extensive and includes the approach to the euro-adoption, migrants, the gender quota and finishing building the nuclear power plant in Temelín. Sometimes he speaks about issues which he does not really want to take action on (such as the abolition of the Senate) because doing so can gain him more popularity. The voters do not penalise him for his incongruences. Instead, they praise him for listening to the voice and the will of people.

Politics of permanent conflict

Babiš understands that, in order to rule with the consent of the citizens, he must be favoured by (his) voters. To achieve this, his style is confrontational, and it does not include compromises with his political opponents. Thus, his marketing operations have three permanent goals:

1   To present him as a selfless, successful, potent and competent candidate (even by manipulating the public agenda).
2   To criticise (or even attack) his opponents, even if they were coalition partners.
3   To portray him as an average citizen or everyman, although he is a billionaire (the resulting image is rather a simulation of a candidate; cf. Zavattaro 2010).

Partly due to his aggressive approach, Czech politics reached a state of permanent conflict at many levels.

Limited coalition potential

The state of permanent conflict among most Czech political parties, the unpredictable nature of Babiš's politics and his often-controversial approach to coalition partners make it difficult for other political actors to deal with him. Furthermore, to form a stable political coalition (without the support of communists and other extremists) is more than difficult after the 2017 election. Also, leaders of many parties took strong positions against Babiš before the election and categorically denied possible post-electoral cooperation with him. To break this pledge could be considered as a betrayal of the voters and lead to decrease in support in the next election.

To conclude

Babiš's approach to politics is the result of a well-chosen marketing strategy. Continuous use of marketing techniques, market research and targeted communication from Babiš, together with the inability of other political actors to do the same, quickly helped ANO 2011 to win the dominant position in the Czech political system. At the same time, it causes a lot of problems. Without any doubt, this strategy would work perfectly in a two-party system; it would be the winning strategy. But in the Czech Republic, to win an election is not enough. When planning a campaign strategy, the parties and marketing experts should realise that after the election they will have to deal with others, and an exaggerated campaign could make it difficult or even impossible to do so. As we see in the Czech Republic, perfect use of political marketing techniques led to a partly paralysed political system and a divided society. Applied marketing strategy should lead to victories, but not to victories at any cost.

References

Henneberg, Stephan C. (2006a). 'The Views of An advocatus Dei: Political Marketing and Its Critics'. *Journal of Public Affairs*, 4(3): 225–43. doi:10.1002/pa.187.

Henneberg, Stephan C. (2006b). 'Leading or Following?' *Journal of Political Marketing*, 5(3): 29–46. doi:10.1300/J199v05n03_02.

Henneberg, Stephan C., Margaret Scammell and Nicholas J. O'Shaughnessy (2009). 'Political Marketing Management and Theories of Democracy'. *Marketing Theory*, 9(2): 165–88. doi:10.1177/1470593109103060.

Kopeček, Lubomír (2015). *Deformace Demokracie?* Brno: Barrister & Principal.

Zavattaro, Staci M. (2010). 'Brand Obama'. *Administrative Theory & Praxis*, 32(1): 123–8. doi:10.2753/ATP1084-1806320108.

Notes

1 See for example a collation of political ads for women Oct 2012 on www.youtube.com/watch?v=qUmh4KCzrjc.
2 See Michelle Obama – Join Women for Obama – www.youtube.com/watch?v=KaXtEwTszac&feature=relmf.

References

Ahmad, Nyarwi (2017). 'Political Marketing Management of Parliament Under the Presidential Government System: A Lesson Learned from the Indonesia House of Representative Post–New Order Soeharto'. *Journal of Political Marketing*, 16(2): 71–94.

Asano, Masahiko and Bryce Wakefield (2010). 'Political market-orientation in Japan'. In Jennifer Lees-Marshment, Jesper Strömbäck and Chris Rudd (eds) *Global Political Marketing*. London: Routledge, 234–48.

Ashcroft, M. and I. Oakeshott (2015). *Call Me Dave: The Unauthorized Biography of David Cameron*. London: Biteback.

Baines, Paul, Ian Crawford, Nicholas O'Shaughnessy, Robert Worcester and Roger Mortimore (2014). 'Positioning in political marketing: How semiotic analysis adds value to traditional survey approaches'. *Journal of Marketing Management*, 30(1–2): 172–200.

Balestrini, Pierre P. and Paul R. Gamble (2011). 'Confronting EU unpopularity: the contribution of political marketing'. *Contemporary Politics*, 17(1): 89–107.

Bannon, Declan (2004). 'Marketing segmentation and political marketing'. Paper presented to the UK Political Studies Association, University of Lincoln, 4–8 April 2004.

Barber, Stephen (2005). *Political Strategy: Modern Politics in Contemporary Britain*. Liverpool, UK: Liverpool Academic Press.

Barber, Stephen (2009). 'The strategy of the British Liberal Democrats' Case Study 3.4. In Jennifer Lees-Marshment (ed.) *Political Marketing: Principles and Applications*. London and New York: Routledge, 73–4.

Bendle, Neil, Joseph Ryoo and Alina Nastasoiu (2018). 'The 2016 US primaries: Parties and candidates in the world of big data'. In Jamie Gillies (ed.) *Political Marketing in the 2016 U.S. Presidential Election*. New York: Palgrave Macmillan, 65–80.

Bigi, Alessandro, Michelle Bonera and Anjali Bal (2015). 'Evaluating political party positioning over time: A proposed methodology'. *Journal of Public Affairs*, 16(2): 128–39.

Bigi, Alessandro, Emily Treen and Anjali Bal (2016). 'How customer and product orientations shape political brands'. *Journal of Product and Brand Management*, 25(4): 365–72.

Boaz, Annette and William Solesbury (2007). 'Strategy and politics: the example of the United Kingdom'. In Thomas Fischer, Gregor Peter Schmitz and Michael Seberich (eds) *The Strategy of Politics: Results of a Comparative Study*. Gütersloh: Verlag Bertelsmann Stiftung, 107–32.

Collins, Neil and Patrick Butler (2002). 'Considerations on market analysis for political parties'. In Nicholas O'Shaughnessy and Stephan Henneberg (eds) *The Idea of Political Marketing*. London: Praeger, 1–18.

Conley, Brian M. (2014). 'Does Obama care? Assessing the delivery of health reform in the United States'. In Jennifer Lees-Marshment, Brian Conley and Kenneth Cosgrove (eds) *Political Marketing in the United States*. New York: Routledge, 272–88.

Conley, Brian M. (2018). 'Thinking what he says: Market research and the making of Donald Trump's 2016 presidential election'. In Jamie Gillies (ed.) *Political Marketing in the 2016 U.S. Presidential Election*. New York: Palgrave Macmillan, 29–48.

Cwalina, Wojciech and Andrzej Falkowski (2015). 'Political branding: Political candidates positioning based on inter-object associative affinity index'. *Journal of Political Marketing*, *14*(1–2): 152–74.

Davidson, Scott and Robert H. Binstock (2012). 'Political marketing and segmentation in aging democracies'. In Jennifer Lees-Marshment (ed.) *Routledge Handbook of Political Marketing*. London and New York: Routledge, 20–33.

Delacourt, Susan (2016). *Shopping for votes: How politicians choose us and we choose them*. Madeira Park: Douglas and McIntyre.

Devine, Tad (2013). 'Obama campaigns for re-election'. In Dennis W. Johnson (ed.) *Campaigning for President 2012: Strategy and Tactics*. New York: Routledge, 137–50.

Downer, Lorann (2014). 'Positioning for Power in Australia' Case Study 2.1. In Jennifer Lees-Marshment (ed.) *Political Marketing: Principles and Applications*. London and New York: Routledge, 49–52.

Fischer, Thomas, Gregor Peter Schmitz and Michael Seberich (eds) (2007). *The Strategy of Politics: Results of a Comparative Study*. Gütersloh: Verlag Bertelsmann Stiftung.

Glaab, Manuela (2007). 'Strategy and politics: the example of Germany'. In Thomas Fischer, Gregor Peter Schmitz and Michael Seberich (eds) *The Strategy of Politics: Results of a Comparative Study*. Gütersloh: Verlag Bertelsmann Stiftung, 61–106.

Gorbounova, Daria and Jennifer Lees-Marshment (2009). 'Political marketing strategy of Hillary Clinton in the 2008 Iowa and New Hampshire primaries' Case study 5.3. In Jennifer Lees-Marshment (ed.) *Political Marketing: Principles and Applications*. London and New York: Routledge, 126–8.

Harada, Susan and Helen Morris (2012). 'Niche Marketing the Greens in Canada and Scotland'. In Jennifer Lees-Marshment (ed.) *Routledge Handbook of Political Marketing*. London and New York: Routledge, 93–106.

Hughes, Andrew and Stephen Dann (2010). 'Australian political marketing: substance backed by style'. In Jennifer Lees-Marshment, Jesper Strömbäck and Chris Rudd (eds) *Global Political Marketing*. London: Routledge, 82–95.

Johns, Robert and Heinz Brandenburg (2014). 'Giving voters what they want? Party orientation perceptions and preferences in the British electorate'. *Party Politics*, 20(1): 89–104.

Kiss, Balázs (2009). 'The Hungarian Socialist Party winning young people' Case Study 5.2. In Jennifer Lees-Marshment (ed.) *Political Marketing: Principles and Applications*. London and New York: Routledge, 123–5.

Kiss, Balázs and Zsuzsanna Mihályffy (2010). 'Political salesmen in Hungary'. In Jennifer Lees-Marshment, Jesper Strömbäck and Chris Rudd (eds) *Global Political Marketing*. London: Routledge, 143–56.

Kotler, Philip and Sidney J. Levy (1969). 'Broadening the concept of marketing'. *Journal of Marketing*, 33(1): 10–15.

Kotzaivazoglou, Iordanis and Torgos Zotos (2010). 'The level of market-orientation of political parties in Greece'. In Jennifer Lees-Marshment, Jesper Strömbäck and Chris Rudd (eds) *Global Political Marketing*. London: Routledge, 28–42.

Lees-Marshment, Jennifer (2001). *Political Marketing and British Political Parties: The Party's Just Begun*. Manchester, UK: Manchester University Press.

Lees-Marshment, Jennifer (2008). 'Managing a market-orientation in government: cases in the UK and New Zealand'. In Dennis W. Johnson (ed.) *The Routledge Handbook of Political Management*. New York and Abingdon, UK: Routledge, 524–36.

Lees-Marshment, Jennifer (2009a). 'Political marketing and the 2008 New Zealand election: a comparative perspective'. *Australian Journal of Political Science*, 44(3): 457–75.

Lees-Marshment, Jennifer (2009b). 'Marketing after the election: the potential and limitations of maintaining a market-orientation in government'. Rethinking Public Relations special issue for *The Canadian Journal of Communication*, 34(2): 205–27.

Lees-Marshment, Jennifer (2010). 'New Zealand Political Marketing: marketing communication rather than the product?' In Jennifer Lees-Marshment, Jesper Strömbäck and Chris Rudd (eds) *Global Political Marketing*. London: Routledge, 65–81.

Lees-Marshment, Jennifer (2011). *The Political Marketing Game*. Houndmills, UK and New York: Palgrave Macmillan.

Lees-Marshment, Jennifer (ed.) (2018). *Political marketing and management in the 2017 New Zealand election*. Basingstoke, UK: Palgrave Macmillan.

Lees-Marshment, Jennifer, Yannick Dufresne, Gregory Eady, Danny Osborne, Cliff van der Linden and Jack Vowles (2015). 'Vote compass in the 2014 New Zealand election: Hearing the voice of New Zealand voters'. *Political Science*, 67(2): 94–124.

Lees-Marshment, Jennifer, Jesper Strömbäck and Chris Rudd (eds) (2010) *Global Political Marketing*. London: Routledge.

Lilleker, Darren and Jennifer Lees-Marshment (eds) (2005). *Political Marketing: A Comparative Perspective*. Manchester, UK: Manchester University Press.

Lindholm, Mikael R. and Anette Prehn (2007). 'Strategy and politics: the example of Denmark'. In Thomas Fischer, Gregor Peter Schmitz and Michael Seberich (eds) *The Strategy of Politics: Results of a Comparative Study*. Gütersloh: Verlag Bertelsmann Stiftung, 11–60.

Maier, Michaela, Jens Tenscher and Kirsten Schüller (2010). 'Political marketing in Germany'. In Jennifer Lees-Marshment, Jesper Strömbäck and Chris Rudd (eds) *Global Political Marketing*. London: Routledge, 34–51.

Mathesian, Charlie. (2016). 'Glenn Thrush Interviews David Plouffe'. *Politico*, 29 March 2016. www.politico.com/story/2016/02/off-message-david-plouffe-2016-219942 (accessed in June 2018).

Matušková, Anna, Otto Eibl and Alexander Braun (2010). 'The Czech case: a Market-Oriented Party on the rise?' In Jennifer Lees-Marshment, Jesper Strömbäck and Chris Rudd (eds) *Global Political Marketing*. London: Routledge, 157–74.

Messina, Jim (2013). 'Obama Campaign Manager Jim Messina Talks Big Data at the Milken Institute's 2013 Global Conference'. Milken Institute, published 23 May 2013. www.youtube.com/watch?v=mZmcyHpG31A&feature=youtu.be.

Mullen, Andrew (2016). 'Election strategies, campaign themes and target voters'. In D. G. Lilleker and M. Pack (eds) *Political Marketing and the 2015 UK General Election*. Basingstoke, UK: Palgrave Macmillan, 11–34.

Newman, Bruce I. (1994). *The Marketing of the President: Political Marketing as Campaign Strategy*. Thousand Oaks, CA: SAGE Publications.

Newman, Bruce I. (ed.) (1999). *Handbook of Political Marketing*. Thousand Oaks, CA: SAGE Publications.

Newman, Bruce I. (2016). 'Reinforcing lessons for business from the marketing revolution in U.S. presidential politics: A Strategic Triad'. *Psychology and Marketing*, 33(10): 781–95.

Ormrod, Robert P. (2005). 'A conceptual model of political market orientation'. In Walter Wymer and Jennifer Lees-Marshment (eds), *Current Issues in Political Marketing*. Binghamton, NY: Haworth Press, 47–64.

Ormrod, Robert P. (2006). 'A critique of the Lees-Marshment Market-Oriented Party model'. *Politics*, 26/2(May): 110–18.

Ormrod, Robert P. and Stephan C. Henneberg (2006). 'Different facets of market orientation: a comparative exploratory analysis of party manifestos in Britain and Germany'. Paper presented at the 3rd International Conference on Political Marketing, Cyprus, 5 April 2006.

Ormrod, Robert P., Ghasem Zaefarian, Stephen C. Henneberg and Philippe de Vries (2015). 'Strategy, market orientation and performance: the political context'. *Journal of Public Affairs*, 15(1): 37–52.

Patrón Galindo, Pedro (2009). 'The re-launch of the APRA Party in a new political era in Peru' Case study 3.2. In Jennifer Lees-Marshment (ed.) *Political Marketing: Principles and Applications*. London and New York: Routledge, 69–70.

Patrón Galindo, Pedro (2010). 'Political marketing in a weak democracy: the Peruvian case'. In Jennifer Lees-Marshment, Jesper Strömbäck and Chris Rudd (eds) *Global Political Marketing*. London: Routledge, 202–17.

Pettitt, Robin (2012). 'Internal party political relationship marketing: Encouraging activism amongst local party members'. In Jennifer Lee-Marshment (ed.) *Routledge Handbook of Political Marketing*, London: Routledge, 137–50.

Promise (2006). *Reconnecting the Prime Minister*. Paper 21 for the Market Research Society. www.promisecorp.com/documents/Reconnecting_the_Prime_Minister.pdf (accessed September 2013).

Rosin, Hannah (2012). 'Rise of the single-woman voter'. *Slate*, 13 March 2012. https://slate.com/human-interest/2012/03/single-women-are-the-new-swing-voters-but-which-way-do-they-lean.html (accessed June 2013).

Russell, Andrew and Edward Fieldhouse (2005). *Neither Left nor Right? The Liberal Democrats and the Electorate*. Manchester, UK: Manchester University Press.

Savigny, Heather (2005). 'Labour, political marketing and the 2005 election: a campaign of two halves'. *Journal of Marketing Management*, 21(9/10): 925–41.

Stockemer, Daniel and Mauro Barisione (2017). 'The "new" discourse of the Front National under Marine Le Pen: A slight change with a big impact'. *European Journal of Communication*, 32(2): 100–15.

Strömbäck, Jesper (2010a). 'A framework for comparing political market-orientation'. In Jennifer Lees-Marshment, Jesper Strömbäck and Chris Rudd (eds) *Global Political Marketing*. London: Routledge, 16–33.

Strömbäck, Jesper (2010b). 'Political market-orientation in a multi-party system: the Swedish case'. In Jennifer Lees-Marshment, Jesper Strömbäck and Chris Rudd (eds) *Global Political Marketing*. London: Routledge, 52–64.

Strömbäck, Jesper, Christina Grandien and Kajsa Falasca (2013). 'Do campaign strategies and tactics matter? Exploring party elite perceptions of what matters when explaining election outcomes'. Journal of Public Affairs, 13(1): 41–52.

Temple, Mick (2010). 'Political marketing, party behaviour and political science'. In Jennifer Lees-Marshment, Jesper Strömbäck and Chris Rudd (eds) *Global Political Marketing*. London: Routledge, 263–77.

Wakefield, Bryce (2009). 'Principle versus patronage: the Lees-Marshment method and political marketing in Japan' Case Study 3.3. In Jennifer Lees-Marshment (ed.) *Political Marketing: Principles and Applications*. London and New York: Routledge, 71–2.

Winder, Georg and Jens Tenscher (2012). 'Populism as political marketing technique'. In Jennifer Lees-Marshment (ed.) *Routledge Handbook of Political Marketing*. London and New York: Routledge, 230–42.

Wilcox (2014). 'The Green Party's SOP/MOP strategy at the 2011 general election in New Zealand' Case Study 2.3. In Jennifer Lees-Marshment (ed.) *Political Marketing: Principles and Applications*. 2nd edition. London: Routledge, 54–6.

Winther Nielsen, Sigge (2012). 'Three faces of political marketing strategy'. *Journal of Public Affairs*, 12(4): 293–302.

Winther Nielsen, Sigge (2013). 'Toward a new institutional strategy framework for political marketing'. *Journal of Public Affairs*, 13(1): 84–99.

Winther Nielsen, Sigge (2015). 'Party planners – how political strategies are chosen'. Journal of Public Affairs, 15(4): 340–63.

3 Political market research

by André Turcotte and Jennifer Lees-Marshment

The last few years have been difficult for political market research (PMR). The most obvious misses have been the inability of opinion polling to predict that the Britons were ready to leave the European Union (Brexit) and that Donald Trump would become the 45th President of the United States. But there have been numerous other instances when pollsters have been embarrassed by their predictions. For instance, market intelligence specialists have failed to accurately predict the outcome of the UK general election, the Scottish referendum and several aspects of the 2016 US presidential election, such as Bernie Sanders's win over Hillary Clinton in the Michigan primary. A more recent area of disparagement associated with the practice of PMR centres around innovation associated with data-mining and voter profiling. Previously unknown firms like Cambridge Analytica have come under media scrutiny for what appears to be questionable use of first-, second- and even third-party data to influence the outcome of elections (Gonzalez 2017). This practice has also engulfed Facebook, which had to defend its privacy practices.

While opinion polling as reported in the media only represents the public face of what we refer to as political market research and is only a small part of the area, it is important because whatever prestige political market research may have, it originates with this public dimension. As Wheeler noted more than four decades ago: 'polls are often misrepresented and some are deliberately rigged, yet they are all treated with unquestioning respect' (Wheeler 1976, 13).

Despite the controversies, political market research remains fundamental to political marketing; it ensures that any decisions taken are well informed. In this chapter, we will explore the multiple facets of political market research and go beyond opinion polls. We will see that it involves a wide range of qualitative and quantitative, and formal and informal, methods enabling candidates, parties and governments to understand the nature of the political marketplace. Such research is used to understand the attitudes, behaviour, needs and wants of the public and other key stakeholders and then inform decisions about strategy, creation of the brand, policies, internal political marketing within organisations, and communication of positions with the view to inform, educate, persuade, change and reinforce existing views. In recent years, new techniques spurred by developments in data analytics have made the process of understanding citizens both more inconspicuous and more pervasive. This chapter offers an up-to-date look at political market research and will cover:

- The political market and the political consumer.
- Quantitative research including polling and surveys, segmenting and profiling the market, and data analytics.

- Qualitative research including focus groups and co-creation.
- Other PMR tools including informal research and opposition research.
- How PMR is used.
- Limitations on the influence of PMR.
- PMR in the Workplace.

Context: The political market and the political consumer

The decline in traditional patterns of political behaviour

Speaking in the aftermath of a US presidential election, Hezekiah Niles, the then editor of the *Weekly Register*, complained that the election had been 'the most anxious and ardent, as well as the most rude and ruthless political contest that ever took place in the United States' (Parsons 2009, xiii). Others mused that the election brought about 'so many changes in society – so many families broken up, and those of the first distinction . . . Oh! 'tis melancholy' (Ibid). While those sentiments are not new, it is striking that they were written in reference to the 1828 contest between Andrew Jackson and John Quincy Adams – almost two hundred years ago. The political environment, or its modern moniker of political marketplace, is constantly evolving and has been the focus of concern among scholars, pundits and politicians since the early days of democracy. Public opinion research has made the most important element in democracy – the will of the people – measurable and available for political decision making on an almost daily basis (Donsbach and Traugott 2008, 3). This political marketplace, which includes every obscure factor a candidate, party or government has to consider as well as the more obvious aspects such as how voters behave, is the arena where democracy operates and thus deserves this continual scrutiny.

While changes in the political marketplace may have been a constant reality, the pace and depth of this transformation has accelerated in the past few decades. The advent of the 24-hour news channels revolutionised the communication of politics, but this has given way to something more akin to a '24-second' news cycle where social media allows for a constant update on evolving news. This has had significant implications on actors in the political marketplace and how they receive and process communication. As Fearn-Banks suggests: 'whereas we used to have a golden hour to disseminate crucial information about a crisis, now we have a golden few minutes before publics expect information' (2017, 1). The scope of the changes has affected the attitude of voters towards institutions in general and politicians in particular.

There is a substantial area of research that reports a declining respect for, and confidence and trust in, established institutions and politicians. A study conducted by Edelman Canada indicates that the decline in trust is far from subsiding and is a worldwide phenomenon expanding beyond politics. Based on more than 33,000 interviews conducted in 28 markets around the world in early 2018, the 2018 Edelman Trust Barometer shows that the level of trust in institutions has declined in all but six markets, with the biggest decline in the US (–9% from 2017) and Italy (–5%). Only five countries (India, Indonesia, China, Singapore and the UAE) have an institutions trust score of over 60 (on a 0–100 scale), and 19 countries score below 50 (Edelman 2018). This general mood of distrust has repercussions for several aspects of the political process, including forms of participation.

Traditional forms of political participation, including becoming a member or formal supporter of a party and even voting itself, have been in decline for more than three decades. This situation has become an important issue of concern for political marketing.

As Richardson notes: 'One of the most pressing issues in both the political science and political marketing literature, for practitioners and commentators alike, is the problem of voter disengagement from the electoral process' (2016, 283). At the same time, it has become more difficult to predict how people will vote when they decide to do so. The influence of traditional social groupings or cleavages, such as class, geography and family background, on voting has declined, while new electoral segments, such as those based on ethnicity, race, lifestyle, life cycle stage and age have emerged. In Canada, for example, deep regional and linguistic cleavages are emerging (see Gidengil 2012, 39) but in varying ways, so that, as Dufresne and Marland (2012, 23) note, political marketers 'can no longer split the population simply along an English and French linguistic line, especially not in cities and suburbs where immigrant populations are concentrated'.

This shift is further explored by Bricker and Ibbitson (2013), who point to the erosion of what was the old elite consensus known as the 'Laurentian Consensus' in Canada. This is being replaced by new geographical and ethnic centres of influence. Moreover, in a number of countries the senior market is expanding and diversifying, and Davidson and Binstock (2012, 24) argue that strategists have to conduct research to keep up to date with seniors' diverse needs. Not only are there various life cycle factors such as retirement, bereavement, giving up driving, giving up one's home, experiencing ill health and crime; older peoples' reactions to these factors vary widely, and thus governmental organisations need to conduct research to better understand the different needs within this group.

Continual media coverage also provides an uncomfortable, unrelenting environment for political parties and politicians, especially in government. Online media outlets enable the voter to be part of the broadcast and make the news, not just watch it; and the instant nature of mediums such as Twitter encourages the public to expect an instant response from politicians. Furthermore, research by Sherman *et al.* (2008) suggests that voters do not trust any source of information on (or from) political candidates. Similarly, Lloyd's (2009) research suggests that political elites cannot control how their communication is perceived. Lloyd interviewed members of the public and found that all of them regularly failed to understand, believe or agree with political communication; they form their perception of a political brand from a range of sources to obtain alternative perspectives. The attention they pay to political communication was also mitigated by other things going on in their lives. Hillygus and Shields (2009) argue in *The Persuadable Voter* that, as a result of all these changes, voters are increasingly subjected to cross-pressures, and parties can attract voters by putting emphasis on the issues that are a source of internal conflict. Others argue that parties can appeal to citizens as consumers.

Political consumerism

The public is increasingly consumerist towards political elites and institutions. As Pharr and Putnam (2000) argue, citizens have new expectations and information that have altered the criteria by which they judge their governments. The public act more like consumers, not just in how they vote but in their overall attitude to politicians – what they demand, how they want to be involved, how they question authority, how they want to be consulted and how they scrutinise lack of delivery.

Consumerisation has a number of effects on politics. Voters themselves want a more tangible, rather than a rhetorical, product: hence the rise of pledge cards, guarantees or contracts between the government and people. Some political parties have also suggested 'right-of-recall' legislation as a way to give voters some democratic tools to remove elected politicians from office. Voters also want more evident and instant delivery, and they prefer achievement to aspiration and pragmatic effectiveness to moral principle, so delivery management is increasingly important. Parties and politicians need to convey their governing capability and political promises need to be costed and realistic. As Bennett (2012, 26) notes when discussing the consumerisation aspect of personalised politics, 'individuals have become fully immersed in consumer cultures and have developed a discerning eye for their political and personal products' which 'undermines the appeal of adopting collective identifications with party, ideology, or conventional movements'.

The other side of this equation is that political market research is continuing to expand its reliance on concepts and approaches from business and marketing to better understand voters. For instance, Rao (2017, 528) discusses how borrowing from consumer psychology can shed light on the way some segments of the electorate can be persuaded during campaigns specifically by understanding that most segments of the electorate are dynamic – they 'transition from one state to the other because of changes in life-stage, the environment, marketing persuasion and the like'. Similarly, Winchester (2016) looks at how the well-researched marketing terms 'user' and 'usage' can be applied to political marketing and to the behaviour of voters as consumers.

With emerging areas of analysis and a growing understanding of political consumerism, more scrutiny is given to the role of political marketing – and specifically its applications – on the erosion of traditional forms of political behaviour. While scholars have suggested that political marketing may be at least partly to blame for the problem of disengagement (Richardson 2016), others have shown that political marketing techniques are generally understood by the public (Johns and Brandenburg 2012) and can play a positive role in developing identity-based mobilisation strategies among disengaged citizens (Richardson 2016; Valenzuela and Michelson 2016).

Political consumer behaviour

While we have seen some research progress in applying concepts and approaches from business and marketing to better understand voters, there has been slower advancement made in trying to understand political consumer behaviour in a systematic manner. This is somewhat surprising since in business there is a substantial body of literature on consumer behaviour. Nevertheless, Busby (2009, 28) notes how, given that poll questions frequently ask voters whether they perceive candidates as being able to understand their needs or relate to ordinary people, expectations and perceptions of ordinariness are important to voters. Research by Chiu *et al.* (2010, 35) found that in addition to party identification and demography, respondents' voting behaviour choices were significantly related to personal values; specifically, whether they were:

- conscientious (sense of accomplishment, wise, ambitious, honest, self-controlled, logical, polite and responsible);
- self-confident (capable, imaginative, independent and intellectual);
- considerate (cheerful, clean, forgiving, helpful and loving);
- affectionate (happy, projecting inner harmony, mature love, self-respect and true friendship);
- artistic (envisioning a world at peace and a world of beauty).

Political consumer behaviour raises wider questions. Susan Delacourt's *Shopping For Votes: How Politicians Choose Us and We Choose Them* (2013) set out to define the way political consumer behaviour should be researched and examined. In her book, Delacourt explores how voters behave like and are treated as consumers. Although it focuses on Canada, the analysis is relevant to all modern democracies, and raises normative as well as practical questions. It discusses how political marketing first focused on advertising in the 1950s–1970s, then moved to a fusion of marketing and governance under Conservative Prime Minister Stephen Harper, followed by increased use of data management. *Shopping For Votes* asks us to reflect on whether the political marketplace needs rules and guidelines like the consumer marketplace.

All of this research points to the fact that the political marketplace is a very challenging one for politicians. Voters are like buyers who will switch supermarkets easily instead of building a long-term relationship of loyalty and trust with their local grocery store. In their book on voters as consumers, Lilleker and Scullion (2008, 1–2) conclude that politicians cannot just argue that they know what is best for the country and deliver that; they must listen to the key concerns of the public and deliver specific outcomes.

Political market research tools

PMR is used to ensure politicians are well informed. Lees-Marshment (2011) notes that it enables practitioners to see whether the daily critique common to 'planet politics' – the centre of political activity, whether it be Parliament Hill in Ottawa in Canada; Wellington BeeHive and Parliament in New Zealand, Westminster in London in the UK or Capitol Hill in Washington DC in the US – is being felt by the general public. In technical terms, it protects the political world from reacting to confirmation bias – a tendency to search for data to confirm your point of view.

There are a range of market research tools that can be used in politics, both quantitative and qualitative, offered by a substantial market research industry developed for corporations (see Box 3.1), and each method has always had pros and cons. The market intelligence industry is currently undergoing significant change. In its 2016 AMA Gold Report, the American Marketing Association stated that 'the market research industry, as we have known it for decades, is disappearing. It is being absorbed into a rapidly transforming collection of market intelligence sub-disciplines' (Bowers 2016). The transformation will affect the industry at different levels. We will likely see the emergence or consolidation of, on the one hand, new and more global organisations, and on the other hand, very specialised and highly technical boutique firms (see Box 3.1). It will also affect the way market research tools are used and how they will develop. The AMA suggests that the changes will impact traditional and advanced predictive research, as well as sampling, with new tools emerging in areas such as specialised data visualisation and the management of vast quantities of big data. Such changes experienced in the broader market research sector are seeping into the field of political market research. The new emphasis on the potential of advanced analytics and data proliferation means that quantitative research approaches have become more dominant than ever since they tend to yield more robust findings. In contrast, qualitative research, while still widely used, is struggling with establishing its legitimacy. We will review both approaches in turn.

Box 3.1 The market intelligence industry

Harris Interactive: harris-interactive.com

Nielsen: Nielsen.com

Gallup: gallup.com

Penn Schoen and Berland: psbresearch.com

Greenberg Quinlan Rosner Research: gqrr.com

Visioncritical: visioncritical.com

Ipsos: Ipsos.com

ORC International: orcinternational.com

Mission Research: MissionResearch.ca

Opinion Leader: opinionleader.co.uk

Pollara Strategic Insights: pollara.com

IDC: idc.com

Efficience 3: Efficience3.com

Colmar Brunton: colmarbrunton.co.nz

YouGov: today.yougov.com

GfK Global: gfk.com

IBI Global Research Solutions: ibigrs.com

IRI: iriworldwide.com

Westat: westat.com

Quantitative research

The fundamentals of conducting quantitative research have remained the same for many years. Generally, this approach uses closed questions to try to measure opinion and the strength of opinion. It provides big numbers – surface-level data. Examples include: polling; consumer panels; telephone surveys; online panels studies; and mail surveys. It provides accuracy just before an election and trends over time; it is also easy to administer, deliver data and compare results from quantitative research.

The constraints with quantitative research include the potential for bias in question design, the financial cost of the research, and the fact that you have to know what you want to measure before you do it so it is less likely to uncover new insights. Quantitative research has to be designed carefully to produce accurate results. It is impossible to ask everybody in the market, because the market is too big. Instead, a sample is drawn to reflect the overall population. Whereas the *population* includes all elements, units or individuals that are of interest to researchers for a specific study, a *sample* is a smaller-size population: a segment of people that will reflect or represent characteristics of an entire population. There are different options for the types of question asked, including structured multiple choice; opinion scales (e.g. very happy – happy – neutral – unhappy – very unhappy); rank order ('In your opinion, rank the following . . .'); and alternatives or paired comparisons ('Is *x* candidate lively or dull?'). The simplest polls merely ask for voting preferences, but more detailed questions give an idea of how voters perceive particular characteristics and track ongoing levels of support.

Quantitative polling is used in different ways at different times. There are a number of uses at different stages during a campaign, for example. Turcotte sets out five types of opinion polls frequently used in political campaigns (see also Rademacher and Tuchfarber 1999, 203–5; and Braun 2012, 17): see Box 3.2.

Box 3.2 Turcotte's stages of quantitative polling research during a political campaign

1 **Benchmark poll:** Typically the most in-depth poll (in terms of sample size and number of questions) conducted prior to the official beginning of the election campaign and designed to gather information on every relevant aspect of the campaign (issues, leaders' images, voting intentions, key segments, etc.). Braun (2012, 17) notes that the results are usually presented to the campaign leadership in significant detail and help develop the overall strategic plan of the campaign, its positioning, targeting and framework for communications.

2 **Strategic poll:** Poll conducted after the benchmark poll and designed to delve into the key findings gleaned in the benchmark poll. A strategic poll is often timed in conjunction with focus group research.

3 **Tracking poll:** Small poll typically conducted on a daily basis throughout the campaign and designed to look at the dynamics of voter choice, allowing for immediate strategic changes or readjustment in tactics.

4 **Brushfire poll:** Small poll designed to focus on an emerging issue or problem during the campaign.

5 **Post-election poll:** Large poll designed to ascertain the nature of the electoral mandate and evaluate the reasons for success or failure.

Source: Adapted from Turcotte (2012, 79)

Despite the value of research and the long tradition deeply steeped into statistical methods and advance data analysis, public opinion can be very volatile and hard to measure. Public opinion remains 'one of the fuzziest terms in the social sciences' (Donsbach and Traugott 2008, 1) and it is a testimony to its importance that it continues to garner close scrutiny across many disciplines. But the real contribution of political market research in understanding public opinion goes beyond the mere reporting on opinion to what it allows strategists to do with the data.

Segmenting and profiling the market

Segmentation is a crucial tool used to break up the heterogeneous, mass electoral market into smaller sections which can be targeted in terms of product, message and medium. With the decline in traditional forms of political participation, segmentation is more effective and actionable than left-right ideological divisions. Segmentation tries to identify common characteristics (see Box 3.3). It helps to create new and more precise groupings and can help to provide new understanding where traditional political labels no longer apply or work as effectively.

Box 3.3 Segmentation meta-categories

- Geographic: physical location of the individual, including country (macro-level), state, province or region (meso-level), city, town or electoral district (micro-level).
- Demographic: socially meaningful characteristics that identify an individual – e.g. age, stage in the life course, gender, income, family size, race, ethnicity or religion.
- Psychographic: phenomenological facts about an individual's values, attitudes, interests and aspirations; typically linked to socio-demographic characteristics, though important divergences can exist and should be identified.
- Behavioural: activities related to lifestyle such as consumption patterns and voting preferences; frequently linked to both socio-demographic characteristics and perceived benefits of behaviour, though identification of divergent groups is critical to achieving actionable segments.

Source: www.missionresearch.ca/segmentation-analysis/

This approach has a long tradition. As far back as the late 1970s, Margaret Thatcher, the UK's first female prime minister, gained support from a new segment – the skilled working class – through a policy enabling tenants to buy their council estate house. Similarly, Newman (1999, 263) observed how Bill Clinton's presidential re-election bid in 1996 succeeded by creating a message that appealed to the desire for an American dream across four segments of voters: rational voters, driven by their American dream expectations; emotional voters, driven by the feelings aroused by their desire to achieve the American dream; social voters, driven by the association of different groups of people and their ability to achieve the American dream; and situational voters, driven by situations that might influence their decision to switch to another candidate.

More recently, Braun (2012, 13) notes how researcher Mark Penn's company conducted a unique micro-targeting project for Republican candidate Michael Bloomberg's election campaign for mayor of New York City in 2001. At that time, 70 per cent of registered voters in New York were Democrats, so research was used to create a target group based on a combination of demographics, party affiliation and established attitudes and needs. This generated surprising outcomes such as that older, affluent Jewish males on Wall Street and younger, low-socio-economic-status Hispanic waitresses shared concerns about the effects of terrorism on their businesses and incomes, and thus the campaign was able to send all these groups communication on Bloomberg's security plan.

Segmentation can also be carried out at a much more detailed level. Turcotte (2012, 85) noted how strategists for the Canadian Conservatives in the 2006 and 2008 federal elections created fictional people to epitomize swing voters, such as:

- 'Dougie' – single, in his late twenties, working at Canadian Tire, who agreed with Conservative policies on crime and welfare abuse but was more interested in recreation than politics and might fail to turn out.

- 'Rick and Brenda' – a common-law couple with working-class jobs.
- 'Mike and Theresa' – who were better off and could become Conservative supporters if not for their Catholic background.

This identified about 500,000 voters out of the 23 million eligible voters the Conservative strategy could focus on to achieve victory.

Segmentation has recently become more sophisticated and precise. Psychographic segmentation is seen as more valuable because it considers the individual's actual behaviour and lifestyle rather than inferring that from other characteristics (see Practitioner Perspective 3.1).

Practitioner Perspective 3.1 on segmenting the market

Although the standard meta-categories of segmentation – geographic, demographic, psychographic and behavioural – provide the fulcrum for the first phase of analysis, a truly precise and actionable segmentation of any population (for example, an electoral bloc) requires a nested, multilevel approach that breaks down simple segments to reveal their complexity. It is no longer adequate, for example, to segment younger and older cohorts as more or less progressive in their political leanings; there is little actionable value in these labels. Instead, such meta-segments require another level of segmentation to identify the granularity in their characteristics – for example, a segment of older men with a net worth of a million dollars who live in a suburban area may be identified as conservative voters; still, the political riding in which these men live could play a significant role in mediating this relationship. Additional segmentation according to political riding (size, location, candidate) is necessary to define sub-segments that could affect the probability of the outcome (i.e., voting Conservative) for the meta-segment.

Heather Scott-Marshall, President of Mission Research (Source: telephone interview by author André Turcotte, 28 May 2018)

Texas is a good example, where we don't have any party registration, so we don't know whether somebody is a Republican or a Democrat . . . so micro targeting is very helpful in saying OK . . . somebody lives in this type of house, drives this type of car, reads these kinds of magazines, goes to this kind of church, has this many kids, and they voted in these last three elections, therefore we can make some basic assumptions about them.

Rick Beeson, RNC Political Director (Source: interviewed by author Jennifer Lees-Marshment, 2007, quoted in Lees-Marshment 2011, 20–1)

Segments should be selected strategically depending on goals and resources. As Burton (2012, 35) explains, strategic voter selection is 'the act of prioritizing members of the voting-eligible population, as individuals or as groups, in order to guide the allocation of outreach expenditures'. It helps maximise the effectiveness of resources by dividing the electorate into politically meaningful segments and estimating the benefit and costs of reaching them before identifying the most cost-effective means of accumulating enough votes to win the election. In the 2004 US presidential election, Republicans divided Michigan voters into 31 political categories, noting numbers and likelihood of voting

Republican in each one, such as religious conservative Republicans, tax-cut conservative Republicans, flag and family Republicans, anti-terrorism Republicans, and harder to reach groups such as wageable weak Democrats (Johnson 2007). Burton and Miracle (2014) note how the 2012 Obama re-election campaign invested $25 million into data analysis to maximise the efficiency of campaign expenditures.

Segmentation is also used to make sure a candidate's own supporters actually turn out to vote (GOTV) which is especially important when elections are close. Knuckey (2010, 107) argues that the goal of Bush's re-election campaign in 2004 was to 'mobilise the Republican base' using the RNC's database Voter Vault to target Bush voters. Finally, segmentation relies on data about voters which is gathered using software such as Voter Vault, Mosaic, Demzilla and the Constituent Information Management System (CIMS). Systems are sometimes tailor-made for specific parties – the US Republicans used Voter Vault, US Democrats used Demzilla and Canadian Conservatives used CIMS. Relative newcomers such as NationBuilder are expanding the capacity of those tools to incorporate voter segmentation, fundraising and communication targeting into one seamless product.

Data analytics

There has been an explosion of references to 'big data' in the last few years. At the time of writing, if you googled the term, you would get over 828 million results. And yet, the expression is not well understood. Big data 'refers to things one can do at a large scale that cannot be done at a smaller one, to extract new insights or create new forms of value, in ways that change markets, organisations, the relationship between citizens and governments, and more' (Mayer-Schönberger and Cukier 2013, 6). There is now a lot more data on individual behaviour available because we interact online, and this new information, together with extensive databases built by political parties, has enabled practitioners to engage statistical modelling to predict how voters will behave in response to a range of potential actions and messages from political organisations and politicians. Data is no longer being used just for one campaign; US parties are now combining data from one election to the next to build up a long-term resource. This makes the data much more nuanced and enables analysis to explore the consequences of several courses of action the leader may take in advance of the decision.

As Dalton notes, 'the US presidential elections of 2008 and 2012 were a coming out party for big data applications in electoral studies' (2016, 8). And while Dalton is cautious about his evaluation of the potential of big data applications, he acknowledges that 'Big data can be a powerful tool that dwarfs past methodologies' (Ibid, 18). This cautious approach is echoed by McNeely and Hahm, who suggest that 'Big data is rife with both promise and problems' (2014, 309) but that nevertheless it should be 'engaged with an appreciation not just of its power but also its limitations' (Ibid, 307). And the potential is impressive. For instance, in the 2012 Obama re-election campaign, staff analysed data to predict what communication would be most effective. Organisations like The Analyst Institute, founded in 2006 by liberal groups in the US, and the Canadian Firm Environics Analytics offer dedicated services combining data analysis and predictive modelling. They conduct randomised controlled experiments, or field experiments, to predict what will work in communication, and identify new groups of voters not discernible from other methods. Friesen (2011) discusses how, in Canada, Environics Analytics creates narrow, sophisticated segments based on a host of factors, from where people live to what they buy and believe. They assign one dominant group to each area, assuming that people who live nearby tend to have similar profiles; and in Surrey North the dominant group was seen to be 'fairly well-off, blue collar, South Asian families, both Canadian-born and immigrant. They're more likely to have large households and to speak a non-official language at home. Let's call them Aspirasians.' Friesen described how, in the 2008 Canadian federal election, the Conservatives got 10 per cent of this group to shift to them, as well as just under 1,000 votes from the next two largest groups: 'Canadian Tirekickers, mostly white exurban families' and 'Rust Collars, a low-income, mobile, working-class population'. This made the difference between winning and losing.

The rise of data analytics raises many implications to consider. Firstly, Turcotte (forthcoming) posits that one impact to consider is the surveillance capacities of big data on public opinion research. Accordingly, new technological developments and accompanying analytical techniques will 'make it feasible to understand individual behaviour in real-time and surreptitiously'. Turcotte divides the evolution of political market research into three periods: the traditional polling period, the market intelligence era and the emerging market surveillance period, and argues that:

> Recent developments in business, data management, and computer programming are combining to further improve the ability of opinion researchers to understand the needs and wants of individual voters. In particular, Data Management Platforms – or DMPs – are allowing businesses to know a lot about the behavior of individuals and DMPs make it possible to discern and deduct a lot about an individual without having to ask a single question.

The consequences of this shift for PMR will be discussed in a later section of this chapter. There are also ethical issues. The case study by Bozo (see Case Study 3.1) is a recent example of the potential applicability of data analytics, or 'big data', on political mobilisation. Further such examples are needed for the field to come to grips with the positive and negative influences big data may have on PMR but also on the practice of politics in general. The ethical implications of big data are also discussed in Democratic Debate 3.1.

Limitations of micro-targeting

All of these systems and methods are, however, limited by assumptions made on data that may be inaccurate, given that the data fed into the system is often collected by canvassing by party supporters or members on the ground, and thus elites risk spending a lot of money communicating inappropriate messages to people. As US Republican consultant Terry Nelson explained:

> It's not like I have called you up on the phone and you have said 'I believe in X, Y and Z'. All we know about you is that you fall into a segment in a voter file that says there is a high likelihood that you want low taxes . . . you can't say with great specificity that they support a reduction in capital gains taxes or the earned income tax credit . . . if you take the issue of abortion you might have a segment that is 75 per cent or 85 per cent pro-life, but you don't necessarily know how pro-life . . . [so] a very hardcore message . . . [is] likely to alienate some people in that segment.
>
> (Lees-Marshment 2011, 24)

Furthermore, micro-targeting can't solve every problem. As US consultant Gene Ulm noted: 'we couldn't micro target our way out of this last election . . . you can't micro target our way out of a third of Americans strongly supporting the President. That's a brand issue' (Lees-Marshment 2011, 24).

Qualitative research

Qualitative research comes in many forms, mainly: focus groups, participant observation, interviewing and ethnography. It is a field of inquiry in its own right and had a strong multidisciplinary tradition. It is used to *understand* rather than measure and thus uses open-ended questions and produces narrative data. It is designed to probe more deeply than quantitative research, exploring values, beliefs, attitudes and influences behind opinions measured by quantitative methods. Qualitative research can help explore whether an opinion can be changed. It is particularly powerful at uncovering the process people go through to get to a decision, an opinion or a particular point of view. While PMR occasionally relies on the whole spectrum of qualitative research tools, it mostly uses the focus group method.

Focus groups

Focus groups are small samples of typical consumers under the direction of a group leader who elicits their reaction to a stimulus, such as a potential ad, branding positioning, slogans or – in the context of politics – reactions to leaders, parties or policies. It is typically conducted with a group of between eight and ten participants. They are recruited to meet a certain list of characteristics that have been identified as important to the particular issue at hand. The focus groups are conducted in specially equipped facilities with recording equipment and a two-way mirror to allow observers to witness the proceedings.

As Kamberelis and Dimitriadis point out, 'focus groups are efficient in the sense that they generate large quantities of material from relatively large numbers of people in a relatively short time' (2005, 903). Moreover, focus groups often generate insights that are rarely produced through other methods (Ibid). Analysis is conducted not just on what is said but of body language. Mills (2011, 27) offers a definition:

> The political focus group is a facilitated discussion, usually amongst undecided voters ... [who have] some prospect of voting for the commissioning party. Typically in a campaign, a group would explore campaign impressions and views on critical issues, and test the messaging and campaign advertising.

Mills (2011, 36) notes how focus groups can help test how well a policy is understood, how best to argue for it, what the weak points are that need to be defended, what the best language is and how to explain the potential impact. Focus groups can also be used to understand why a party has lost support, as well as to develop new strategies to regain votes in the future. While focus groups undeniably play an important role in political market research, practitioners continue to struggle on how best to use them. For better or for worse, the comparative robustness of quantitative research results has pushed qualitative research into a secondary supportive role. This is even more the case with the data analytics upsurge. Nevertheless, focus groups are most efficient when they are used for very specific purposes. Morgan and Fellows organised the different uses of focus groups into three broad categories (2008, 340–3):

1　**Discovery-oriented groups:** Focus groups are used to uncover and understand the range of thinking cues voters rely on when assessing a particular research issue.

They aim is to draw up a list of elements or dimensions that are part of the voters' thinking process on a set of issues.

2   **Development-oriented groups:** Focus groups are used to develop the operationalization of the previously identified elements or dimensions pertinent to a set of issues. The discussions still remain mostly at the conceptual level and the objectives are to listen as much as possible to participants' thoughts about an issue.

3   **Definition-oriented groups:** Focus groups are used to finalize question wording before the quantitative phase begins. This is an important step to ensure that questions capture the intended dimensions and helps avoid potential wording bias.

As the field of political market research continues to evolve at an increased pace, more questions will be raised about how to maximise the insights coming from qualitative research. Recent studies such as Gorbaniuk *et al.* (2015)'s show how the two methods can be used complimentarily, in this case to look at political party personalities. However, Stanley (2016) poses a more fundamental question about the continuing struggle for legitimacy facing qualitative research. For him, 'following widespread use in political marketing, focus groups are slowly gaining recognition as a useful and legitimate method in political science' (236). He makes the case that focus groups 'can be far more than just a secondary method to primary quantitative public opinion research' (Ibid). He wants the method to be used to study 'everyday narratives in world politics' (Ibid, 248) and invites the field to 'think critically about methods and methodology because there is no need to involuntarily accept or instrumentally acquiesce to orthodox positions' (Ibid).

Co-creation and deliberative market research

Qualitative political market research has expanded to include more deliberative and creative approaches. Langmaid (2012, 61) explains that co-creation uses a range of techniques 'that involve the user, or voter, in creating the solution to the problem, rather than simply voicing their demands and issues'. It holds the potential to provide higher-quality information which will be more valuable to politicians. The techniques used to generate co-creation research include two-chair work, spirit walks, gossip games, role-play, social dreaming and art-from-within.

Langmaid (2012, 66–7) discusses how the firm Promise used co-creative techniques when invited in February 2005 by the then UK prime minister Tony Blair's advisors, including Philip Gould, Alan Milburn and Alastair Campbell, to understand and also find solutions to the disconnection between Blair and UK voters. The creative techniques they used not only explored the underlying feelings of voters towards Blair to help understand the problem on a much deeper level than polls would ever identify – because they took the approach of asking the public how to make things better – they also identified a potential solution to Blair's unpopularity. They asked participants to write letters to Blair (see Table 3.1; see also Promise 2005 and Scammell 2008 for further detail).

They also used 'two-chair work', where one of the people in a chair was a voter, and the other one played Tony Blair. In the first role-play, the participants played Blair as voters currently saw him:

I'm afraid you've only got part of the picture. From where I sit the war in Iraq was crucial to the cause of world peace. But I understand that it's difficult to see the whole thing for you. You put me in charge and I just do what I think to be the right thing. I am sure that history will prove us right in the end.

Table 3.1 Fictional letters to Blair in expressive market intelligence by Promise

Key phrases from letter	Underlying emotion direction tone/experience	Desires/wishes/
Theme 1: You left me!		
• E.g. you should have come home (tsunami) • You should put our people first • All the promises you made that never came to fruition	• Abandoned and unimportant	• Get back in touch • Get more involved with us/be more hands on
Theme 2: Too big for your boots/celebrity		
• Globe-trotting holiday-makers • Celebrity hero worship (Bush) • Thought you were a people person, not a movie star	• His self importance and global lifestyle leaves me feeling inferior, undervalued	• Reorder priorities • Get back to basics
Theme 3: Reflect and change		
• You have lost sight of reality, how the person in the street lives	• Not held in mind • Uncontained • Out of control	• Think, reflect – are you still the bloke we elected?

Source: Adapted from Promise (2005)

Langmaid (2012, 66–7) explains this made it clear that the problem was that Blair was not listening any more, no longer a people person, and didn't seem to care about domestic issues, and that he tried to explain his position in a dismissive way. In the second role-play, however, participants played Blair as they'd like him to be, where 'he' acknowledged their discontent and was more humble. By getting volunteers to play Blair in a more ideal way as they would like to see him – where he noted public concerns and would seek to listen and explain more in future – he could be seen as a politician who would make voters feel like they were heard, not just ignored, even if the actual policy and decision did not change. Building on this research, the Labour Party enacted the reconnection or 'masochism strategy' to rebrand Blair as someone who acknowledged what he had done wrong and how he wanted to be different in the future.

This more creative form of market research thus seeks to work with the public to identify solutions to problems – while still leaving room for leadership decisions – but operating on a more co-operative level. Voters have responsibility to identify solutions, not just complain. Langmaid (2012, 68) suggests that co-creation works best with those less informed and with less expertise – perhaps as they are more open to new ways of working in future.

König and König (2012, 48) describe another form of research: deliberative dialogue. They note how President Obama sought to make government more transparent and involve the public more through his 'Open Government' initiative in 2009, and that in Europe deliberative political marketing is getting onto the governance agenda. They explore the use of citizen juries in Germany and from this argue that governments need to become more deliberative. After openly listening to voters, leaders need to explain their decision in relation to it – especially if they decide to go against what the public consultation recommended – so that stakeholders can understand why the leader has taken a different position. If they do this, they help generate more trust.

Other political market research tools

While the quantitative and qualitative division remains the dominant way to organise political market research tools, other innovations cross the divide and are worth reviewing to provide a full picture of the PMR 'toolkit'.

Informal low-cost political market research

Not all candidates and campaigns have the funds to carry out all commissioned PMR. However, they can use 'free' data sources such as past election results to see how voters in geographic areas have cast votes in different elections (see in Case Study 3.2). For example, in the US, where there are a lot of elections for different offices, the geographic boundaries for each level of election (local, county, state, congressional and presidential/statewide) provide different pieces of information. Indirect market research on public views can be conducted by analysing local newspapers' discussions of local policy issues, which would indicate which problems people want the government to address. Turcotte (2012, 77) notes that politicians and parties gather informal intelligence in various ways such as polling members via mailed party correspondence, straw polls during meetings and conventions, door-to-door canvassing, and analysing letters and online feedback from constituents. Another source is analysis of past elections: a Canadian practitioner recalled how they interviewed people all across the country in the Conservative party, as well as practitioners in the UK and the US, and 'tried to get a sense of best-practices – what were the common things among failing enterprises, and what did winning campaigns have in common' (Lees-Marshment 2011, 17). Gut instinct and just observing what is happening in the local community or what people are complaining about is also a useful source of public input, as is 'little data' as discussed in Case Study 3.2.

Opposition research

One of the many repercussions of the first few years of the Trump administration has been to both showcase and denigrate the practice of opposition research (such as the infamous Trump Tower meeting). Opposition research is conducted to identify potential weaknesses and controversies and also comparable strengths of the party/candidate and the opposition, and, like other forms of market research, there are companies specialising in this work. However, it rarely implies meeting with nefarious characters who claim to 'have dirt' on a candidate. While candidate research is better known for digging up personal scandals, analysis of public documents can be as valuable for identifying potential problems. Such research draws on a range of sources including elected officials' voting records, campaign contribution records, court files, and personal and business records, including property records and property tax payment histories; behavioural records such as club membership and military service; comments from previous associates, whether work colleagues, family, friends or former partners; and more recently, audiovisual footage.

A candidate can expect their entire professional career to be scrutinised, even if it wasn't in the political realm and whether or not they were responsible for everything that happened. Even their education or training will be considered. Moreover, one of the neglected consequences of entering political life is the challenges it will pose for the candidate's family (see Manning 2002, 242–69). Personal family issues, such as choice of school for their children (rather than the more obvious skeletons such as affairs) can be included in the campaign (Johnson 2007, 70–1). This is particularly pertinent if and when behaviour contradicts public political positions, but these issues are not always restricted to what the candidate does. In May 2008, Obama resigned from the Trinity United Church of Christ in Chicago, which he had been a member of for 20 years, when controversial comments made by the pastor, the Reverend Jeremiah Wright, were widely circulated by the media and threatened to damage his brand.

Practitioner Perspective 3.2 on candidate research

I'm a believer in doing very solid research on yourself and your opponent, in order to know what your strengths and weaknesses are . . . [however] in one race I . . . found a complaint [that] one of the kids of the [opposing] candidate had filed one time, and there was a divorce in the family and stuff. The candidate . . . looked at that and said . . . I don't want anybody in the campaign ever talking about this.

Peter Fenn, US Democratic consultant, interviewed in 2007

[We] do opposition research on our own candidates, so now there's no surprise . . . if we know something ahead of time, we can make plans to blunt it, counteract it, do whatever we need to do to explain it . . . Americans actually care much less about their personal lives than most. What they do do though is, you know, if you're a businessman, have you run your business well? Have you ever been sued? Did you stick by your vendors?. . . there are firms that are year-round enterprises that work and do just this.

Gene Ulm, US Republican consultant, interviewed in 2007

Source: Lees-Marshment (2011, 24–6)

As Practitioner Perspective 3.2 indicates, candidate research helps prepare candidates for attacks and helps them prepare rebuttals so that their campaigns are less likely to be sent off course. In the 2004 US presidential election, John Kerry, the Democrat candidate, made his military service in Vietnam a key part of his campaign, assuming it to be a win-win characteristic. When he was attacked by a Swift Boat Veterans ad, there was no response from Kerry's team, and the media were able to continue criticism. Henneberg and O'Shaughnessy (2007, 261) note that Kerry could have anticipated the attack, as there was an 'inherent contradiction in his Vietnam-era role and his post-service militant peace activism'. If changes can be justified and explained, they can be defended, but the candidate risks being accused of flip-flopping, lacking certainty and conviction, or only changing their position for electoral expediency.

Candidate research can also be used positively: as Johnson (2007, 57–8) observes, 'it builds the case that the incumbent has established a solid record of achievement . . . and it devises strategies to protect that record'. If they are already in office, candidates' accomplishments include legislation assisted or blocked, grants obtained, votes cast, favourable ratings, supporting or criticising the government, and constituency work. Research also investigates what would attract support from different groups of people or constituents as not all behaviour is interesting to all voters (see Varoga and Rice 1999, 255).

How political market research is used

Market research is used to inform a range of activities in politics. Interviews with practitioners suggest that 'market analysis in politics is a multi-varied activity . . . the value, purposes, uses, methods and attitudes to market analysis are broad-ranging' (Lees-Marshment 2011, 41). In terms of product and brand development, PMR can identify weaknesses in a party brand as well as opportunities for development.

Market research can become an integral part of the party and campaign apparatus and thus be closely connected to the strategy. Turcotte (2012, 83–4) notes how market intelligence became more closely integrated into the strategic thinking by the Canadian Conservatives under the leadership of Stephen Harper after losing the 2004 election. Harper's staff thought that there needed to be a 'market intelligence structure', and thus research was integrated with strategy to keep everyone focused on meeting set goals. Patrick Muttart, a former director for a hotel chain, used research to measure public mood, test policies and find ways to communicate the Conservative product to appeal to a sufficiently large number of voters to form government. It also uncovered new insights: when interviewed, Muttart recalled how research found that right-of-centre voters respond to 'three key fanatic drivers': aspiration for 'something better for their families and their children' from their hard work; family, including those who get legally married; and 'a sense of localism' or cohesion. They then devised their strategy to tap into those broader themes emotionally as well as cognitively (Lees-Marshment 2011, 15).

In the 2007 French presidential election, the candidate Nicholas Sarkozy used a range of tools for different purposes during the campaign from January to April, such as online panels to identify why voters might leave/join a particular candidate and then tested their reactions to the candidate's main TV or radio appearances during the campaign. Teinturier (2008, 150–1) explains that such intelligence was used to support the foundations of strategy using public opinion results, to select candidates, to help improve the language and create the effect of reality in political communication, and to identify strong public support, which would then reduce criticisms from commentators.

For his part, Braun (2012) notes that in campaigns, research is used to inform a wide range of decisions which are strategic, policy and communication focused. One example is making sure candidates talk about issues that voters care about most; another is which voters to target (Braun 2012, 11–12).

PMR is not confined to establishing democracies – it is also used in developing democracies. Rottinghaus and Alberro (2005) explored how polls were used for Vicente Fox's campaign in the 2000 Mexican election to inform the selling of the candidate at key chronological points, such as to establish which candidate traits were the most desirable. Campaign staff identified that using a message of change Fox could attract support and determine what was most important to voters, which was honesty, followed by reliability and good proposals. Fox connected all three in his speeches, talking of honest new faces to form a new government, declaring he was strong enough to do the job.

PMR is also used in government. Rothmayr and Hardmeier (2002, 130–1) analysed how the Swiss federal government used polls to inform government communication, and Birch and Petry (2012) note how government agencies commission substantial research on policy and behaviour to improve policymaking, which is regulated at the federal level in the US and Canada to ensure methodological quality and objectivity. Bennett (2017) provides the first attempt to examine the linkages and uses of PMR by government in the policymaking process. The analysis is based on elite interviews conducted with a small number of people actively involved in public opinion and governance in four countries: Australia, Canada, New Zealand and the United Kingdom (Ibid 48). His analysis leads to a series of clear conclusions:

1   'Public opinion is viewed as being of general importance in governing by elite decision makers' (Ibid 50).
2   'Despite the perceived importance of various functions of public opinion for governance, the actual effective use of public opinion and related techniques to serve governing is seen as being at a rather neutral level' (Ibid 52).
3   'Elites agree that it is important for those involved in governing to have access to public opinion' but particularly legislators (Ibid 55).
4   'The evaluations of government performance in conducting good surveys and disseminating the information on public opinion tend to be nearly neutral' (Ibid 57).
5   'Australians believe that there has been an increase in the use of public opinion in governance in recent years while New Zealanders tend not to have noted any change. Canadians and UK respondents were the most likely to say that there had been a decrease' (Ibid 59).
6   There is some evidence that partisanship makes a difference in the use of public opinion in governing, but the results are mixed, and 'such differences may exist but not necessarily in terms of conventional ideas of partisanship. Individual and agency differences may be just as important as the overall partisan stripe of elected government' (Ibid 66).

Bennett's book addresses an important gap in our understanding of the use of PMR and is a good example of the expanding scope of the field.

Limitations to the influence of political market research

Historically there have been many barriers to politicians and parties commissioning, let alone responding to, market intelligence. Wring (2005) explains how the UK Labour Party's traditional culture, mission and ethos involved education and persuasion, which made it difficult for professionals and party figures to gain acceptance for the use of marketing in presentation, let alone product design. Not every politician or party wants to just win an election – they also want to change the world. Individual politicians often think they know best and that their gut instinct is the right one – and their agenda and goals can be to advance a particular cause, not subject their behaviour to the dictates of the market, let alone the median or target voter. Kavanagh (1996, 105–10) argues that there are a number of factors that enhance or constrain the attention politicians pay to market intelligence results, such as that in power ministers are more interested in justifying existing programmes than considering where new proposals would attract market support; individual politicians and different party groups prefer one policy to another and look for results that support a particular position.

Even though the use of PMR is now more widespread, interviews with practitioners suggest that PMR is only one of many different inputs into a politician's decision making (Lees-Marshment 2011). An advisor to President Bill Clinton recalled that 'he was interested in as wide a network of people informing him as he could. He wanted as many facts and opinions from informed people as he could get . . . Clinton read voraciously and would mark up articles every single day and send them around and circulate them and ask questions and stress things and want to know more about things'. Consequently, Lees-Marshment suggests a model for PMR whereby the first stage is that the politician sets the goals before PMR is commissioned from several sources; consultants then offer multifaceted advice about potential actions in response, and politicians consider this along with other inputs before making their decision. In her analysis of the 2016 US presidential election, Jessica Baldwin-Philippi (2017) offers another perspective on those limitations by suggesting that while 'contemporary campaigns are operating in a data-rich environment [. . .] campaigns do not always execute analytic-based campaigning tactics as fully or as rigorously as possible' (2017, 631) because of the complexity of doing so. Thus, the role that market research plays in politics needs to be seen in the context of politics and government.

Another issue is whether marketing strategies developed in one country can be transplanted whole to another. Systemic differences such as political culture and the electoral system vary from one country to another and can affect how political marketing ideas can be used. The most recent comparative study which explored the strategies adopted by parties concluded that fixed systemic differences were less influential than contextual ones such as the nature of the leader, whether a party had been out of power a long time, and the internal support for an MOP strategy (see Lees-Marshment *et al.* 2010). For example, Hutcheson (2010, 221–2) argues that in Russia 'political marketing – or, to use the Russian term, 'electoral technology' *(izbiratel'naya tekhnologiya)* – is not a straightforward transfer of American or even West European expertise. There is a multibillion-dollar political consulting market with its own techniques and values'. Interviews with practitioners involved in global knowledge sharing concluded that while political marketing is going global and being utilised across countries, to be effective it has to be adapted to the local context, not least because of system differences (Lees-Marshment and Lilleker 2012). Political marketing ideas flow back and forth – not just from the US to other countries. Thus Lees-Marshment and Lilleker argue that the more effective international consultants select lessons from a range of countries to suit the particular campaign they are advising on, or look for particular tools to suit similar features within their own market.

PMR in the workplace

The evolution of PMR as described in this chapter will inevitably lead to changes in the skills required for those who want to pursue a career in the field. In particular, the implications of the rise of data analytics on PMR are beginning to be considered. As mentioned previously, Turcotte (forthcoming) posits that one impact to consider is the surveillance capacities of big data on public opinion research (see Table 3.2). The impact will be felt not only in how PMR is conducted but also in the role of the political market researchers and the skills they need to pursue a career in this field.

Specifically, researchers will be less likely to emerge from the social sciences tradition but more from the applied math field. Three specific new sets of skills will be in high demand.

Table 3.2 Looking ahead at market surveillance

Component	Traditional Polling Period	Market Intelligence	Market Surveillance
Target of Analysis	Median Voters	Segmented Voters	Individual Voter
Influences	Sociology, Anthropology and Political Science	Marketing, Business and Communication	Information Technology, Software Engineering, Applied Math
Function	General Information Gathering	Strategic Marketing and Communication applications	Tracking of Individual Behaviour; Message Targeting
Methods	Mainly Quantitative Analysis w/ occasional qualitative analysis	Mixed Methods	Quantitative Only
Key Statistics	Measures of Association and Correlation	Inferential Statistics	Correlation Analysis
Data Collection	Random Sampling	Random Sampling	N=all
Research Focus	Key Trends, Issue Priorities and Overall Impressions	Segmented Issue Priorities, Key Messaging and Communication	Individual Preferences: Behavioural Triggers
Role	Pollster as Oracle	Pollster as Strategist	Pollster as Data Scientist?

(Turcotte, forthcoming)

A **Coding and advanced analytics**

Political market researchers will increasingly need coding and analytics skills beyond knowledge of SPSS, which has been the dominant computer programme in the field for several decades. Programmes like Python, R and Tableau are used widely to push data analysis towards more depth and analysing capacities.

B **Data management platforms**

As noted above, data management platforms (DMPs) are having an impact on how the field can measure individual preferences and behaviour. Doing analysis using a DMP requires specific skills which are part programming, part analysis and part data investigation. Each DMP is somewhat unique, and researchers will require training that is not currently available in universities.

C **Online panels and communities**

Data collection in the PMR field is moving from online samples to online panels and communities. While the technical aspects of this emerging mode of data collection are beyond the scope of this chapter, it remains that panels and communities need to be built and managed. Henceforth, panel managers are likely to become ubiquitous in the practice of PMR.

Summary

This chapter has explored how a number of changes in the political market have altered the way that voters respond to and judge political parties and candidates, so that voters are more demanding and questioning, and their behaviour is less predictable. Additionally, citizens appear to behave in a more consumerist manner. Such changes have encouraged parties and candidates to consider using marketing to help them achieve their goals. Market intelligence provides politicians and their staff with information that they can then use to make decisions about all other aspects of marketing, including product development and communication. Options such as segmentation, targeting and opposition research provide different ways of looking at the market. Box 3.4 provides a best practice guide to understanding political consumers and carrying out PMR.

However, PMR tools also have limitations and are not quick fixes to secure success. There remains debate about the value of market intelligence, but it is unlikely any modern candidate or party would not gather any, given the choice. Without using such methods to understand an increasingly diverse public, politicians would be relying on gut instinct and guesswork, which would be more prone to bias and inaccuracy and unable to provide the detailed breakdown of the electorate now offered by computerised segmentation models. This chapter has also suggested that more changes may be on the horizon. The role of political market researchers has evolved from merely providing information to helping making sense of it. The next era is likely to bring new perspectives.

It remains that market intelligence isn't a perfect conversation between government and the public, but it does go some way to bringing the two closer together. While there are democratic issues with the use of market intelligence, most of these develop because of the way elites choose to use it. Parties and politicians need to listen, interpret and respond carefully before using it to develop their product and brand. If they do so, 'it may actually enhance the public sphere that political marketing scholars were previously concerned it might destroy' (Lees-Marshment 2015, 9).

Box 3.4 Best practice guide to political market research

1   Regardless of recent criticisms, be confident that PMR remains the best way to understand voters.
2   Understand that voters are critical, negative and consumerist towards political elites, and they use a variety of sources of information to form their views and are questioning of them all.
3   Accept that how they vote is less predictable, that whether they vote is uncertain; if they volunteer it has to be on their terms, not the candidate's/party's.
4   Develop increasingly specific segments to improve the effectiveness of campaigns.
5   Conduct market analysis continuously, using all the research tools at your disposal.
6   Create and respond to, and communicate with, micro-targets: tiny segments that will most likely influence the election outcome, including core voters.
7   Analyse data to identify future needs and alternative options, and to test potential reactions. This can be big data gathered by well-resourced organisations/candidates or little data from local candidates analysing free information on their own social media sites.
8   Research all stakeholders, not just voters.
9   Keep up with all the innovations happening in the field.
10 Develop coding and programming skills.
11 Descriptive analysis is no longer adequate; interpretation and analysis are requirements.

12 Use market analysis proactively to inform – not dictate – decisions, and create room for proactive, visionary leadership.
13 Use PMR to inform a range of positions in response to public opinion and types of communication.

Discussion points

1   Discuss how you decide what to think about politics. What sources of information are most relied on? What has changed in the last two or three years? What does this reveal about how voters form political opinions and therefore what politicians should consider when using marketing?
2   How do you decide to vote? List the different factors that influenced you, and discuss which are most important. How do you reconcile cross-pressures?
3   To what extent are practitioners and academics right about voters becoming more demanding and wanting to be empowered and drive the political system?
4   Create a plan for how you would conduct PMR for an election campaign, organisation or issue, including when, what type and on what issues/aspects.
5   Thinking about an issue that matters to you, how would you draw from PMR findings to influence policymaking?
6   If an election were held tomorrow in your electorate/country, consider what segments might be most important and why.
7   Give an example of how you would use deliberative and co-creation forms of market research. What might be the limitations?
8   To what extent is the global transfer of political marketing consultations effective?
9   Is big data all hype or the future of PMR?

Assessment questions

Essay/exam

1   To what extent has the political market changed in recent decades, and how?
2   Explore the potential effects that the rise of the political consumer has on politics.
3   Outline and compare the nature and effectiveness of the different political market research tools. Where do you stand on the quantitative vs. qualitative divide?
4   How important and effective is segmentation in politics?
5   What do you think it means for a voter to act as a consumer?
6   What is the nature of quantitative political market research, and what are the benefits and limitations of its use in political marketing?
7   Do you agree or disagree that we may be on the cusp of a new era in political market research when data analytics will dominate the field?
8   To what extent do you think Brexit and the Trump victory are examples of the rise of the political consumer? Can you describe any similar examples in your own country?
9   Outline and discuss the range of ways that political market research is used in policymaking.

Applied

1 Conduct and analyse market research data (whether a poll or other form) during a political campaign, using Turcotte's stages of quantitative research during a political campaign – the benchmark poll, strategic poll, tracking poll, brushfire poll and post-election poll.
2 Conduct a strategic analytic marketing plan for a local candidate, using free online data from sources such as their emails, Facebook, Twitter and LinkedIn, and make recommendations for what they should do over the next 12 months in light of this.
3 Find a questionnaire used in a national election study conducted prior to the 1990s and compare it to a questionnaire used in your country's most recent national election. Isolate and discuss the changes in questions used and how these changes may have been influenced by the rise of political marketing.
4 Produce a market research report for a current political leader/party/government with analysis of all publicly available market research, and make recommendations for what they should do over the next 12 months in light of this. Try to take into account contextual factors such as their goals, position in the electoral cycle, constraints, likely crises, potential positives, nature of the leader themselves and how to manage markets (e.g. their party, other MPs, media, the public, civil service).
5 Isolate one key policy question that has dominated politics in your country. To what extent do you think PMR influenced policy implementation in this particular case? Why or why not?
6 If the era of market surveillance is upon us and PMR specialists are to become data scientists, which changes would you make to the course curriculum in the programme you are currently in?

Case studies

Case study 3.1 Big data analytics, technology, electoral choice and political marketing in 2017 Kenyan elections

By Bozo Jenje Bozo (University of Nairobi)

This case study shows how the Kenyan major political parties in a democratic election used political data science in the 2017 presidential elections in electing the 'computer generated chicklet president' and the nullification of the elections by the Supreme Court. Big data in the evolution of politics uses new technology and demographic data to give an impetus to the political elites that influence election decisions and perceive the electorates as not only voters living in their constituencies but 'voter consumers' that have a role to elect them to access power and control resources.

Kenya, a regional hub for trade, diplomacy and security in Africa, has a population of 49 million. According to the Independent Electoral and Boundaries Commission (IEBC 2017), 19,611,423 registered voters were eligible to participate in the 8 August 2017 elections and the 26 October 2017 rerun pitting Jubilee candidate Uhuru Kenyatta against his challenger Raila Odinga. Kenya is East Africa's largest economy, with 43 ethnic tribes voting along tribal affiliations and not on issues. In previous elections, ethnic profiling and micro-targeting by political parties and individuals occurred in each election cycle. Candidates pay attention to demographic data of registered voters identified by the Biometric Voters Registration System (BVRS) that collects and stores biometric features.

Moreover, the candidate data is recorded in the Candidate Registration System (CRS), which ensures primary data of candidates nominated by parties is entered in a format that makes it easy for IEBC to verify candidate details, check accuracy, ensure compliance and generate ballot paper proof. The data obtained is important for political parties in the regions they target in formulating marketing programmes that help solidify political bases. According to Todd and Dann (2017), micro target approaches in segmented constituencies are made easier by big data and also precipitate the problem of demarcation and polarisation. Big data, though, is crucial in revolutionalising understanding and predicting voters; it assists in the mobilisation of supporters quickly and in an inexpensive way.

During the August presidential elections, the main political party Jubilee and the opposition National Super Alliance (NASA) based their campaigns on 'tyranny of numbers' in their major strongholds, targeting 100 per cent voter turnout. To mobilise supporters, the Jubilee Party gathered market intelligence and positioned themselves on the platform of development while NASA campaigned as agents of change. On track record, the Jubilee leadership challenged the opposition by stating that its implemented projects exceeded those of opposition leaders in their power regimes. To critique the government, NASA spearheaded a campaign that propagated 'half-truths' and allegations of corruption and squandered Eurobond funds, among others. After the August elections, NASA boycotted the fresh elections and marketed the repeat elections as predetermined by the IEBC.

With the political crisis, NASA diehards felt disenfranchised by the Jubilee government. At their strongholds, voters resisted the Jubilee inroads despite the foray of development programmes initiated by the current regime. In both the elections, Kenyatta trounced the opposition maverick politician Odinga with 8.2 million or 54 per cent of the presidential vote and 6.7 million or 47 per cent, respectively. The outcome was nullified by the Supreme Court, which cited anomalies in the electoral process. In accordance with the promulgated 2010 Kenyan Constitution, the Election Act 2011 incorporated technology as key for a verifiable election process. To enhance efficiency, the IEBC used the Kenya Integrated Elections Management System (KIMS) kits to identify voters, authenticate voters, and stem any election fraud and transmission of results. The KIMS gadget is intelligent and automated to detect and prevent a person from voting twice. The gadget sends three-hour periodic updates of voter turnout that match with the results (Wanyonyi 2017).

To reinvent the party, NASA advanced Collins and Butler's (2002) theory of positioning tactically to influence the Supreme Court that nullified the elections on alleged irregularities in voting, counting, tabulation, relaying and transmission of results. This electoral evidence found using the technology on IEBC systems' data and logs, an audit of the technology for discrepancies in the presidential results transmission, phone networks failure and the provisions of backups, gave NASA a competitive advantage after the defeat. The voting, counting and the tabulation of results compiled were within the law. The IEBC responded that the 2017 elections were transparent, open and accountable in accordance with the applicable electoral laws. After the nullification, Jubilee employed the encirclement attack strategy by luring the electoral losers from NASA with development projects in their constituencies. Secondly, a frontal attack technique was used on the opponent by injecting heavy campaign funds at the behest of NASA seeking financial aid from its supporters on the M-PESA transaction platform.

In its ruling, Kenya made history to become the third country in the world to nullify presidential elections, after Ukraine and the Maldives in 2004 and 2013, respectively. The verdict was delivered after the IEBC failed to provide presidential data from the servers and after harmonising the Results Transmission and Presentation System (RTS) – technology that transmits electronically provisional data to observation centres, media and other stakeholders after the presiding officers sign the results sheet (Form 35) configured in mobile phones from the constituencies, county and national levels.

After the rerun, NASA employed military strategies. The strategic plan was to allege that the Jubilee government was invalid and illegitimate, forcing its supporters to boycott products from a telecommunication company, Bidco and Brookside. Additionally, NASA established the National Resistance Movement (NRM), after the strategic withdrawal of Odinga in the fresh elections. NASA also adopted the shuttle diplomacy tactic to lobby foreign leaders at the Centre for Strategic and International Studies (CSIS) headquarters for intervention since the elections held were not credible, free and fair, and about 25 constituencies failed to vote due to protests. People assemblies were formed in counties after Kenyatta garnered 7,483,895 votes or 98 per cent of the casted votes and Odinga got 73,259 votes. Only 39 per cent of the total registered voters participated in the repeat elections. But after contestation, the jury upheld Uhuru's victory on 20 November to serve a second term.

Lessons for political marketing

Political demographic data is significant for micro-targeting ethnic voters, but its disadvantage is polarisation. From the election management body, data on registered voters can be gathered from the voter registration database, Facebook and Google, and this data is key in facilitating voter mobilisation. From analysis, voting data alone and tallying do not determine election outcomes but only an accurate, credible and verifiable election process. Finally, technology manipulation in elections leads to lack of confidence in the integrity of the poll body.

References

Collins, Neil and Patrick Butler (2002). 'Considerations on market analysis for political parties'. In Nicholas O'Shaughnessy and Stephan Henneberg (eds) *The Idea of Political Marketing*. London: Praeger, 1–18.

Gulbaksh, C. (2013). Election 2016: 'Marriage of big data, social data will determine the next president'. Wired. www.wired.com/insights/2013/05/election-2016-marriage-of-big-data-social-data-will-determine-the-next-president/ (accessed in November 2018).

Havi, W. (2017). 'Uhuru's repeat election victory is by all means invalid and illegitimate'. *Standard Digital*, 29 October 2017.

IEBC (Independent Electoral and Boundaries Commission) (2017). Registered Voters per Constituency for 2017 General Elections. www.iebc.or.ke/docs/Registered Voters Per Constituency For 2017 General Elections.pdf.

Todd, C. and C. Dann (2017). 'How Big Data Broke American Politics'. *NBC News Digital*, 14 March 2017. www.nbcnews.com/politics/elections/how-big-data-broke-american-politics-n732901.

Wanyonyi, T. (2017). 'IT experts and scrutiny of forms may have sunk IEBC'. *Saturday Nation*, 2 September 2017.

Case Study 3.2 Little data: Using social media to gain market research and inform campaign strategy at local government level

By Nicholas Mignacca, University of Auckland

Social media is increasingly becoming a central tool for communications within political campaigns, but it can also be used more strategically by local candidates as a means to conduct free market research. In the New Zealand context, attention has been given to the use of social networking websites at a parliamentarian level (Blair 2012) and in general elections (Cameron *et al.* 2013), but social media marketing in local body elections remains an overlooked area of research, just as in all countries. This case study examines Auckland candidates' use of social media in the 2013 local body elections, focusing on mayoral, council and local board campaigns. The research shows that services such as Facebook and LinkedIn allow local-level candidates to collect free quantitative and qualitative analytical information that can be used to target communications to the tastes of the electorate. Social media is therefore a very practical tool for individual politicians who want to utilise market-oriented political marketing but don't have the big budget of national-level parties and campaigns.

This study collated social media data about the 464 Auckland candidates running for mayor, council and local board in the 2013 local body elections, as found on the Vote.co.nz and VoteAuckland.co.nz databases. Firstly, it found that social media has become intrinsic to grass-roots New Zealand politics. Of the 464 candidates, 120 (26 per cent) integrated social media into their campaigns. Indeed, 47 (10 per cent) used two or more social media; and 22 (5 per cent) displayed a sophisticated use of synchronised multi-medium social media platforms, especially targeted at maximising candidate visibility among specific voter segments. Key social media websites used to campaign in the elections were Facebook, Twitter, LinkedIn, YouTube, Google+ and Webo. In the most successful cases, an official website and Facebook advertising supplemented candidates' use of social media. Final results showed that, out of the ten candidates with the strongest social media use, six won their respective seats (Brown, R. Thomas, Krum, Cooper, Hulse and Brewer).

Secondly, it found that candidates utilised social media to help them market themselves in several ways. The greatest benefit of a social media communications campaign to local body candidates is increased visibility. New Zealand local elections traditionally enjoy lower voter turnouts than general elections and voters tend to be older. Consequently, campaigning candidates tend to focus their limited resources on targeting narrow voter segments, politically active at a grass-roots level. In this context, social media campaigning is an attractive option as, for no cost, it provides candidates with around-the-clock personal access to voters, high visibility and name recognition. The 2013 Auckland local body elections saw candidates creatively supplement traditional campaigning techniques such as hoardings, door-knocking and live hoardings with new uses of social media. This included Facebook, Twitter and LinkedIn links on candidate billboards; use of social media to recruit volunteers for door-knocking and live hoarding activities; and the use of Facebook and Twitter to organise fundraising events. When one considers that the Maungakiekie-Tāmaki Ward was won by 7,923 to 7,049 votes, by a candidate with a combined Facebook, Twitter and LinkedIn following of 2,048 users, one can see that social networking websites' contribution to raising a candidate's profile is significant.

Furthermore, Facebook and LinkedIn help to generate free quantitative and qualitative data that can inform the candidate's marketing strategy. The rising use of Facebook public profiles and LinkedIn in local body campaigns indicates that candidates are becoming increasingly aware of social media's potential for targeted, market-oriented communications. Facebook and LinkedIn both offer their users the capacity to collect diverse quantitative and qualitative data about followers, feedback to posts and third-party connections. On both websites, one can:

1   Calculate how many people saw one's posts.
2   View how other users responded to each post in 'likes', 'shares' and 'deletes'.
3   Divide followers according to gender, age brackets and geographical provenance.

For political marketing purposes, this allows candidates to determine what posts received the most feedback and develop consequent strategies to boost the reach of their communications, mindful of the specific makeup of the audience. In 2013, campaigning saw a rise of targeted posts with short personal messages, colourful images and questions aimed at generating user response on candidates' pages. Additionally, as shown by Brown, Palino, Krum and Thomas, some candidates used the data collected by their Facebook pages to conduct narrowly targeted Facebook advertising campaigns. Facebook advertising for non-profit organisations costs NZ$1 a day. For less than the daily cost of a single billboard, one can gain quotidian name recognition from 138,000 Auckland Facebook users, for three months.

Additionally, candidates can engage in strategic and synchronised multi-faceted social media campaigning. What the cleverest Auckland local body campaigns demonstrated is that there is no single best all-encompassing social medium for political marketing. Rather, each medium is different and serves a separate communications purpose. Each social networking website connects different voter segments according to demographics, occupation and personal interests, reaching people in different settings. Social media are complementary to one another, and can be connected to make up for each one's structural limitations. In practical terms, while Facebook is by far the most popular social network website in New Zealand, its use to political marketing is different from that of Twitter or LinkedIn. Facebook is a hub for personal communications, linking people of all ages and social backgrounds. Its communications are personal, visual and informal. LinkedIn instead is rapidly emerging as New Zealand's leading corporate online social network, and it complements Facebook by reaching people in a professional manner. While LinkedIn lacks the audience volumes Facebook provides, it allows targeted sectorial and one-on-one communications in a similar process to emailing (with To:, Cc:, and Bcc:). Twitter is the more fluid of the three, as it is both a formal and informal social medium depending on the context. Like Facebook, Twitter allows larger online user followings than LinkedIn. However, because of Twitter's instant newsfeed structure, the dynamics of communicating via Twitter are different to those of other social media. Since Facebook and LinkedIn can be synchronised through Twitter, a candidate can set up a multifaceted social media platform to access more voters in diverse settings while halving the workload.

Lessons for political marketing

In their study of social media use in the 2010 New Zealand General Elections, Cameron *et al.* (2013) found that social media had a visible effect in closely contested campaigns, often shifting the odds in favour of the candidate with the best social media strategy. This study of the way social media was used in the 2013 Auckland local body elections reinforces Cameron *et al.*'s findings, showing that not only have social media communications become a central feature of New Zealand political campaigns but that they can be used to generate valuable market research data which can help candidates produce informed, synchronised and targeted marketing campaigns. With the trial of online voting commencing in the 2016 New Zealand local body elections, internet-based forms of political marketing will undoubtedly grow in importance at the local level. Looking to the future, the capacity of social networking websites such as Facebook and LinkedIn to provide candidates with vital quantitative and qualitative data about their audience will become increasingly key to competing for digital votes and potentially enable individual candidates to utilise the same range of marketing tools and concepts we see in national-level campaigns.

Further reading

Blair, Sophia (2012). *'Making the Net Work: What New Zealand Political Parties Can Learn From Obama'*. Master of Arts thesis on online political marketing and political party participation, University of Auckland.

Cameron, M. P., P. Barrett and B. Stewardson (2013). *Can Social Media Predict Election Results? Evidence from New Zealand*. Working Paper in Economics 13/08, University of Waikato. https://ideas.repec.org/p/wai/econwp/13-08.html (accessed 12 September 2013).

Democratic Debate 3.1 The ethical issues around big data in politics

By Jennifer Lees-Marshment*, Edward Elder* and Vincent Raynauld+
*University of Auckland and +Emerson College

The public's behavioural data is not just collected when they interact online in politics, such as answering an online government survey or liking a politician's Facebook page; it is also accumulated from all other spheres or life, and then this data is mined for use in campaigning, government and policymaking. Research on political campaigning has noted how political parties internationally are increasingly turning to sophisticated canvassing strategies and software to identify, collect, process and analyse data. Moreover, political parties and candidates commit time and growingly large volumes of human and financial resources to their data operations. Of note is US presidential candidate Donald Trump spending US$5,912,500 on data services provided by Cambridge Analytica during the 2016 US presidential election cycle (Center for Responsive Politics 2017). Political databases include ever-expanding collections of, and complexity in analysis derived from, data about several dimensions of daily lives of citizens. The Liberal Party of Canada's data operation unit used data which was acquired in various ways, both online and offline, to break down electoral districts into six categories based on the party's electoral prospects. This categorisation would ultimately inform messaging as well as voter outreach and engagement (Delacourt 2016). Aristotle CEO John Phillips (2012) describes it as 'the DNA of the electorate' and explains that if data suggests there is 'a correlation between people who own corvettes and voting behaviour [. . .] they're going to be trying to find as many corvette owners as they can.'

On one hand, data-driven market research has the potential to help marketers and government policymakers identify, understand and respond to the public's preferences, interests and objectives that can often be very narrow in nature. In practice, the way established political elites – including political candidates, elected officials and civil servants – use such technologically-driven data can be both for the wider public good or their own self-interest, and thus it raises profound ethical questions. The table below outlines the positive and negative implications of big data in politics.

Potential democratic impact of big data on electoral politics and governance

Theme	Positive implications	Negative implications
Empowerment	Engages and empowers a wider range of citizens to participate in the political process through campaigns, parties, online policy discussion and voting.	Gives elites more power to manipulate the public for their interests and disempowers citizens who have little awareness of, or control over, how their data is used.
Engagement	Encourages elites to engage with segments of society who have previously been overlooked.	Leads to focus on certain citizens and ignores others, making citizen input into the system unequal.
Progression	Helps draw attention to new ideas, candidates and policies; mitigating incumbency.	Hinders the development of new policy ideas as it encourages elites to respond to prevailing views.
Policy making	Improves policy decisions by giving elites new information.	Damages policy making as elites are given unreliable data.

For example, many arguments have been made for the potential value of using big data in public policy, such as health care, traffic management and planning, diplomacy, and surveillance. By providing a larger sample size and analysis of citizens' actions, big data can help governments make better policy decisions with more reliable results. Furthermore, the growing availability, flexibility and affordability of data enables established political players to consider and engage with segments of the population that were previously overlooked when market research had to be focused on pre-selected segments in order to keep costs down. However, big data raises ethical issues around privacy, security, transparency and control because it is often collected and used by political actors without the public's awareness or consent. Data-driven individualised political communication can also become manipulative, selectively presenting information to voters based in their individual preferences. There are also concerns about how big data might be used by governments for surveillance. Additionally, the use of data can encourage focus on some segments of the citizenry at the expense of others as established political players target individuals and organisations more useful to them from an electoral and government perspective.

In essence, it depends on how the data is used. As US Democratic Party presidential candidate Hillary Clinton noted: 'there's nothing inherently wrong with using big data and microtargeting. The problem would come if the data were obtained or used improperly' (Clinton 2017, 368). We therefore argue that big data needs to follow a policy framework with clear ethical principles; it needs to be open, professionally managed and regulated, publicly accessible and beneficial, utilised carefully in government and used in all areas of politics, not just campaigns. This is important, otherwise there will be more calls for increased regulation of data-using companies such as Facebook and Cambridge Analytica.

References and further reading

Bendle, N., J. Ryoo, and A. Nastasoiu (2018). 'The 2016 US Primaries: Parties and Candidates in a World of Big Data'. In J. Gillies (ed.) *Political marketing in the 2016 US presidential election*. Cham, Switzerland: Palgrave Macmillan, 65–80.

Bennett, C. J., and R. M. Bayley (2012). *Canadian federal political parties and personal privacy protection: a comparative analysis*. Report for the Office of the Privacy Commissioner of Canada.

Center for Responsive Politics (2017). 'Expenditures Breakdown, Donald Trump, 2016 cycle'. OpenSecrets.org. www.opensecrets.org/pres16/expenditures?id=n00023864. (accessed in June 2018).

Clinton, H. R. (2017). *What happened*. London: Simon & Schuster.

Delacourt, Susan (2013). *Shopping for Votes: How Politicians Choose Us and We Choose Them* Douglas & McIntyre.

Delacourt, S. (2016). 'How the big red machine became the big data machine'. *The Star*, 21 May 2016. www.thestar.com/news/insight/2016/05/21/how-the-big-red-machine-became-the-big-data-machine.html.

Lees-Marshment, Jennifer, Edward Elder and Vincent Raynauld (n.d.). 'Political Marketing, Technology, and Big Data: A policy framework for research and ethical practice'. Unpublished paper.

References

Asher, Herbert (1995). *Polling and the Public: What Every Citizen Should Know*. Washington DC: Congressional Quarterly Press.

Baldwin-Philippi, Jessica (2017). 'The Myths of Data-Driven Campaigning'. *Political Communication*, 34(4): 627–33.

Bennett, Scott Edward (2017). *Applying Public Opinion in Governance*. Cham, Switzerland: Palgrave Macmillan.

Bennett, W. Lance (2012). 'The personalization of politics: political identity, social media, and changing patterns of participation'. *The Annals of the American Academy of Political and Social Science*, 644: 20–39.

Birch, Lisa and François Petry (2012). 'The use of public opinion research by government: insights from American and Canadian research'. In Jennifer Lees-Marshment (ed.) *Routledge Handbook of Political Marketing*. New York: Routledge, 342–453.

Bowers, Diane (2016). *The AMA Gold Report: 2016 Top 50 Markt Research Firms*. American Marketing Association, 1 June 2016. www.ama.org/marketing-news/the-ama-gold-report-2016-top-50-market-research-firms/.

Braun, Alexander (2012). 'The role of opinion research in setting campaign strategy'. In Jennifer Lees-Marshment (ed.) *Routledge Handbook of Political Marketing*. New York: Routledge, 7–19.

Bricker, Darrell and John Ibbitson (2013). *The Big Shift*. Toronto: HarperCollins Publishers Ltd.

Burton, Michael John (2012). 'Strategic voter selection'. In Jennifer Lees-Marshment (ed.) *Routledge Handbook of Political Marketing*. New York: Routledge, 34–47.

Burton, Michael John and Tasha Miracle (2014). 'The emergence of voter targeting: learning to send the right message to the right voters'. In Jennifer Lees-Marshment, Brian Conley and Kenneth Cosgrove (eds) *Political Marketing in the US*. New York: Routledge.

Busby, Robert (2009). *Marketing the Populist Politician: The Demotic Democrat*. Houndmills, UK and New York: Palgrave Macmillan.

Chiu, Kevin Kuan Shun, C. Richard Huston, Hani I. Mesak and T. Hillman Willis (2010). 'The role of a psychographic approach in segmenting electorates' voting behaviour and party identification'. *Journal of Political Marketing*, 9(1–2): 34–54.

Dalton, Russell J. (2016). 'The Potential of Big Data for the Cross-National Study of Political Behaviour'. *International Journal of Sociology*, 46(1): 8–20.

Davidson, Scott and Robert H. Binstock (2012). 'Political marketing and segmentation in aging democracies'. In Jennifer Lees-Marshment (ed.) *Routledge Handbook of Political Marketing*. New York: Routledge, 20–33.

Donsbach, Wolfgang and Michael W. Traugott (eds) (2008). *The SAGE Handbook of Public Opinion Research*. London: SAGE Publications Inc.

Dufresne, Yannick and Alex Marland (2012). 'The Canadian political market and the rules of the game'. In Alex Marland, Thierry Giasson and Jennifer Lees-Marshment (eds) *Political Marketing in Canada*. Vancouver: UBC, 22–38.

Edelman (2018). 2018 Eledman Trust Barometer. www.edelman.ca/sites/default/files/2018-02/2018-Edelman-Trust-Barometer-Canada_ENGLISH.PDF (accessed February 2018).

Fearn-Banks, Kathleen (2017). *Crisis Communication*. New York: Routledge.

Friesen, Joe (2011). '"Micro-targeting" lets parties conquer ridings, one tiny group at a time'. *The Globe and Mail,* 22 April 2011. www.theglobeandmail.com/news/politics/micro-targeting-lets-parties-conquer-ridings-one-tiny-group-at-a-time/article4359559/ (accessed 12 June 2013).

Gidengil, Elisabeth (2012). 'The diversity of the Canadian political marketplace'. In Alex Marland, Thierry Giasson and Jennifer Lees-Marshment (eds) *Political Marketing in Canada*. Vancouver: UBC, 39–56.

Gonzalez, Robert J. (2017). 'Hacking the Citizenry?' *Anthropology Today*, 33(3): 9–12.

Gorbaniuk, O., K. Kusak, A. Kogut and M. Kustos (2015). 'Dimensions of Political Party "Personality" Perception'. *Journal of Political Marketing*, 14(1/2): 35–63.

Gould, Philip (1998). *The Unfinished Revolution: How the Modernisers Saved the Labour Party*. London: Little, Brown and Company.

Harmer, Emily and Dominic Wring (2013). 'Julie and the Cybermums: Marketing and Women Voters in the UK 2010 General Election'. *Journal of Political Marketing*, 12: 262–73.

Henneberg, Stephan and Nicholas O'Shaughnessy (2007). 'Theory and concept development in political marketing: issues and an agenda'. *Journal of Political Marketing*, 6(2–3): 5–31.

Hillygus, D. Sunshine and Todd G. Shields (2009). *The Persuadable Voter*. Princeton, NJ: Princeton University Press.

Hutcheson, Derek S. (2010). 'Political marketing techniques in Russia'. In Jennifer Lees-Marshment, Jesper Strömbäck and Chris Rudd (eds) *Global Political Marketing*. London: Routledge, 218–33.

Issenberg, Sasha (2012). *The Victory Lab: The Secret Science of Winning Campaigns*. New York: Crown Publishing Group.

Johns, Robert and Heinz Brandenburg (2012). 'Giving voters what they want? Party orientation perceptions and preferences in the British electorate'. *Party Politics*, (22 February 2012): 1–16.

Johnson, Dennis W. (2007). *No Place for Amateurs,* 2nd edition. New York: Routledge.

Kamberelis, George and Greg Dimitriadis (2005). 'Focus Groups'. In Norman K. Denzin and Yvonna S. Lincoln (eds) *The SAGE Handbook of Qualitative Research*, 3rd edition. Thousand Oaks, CA: SAGE Publications.

Kavanagh, Dennis (1996). 'Speaking truth to power? Pollsters as campaign advisers?' *European Journal of Marketing*, 30(10/11): 104–13.

Knuckey, Jonathan (2010). 'Political marketing in the United States: from market- towards sales-orientation?' In Jennifer Lees-Marshment, Jesper Strömbäck and Chris Rudd (eds) *Global Political Marketing*. London: Routledge, 96–112.

König, Mathias and Wolfgang König (2012). 'Government public opinion research and consultation: experiences in deliberative marketing'. In Jennifer Lees-Marshment (ed.) *Routledge Handbook of Political Marketing*. New York: Routledge, 48–60.

Langmaid, Roy (2012). 'Co-creating the future'. In Jennifer Lees-Marshment (ed.) *Routledge Handbook of Political Marketing*. New York: Routledge: 61–76.

Lees-Marshment, Jennifer (2001). *Political Marketing and British Political Parties: The Party's Just Begun*. Manchester, UK: Manchester University Press.

Lees-Marshment, Jennifer (2009). 'Political marketing and the 2008 New Zealand election: a comparative perspective'. *Australian Journal of Political Science*, 44(3): 457–75.

Lees-Marshment, Jennifer (2010). 'New Zealand political marketing: marketing communication rather than the product?' In Jennifer Lees-Marshment, Jesper Strömbäck and Chris Rudd (eds) *Global Political Marketing*. London: Routledge, 65–81.

Lees-Marshment, Jennifer (2011). *The Political Marketing Game*. Houndmills, UK and New York: Palgrave Macmillan.

Lees-Marshment, Jennifer (2015). 'The Democratic Contribution of Political Market Researchers'. *Journal of Public Affairs,* 15(1): 1–10.

Lees-Marshment, Jennifer and Darren G. Lilleker (2012). 'Knowledge sharing and lesson learning: consultants' perspectives on the international sharing of political marketing strategy'. *Contemporary Politics,* 18(3): 343–54.

Lees-Marshment, Jennifer, Jesper Strömbäck and Chris Rudd (eds) (2010). *Global Political Marketing*. London: Routledge.

Lilleker, Darren and Jennifer Lees-Marshment (eds) (2005). *Political Marketing: A Comparative Perspective*. Manchester, UK: Manchester University Press.

Lilleker, Darren G. and Richard Scullion (eds) (2008). *Voters or Consumers: Imagining the Contemporary Electorate*. Newcastle, UK: Cambridge Scholars Publishing.

Lloyd, Jenny (2009). 'Keeping both the baby and the bathwater: scoping a new model of political marketing communication'. *International Review on Public and Nonprofit Marketing*, 6(2): 119–35.

Manning, Preston (2002). *Think Big*. Toronto: McClelland & Stewart Ltd.

Mayer-Schönberger, Viktor and Kenneth Cukier (2013). *Big Data*. New York: Houghton Mifflin Harcourt.

McNeely, Connie L. and Jong-on Hahm (2014). 'The Big (Data) Bang: Policy, Prospects, and Challenges'. *Review of Policy Research*, 31(4): 304–10.

Mills, Stephen (2011). 'Focus groups: myth or reality'. In Alastair Carthew and Simon Winkelmann (eds) *Political Polling in Asia-Pacific*. Singapore: Konrad Adenauer Stiftung, 27–38.

Morgan, David L. and Colin E. Fellows (2008). 'Focus Groups and Public Opinion'. In Wolfgang Donsbach and Michael W. Traugott (eds) *The SAGE Handbook of Public Opinion Research*. London: SAGE Publications Ltd.

Newman, Bruce I. (1999). 'A predictive model of voter behavior – the repositioning of Bill Clinton'. In Bruce I. Newman (ed.) *Handbook of Political Marketing*. Thousand Oaks, CA: Sage, 259–82.

Norris, Pippa (ed.) (2005). *Critical Citizens*. Oxford: Oxford University Press.

Parsons, Lynn Hudson (2009). *The Birth of Modern Politics*. New York: Oxford University Press.

Phillips, John (2012). Comments made in PBS documentary 'Big Money 2012 The Digital Campaign, PBS Newshour/Election 2012'. *Frontline*, 22 October 2012. www.pbs.org/wgbh/pages/frontline/digital-campaign/.

Pharr, Susan and Robert Putnam (eds) (2000). *Disaffected Democracies: What's Troubling the Trilateral Countries?* Princeton, NJ: Princeton University Press.

Promise (2005). *Reconnecting the Prime Minister.* Report. www.promisecorp.com/documents/Reconnecting_the_Prime_Minister.pdf (accessed 19 March 2008).

Rademacher, Eric W. and Alfred J. Tuchfarber (1999). 'Pre-election polling and political campaigns'. In Bruce Newman (ed.) *Handbook of Political Marketing.* Thousand Oaks, CA: Sage, 197–222.

Rao, Akshay R. (2017). 'Red, blue and purple states of mind: segmenting the political marketplace'. *Journal of Consumer Psychology*, 27(4): 521–31.

Richardson, Brendan (2016). 'Corbynmania: Citizen-consumers and the case for an alternative political marketing'. *Journal of Customer Behaviour*, 15(3): 283–97.

Rothmayr, Christine and Sibylle Hardmeier (2002). 'Government and polling: use and impact of polls in the policy-making process in Switzerland'. *International Journal of Public Opinion Research*, 14(2): 123–40.

Rottinghaus, Brandon and Irina Alberro (2005). 'Rivaling the PRI: the image management of Vicente Fox and the use of public opinion polling in the 2000 Mexican election'. *Latin American Politics and Society*, 47(2): 143–58.

Scammell, Margaret (2008). 'Brand Blair: marketing politics in the consumer age'. In D. Lilleker and R. Scullion (eds) *Voters or Consumers: Imagining the Contemporary Electorate.* Newcastle, UK: Cambridge Scholars Publishing, 97–113.

Sherman, Elaine, Leon Schiffman and Shawn T. Thelen (2008). 'Impact of trust on candidates, branches of government, and media within the context of the 2004 US presidential election'. *Journal of Political Marketing*, 7(2): 105–30.

Teinturier, Brice (2008). 'The presidential elections in France 2007 – the role of opinion polls'. In Marita Carballo and Ulf Hjelmar (eds) *Public Opinion Polling in a Globalized World.* Berlin: Springer-Verlag, 135–52.

Thompson, Derek (2018). *Hit Makers.* New York: Penguin Random House.

Turcotte, André (2012). 'Under new management: market intelligence and the Conservative resurrection'. In Alex Marland, Thierry Giasson and Jennifer Lees-Marshment (eds) *Political Marketing in Canada.* Vancouver: UBC, 76–90.

Turcotte, André (forthcoming). 'Beyond Market Intelligence: New Dimension in Public Opinion Research'. In Mireille Lalancette, *Vincent Raynauld and Erin Crandall* (eds) *#Trending in Canadian Political Communication.* Vancouver: UBC Press.

Valenzuela, Ali A. and Melissa R. Michelson (2016). 'Turnout, Status, and Identity: Mobilizing Latinos to vote with group appeals'. *American Political Science Review*, 110(4): 615–30.

Varoga, Craig and Mike Rice (1999). 'Only the facts: professional research and message development'. In B. Newman (ed.) *Handbook of Political Marketing.* Thousand Oaks, CA: Sage, 243–58.

Wheeler, Michael (1976). *Lies. Damn Lies and Statistics.* New York: W.W. Norton & Company.

Winchester, Tiffany (2016). 'Conceptualizing Usage in Voting Behaviour for Political Marketing: An Application of Consumer Behaviour'. *Journal of Political Marketing*, 15: 259–84.

Wring, Dominic (2005). *The Politics of Marketing the Labour Party.* Hampshire, UK: Palgrave Macmillan.

Wring, Dominic (2007). 'Focus group follies? Qualitative research and British Labour Party strategy'. *Journal of Political Marketing*, 5(4): 71–97.

4 Political branding

by Jennifer Lees-Marshment[1]

Practitioner perspective 4.1 on the importance of brands in politics

Political leaders are iconic in the same way that nationally or internationally known brands are. And that people project a lot of fantasies onto them . . . Of no politicians in the UK has that been more true (truer) than of the Blairs. You only have to replay the footage of their arrival at Number 10 in 1997 to see that nothing really short of adulation was going on . . . they become the best of us in a way that a brand is the best of its class. And they then carry all of our hopes with them.

Roy Langmaid, Consultant from Promise, UK, advisor to UK Labour
2004–2005, interview in Lees-Marshment (2011)

Running for President of the United States means building a brand that at least 51% of the country is willing to buy on Election Day. Not an easy task in a country as large and diverse as America. Too narrow a focus and you won't get a majority vote. A narrow focus builds a brand, but a wide base wins the election. The task is huge. Even the iPhone doesn't have a 51% share of the smartphone market in the U.S.

Laura Ries (2015), branding strategist

A political brand is the overarching feeling, impression or image the public has towards a politician, political organisation or nation. It is broader than the product and more intangible, as well as psychological. Political brands provide a short cut to what a political entity is about: they are the overall perception voters have of a political entity derived from 'nodes' individuals receive from a range of sources including behaviours, organisation, communication and visuals.

Political parties, candidates, government policies, departments and agencies, cities, states and countries use branding to connect with and gain support from potential consumers. Political branding helps the political organisation or politician create a relationship and identity with the public, connect with new markets, and change or maintain reputation and support. This chapter will explore:

- Core principles of effective political brands and brand equity.
- Branding political leaders and candidates, including political brand personality, authenticity, brand heritage, leader and candidate brand delivery, and differentiating deputy leader brands.

- Branding parties, including principles of successful party branding, party brand equity, party brand personality, party brand consumer perception, and political branding and movements.
- Policy, government and programme branding.
- Nation and city branding.
- Maintaining and rebranding political brands, including decontaminating negative brands, considering internal stakeholders and reconnecting in government.
- Political branding in the workplace.

Core principles of effective political brands and brand equity

Practitioners draw on many different elements of political marketing – strategy, goals, political market research, product development and communication – to create and improve political brands. As Cosgrove (2012) notes, branding can occur at different levels:

- The government, e.g. the Trump Administration, the Harper Government.
- The House party brand, e.g. the Democrat or Republican Party.
- Platform brands occupied by candidates in each election, e.g. Trudeau 2015, Trump 2016 or Ardern 2017.
- Product brands related to policies, e.g. the Affordable Care Act (or Obamacare), Brexit, and the American Reinvestment and Recovery Act.

Although it is important to consider the different elements of political brands, they all interact with and influence each other. Pich and Armannsdottir's (2015) research makes clear that the external perception of party brands are also affected by the leader and policies, with the UK Conservative Party's brand image during the 2010 election impacted by unclear policies, former associations with the rich, privileged and upper classes, and mixed perception of the leader David Cameron. Voters themselves can also influence brand perception. Guzmán *et al.*'s (2015) research on Mexico found that how voters saw themselves affected their perception of political brands: voters support candidates who share similar characteristics to themselves.

Political brands are therefore influenced by a range of factors and not easy to control. Nevertheless, Needham (2005) outlines clear criteria for a successful political brand: see Box 4.1.

Box 4.1 Needham's criteria for successful brands

1 Brands act as simplifiers to make it easy for voters to understand what is being offered.
2 Brands are unique and clearly differentiated from the competition.
3 Brands are reassuring so voting for them is not risky.
4 Brands are aspirational and convey a positive vision for a better way of life.
5 Brands symbolise better internal values of the product or organisation.
6 Brands are perceived as credible, delivering on their promises.

Source: Adapted from Needham (2005, 347–8)

Canadian Liberal Party leader Justin Trudeau utilised branding effectively to win the 2015 election. Case study 4.1 by Amber Wharepapa discusses how he adopted a simple *Real Change* slogan which emphasised that the brand on offer was focused on delivering aspirational change for the middle class, framed within the unique idea of a 'better Canada' with superior, positive values. Campaign ads talked about how Trudeau was ready with a plan to deliver the policies, building credibility. Similarly, Conley (2012, 128) argues that Barack Obama's 2008 brand was successful because it was simple and reassuring, centred on an aspirational rhetoric of 'hope' and possibility, with the slogan *Yes We Can*. Political branding can also be used by minor parties. Davies (2014) detailed how the New Zealand Green Party in 2011 reduced radical environmentalism and integrated an economic focus with key words *jobs, rivers and kids* as their focus and *For a Richer New Zealand* as their slogan. This made their brand both aspirational and reassuring, and they secured a big increase in MPs.

Political organisations also need to aim for superior brand equity compared to the competition and thus be the organisations voters are most aware of, loyal to, and positively perceive and associate with. French and Smith (2010, 462) analysed the brand equity of the main UK parties in 2007. Both scored highly on brand awareness and reasonably on loyalty but had mixed perceptions. Conservative supporters provided positive comments such as 'good policies on education' and 'supports green policies' as well as negative ones including 'party of the 80s/dated' and 'hug a hoodie'. Labour received negative comments such as 'war in Iraq' but also positive ones including 'promotes equal opportunities' and 'promotes a fair society'.

Branding political leaders and candidates

Practitioner perspective 4.2 on the need for presidential branding

Political branding tells the public not just who a political actor is, but shapes how a political actor is perceived through her or his narrative . . . [that] manipulates symbols and concepts to tell a story . . . 'Make America Great Again!' emotionally connect[ed] with a key demographic of the American electorate: the white male working-class . . . 'Make America Great Again!' invoke[d] a sense of nostalgia, inspires hope and elicits a desire for change, while being simultaneously anxiety-provoking.

Dellvin Roshon Williams (2017), Communications Strategist

Political branding is a necessity that you can't afford to ignore. It's a critical piece to political marketing in Joplin, Missouri, and elsewhere, one that ensures your audience of voters understands who you are as a candidate.

Carol Daily, Director of Sales, Zimmer Radio Inc. (2017)

Creating an effective political brand is very important for political leaders and candidates. Leader and candidate branding needs to include offering an appealing vision and personality that will create positive associations in voters' minds but also integrate the reality of what a politician is actually like for it to be authentic.

Political brand personality

Political leaders need to build up a positive political brand personality. This can be done through events, politicians'/party actions and behaviour, promises, policies, statements and advertising. These all help to form a brand's personality as well as being impacted on by partisanship (Smith 2009). Smith (2009, 220) argues that there are six important components of political brand personalities (see Box 4.2), and political leaders need to try to score highly on sincerity, excitement, competence, sophistication and ruggedness.

Box 4.2 Smith's components of the political brand personality

- *Honesty*: traits such as honest, reliable, wholesome, sincere, real, sentimental, down to earth and friendly.
- *Spirited*: being spirited, daring, imaginative, up to date and cheerful.
- *Image*: smooth, good looking, trendy, young, cool, exciting, contemporary.
- *Leadership*: the leader, confident, intelligent, successful, hardworking, technical and secure.
- *Toughness*: masculine, rugged, tough and outdoorsy.
- *Uniqueness*: unique, independent and original.

Source: Smith (2009, 220)

Guzmán and Vicenta (2009) also propose principles for effective brand personality including capability, openness and empathy (see Box 4.3). They surveyed a representative sample of 1,144 Mexican registered voters in the 2006 election and concluded that political candidates need to develop a brand that conveys the ability to do the job as well as being in touch with the public.

Box 4.3 Guzmán and Vicenta's principles of effective political brand personality

1 *Capability*: hardworking, intelligent, leader, successful, dynamic, energetic, enterprising, constant and responsible.
2 *Openness*: sharp, creative, innovative, modern and original.
3 *Empathy*: cheerful, sentimental, friendly, cool and young.

Source: Guzmán and Vicenta (2009)

Barrett's (2018) analysis of candidate brand personality and the 2017 New Zealand election concluded that a range of personality aspects are important. Competence was crucial, with Labour leader Andrew Little's inability to demonstrate competence contributing to his poor performance in the polls and his eventual handover to Jacinda Ardern just before the campaign began. In contrast, competence was National leader Bill English's key brand strength. Ardern was weaker on competence but improved Labour's electoral prospects without any major policy changes using her high energy, openness, empathy and agreeableness to 'reinvigorate' the party brand. Ardern's ultimate victory over English suggests competence alone cannot win over voters when opponents turn in stronger performances in all other personality dimensions.

Thus, while political leaders need to project competence, recent cases suggest that strong competence alone is ineffective against opposition or outsider candidates with high energy and charisma:

- Canada 2015: open and charismatic Justin Trudeau won over highly competent incumbent Stephen Harper.
- US 2016: charismatic and high-energy outsider Donald Trump beat the insider and highly competent Hillary Clinton.
- NZ 2017: open and charismatic Jacinda Ardern won over the proven competence of incumbent Bill English.

Authenticity and integrating the candidate's own personality

A politician is a human being, rather than a commercial product, and as a result brings their own personality to the branding exercise. Branding can be limited by their own physical attributes; new, younger leaders find it easier to convey change and be fresh, and older leaders find it easier to appear competent and capable of governing. As Speed *et al.* (2015) note, politicians also bring their own brand heritage into brand formation, such as Ronald Reagan's past as a movie actor, Barack Obama's ethnic heritage and David Cameron's old Etonian background, among other things. Scammell's (2015, 15) analysis of George Bush's brand identity details how it both connected to voters' views and drew on the candidate's own personality, being focused on defending 'family, freedom and country', which connected with hard-working, family-oriented and religiously observant families and the war on terrorism. Branding can also be applied to leaders of international organisations. De Landtsheer and De Vries (2015) explored the brand of the European Union leader Herman Van Rompuy, using a psycho-political profiling method to establish his psychological profile. Rompuy had a positive profile that was accommodating, confident, respectful and ambitious because of how he came across in the media but also how he sought consensus and compromise. Strategists need to adapt branding strategy to suit the candidate.

Branding designs do not always work in practice. One notable case was the strategic choice of Sarah Palin for the vice-presidency on the John McCain ticket in the 2008 US presidential election. Busby (2012, 220) notes that she first attracted positive public and media support as a popular governor of Alaska and down-to-earth working mother of five children. Her brand was designed to appeal to the market-research-identified *Walmart Mom*: lower-middle-class white women who shopped at the discount retailer and were a pivotal swing group with split electoral loyalties. Initial research found she was seen as strong, fresh and interesting. During the campaign, however, her core product-oriented approach became apparent and she moved more in line with very traditional core Republican voters. She was then dressed in expensive designer clothes, contradicting her original *Walmart Mom* image. Questions over her foreign affairs knowledge then damaged perceptions of her leadership capability. The resulting brand was weak in terms of competency, coherence and authenticity.

It is no good conducting research and asking politicians to change to suit it in a way that does not suit them. Speed *et al.* (2015) argue that leadership branding requires authenticity to be valued and perceived as clear and trustworthy. Leaders such as Bernie Sanders, who garnered significant support in the 2015–16 US Democratic primaries, and Jeremy Corbyn, who won the UK Labour leadership, are seen as authentic leaders but struggle to also meet the basic demands of a market-oriented strategy to win overall.

Utilising party brand heritage

Cosgrove (2007) argues that successful political brands in the US have been supported by established party brand heritages. Under President Ronald Reagan, the Republicans built a brand that stressed traditional principles such as a smaller state and lower taxes while focusing on the themes of American renewal and a strong America. This brand was so effective it became the heritage brand for the party with which subsequent leaders try to connect, such as George W. Bush using colours and cowboy imagery similar to Reagan. Cosgrove (2018) details how Trump drew on this brand heritage when campaigning for office in 2016, projecting himself as someone who would restore America's glory, using his personal traits and Reagan's Conservative brand as well as Richard Nixon and George Wallace's issue and populist approach. Trump also made use of the Reagan colours, fonts, slogans and positioning. He was therefore able to attract and mobilise loyal customers for the party while updating the brand by arguing that a vote for him was a vote for change. *Make America Great Again* resonated with those dissatisfied with Obama and connected emotionally with voters. Trump's emotional branding raises multiple democratic questions, including how it potentially had a positive impact by expanding the participation of an underserved market (see Democratic Debate 4.1).

Communicating the leader and candidate brand

Communication strategies need to be used to build a brand. Images taken by Canadian Prime Minister Stephen Harper's official photographer were carefully controlled and presented to convey core brand attributes such as family values and that he was hard working and interested in hockey (Marland 2014). As Simons (2016) has detailed, Russian President Vladimir Putin utilised branding in the 2000 election to present himself as a young, vital, energetic and responsible family man of action with a macho toughness that made him capable of serving the people of Russia. He travelled around Russia interacting with different citizens, discussing the challenges they faced, and as a result building up a sense of being in touch with the people. He also used symbolism, such as associations with sport, and sought to raise hopes and appeal to voters. Brands serve as short cuts for voters, and thus Kumar and Dhamija (2017) found that in democracies such as India party symbols and leaders' appearances influence voters as much as policies.

Branding is used at all levels of power, and Phipps *et al.* (2010) found that local politicians in Australia utilised active members of the community who are well connected in the electorate to help to advocate for their brand and help build a positive brand equity over time. As Cosgrove (2014) notes, personal branding allows candidates to sell themselves to voters, enabling candidates to win in states where their party does not normally succeed.

Associative political branding with refreshments and sports

Political branding also draws on highly salient commercial brands. For example, in Canada politicians aim to be seen in the home-grown Canadian coffee shop Tim Hortons. Cormack (2012) noted how former Conservative Prime Minister Stephen Harper linked himself to Tim Hortons to target less well-off voters who got their coffee from Tim Hortons as opposed to Starbucks. In 2010, Harper even chose to visit Tim Hortons headquarters in Ontario over attending an address to the UN by President Obama. Cosgrove (2017) has also noted that another linkage often made is with sports such as hockey in Canada, basketball in the US and football in the UK.

Leader and candidate brand delivery

As the Needham criteria for effective brands suggests, it is important that leaders stick to and are seen to deliver on brand promises once in power, otherwise their relationship with consumers could be damaged. Cosgrove (2009) notes that George W. Bush's brand became problematic because of the unfounded rationale for the War in Iraq, a weak response to Hurricane Katrina and failure to pass social security reform. The Democrats were then able to brand the Republican Party as corrupt and failing to deliver. In 2012, the Obama Administration then faced the same challenges as they were not seen as delivering hope and change: as Cosgrove explains, change is 'a daunting promise for any branded candidate to deliver in the real world'. Speed *et al.* (2015) therefore argue that candidates need to convey brand authority over their party to be seen as capable of delivering their political product. A leader's credibility emanates from voters' perception about their ability to deliver, which is an outcome of their authority as a brand in the party organisation.

   Butler and Powell's (2014) research on voters and politicians in the US showed that politicians try to pass legislation throughout their term in office, not just near elections, because it helps to build the party brand over the long term; this, in turn, helps them as individual politicians. Candidates benefit from a positive brand valence: they can claim credit for what their party did. Similarly, they can lose credit when things go wrong, such as during the 2013 government shutdown. At such times politicians need to demonstrate they are working to resolve the issue.

Differentiating the brand of deputy leaders

Unfortunately for those politicians who become leaders after working closely with former leaders, electoral history suggests that they are unlikely to be able to differentiate and position their brand effectively. Needham (2006) observes how George Bush Senior and John Major each failed to win a second election because they failed to offer an alternative brand offering to their predecessors. It is harder for new leaders to rebrand in government after a particularly strong leader has gone before them without a period in opposition in which to rebuild. The same was true of UK Prime Minister Gordon Brown, who came after Tony Blair; Bill English, who succeeded John Key in New Zealand; and to some extent even Hillary Clinton, who, having served as Secretary of State in Obama's administration, found it hard to distance herself from Obama's weaknesses. If candidates have been part of their predecessor's team, then voters will hold them responsible for any problems in the government's record and they find it hard to convey their own version of the same party brand (see Lloyd 2009).

Branding parties

Practitioner perspective 4.3 on the powerful impact of party brands

Labour would painstakingly work away and, 'oh, they can't pay for their policies', and then the media would run a story saying, 'Labour's accused of mucking up its numbers', and people would go, 'oh god, Labour's stuffed up again', when we hadn't. And it's a really unfair playing field, but that's the nature of it. Like you say, it's brand and brand is very hard to build and brand is very hard to shake.

NZ Labour Chief of Staff Neale Jones, interviewed
in Lees-Marshment (2018, 131)

We saw it as a marketing exercise where we would sell the right product. And so, we did market research, we focus grouped . . . we had this kind of shop front that we then stocked with policies . . . At different times we were the tough on crime party; the smart crime party; the low tax cut, government waste party; the party of Uber using sophisticated urban liberals; the party of cutting down on benefit fraud and abuse with tougher incentives; the party of educational choice; the party of intergenerational justice and giving millennials a fair go by raising the pension age; and also the party that was supposed to be best on housing . . . There's an old saying that a good library has something to offend everyone. We managed to be a good library. But that's not what a political party should be . . . be consistent in your brand, know what you stand for, don't deviate.

David Seymour, leader of the New Zealand ACT Party, interviewed
in Lees-Marshment (2018, 132)

If parties can create and maintain an effective brand image, this helps new leaders succeed in presidential, federal and national elections, even in political systems such as the US where parties are thought to be weaker than in countries like the UK.

Principles of successful party branding

Conley (2012) argues that there are five principles of successful party branding (see Box 4.4).

Box 4.4 Conley's five principles of successful party branding

1 **Market research**
   Parties must develop a clear understanding of the changing contours of the public's opinion of itself; including past, current and future perceptions; and then identify those segments of the public with which the party can relate and build a lasting relationship.

2 **Brand design**
   The party should design and modify brand concepts in response to this research, creating a brand based on market desires as well as the party's unique history and political identity.

---

3   **Brand implementation**
The brand concept must reflect the input of the internal market to get support and then a broad section of a party's leadership and membership. Once established the party brand will function as a mechanism for co-ordinating the party's activities. So brand co-ordinators must develop mechanisms through which they test and gather feedback on working brand concepts from all stakeholders.

4   **Brand communication and management**
The brand must become the main prism through which the party interacts with, and is understood by, the public and be the vehicle through which the party will, when necessary, reposition itself with its target audiences.

5   **Brand delivery**
A party's brand, its promises, ideals and images must permeate the party's behaviour and be delivered in government in order to create brand loyalty.

Source: Adapted from Conley (2012, 131)

Conley (2012, 129) argues that the US Democratic Party struggled to link itself with the success of the Obama brand, foreseeing the failure of the party to help Hillary Clinton win the presidency in 2018. Conley observed a lack of connection between Obama and Democrat candidates running for US Senate in the 2010 midterm elections, for example, as well as the overall lack of coherent Democratic brand due to ineffective centralised party organisation or strategising. On the other hand, a strong party brand can also hinder candidates. Cosgrove (2012) notes that the US Republican branding under Reagan emerged from the top level, which helped ensure consistency but can make it difficult for new leaders or candidates to create their own unique identify or to rebrand the party following defeat.

Indeed, party brands are longer-lasting than leadership or candidate brands and hard to change. Lloyd (2006) examined branding in the 2005 UK general election and found that voters' associations were predicated on previous party behaviour at past elections, not just what the parties offered in 2005. Cosgrove (2012, 110) therefore argues that Ronald Reagan created such a positive brand heritage around defence, free-market economics, weak regulatory states and family values that it forged deep and enduring voter loyalty and relationships which Trump benefited from in 2016. This does, however, create risks for the Republican Party: if the Trump brand is not seen to be delivering in government this could negatively impact their own brand.

Similarly, Lees-Marshment (2018) notes how party fortunes were affected – and hindered – by their overall brand in the 2017 New Zealand election. The National Party built on their reputation for delivery and competence they had developed since 2008, while Labour's reputation lacked such qualities. Labour campaign manager Andrew Kirton said when interviewed that like all parties 'we went into the election campaign with our brand . . . and Labour parties and Social Credit parties across the world, are common in that they are attacked by conservative and in right wing parties for management of the economy'. Additionally, as Practitioner Perspective 4.3 describes, while the NZ minor party ACT conducted significant market research into what policies might be popular, it suffered from not considering how all its policies fitted together as an overall brand.

Party brand equity in campaigning and government

Party brand equity explores how one party measures up against another in terms of whether voters are very aware of it, loyal to it, consider it highly and associate with it positively. Downer's (2016) in-depth analysis of the rise and fall of the Australian Labor Party's *Kevin07* brand in campaigning and government provides important insights into creating and maintaining branding. Downer created a new brand-oriented party model for building and protecting party brand equity over time (see Table 4.1).

Table 4.1 Downer's Brand-Oriented Party Model

Strategy 1. Identify and establish brand positioning and values

Mental mapping: understand voters' core associations linked to your brand, using qualitative techniques to elicit core brand associations from target market voters.

Competitive frame of reference: create an internal understanding of what your brand represents and how it should be positioned regarding competitors, to create brand superiority in the minds of voters/media by analysing competitors and identifying segments and what will appeal to them.

Points of difference: identify distinctions that create strong, favourable and unique associations for your brand by identifying functional or emotional attributes or benefits that voters strongly and positively associate with your brand and not competitors, and believe you can deliver.

Points of parity: alleviate possible disadvantages against competitors by identifying the shared or similar points between your brand and its competitor/s.

Brand values and mantra: pinpoint a 3–5 expression of the brand values using words from the mental map that conveys the brand's function and associated emotions and captures your brand's heart and soul as well as points of difference.

Strategy 2. Plan and Implement Brand Marketing Programs

Mixing and matching of brand elements: create trademarkable elements that identify and differentiate your brand by choosing elements - brand names, URLs, logos, symbols, spokespeople, slogans, jingles, packaging and signage - using specific tactics for each element.

Integrating brand marketing activities: build strong, favourable, unique brand associations that produce the desired positioning for your brand through relationship marketing programs for brand experiences that create stronger voter/media ties alongside integrated distribution channels and communication.

Leveraging secondary associations: connect your brand with other entities to build equity such as spokespeople, sporting/cultural events, or third-party sources.

Strategy 3. Measure and Interpret Brand Performance

Brand equity chain: assess the outcome of party activities aimed at creating brand equity by tracing the chain of equity creation through its four stages - investment, the voters' mind-set, the brand's performance in the marketplace, and the media's assessment of brand performance.

Brand audit: profile voter knowledge of the brands and products through a voter-focussed comprehensive assessment of brand health to inform long-term strategy.

Brand tracking: collect consistent and regular information about the brand's performance over time to assist with short-term tactical decisions.

(continued)

Table 4.1 (continued)

Brand equity management system: improve understanding and use of the brand equity concept within the party by creating a brand equity charter and create responsibilities and processes throughout the party.

Strategy 4. Grow and Sustain Brand Equity

Brand-product matrix: explore the breadth and depth of the party's branding strategy by developing a matrix of all brands and products offered by the party including hierarchy and relationships between them.

Brand hierarchy: combine and utilise different brand elements across all the party's offerings to promote brand awareness and image.

Brand expansion: target a new market segment by introducing a new product under the party brand name using the rows of the brand-product matrix to identify potential leverage of, and contribution to, existing brand equity.

Brand reinforcement: reinforce brand equity if it erodes over time through consistent marketing support and adjusting tactics to identify new sources of brand equity.

Brand revitalisation: rebuild brand equity to restore lost brand status when identified as necessary through brand equity measurements or brand audits.

Source: Adapted from Downer (2016)

Downer notes how Australian Labor and Kevin Rudd ran a sophisticated and disciplined co-branding campaign in the lead up to the 2007 election built around the charismatic persona of *Kevin07*, which helped them win. A mapping study involving Labor's primary vote showed that under Rudd's leadership the party's equity increased but then declined. Brand discipline dissolved throughout their first term in government and Rudd failed to keep key promises such as action on the brand-defining issue of climate change. This left voters with a severe case of post-purchase dissonance: what they had voted for in the election did not match what was delivered in government. Practitioners therefore need to embrace the concept of political branding in totality and understand why and how to employ the strategy. If party brands become tainted or develop negative associations, they need to be revitalised. Otherwise, if they do not live up to their brand promise, voters will seek alternatives.

MacDonald *et al.* (2015) explored the political brand equity of the four largest Irish political parties in 2012: Fine Gael, the Labour Party, Fianna Fáil and Sinn Féin, focusing on the strength, favourability and uniqueness of the brand associations of the four parties. Exploring the mental maps voters had of parties, they found that Fianna Fáil's brand was the most negative, affected by corruption and former leaders, while the Fine Gael brand was hindered by a lack of differentiation or being seen as 'the same as every other party', which made it weak. The Sinn Féin aggregation map possessed the largest number of brand associations for any party and managed to avoid some of the negative associations attributed to Fine Gael and Fianna Fáil. Where associations are identified as negative, strategies can be developed to reverse them while positive associations can be maintained.

Downer (2016) also contends that effective political branding requires adopting a long-term strategic approach, resources such as time, money and expertise, and once created needs to be disciplined, consistent and authentic to build positive associations, resonate with voters and bring clarity in their minds. Nielsen and Larsen's (2014) research on party brands and voting behaviour in Denmark reached the same conclusion. Brand perception is based on learning: voters pick up the general feelings of the public about different political parties and look up for the most appealing party at a time to make decisions.

Similarly, Ahmed *et al.*'s (2017) research on party brands and voter choice in Pakistan found that the party socialisation process is vital to create party brand equity.

Party brand personality

Brand personality theories can also be applied to parties. Rutter *et al.* (2018) analysed online communication by UK political parties and identified different personality traits such as sincerity, competence, ruggedness, sophistication and excitement. The research found that:

- The Conservative Party communicated competence strongly and was situated between sophistication and ruggedness.
- The Liberal Democrats communicated competence and sophistication relatively weakly.
- The Labour Party and the Green Party communicated both competence and ruggedness strongly, although Labour communicated slightly stronger competence.
- The Green Party communicated slightly stronger ruggedness.
- The United Kingdom Independence Party (UKIP) communicated excitement to a moderate level but were very strong on sincerity.

Overall, online party brand personalities suffered from a trade–off between communicating competence and communicating sincerity as well as between communicating sophistication and ruggedness. Parties must be mindful of their online communication. Lilleker (2015) argues that interactive online communication impacts positively on brand personality, with the Liberal Democrats enabling their supporters to upload pictures and showing evidence of achievements.

Party brand consumer perception

Grimmer and Grube (2017) assessed what brand attributes voters associated with Australian political parties (the Australian Labor Party and the Liberal Party of Australia, and two minor parties: the National Party of Australia and the Australian Greens), surveying over 1,000 participants in 2012. They found that the minor parties had high brand equity and strong penetration levels, but this did not yield voters, whereas the major parties had lower brand equity but high levels of brand associations in voters' minds. Party heritage also played a part in brand perceptions. For example, the Labor Party was largely associated with workers and workers' rights but these associations co-existed with the negative perception about the power of unions within the party. The Liberal Party brand, on the other hand, was strongly associated with sound economic management but was damaged by the perception that the party supported those well-off. However, current party behaviour also affected brand perception, such as the Liberals being affected by their asylum seeker 'stop the boat' policies and Labor's leadership instability under Rudd/Gillard. Such negatives impact major party brands. However, given that minor parties cannot translate their high brand equity into votes, the votes of unsatisfied voters were likely to go to populist parties instead and, thus, the major parties needed to work harder to improve their brand appeal to voters. Party brands are also important in developing democracies: Narteh *et al.* (2017) found in their analysis of party brands in Ghana that party branding elements such as ideology, policy and colours have positive influences on voters' choices.

Political branding and movements

Movements can also use branding. Miller (2014) argues that the success of the US Tea Party was due in part to branding which helped citizens understand the goals and functions of the movement through memorable tactics which played on people's beliefs about spending and taxing. Movements might be able to utilise branding more easily than parties as they have a more focused, niche market, and thus branding might empower non-party organisations to compete with established political parties as they can use branding to generate support quickly. Busby and Cronshaw (2015) argue that the Tea Party also drew on participation branding, which built on supporters' desire to be part of a distinct community, contribute and acquire status – connecting branding with internal political marketing. The movement's creation, authenticity and values also responded to dissatisfaction with Obama's financial bailout issues and attracted significant media attention.

Policy, government and programme branding

Branding can be used to help gain support for leaders' policies, their government and government programmes. US presidents have utilised branding to sell policies to various stakeholders they need support from to get legislation passed; this includes Congress but also lobbyists, the media and the public themselves. Barberio and Lowe (2006) outline principles of presidential policy branding (see Box 4.5).

Box 4.5 Barberio and Lowe's principles of presidential policy branding

1   Appeal to universally desired values such as strength, reliability and fairness.
2   Make claims and offer a comparison about how the policy more fully provides these values, or how the competition's offering is completely devoid of these values.
3   Encourage the consumer to see a benefit beyond the one immediately evident in the policy offered, either directly or indirectly by the use of symbols.

Source: Adapted from Barberio and Lowe (2006)

Examples of presidential policy brands include *The New Deal, The Great Society* and *No Child Left Behind.* They are used by presidents to gain public support before engaging in traditional political combat with organisations and institutions, as the media and members of Congress are also influenced by public opinion. Well-thought-out phrases help to convey the values of the brand and create symbols that resonate with voters and their values. Presidents then draw on staff in the White House Offices of Communications, Public Liaison and Media Liaison to help communicate the brand.

Similarly, political leaders can try to brand the administration of government as 'their' government. Cosgrove (2012, 114–5) observed how the Canadian Conservatives attempted to brand the government under Harper, focusing on economic policy to stimulate the economy through Canada's Economic Action Plan with its own logo featuring multi-coloured arrows upward and a consistent font for its verbiage with both official languages.

The Canadian media critiqued how public servants were asked to use the 'Harper Government' wording when announcing federal funding, policies and government projects in more than 500 news releases in the first seven months of 2013, breaching the principle of a non-partisan bureaucracy.

However, neither policy nor government branding is fail-proof. Barberio and Lowe (2006) observe that branding did not work for President George W. Bush when he tried to implement new social security reforms, despite utilising careful phrasemaking featuring terms such as 'personal' rather than 'private' accounts. There were also problems in the branding of the first Obama administration: Cosgrove (2012) argued that Obama struggled to deliver legislation such as the Affordable Care Act and the American Reinvestment and Recovery Act because – in part, at least – both policies were complex and the values and benefits of such policies were not made clear enough. Consequently, the administration failed to generate strong public awareness of the legislation or to connect it to Obama's brand. This in turn made it harder to pass the legislation in Congress. Government branding can also attract controversy, blurring the line between government and partisan work, as with the use of the 'Harper Government' wording.

Government services or programmes can also be branded, as observed by Marsh and Fawcett (2012). They note how the UK government also sought advice from a branding consultant and created a plan to market the *Gateway Review Process* to the UK and then overseas. A Brand Assurance Team was established in 2007 to ensure that when it was franchised the overall brand was maintained. Marsh and Fawcett suggest a number of principles for effective programme branding (see Box 4.6).

Box 4.6 Marsh and Fawcett's principles for effective government programme branding

1   The brand should only be adopted after all relevant stakeholders are aware of its nature and have been extensively consulted.
2   Extensive documentation must be provided about the brand so that it will remain intact through franchising.
3   A Brand Assurance Team should be established to involve all relevant stakeholders.
4   The government department needs to show continued commitment to the brand.
5   There should be reviews of the policy to enable the exchange of best practice and policy learning which can help reinvigorate and strengthen the brand.
6   Franchisees need to be free to adapt the overarching brand to meet their needs as long as they accept the broad principles of the system.

Source: Adapted from Marsh and Fawcett (2012, 335)

Nation and city branding

Branding is also used to define and promote nations, regions and cities to attract tourists, new residents and investors in the area. This requires working with a range of stakeholders with divergent needs and wants including hotels, the tourist board, museums, major companies and local government to influence not just communication but the design and deployment of space, organisations and finances to make places more attractive.

Nation branding seeks to create a more positive international brand perception of a whole country to help countries compete in a competitive global marketplace (see Fan 2008). A nation brand is how a country is seen in the minds of international stakeholders, and, like party and leader brands, it may be influenced by a range of factors including the place, culture, language, history, food, fashion, tourists' experiences, companies and famous people from that nation such as celebrities, actors and athletes. It draws not just on branding but market research to identify strengths and weaknesses as well as strategically consider competitors and overall positioning. Hulsse (2009, 294 and 302) observes how Germany adopted the slogan *Germany – Land of Ideas* in the run-up to the 2006 Football World Cup and launched various communications initiatives including a *Walk of Ideas in Berlin*: a guide to over 350 locations developing innovative ideas.

Nation branding is particularly important for countries with a historically unfavourable image due to wars or poor human rights records, to remedy outdated images held by the rest of the world. Fan (2008) argues that South Korea and Spain did this in the 1980s and 1990s, and China tried to do the same with the Beijing Olympics in 2008 and Shanghai World Expo in 2010, adding soft power to economic and military power. Choi and Kim (2014) detail how South Korea recently created a Presidential Council on Nation Branding, which worked between 2008 and 2013 to make the country more attractive to foreign investment and trade.

Nation branding can also be used to address other negatives. For example, New Zealand suffered from being seen as geographically remote and just full of sheep. It was firstly branded as *100% Pure New Zealand* then boosted by connecting the country and the national airline Air New Zealand with movies *The Lord of the Rings* and *The Hobbit* to increase tourism. Most recently, the nation's branding was broadened under the tagline *NZ Story* with a video depicting '*open hearts, open minds and open places' (Immigration New Zealand 2013)*.

Challenges with nation and city branding

As with all other areas of branding, nation and city branding is not without difficulties. Nation brands are built up over an even longer period of time. A negative nation brand is hard to change, yet a positive nation brand can be quickly damaged. In August 2013, New Zealand's nation brand was undermined by Fonterra's discovery of the contamination of a component used in their manufacturing of baby formula. As Fonterra was such a big company in New Zealand, and strongly associated with the national brand, this threatened to damage the country's overall image, not just the reputation of that individual company. The government held crisis meetings about the issue and sent its own officials into Fonterra facilities in New Zealand and Australia, trying to control the crisis because it threatened the country's trade reputation. Similarly, Germany's nation brand could be threatened by the recent influx on unidentifiable migrants with associated problematic consequences (Wood 2017).

Nation branding also needs to be authentic. The *100% Pure New Zealand* brand promise was criticised for being exaggerated: Desmarais (2015) noted that while '100%', 'pure' and 'New Zealand' triggered emotional and cognitive processes to create a memorable slogan, the country could not live up to such ambitious claims when it came to the environment.

City branding also raises complications. Case Study 4.2 on Auckland Council's branding by Sophie Sager discusses how the money spent on branding to create the slogan

The Place Desired by Many was extremely controversial. Designing and implementing the changes needed to rebrand can also create power struggles (Eshuis *et al.* 2013, 509). City branding in Buenos Aires in Argentina explored by Dinardi (2017) showed how the process of creating a city brand needs bottom-up participation to be effective to ensure it integrates multiple organisations and cultures within the city, otherwise it might experience resistance.

Maintaining and rebranding political brands

Practitioner perspective 4.4 on maintaining political brands

Iconic brands in politics follow similar patterns to iconic brands in the marketplace . . . what had been a good Tony, became a bad Tony. The idealisation is always followed by denigration . . . in the marketplace we do brand tracking . . . when a product or a service loses its way, if it has any sense, it instantly starts to re-engage with its customers and find out what's gone on in their psychological process that's made them leave.

Roy Langmaid, Advisor to UK Labour 2004–2005, interview in
Lees-Marshment (2011, 67).

You have to re-calibrate the branding exercise as you govern for all and have to deliver.

John Utting, Australian Labor consultant, interview in Downer (2016).

Maintaining a positive brand over time is very difficult. To enjoy continued success, or manage a decline in brand perception, political brands need to be managed and sometimes renewed. Freshness is important: Smith and French (2009, 218) note how 'there is a shelf-life with most brands'. However, rebranding is not easy in practice, especially for parties who have long-standing brand heritage. Perceptions of former leaders also impact on current party brands: French and Smith (2010) found that negative associations from Prime Minister Margaret Thatcher's time in power from 1979–1990 still impacted on the UK Conservatives when David Cameron was trying to rebrand the party in 2005. Rebranding therefore includes decontaminating negative brands, considering internal stakeholders and reconnecting in government.

Decontaminating negative brands

If a political party fails in government, this can haunt it for a long time in opposition, especially if their competitor negatively brands them, as happened with the New Zealand National Party's attacks on Labour's delivery ability. Any negativity which is strongly attached to a party brand has to be removed before rebranding can be begin, otherwise just a single image can reactivate the negative memory in the public mind (Smith 2009, 212). If a leader wants to improve a negative party brand they need to engage in a careful, sustained and coherent effort. Successful rebranding examples include:

- UK New Labour under Tony Blair: significant steps were taken between 1994 and 1997 to remove negative associations with the party that had contributed to successive election losses, such as high taxes and anti-aspiration, and replace them with key fixed policies that repositioned the brand in a new direction.

- Canadian Conservatives under Stephen Harper: when they lost in 2004, Harper initiated a rebranding exercise for 2006, appealing to Québec voters in particular (Paré and Berger 2008, 51).
- UK Conservatives under David Cameron: when Cameron became leader in 2005, he first sought to decontaminate the brand by conceding past mistakes and arguing the party needed to change, and he adopted new policy focuses such as environmentalism and social welfare alongside communication of community action days to ensure behaviour and communication consistently conveyed the new brand position (see Lees-Marshment and Pettitt 2010, 122; Smith 2009, 210).

Internal stakeholders and rebranding

Pich *et al.* (2016) also argue that leaders need to take care to communicate new brand values to members so that they can be clear as to the new brand identity, but also allow enough flexibility in the communication strategy to enable locally-appropriate adjustment to help retain internal stakeholder loyalty. Assessing the impact of internal stakeholders on the rebranding of the UK Conservative Party brand by David Cameron in the lead up to the 2010 election, Pich *et al.* note that Cameron's efforts to remove the 'nasty party' label left some members feeling disconnected, even though Cameron's efforts as leader were appreciated.

Market-research-informed reconnecting in government

It is harder to rebrand in office than in opposition. Governing is not easy, and misconduct or a crisis such as questions over MPs' expenses, personal affairs or war can tarnish and threaten the integrity of the brand. Furthermore, brands need to deliver the brand promise, which, as the political delivery marketing chapter will demonstrate, is not easy. White and de Chernatony (2002, 50) observed how the UK New Labour/Tony Blair brand offered in 1997 'came to be devalued when some of the important promises made were not delivered,' creating negative feelings towards the whole brand. Yet rebranding in office has to be done under significant constraints: politicians cannot redesign and relaunch a completely new brand because one already exists.

Nevertheless, the Blair New Labour case provides the only publicly-known example of successful rebranding in office. In 2004, the Labour Government asked external consultants – a market relations company, Promise – to consider the problem of Labour's and Blair's declining public support. The practitioner Roy Langmaid (2006), who worked for Promise, reports how they conducted brand analysis and qualitative research on the incumbent New Labour brand and the reputation of Prime Minister Tony Blair (see Practitioner Perspective 4.4). Promise found that peoples' needs in 2004/2005 were very different from when New Labour was first elected in 1997 and they were no longer so attracted to the New Labour brand as personified by Tony Blair in 2004. In part, the problem was a decline in the public's relationship with Blair on a personal level. The public's idealisation of Blair in 1997 had turned into a negative view by 2005, with female voters characterising this broken relationship as a 'damaged love affair'. People felt that the New Labour/Blair brand had stopped listening. Langmaid notes how key brand attributes of competence, integrity and teamwork 'had been undermined for voters by the perceived inability of the Prime Minister to listen (principally over Iraq), the divisiveness of the media and the infighting within the party'. Promise therefore advised the government to embark on key strategies such as:

1   Show Team Labour through party figures other than Blair.
2   Be seen to deliver, especially domestically, and keep future promises manageable.
3   Make sure communications are unified within the brand.
4   Reconnect the leadership.

Blair followed this advice, sitting through and listening to harsh public critique from live audiences on Channel 5 and on the BBC's *Question Time*. This advice worked: Blair's reputation with the public improved during the 2005 election. Politicians and their advisors need to monitor the brand before it is too late and be prepared to listen to good strategic suggestions for new ways to deal with old issues.

Political branding in the workplace

Branding is a commonly understood term in society, and political branding is a significant area of practice. Nevertheless, 'branding coordinator' is rarely a title you will find in political job ads. Like the topic, political branding practice interlinks with political market research, strategy and communication. Consequently, political branding is most commonly carried out by multiple practitioners including outside consultants involved in market research, advertising and media as well as insider party staffers involved in campaign management and strategy. For example, media advisors Brian Edwards and Judy Callingham coached former New Zealand Prime Minister Helen Clark on her media appearances when she was opposition leader, helping to build a positive leadership brand foundation from which she led her party to win in 1999, 2002 and 2005. Market researchers such as Roy Langmaid advised Tony Blair on how to reconnect with voters after two terms of office. The one exception is nation branding, where government departments that work on trade and tourism can have branding directors – such as the New Zealand Trade and Enterprise, which had positions in branding and marketing – or use market research companies to conduct branding research for them.

In terms of tasks and skills, branding therefore requires understanding market research data, including brand perceptions and tracking brand performance over time; brand management, including rebranding at times; and also brand communication. It also requires strong relationship maintenance as to change or develop the political brand involves working with politicians, parties and broader stakeholders on vision, values, policies and delivery. Skills that are useful to branding therefore include data skills, analysis, relationship management, inter-personal communication, overall big-picture thinking and media management.

Summary

This chapter demonstrated the broad scope of branding in politics and government. Political branding is both strategic and communicative. Party branding is affected by brand heritage built up over time, and candidate branding involves brand personalities with key characteristics including honesty and openness. Political brands need to be rebranded over time. As discussed in the workplace section, political branding is a growing area of political practice, and staff who work in research, strategy and communications all intersect with it. Like other areas of political marketing, it is also not without democratic implications, as made clear in Democratic Debate 4.1. Box 4.7 presents a best practice guide to doing political branding. Like most marketing techniques and concepts, there is no magic formula with political branding but there are some key principles for success. The next two chapters will explore the communication aspects of political marketing.

Box 4.7 Best practice guide to political branding

1   Understand that a political brand is an overarching feeling and impression the public has of a politician, party, government, international political organisation or nation. Public perceptions of brands are created by multiple experiences of the brand over time, can be affected by policies, leaders, the party and voters' self-perceptions, and builds a brand heritage not easily controlled or changed.

2   Develop an overall brand that is clear and coherent, differentiated, reassuring, aspirational, symbolic of superior internal values, credible and competent, sincere and trustworthy.

3   Candidates need to build an effective brand personality, such as one that is sincere, exciting, competent, sophisticated, strong, open and empathetic. Opposition or outsider candidates should focus on developing energy and charisma and connecting emotionally to triumph over an incumbent or insider's image of competence.

4   Party brands need to build and retain a positive brand equity over the competition, where the public is very aware of their brand, loyal to it and considers it positively.

5   In power, build a brand reputation for competence and delivery to help parties and politicians be re-elected.

6   Political leaders should use policy branding to gain public support for key policies which can then help gain support from other politicians and ensure legislative success.

7   Use nation branding to help promote trade, foreign investment and tourism.

8   Manage the political brand's product life cycle: try to ensure it delivers, especially once in power, but expect it to decline and plan to reconnect as part of a long-term brand relationship.

9   Decontaminate a negative brand before rebranding and implement a comprehensive plan to demonstrate convincing and coherent new behaviour and communication to make the rebrand convincing. Also communicate the new brand to internal supporters to retain brand identity and loyalty.

10 Make sure the political brand is authentic and fits with the politician's own personality, product and behaviour. Don't just conduct research and ask politicians to change to match the market if that does not suit them.

Discussion points

1   Why are political brands so important in modern politics?

2   Discuss whether current parties or politicians meet Needham's Criteria: simple, unique, reassuring, aspirational, value-based and credible.

3   Rate the brand personality of current leaders or parties.

4   Is charisma and emotional connection more important to a leader's brand than competence, and, if so, what does this mean for democracy?

5 Discuss the brand equity of current parties. What might they try to improve?
6 Identify party brand heritage and discuss the impact this has on current party leaders' branding strategies.
7 How might political leaders currently in power develop a brand around key policies – as Barberio suggests – to gain more support and credit for themselves?
8 Should governments continue to fund nation branding, or is it a waste of money?
9 Develop a plan to rebrand a candidate/politician/party or government, utilising a range of branding concepts.
10 To what extent can politicians be branded without losing authenticity?

Assessment questions

Essay/exam

1 What is political branding, and why do politicians and political organisations use it?
2 Discuss and critique the effectiveness of the brands of current politicians or parties against the Needham criteria.
3 Define brand personality and assess how effectively current political leaders have developed different aspects of brand personality.
4 Compare and contrast branding by political leaders, parties and candidates, noting similarities, differences and challenges between branding in the three areas.
5 'Candidate Obama represents an excellent model of what works in branded politics, but President Obama is more of a cautionary tale about branding's pitfalls' (Cosgrove 2012, 116). Discuss this statement in light of current or recent presidents'/prime ministers' brands when campaigning and in government.
6 What problems can occur with nation and city branding and how might they be overcome?
7 To what extent is it possible to rebrand a leader or a party? Discuss both the potential and limitations using a range of examples.

Applied

1 Assess the effectiveness of a political organisation or practitioner against Needham's Criteria for Successful Brands.
2 Assess the brand equity of political organisation or practitioner using concepts by theorists such as French and Smith (2010).
3 Evaluate the effectiveness of the political brand personality of a politician (such as honesty, spiritedness, image, leadership, toughness and uniqueness; and/or capability, openness and empathy), and make suggestions for how they might improve it in future.
4 Assess the political brand of a political party utilising Conley's five principles of successful party branding, determining what they are succeeding at and what they need to improve – and how they should do this.
5 Apply Barberio's (2006) principles of presidential policy branding to the marketing of a political leader's key policy.
6 Identify and assess effectiveness of branding by government departments to brand government programmes.
7 Assess the effectiveness of nation or city branding.
8 Create a plan for rebranding a politician who has been in power for more than one term, drawing on theory and empirical examples for what might work as well as what to avoid.

Case studies

Case Study 4.1 The success of Brand Trudeau in 2015 through clear, consistent messaging at a time for change

Amber Wharepapa (University of Auckland)

Political branding is vital for opposition parties to gain power. An integral part of this is the branding of the party leader. The Canadian Liberal Party's Justin Trudeau is an example of how utilising branding tools can transform a political party. The Liberal Party had declining results in general elections from 2006 onwards, winning only 18.9 per cent in 2011. With effective branding, they jumped into government with 39.5 per cent. To achieve this, the Liberal Party had to use effective branding to reflect the policies and values they wanted to market to potential voters. This case study uses Needham's criteria (2005) to outline how the Trudeau brand was successful during the Canadian 2015 election, focusing on the elements of brands as simplifiers, unique, aspirational, values-based, reassuring and credible. Using the criteria, with empirical evidence from the 2015 campaign, this case study will aim to provide an example of effective oppositional branding that is common in recent election campaigns.

Real Change – Slogans, terminology and message

The Trudeau campaign focused on the slogan *Real Change*, which featured consistently throughout the campaign. The *Real Change* slogan was simple and provided a representation for the rest of Trudeau and the Liberal Party's policy ideas. This slogan follows Needham's simplicity criteria, which argues that 'brands act as simplifiers to make it easy for voters to understand what is being offered' (2005, 347–8). *Real Change* is a simple signifier to the public of what Trudeau and the Liberal Party stand for: a change in government and introducing policies which would make life better for Canadians; in particular, targeting the middle class. The slogan was altered in parts of the campaign to emphasise this idea with 'Real Change – for the middle class'.

Terminology can have an impact on how messages are received. The Trudeau campaign used simple terminology through the *Real Change* slogan to get their message of what the party, Trudeau and their policies meant. The terminology also helped to convey the idea of working towards a better Canada. The intended result of this was to get voters to believe in this idea and get behind their policies.

Challenging the incumbent – projecting the idea of a 'better Canada'

The Trudeau campaign focused on the idea of change by frequently positioning its ideas to be the opposite of what the incumbent government believed in or would do. Needham (2005) discusses this as part of the component of uniqueness in the criteria. The campaign positioned Justin Trudeau as being extremely distinct from the current Steven Harper government, which gained support from those who felt disconnected or unrepresented by Harper's government. This oppositional positioning included videos that focused on the lack of progress that the Steven Harper government had made.

In doing so, the Trudeau campaign positioned Harper as old, out of date and disconnected from voters, and Trudeau as new, fresh and connected to the public. This also rejuvenated the Liberal Party and helped to gain voters' trust. Numerous photo opportunities of the candidate with the public helped to convey an image of being connected to the lives of the middle class and reflecting their values. This aligns with Needham's criteria that a successful brand projects authentic values. Using these images establishes a sense of authenticity of Trudeau's connection to the public. It shows the party as being connected and 'one of us' which was particularly important for the slogan *Real Change – for the middle class.* In this case, having a brand which projects an image of being connected to the people is vital for the policies to be credible and trusted to make a positive change.

One of the challenges that Trudeau faced was building credibility to avoid being seen as a risk by voters. These challenges were often pushed by opposition parties to discredit Trudeau. To respond to this, the Trudeau campaign released videos challenging this notion by demonstrating Trudeau's 'readiness' by presenting the important values that a leader should have along with a consistent policy plan. This consistency of the Trudeau campaign portrays a stable image with strong policy and opinions and created a sense of credibility. The response to these concerns over Trudeau's 'readiness' still projected the same image of a 'better Canada' and a positive change for all Canadians. Emphasis on having a 'plan' was also projected through the use of campaign advertisements. This reinforced the idea of Trudeau being ready and prepared for power and, as such, aimed to build credibility with voters. The result of this response was building stronger credibility with voters without pursuing a negative campaign through still projecting the idea of 'progress' and a positive future under Trudeau and the Liberal Party.

Lessons for political marketing

What is evident from this case study is that through clear consistent messages and oppositional branding politicians and political parties can gain voter support and turn around election results. Although running a campaign on the ideas of progress and change can provide a challenge once in government, it is an effective strategy when in opposition. This is important when considering subsequent elections, such as Donald Trump's win in 2016 and Jacinda Ardern's win in 2017, as these also used the same tools to target their voter market. This case study suggests that it is essential to understand the desire for change in voters and effectively reflect that through consistent branding.

Bibliography

BBC (2015). 'Canada election: Liberals sweep to power'. *BBC News*, 20 October 2015. www.bbc.com/news/world-us-canada-34578213 (accessed 4 April 2017).

Liberal Video. YouTube Channel. www.youtube.com/user/liberalvideo/videos (accessed 3 April 2017).

Needham, C. (2005). 'Brand leaders: Clinton, Blair and the limitations of the permanent campaign'. *Political Studies*, 53(2): 343–61.

Powell, C. (2015). 'Justin Trudeau's winning Campaign'. *Marketing Magazine*, 1 November 2015. http://marketingmag.ca/advertising/justin-trudeaus-winning-campaign-160396/ (accessed 4 April 2017).

Case Study 4.2   The (half a) million-dollar slogan: Auckland Council's branding of Auckland City against Needham's criteria for successful brands

By Sophie Sager (University of Auckland)

Political branding is not just used by political organisations and individuals; it can also be used to define and promote cities. It helps manage perceptions about cities to attract tourists, residents and investors.

In November 2016, it was reported that Auckland Council's promotional arm ATEED (Auckland Tourism, Events and Economic Development) had developed a new slogan for Auckland City, *The Place Desired by Many* (Orsman 2016). While the slogan change was actually just one small part of the Auckland Story, otherwise referred to as the Global Auckland project (ATEED 2016), the New Zealand public were outraged following reports that this new brand took a team of 115 staff two years to develop and, most importantly, that it cost taxpayers $500,000 (Orsman 2016).

This case study will assess the extent to which the Auckland Story followed Needham's (2005) criteria for successful political branding and attempt to account for the public backlash that ensued.

1. Simple

As Needham argues, brands should act as simplifiers, making it easy for the recipient to understand what is being offered. Auckland Council had little control over this aspect because the public first heard of the project when a set of working documents was leaked to the media, who inaccurately reported it (ATEED 2016). The project lacked clarity due to the media attention on the slogan, which was merely intended to be the pillar of the project rather than the main focus. Moreover, when Auckland Council representatives attempted to counter this misinformation they failed to provide any concrete examples of work outside of the slogan change. ATEED also claimed that the slogan was part of a long-form draft of the Auckland Story that was to be shared with stakeholders but did not say what specifically this involved (ATEED 2016). As the project was miscommunicated to the public and Auckland Council did not successfully repair public opinion, it does not meet Needham's first criterion.

2. Unique

Regarding uniqueness, ATEED's aim was 'to articulate what makes Auckland unique on a global level' (ATEED 2016). While they succeeded in making the slogan unique, after it was announced the public questioned why it needed to be changed at all. This suggests that Needham's second criterion is not that relevant in New Zealand, where much of the population abides by the proverb 'if it ain't broke, don't fix it'. Thus, the project meets Needham's second criterion, but this was perceived as a negative by the target audience.

3. Reassuring

The branding failed to reassure the public. One factor that made the public sceptical of the project was the lack of political support. Phil Goff, the new mayor at the time, publicly distanced himself from the project and reportedly had no interest in the rebranding or marketing of Auckland (Edmonds and Sparks 2016). Lack of reassurance from prominent political figures (particularly the mayor of the city in question) cemented the negative public view of the project, and so the slogan fails to meet Needham's third criterion.

4. Aspirational

City brands should be aspirational and give hope of a better life, and this is the aspect Auckland Council most successfully followed. *The Place Desired by Many* suggests that everyone wants to travel to or live in Auckland, creating an air of exclusivity as though it is *the* place to be, thus using supply and demand to increase tourism in Auckland.

5. Value-based

Needham's fifth criterion is that brands are value-based and communicate the values that underpin their product. Auckland Council attempted to capitalise on Auckland's Māori identity and values – the slogan was an ambiguous translation of the Māori word for Auckland, *Tāmaki Makaurau*. The Māori community disagreed with the translation and felt disenfranchised (*Radio New Zealand* 2016). Thus, trying to market Māori identity to the world backfired and alienated a significant portion of the population. While the intention of the slogan may have been value-based, it was executed poorly.

6. Credible by delivering on promises

Needham's final criterion is that brands are perceived as credible by following through with their promises. As the slogan was not adopted, it is difficult to accurately conclude whether or not Auckland Council would have fulfilled the promises it made. However, public opinion was that *The Place Desired by Many* was an inaccurate representation of Auckland. ACT leader David Seymour summarised it as '[Auckland is not] the place where my kids will afford a home before I die, the place where I'm not stuck in traffic all the time, the place where my consents get processed within the 20-day statutory requirement, the place where my rates bear some resemblance to services rendered' (New Zealand Herald 2016). The public found the slogan unconvincing, which discredited the entire project, and therefore it fails to meet Needham's final criteria.

Lessons for political marketing

Although Auckland Council's Global Auckland project successfully met many of Needham's criteria in that the slogan was unique, aspirational and value-based, this was ultimately undermined by the media attention on the cost of the slogan. Local disillusionment, which was echoed by political figures including Phil Goff and David Seymour, also contributed to the mostly negative perception of the brand. Unfortunately, because this slogan did not end up being used, I am unable to explore whether the local view of the brand would have affected the perception of Auckland in the global market, but I think this would be a very interesting aspect of place branding for political marketing to study in the future. Additionally, the idea that Needham's second criterion is not applicable in New Zealand could be researched further.

References

ATEED (2016). 'The Auckland Story or "Global Auckland" project'. Auckland Tourism, Events and Economic Development. www.aucklandnz.com/ateed/the-auckland-story-or-global-auckland-project (accessed June 2018).

Edmonds, E. and Z. Sparks (2016). 'Auckland Council spends $500K on new brand'. *Stuff*, 12 November 2016. www.stuff.co.nz/national/86394744/auckland-council-spends-500k-on-new-brand.

Needham, C. (2005). 'Brand Leaders: Clinton, Blair and the limitations of the permanent campaign'. *Political Studies,* 53(2): 343–61. doi:10.1111/j.1467-9248.2005.00532.x.

New Zealand Herald (2016). 'ACT leader David Seymour slams Auckland Council over $500k slogan', 12 November 2016. www.nzherald.co.nz/nz/news/article.cfm?c_id=1&objectid=11746935.

Orsman, B. (2016). 'Auckland's new $500,000 brand not so desired'. *The New Zealand Herald,* 12 November 2016. www.nzherald.co.nz/nz/news/article.cfm?c_id=1&objectid=11746553.

Radio New Zealand (2016). 'Auckland slogan faces scrap heap', 13 November 2016. www.radionz.co.nz/news/national/317939/auckland-slogan-faces-scrap-heap.

Case Study 4.3 How to sell a U-turn to get re-elected: The case of Syriza from a political branding perspective

By Panos Koliastasis (Hellenic Open University)

Having won the elections, governments are concerned with retaining the trust of the coalition of voters that brought them to power, aiming to improve their re-election prospects. Hence, as Needham (2005) has argued, governing parties tend to develop a communication strategy aimed at promoting an effective brand consisting of six attributes. An effective brand must be: unique in order to differentiate the governing party effectively from its opponents, reassuring enough to allow voters to feel they have made the right political choice, aspirational to create a substantial image for prosperity, be based on specific values to form consistent emotional bonds with voters, credible to convince the public that the governing party is able to deliver on its promises, and finally simple so it can be expressed through clear and short messages that are easily understood and memorised by the broad public.

From this point of view, it is interesting to examine the case of the re-election of the Syriza Party in the September 2015 parliamentary elections in Greece. Nine months earlier, in January 2015, Syriza had come to power on an anti-bailout, anti-austerity platform taking 36.3 per cent of the vote and formed (due to a lack of an outright majority) a coalition government with the anti-Memorandum, anti-austerity right-wing Independent Greeks party (Koliastasis 2015). Employing the campaign motto *Hope is on the way,* Syriza had pledged to end the memoranda consisting of austerity measures and structural reforms as well as negotiate a new agreement with the EU and the IMF including a generous debt write-off along with a stimulus package of tax cuts and spending increases. However, after protracted negotiations with Greece's international creditors, it agreed in July 2015 on a third bailout plan accompanied by a third Memorandum, harsher than the previous two, that consisted of fresh austerity measures and liberal reforms.

Given Syriza's major U-turn on the Memorandum, it would be expected that the radical left-wing party would lose the trust of its electoral base. However, in the snap elections of

September 2015, it managed to secure its re-election by maintaining the greatest part of its vote share (35.5 per cent of the vote). So, the question at this point is how the pro-bailout Syriza managed to retain the trust of the once anti-bailout coalition of voters that had brought it into office in January 2015. In other words, how can this re-election be explained from a branding perspective?

To address this question, the study seeks to evaluate the selling of Syriza's U-turn in order to get re-elected, as expressed by the party's leader Alexis Tsipras, against the six components of an effective brand promotion, though it is unclear whether the party self-consciously employed such a branding strategy.

Having abandoned its anti-bailout platform, Syriza needed to keep differentiating itself from its main competitor for office, the pro-bailout centre-right New Democracy (ND) party, to realign itself with its disillusioned voters. Hence, although Tsipras admitted his failure to avert the memoranda, he projected Syriza as a political force that was less pro-bailout and pro-austerity compared to the ND. Tsipras even argued that the third Memorandum that his government agreed with the EU-IMF contained softer austerity measures and liberal reforms not only than the previous two that had been agreed by the former government of ND and the centre-left PASOK but also from the bailout agreement that ND would have formed if it was still in office (Tsipras 2015a). Moreover, Tsipras claimed that the Syriza-led government had been a harder negotiator than a ND-led one and was more willing than ND to renegotiate the terms of the bailout programme (Tsipras 2015b). Thus, Syriza is more capable of implementing the Memorandum, while defending more efficiently the interests of the most vulnerable. In parallel, Tsipras projected his party as the representative of 'new' politics against the 'old' political establishment of ND and PASOK, which had been alternating in power for 40 years and were blamed by Syriza for both the country's severe economic crisis and the memoranda (Tsipras 2015b).

In parallel, Tsipras reassured his party's electoral base that, despite the adverse political and economic conditions between January and July 2015 when the third Memorandum was adopted, his government had already implemented and would continue to implement a significant part of its policy programme under which it had won the elections of January 2015. He claimed that his government promoted, among other things, social policy measures to protect the most vulnerable social groups (Tsipras 2015b). Furthermore, he argued that the new bailout agreement was better than the previous two since it included lower primary fiscal surplus targets, fewer austerity measures, limited privatisations and minimum labour market deregulation, as well as the financing of the Greek economy under more favourable terms (Tsipras 2015b).

In parallel, Syriza, despite its U-turn on the Memorandum, projected itself as a political force that remained committed to the values of social justice and social cohesion opposing the measures of harsh austerity and neoliberal policies of large-scale privatisations, while advocating measures to combat tax evasion and corruption (Tsipras 2015b). In addition, the radical left-wing party sought to inspire its electoral base, insisting its core goal remained the gradual disengagement from the austerity policy and the memoranda as well as the promotion of growth-friendly policy plans and job-creation measures which would allow Greece to overcome the economic crisis. To convince its electoral base that a Syriza-led government was still capable of delivering on its promises, Tsipras pledged the implementation of a 'parallel' policy programme to the Memorandum, consisting of public investments, social policy measures, expansion of the welfare state and in general helping the poor segments of the society.

Lastly, Tsipras made an effort to express Syriza's brand in a simple and easily understandable way. It is indicative that the party's central campaign message was 'we get rid of the old, we gain tomorrow' (*HuffPost* 2015). In addition, given that Syriza's main slogan in the previous January 2015 election was *Hope is on the way*, it is likely to claim that in these elections Tsipras's new campaign motto sought to revive that 'hope'.

Lessons for political marketing

This case study suggests that a governing party might be able to protect its brand and improve its re-election prospects in spite of a major policy U-turn if it keeps differentiating itself from its main rivals. Given the attributes that characterise an effective brand promotion, it may be appropriate to consider that uniqueness emerges as the core component contributing heavily to the survival of a governing party's brand.

References

HuffPost Greece (2015). 'We get rid of the old, we gain tomorrow: the central campaign slogan of SYRIZA' [In Greek], 4 September 2015. www.huffingtonpost.gr/2015/09/04/politiki-epikoinonia-_n_8087890.html.

Koliastasis, P. (2015). 'The Greek Parliamentary Elections of 25 January, 2015'. *Representation*, 51(3): 359–72. https://doi.org/10.1080/00344893.2015.1113775.

Needham, C. (2005). 'Brand Leaders: Clinton, Blair and the Limitations of the Permanent Campaign'. *Political Studies*, 53(2): 343–61. doi:10.1111=j.1467-9248.2005.00532.x.

Tsipras, A. (2015a). 'Speech in the Panhellenic Conference of SYRIZA: We are here to keep fighting, to move forward' [In Greek]. Syriza website, 29 August 2015. www.syriza.gr/article/id/62169/Al.-Tsipras-sthn-Panelladikh-Syskepsh-toy-SYRIZA:-Eimaste-edw-gia-na-synechisoyme-th-machh-gia-na-prochwrhsoyme-mprosta-.html.

Tsipras, A. (2015b). 'Speech at the International Trade Fair in Thessaloniki: The goal is to disengage from austerity with social justice' [In Greek]. Syriza website, 6 September 2015. www.syriza.gr/article/id/62316/Ομιλία%20του%20προέδρου%20του%20ΣΥΡΙΖΑ%20στη%20ΔΕΘ.html.

Democratic Debate 4.1 Trump's political branding: Expanding the participation of an underserved market?

By Kenneth M. Cosgrove (Suffolk University)

Regardless of what one thinks of him, Donald Trump is the epitome of political branding. Given that politics has been married to marketing for some time now, it should not be surprising that someone who understood how to sell commercial products successfully won office using a similar set of strategies. Donald Trump transformed his personal and celebrity brand into a successful political brand replete with visuals, merchandise, advertising and – most importantly – rallies that both made Trump's brand promises real and attracted a great deal of earned media coverage, thus getting the Trump brand out to the public for free. Trump's rise, as Zito and Todd (2018) note, was predicated on the use of a strategy that literally put him in a different position and set him apart from his 16 rivals for the Republican nomination. Among some conservatives there has long been a sense that their leadership was either too accommodationist or too self-interested. Trump's tough-as-nails branding targeted these people. Coppins (2015) discusses Trump's personal brand and his argument that the GOP was too soft in depth. Trump used his wealth, celebrity and disdainful branding of his opponents – including Republicans (e.g. phrases such as *Lyin' Cryin' Ted Cruz, Little Marco Rubio, and Low Energy Jeb Bush*) – to show that he would feel no need to feel esteemed by such folks. Trump's brand narrative was very clear: he was for the average, forgotten American, and these out-of-touch elites were only out for themselves or their pet causes.

Saying and doing unconventional things showed that a Trump Administration would not represent business as usual (Ibid). Such a self-presentation proved to be strategically wise given that the Democratic nominee epitomised the insiders and status quo Trump was running against. The more Trump said he would drain the swamp and lock up Clinton, who he negatively branded as 'Crooked Hillary', the more his brand story became about dissatisfaction with the present and the likely future direction of the country under either the Democrats or the Washington-establishment Republicans. Trump's emotional brand forged a strong connection with voters and tapped into well-established American cultural themes: the everymen who keep the country running should be represented and the elite had become self-interested and enacted self-serving public policies. Many American politicians have targeted working-class, usually white, voters using these themes. The difference in this case is that Trump built a targeted emotional brand. Trump's campaign found, engaged and turned out an underserved market in working-class white people (Green 2017).

Simultaneously, the campaign knew it was on one side of a battle in the GOP that has been going on since the end of the George W. Bush Administration (Ibid). Trump's new GOP brand supported a very different product aimed at a somewhat different audience that was a response to the lingering effects of a terrorist attack, two wars and a financial crisis that occurred during those years. While these events opened the door to the progressive Barack Obama's presidency, their endurance set the conditions under which a different kind of Republican from the sunny optimistic conservativism of Reagan could flourish. Trump's brand story looked back to an earlier, better America. The brand's dominant emotion was anger over the loss of this great period. The past Trump was recalling was most likely the 1950s but, in its emphasis on nationalism and sovereignty, harkened back to the late 19th- and early 20th-century period. Trump's understanding of where the market had moved since Bush left the White House enabled him to tweak his more multiculturally oriented celebrity brand toward a more working-class, nationalist brand – a process Green (2017) discusses in depth. He thus moved to where the underserved market that he had identified was and showed how changes in the brand and product can reflect changes in the marketplace.

The effectiveness of Trump's brand was criticised because while the core principles (building a stronger economy, an orderly society and a common culture) seem reasonable enough, the way Trump said things and the examples he chose to use to promote himself and his policies both engaged and repelled other customers. His top strategist (Steve Bannon) believes in the power of heroic narrative (Green 2017), and this kind of narrative storytelling fits the branding strategy perfectly. For those defined as the other, these kinds of big narratives can also act as a mobilisation device, as the reaction to Mr. Trump has shown. Not everyone shares the same positive memories of an America gone by: young people had no memories of such a country, many people of colour felt they and their ancestors had been oppressed by it, as did the LGBT communities, and many women were offended by Trump's own personal behaviour and attitudes towards women and his policy positions regarding women's rights. While Republicans from Eisenhower to Reagan to Bush had also argued for a reduced state, none of them did it in the controversially branded way that Donald Trump did, and thus Trump alone generated the antipathy and countermobilisation.

Trump's branding strategy therefore shows both the potential and the democratic limits of political branding. It reduced the room for compromise because to compromise is to undermine the brand's promises and eat away at its market share. Trump's brand personality made this worse because he had a strong personal brand that both attracted and repelled. It engaged people, which is normally seen as good for democracy, but such engagement in this case has become a personal battle and blotted out badly needed policy debates. It encouraged people to retreat into their specific image tribes, thus making compromise and effective government more difficult. Liberals argued that Trump was similar to Adolf Hitler and vowed total resistance to his policies, just as conservatives had totally resisted the Obama Administration. Trump, in turn, has used Twitter, cable news and big rallies to continue sending emotive messages in office. This casts the President as a day-to-day pitchman engaging in the kind of overheated rhetoric that salespeople frequently use, battling with Congress and the intelligence community, rather than acting like a statesman to make the inside aspects of the system work. If all people in both parties do is hunker down in their niches and stay steadfastly true to their brand promises and products, not only will nothing get done but social trust well may erode and result in the country taking steps along the road to despotism.

Trump's emotive branding used so effectively in the campaign has blocked out any serious discussion of the pros and cons of his record in office. Instead of such intellectual discussions, we are mired in discussions about how we *feel* about Donald Trump, as is consistent with the way emotional branding works. The case of Donald Trump therefore shows the upsides and downsides of emotive political branding in a contemporary representative democracy. Trump engaged a market that had been previously underserved and ignored, but, in the process, he also engaged liberal Democrats and alienated specific segments of the Republican Party in ways that could well prove corrosive to the long-term viability of the system and the Republic. While branding is a key political marketing tool with significant benefits, the Trump case shows that it can have multiple mixed (positive and negative) impacts on the societies in which it is used. Scholars and practitioners would be wise to keep both sides of the branding equation in mind when thinking about and using this concept.

References

Coppins, Mackay (2015). *The Wilderness*. Boston, MA: Little, Brown.

Green, Joshua (2017). *Devil's Bargain*. London: Penguin.

Salena, Zito and Brad Todd (2018). *The Great Revolt*. New York: Crown Forum.

Note

1 I would like to thank the University of Auckland's School of Social Sciences for funding a research assistant to complete a review and summary of political branding literature since 2014, and Joyce Manyo for conducting this work, which greatly aided the completion of this updated chapter.

References

Ahmed, M. A., S. A. Lodhi and Z. Ahmad (2017). 'Political Brand Equity Model: The Integration of Political Brands in Voter Choice'. *Journal of Political Marketing*, 16(2): 147–79.

Barberio, Richard P. and Brian M. Lowe (2006). 'Branding: presidential politics and crafted political communications'. Prepared for delivery at the 2006 Annual Meeting of the American Political Science Association, 30 August–3 September 2006.

Barrett, James (2018). 'Chapter 5: Candidate Brand Personality and the 2017 New Zealand General Election'. In Jennifer Lees-Marshment (ed.) *Political marketing and management in the 2017 New Zealand election.* Basingstoke, UK: Palgrave, 67–84.

Busby, R. and S. Cronshaw (2015). 'Political Branding: The Tea Party and Its Use of Participation Branding'. *Journal of Political Marketing*, 14(1–2): 96–110.

Busby, Robert (2012). 'Selling Sarah Palin: political marketing and the "Wal-Mart Mom"'. In Jennifer Lees-Marshment (ed.) *Routledge Handbook of Political Marketing.* New York: Routledge, 218–29.

Butler, D. M. and E. N. Powell (2014). 'Understanding the party brand: Experimental evidence on the role of valence'. *Journal of Politics*, 76(2): 492–505.

Choi, D. and P. S. Kim (2014). 'Promoting a Policy Initiative for Nation Branding: The Case of South Korea'. *Journal of Comparative Asian Development*, 13(2): 346–68.

Conley, Brian Matthew (2012). 'The politics of hope: the democratic party and the institutionalization of the Obama brand in the 2010 mid-term elections'. In Jennifer Lees-Marshment (ed.) *Routledge Handbook of Political Marketing.* New York: Routledge, 124–35.

Cormack, Patricia (2012). 'Double-double: branding, Tim Hortons, and the public sphere'. In Alex Marland, Thierry Giasson and Jennifer Lees-Marshment (eds) *Political Marketing in Canada.* Vancouver: UBC, 209–23.

Cosgrove, Kenneth M. (2007). *Branded Conservatives.* New York: Peter Lang Publishing.

Cosgrove, Kenneth M. (2009). 'Case study 5.4 Branded American politics'. In Jennifer Lees-Marshment (ed.) *Political Marketing: Principles and Applications.* London and New York: Routledge, 129–31.

Cosgrove, Kenneth M. (2012). 'Political branding in the modern age – effective strategies, tools and techniques'. In Jennifer Lees-Marshment (ed.) *Routledge Handbook of Political Marketing.* New York: Routledge, 107–23.

Cosgrove, Kenneth M. (2014). 'Personal political branding at state level'. In Jennifer Lees-Marshment, Brian Conley and Kenneth Cosgrove (eds) *Political Marketing in the US.* New York: Routledge, 148–64.

Cosgrove, Kenneth (2017). 'So much winning if I get elected that you might get bored with winning: Sports as a brand aspect in the 2016 Presidential Election'. Presentation at *the American Elections Symposium 2017: Broken: Barriers, Parties, and Conventional Wisdom in 2016*, New Hampshire Institute of Politics at St. Anselm's College, Manchester.

Cosgrove, Kenneth M. (2018). 'Chapter 4: Trump and the Republican Brand Fresh.' In J. Gillies (ed.) *Political Marketing in the 2016 U.S. Presidential Election.* Basingstoke, UK: Palgrave, 49–64.

Daily, Carol (2017). 'Why Branding Is Critical During a Political Campaign'. Zimmer Radio Inc. blog post, 28 September 2017. https://info.joplinradio.com/blog/why-branding-is-critical-during-a-political-campaign.

Davies, Jack (2014). 'Case study 4.1 Everything in moderation: the brand of the New Zealand Green Party in the 2011 election'. In Jennifer Lees-Marshment (ed.) *Political marketing: principles and applications*, 2nd edition. Abingdon, UK: Routledge, 126–8.

De Landtsheer, C. and P. De Vries (2015). 'Branding the Image of a Fox: The Psychological Profile of EU President Herman Van Rompuy'. *Journal of Political Marketing*, 14(1–2): 200–22.

Desmarais, F. (2015). 'Caught in an inconvenient nation-branding promise: the problematic "100% pure New Zealand" slogan'. *Interdisciplinary Environmental Review*, 16(1): 1–16.

Dinardi, C. (2017). 'Cities for sale: Contesting city branding and cultural policies in Buenos Aires'. *Urban Studies*, 54(1): 85–101.

Downer, L. (2016). *Political Branding Strategies: Campaigning and Governing in Australian Politics.* Basingstoke, UK: Palgrave Macmillan.

Eshuis, Jasper, Erik Braun and Erik-Hans Klijn (2013). 'Place marketing as governance strategy: an assessment of obstacles in place marketing and their effects on attracting target groups'. *Public Administration Review*, 73(3): 507–16.

Fan, Ying (2008). 'Soft power: power of attraction or confusion?' *Place Branding and Public Diplomacy*, 4(2): 147–58.

French, Alan and Gareth Smith (2010). 'Measuring political brand equity: a consumer-oriented approach'. *European Journal of Marketing*, 44(3–1): 460–77.

Grimmer, M. and D. C. Grube (2017). 'Political branding'. *Party Politics*, 1–14.

Guzmán, F., A. K. Paswan and E. Van Steenburg (2015). 'Self-Referencing and Political Candidate Brands: A Congruency Perspective'. *Journal of Political Marketing*, 14(1–2): 175–99.

Guzmán, Francisco and Sierra Vicenta (2009). 'A political candidate's brand image scale: are political candidates brands?' *Journal of Brand Management*, 17(3): 207–17.

Hulsse, Rainer (2009). 'The catwalk power: Germany's new foreign image policy'. *Journal of International Relations and Development*, 12(3): 293–316.

Immigration New Zealand (2013). 'New Zealand: Open spaces, open hearts, open minds'. YouTube video, published 7 November 2013. www.youtube.com/watch?v=x57Wo06aMgs (accessed November 2018).

Kumar, A. and S. Dhamija (2017). 'Political Leaders & Parties as Brands: A Theoretical Perspective'. *Parikalpana: KIIT Journal of Management*, 13(1): 75–82.

Langmaid, Roy (2006). 'Rebranding of Blair in power'. Promise, Brand Strategy. www.promisecorp.com/documents/Reconnecting_the_Prime_Minister.pdf (accessed July 2008).

Lees-Marshment, J. (2018). 'Chapter 8: Conclusion: Political marketing and management lessons for research and practice'. In J. Lees-Marshment (ed.) *Political marketing and management in the 2017 New Zealand election*. Basingstoke, UK: Palgrave, 117–38

Lees-Marshment, Jennifer (2011). *The Political Marketing Game*. Houndmills, UK and New York: Palgrave Macmillan.

Lees-Marshment, Jennifer and Robin Pettitt (2010). 'UK Political marketing: a question of leadership?' In Jennifer Lees-Marshment, Jesper Strömbäck and Chris Rudd (eds) *Global Political Marketing*. London: Routledge, 218–34.

Lilleker, D. G. (2015). 'Interactivity and Branding: Public Political Communication as a Marketing Tool'. *Journal of Political Marketing*, 14(1–2): 111–28.

Lloyd, Jenny (2006). 'The 2005 general election and the emergence of the negative brand'. In Darren Lilleker, Nigel Jackson and Richard Scullion (eds), *The Marketing of Political Parties*. Manchester, UK: Manchester University Press, 59–80.

Lloyd, Jenny (2009). 'Case study 8.4 After Blair . . . the challenge of communicating Brown's brand of Labour'. In Jennifer Lees-Marshment *Political Marketing: Principles and Applications*. London and New York: Routledge, 232–34.

MacDonald, E. A., R. Sherlock and J. Hogan (2015). 'Measuring political brand equity in Ireland'. *Irish Political Studies*, 30(1): 98–120.

Marland, Alex (2014). 'Chapter 4: The Branding of a Prime Minister: Digital information subsidies and the image management of Stephen Harper'. In Alex Marland, Thierry Giasson and Tamara A. Small (eds) *Political communication in Canada: meet the press and tweet the rest*. Vancouver: UBC Press, 55–73.

Marsh, David and Paul Fawcett (2012). 'Branding public policy'. In Jennifer Lees-Marshment (ed.) *Routledge Handbook of Political Marketing*. New York: Routledge, 329–41.

Miller, William J. (2014). 'Branding the Tea Party: political marketing and an American social movement'. In Jennifer Lees-Marshment, Brian Conley and Kenneth Cosgrove (eds) *Political Marketing in the US*. New York: Routledge, 112–29.

Narteh, Bedman, Kobby Mensah and Joyce Nyanzu (2017). 'Chapter 4: Political Party Branding and Voter Choice in Ghana'. In Albert Kobby Mensah (ed.) *Political Marketing and Management in Ghana: A New Architecture*.

Needham, Catherine (2005). 'Brand leaders: Clinton, Blair and the limitations of the permanent campaign'. *Political Studies*, 53(2): 343–61.

Needham, Catherine (2006). 'Brands and political loyalty'. *Journal of Brand Management*, 13(3): 178–87.

Nielsen, S. W. and M. V. Larsen (2014). 'Party brands and voting'. *Electoral Studies*, 33, 153–65.

Paré, Daniel J. and Flavia Berger (2008). 'The Conservative party and the 2006 federal election'. *Canadian Journal of Communication*, 33(1): 39–63.

Phipps, Marcus, Jan Brace-Govan and Colin Jevrons (2010). 'The duality of political brand equity'. *European Journal of Marketing*, 44(3/4): 496–514.

Pich, C. and G. Armannsdottir (2015). 'Political brand image: An investigation into the operationalisation of the external orientation of David Cameron's Conservative brand'. *Journal of Marketing Communications*, 24(1): 35–52.

Pich, C., D. Dean and K. Punjaisri (2016). 'Political brand identity: An examination of the complexities of Conservative brand and internal market engagement during the 2010 UK General Election campaign'. *Journal of Marketing Communications*, 22(1): 100–17.

Ries, Laura (2015). 'Political branding – 2016 preview'. *Blog post, 15 April* 2015. www.ries.com/2015/04/15/political-branding-2016-preview/.

Rutter, R. N., C. Hanretty and F. Lettice (2018). 'Political Brands: Can Parties Be Distinguished by Their Online Brand Personality?' *Journal of Political Marketing*, 17(3): 193–212.

Scammell, M. (2015). 'Politics and Image: The Conceptual Value of Branding'. *Journal of Political Marketing*, 14(1–2): 7–18.

Simons, G. (2016). 'Stability and Change in Putin's Political Image During the 2000 and 2012 Presidential Elections: Putin 1.0 and Putin 2.0?' *Journal of Political Marketing*, 15(2–3): 149–70.

Smith, Gareth (2009). 'Conceptualizing and testing brand personality in British politics'. *Journal of Political Marketing*, 8(3): 209–32.

Smith, Gareth and Alan French (2009). 'The political brand: A consumer perspective' *Marketing Theory*, 9(2): 209–26.

Speed, R., P. Butler and N. Collins (2015). 'Human Branding in Political Marketing: Applying Contemporary Branding Thought to Political Parties and Their Leaders'. *Journal of Political Marketing*, 14(1–2): 129–51.

White, Jon and Leslie de Chernatony (2002). 'New Labour: a study of the creation, development and demise of a political brand'. *Journal of Political Marketing*, 1(2–3): 45–52.

Williams, Dellvin Roshon (2017). 'How Trump's Political Brand Captured the White House'. *International Policy Digest*, 22 January 2017. https://intpolicydigest.org/2017/01/22/how-trump-s-political-brand-captured-the-white-house/.

Wood, S. (2017). 'Rebranding the Nation: Germany's Image Politics'. *International Politics*, 54(2): 161–81.

5   Internal political marketing

by Robin Pettitt and Jennifer Lees-Marshment

By its very nature, internal political marketing is the hidden part of political marketing. It covers the practical implementation of political marketing – the structure, organisation, resourcing and staffing of offices in parties, campaigns and parliament or government; the organisation and involvement of volunteers and members on the ground; and the implementation of product change and branding. Such work goes on behind the scenes and is thus not as visible as other areas of marketing politics, but it is crucial to turning strategies into actual day-to-day activity. Ineffective internal political marketing has the potential to derail political marketing strategies, branding and communication efforts. Successful internal activity ensures that volunteers become and remain effective activists for the party, that donors are recruited, that the right staff are in place, and that new directions in the brand are accepted and complied with even if they challenge traditional party beliefs and ideals. Internal political marketing is particularly tricky because it is heavily focused on managing people. Managing paid employees can be difficult enough, but internal marketing also has to take into account volunteer activists who are giving up their time without a direct financial reward. This chapter will explore:

- Marketing volunteers, including understanding volunteer demands.
- Creating volunteer-friendly organisations.
- Communicating with members and viewing volunteers as part-time political marketers.
- Creating unity.
- Relationship marketing within political parties and campaigns.
- Fundraising.
- Managing political marketing staff and resources.
- Central versus local versus volunteer control.
- Internal political marketing in the workplace.

Marketing volunteers

It has been argued that 'if a volunteer army can be raised and equipped, election battles can be fought and won. If not, your political war is over before it has begun' (Simpson and O'Shaughnessy 2016, 20). Parties are keenly aware of this and have focused heavily on recruiting and making the best use of volunteers. As Practitioner Perspective 5.1 suggests, the 2008 US presidential election saw the beginning of a trend where the parties worked to make campaigning more volunteer friendly. They did this by making it as easy as possible for volunteers to get involved in campaigning. The principle behind this was that structures should be organised to suit the volunteer, not just the party.

Volunteers are crucial to political success. The use of the word 'volunteer' is used here very deliberately, and not just because the US, which is often seen as cutting edge when it comes to political marketing innovation (Pettitt 2014, 198), does not have party members in the traditional European sense (Pettitt 2014, 85). More importantly, parties are increasingly looking beyond the traditional card-carrying members for people to do the practical work of marketing the party (Fisher, Fieldhouse and Cutts 2014). One British party organiser said that 'supporters are important, and moving beyond membership. It is much more valuable to me to get someone who is willing to knock on doors than someone who is willing to pay [a membership fee]' (personal communication). Hooghe and Kölln (2018) argue that parties are increasingly embracing 'multi-speed membership' where people affiliate with a party in different ways depending on national contexts and personal circumstances. In politics, as in other fields of activity, participation is becoming 'non-institutionalised' (Hooghe and Kölln 2018, 3).

Volunteers carry out a number of critical functions including running local offices/branches, providing information about the local community and issues, campaigning on behalf of candidates and locally elected politicians, delivering campaign material, canvassing voters, helping with GOTV (get out the vote), spreading the word in support of candidates through word of mouth, and donating funds to the organisation or campaign (Stromer-Galley 2014, 111, 128).

Practitioner Perspective 5.1 on creating volunteer-friendly organisations

We created a brand new model of organising and it was called the Neighbor to Neighbor programme. What that allowed us to do is any volunteer who wanted to help Barack Obama get elected could go on their computer, and go to his website to my.barackobama.com, and on that website they could type in their home address, and Google, using Google mapping technology, could find their home, and that would find 25 targeted voters.

That's a whole different ballgame, because now I don't have to go 25 miles away to some Obama campaign office or even to another state and volunteer there. I can volunteer from my own home. I can download a list of those people, their names, their addresses, their age, and their telephone numbers; I can print a script of what to say, I can print flyers with information about Barack Obama's position on issues.

Parag Mehta, The Office of the Public Liaison Presidential Transition Team,
interview in Lees-Marshment (2011)

As we push through the last 100 days of this election, our focus remains on helping make grassroots organising as easy and accessible as possible for the volunteers and supporters that are the heart and soul of this campaign.

Stephanie Cutter, Obama for America Deputy Campaign
Manager (Germany 2013, 88)

We'd buddy people up, a new canvasser with a more experienced party member – [. . .] many of the first-timers [. . .] would come back, that was the amazing thing – and after two sessions they were the experienced ones, leading the new ones.

Sarah Jones, Member of Parliament, UK (Hancox 2017)

Understanding volunteer demands

As with voters, it is important in political marketing to understand volunteer wants, needs and behaviours. As noted in the chapter on political market research, the attitude and behaviour of members have also changed with formal membership declining and parties needing to reflect on what their activists want. However, as the Obama and other campaigns show, it is possible to stimulate participation if the right structures are put in place. Political organisations therefore need to conduct research into volunteers' needs and wants. There are different motivations for volunteering. Granik's (2005a, 2005b) research into members of a UK party found that members scoring high on certain motivations are likely to experience higher levels of satisfaction with their role. There are three main areas of motivation:

- *Social* – political party membership is seen as a means of gaining approval.
- *Enhancement* – political party membership boosts the self-esteem of individuals.
- *Understanding* – membership of a political party is seen as a way of learning more about politics.

If campaigns and parties create organisations that focus on these incentives and thus make volunteering enjoyable socially as well as a means of gaining self-esteem and discussing politics, they are arguably more likely to attract and retain volunteers.

Nevertheless, there is plenty of evidence to show that parties are at least trying to use such incentives to motivate their grass-roots. For example, Hillary Clinton's campaign organisers encouraged 'BYOP' (Bring Your Own Phone) house parties to make calls for Clinton (Stromer-Galley 2014, 132). This campaigning approach was low-cost for volunteers to organise but also very sociable.

After the UK Conservatives lost power in 1997, the new leader William Hague introduced several changes which improved the social, political and communication aspects of members. Lees-Marshment and Quayle (2001) observed how several changes were introduced after a period of internal assessment and consultation. A national membership base was created to ease communication with party members, The Conservative Network was launched to offer a social and political programme to encourage young professionals to become involved in the party, the Conservative Policy Forum was established to give members more opportunity to discuss policy, and Conservative Future was created for members 30 years old and under. The party also provided training in skills needed for candidates, such as media management, presentation and speech writing.

Similarly, in a YouTube video posted in May 2018, the UK Labour Party focused heavily on fighting for the party's causes as a motivator to join, but also 'name checked' 'make policy, make friends' as a reason for why people join, which certainly suggests some form of active participation (UK Labour Party 2018a).

Another example of using the above incentives can be found in the Australian Liberal Party. Here politically interested people are asked to contact their regional party to join. The regional parties mention 'Have fun, become involved, meet new people', 'the opportunity to contribute to policy development' and 'get the inside party news first', and 'enjoy the camaraderie at LNP functions with members, elected representatives and party officials' as reasons for joining (Australian Liberal Party 2018). A very similar sentiment is found in a recruitment video from Singapore's People's Action Party, where one volunteer says, 'we are like a big family. We eat together, we laugh together' (People's Action Party 2016).

Foster and Lemieux (2012) discussed how some Canadian interest groups also conduct market research on their members to find out which issues they want them to intervene in and what they need, as well as receiving informal feedback through members' calls, emails and letters to the group. The groups also profile their members to help them meet their expectations more effectively. Indeed, segmentation can be used on members as well as voters, as each group will have specific requirements. Bannon (2005b) argues that political relationships generally can be divided into a number of different types (see Table 5.1). Internal party groups can also be segmented using segmentation according to potential levels of participation and contribution (see Table 5.2).

One way segmentation has been carried out in parties is by creating networks for different socio-demographic groups of party members. Parties often have a youth wing and a women's section, and they sometimes have networks for other groups such as ethnic minorities or LGBT+ members. In doing so, the views and needs of different groups can be catered to within the same, possibly very diverse, organisation.

Table 5.1 Bannon's typology of volunteer relationships with their party/candidate

Relationship	Characteristics
Hyperactivist	Party activist, who is *married* into the party for better or worse
Blood brother	Blood ties, was born into the party through family association with it and treats their party as *the family*
The Idealist	Strongly held political views developed usually in an individual's early life or events, this relationship is based on *true love*
The Mutualist	Seeks mutual outcomes, but doesn't want to sign to an agreed contract, *kissing cousins*
Loosely aligned	A relationship exists but they are not fully committed to the party, the *open marriage*
Multi-relational	A voter who has more than one preference and will get involved in several parties, the *tart syndrome*
The Transient	Floating voter who moves from one party to the next, so has *one-night stands*
The Hostage	Cannot find anyone better to have a relationship with so sticks with the party anyway, the *trapped lover*
Nepotistic relationship	Seeks and gains favour from a party, so acts like a parasite in their own interests and is thus *married for money*
The Blackmailed	Coerced into supporting because the alternatives are worse and the barriers to exit maybe too high, the *forced partner*

Source: Adapted from Bannon (2005b)

Table 5.2 Bannon's principles of political marketing segmentation by social group behaviour

Segment	Behaviour	Desired outcome	Action plan
Politicians	Political representative	Competent and re-electable	Give them a key role in strategic input and implementation
Hyperactivist	Politically active	Evangelist	Involve them in the decision-making process
Activist	Positive advocate	Loyalty	Maintain the existing relationship
Supporter	Active	Vote/member/donor	Nurture and develop the relationship
Potential supporter/ undecided	Passive	Vote	Persuade them to become a supporter through communication
Non-voter	Inactive	Active	Communicate the importance of being an active voter
Non-supporter	Active negatively	Inactive/non-voting	Ignore
Opposition	Negative advocate	Neutralise	Give out misinformation and use negative campaigning

Source: Adapted from Bannon (2004)

Creating volunteer-friendly organisations

Lebel (1999, 134–40) argued that volunteers need to be recruited and promoted to appropriate roles in campaigns according to their skills and performance; also, they need to be trained (see Box 5.1).

The two US Democratic primary campaigns in 2007/8 of Barack Obama and Hillary Clinton made it as easy as possible for volunteers to get involved. The Hillary Clinton campaign created an 'Online Action Centre' on the campaign website where supporters could join Team Hill, make calls using the volunteer calling tool, attend/plan an event, start a blog, join/start a group, or send a fundraising/recruiting email to a friend. Online videos were also posted on the campaign website, showing Clinton supporters in action. One humorous video showed famous movie director Rob Reiner giving volunteers tips on how to be more optimistic and convince more people to support Clinton when door-knocking and making phone calls. Obama gave potential volunteers a specific goal and date such as '*x* calls by Tuesday' and made them actionable and realistic through easy-to-use online tools such as 'click on this button and make 20 calls from this list' (Bryant 2008). Cogburn and Espinoza-Vasquez (2011, 200–2) detailed how the 2008 Obama website was designed in a way that made participation easy: it allowed users to scan it easily and used informal language; and it was easy to find out how to get involved locally and nationally and connect to other volunteers. It gave access to content that was user-generated, encouraging the feeling that volunteers were important too. Communication was also sent from the candidate at key moments, such as before a speech or announcement, which enabled them to feel more connected with him.

Box 5.1 Lebel's principles of managing volunteers

1   **Planning:** plan their recruitment, roles and management, considering what motivates them.
2   **Recruitment:** consider those who fit most easily with campaign needs, including not just their attachment and commitment to a candidate but their skills; segmenting the message sent to volunteers where appropriate; taking into account what they expect to get from the investment of their time; making it easy for them to commit; contacting them within 24 hours of them offering to help to capitalize on their enthusiasm.
3   **Management:** manage volunteers like money; considering the resources available and the needs of the campaign; matching capability with the nature of the task set; including training where needed; relating volunteer activities to the overall campaign; and promoting those who display particular skills.

Source: Summarised from Lebel (1999, 134–40)

The use of Smart Phone apps has also become a feature of campaigning, not only to coordinate the efforts of supporters but also to make those efforts as easy as possible to get involved with. For example, in the UK 2017 general election, Momentum, a group supporting the far-left party leader Jeremy Corbyn, created an app called 'My Nearest Marginal'. This app let people search for nearby seats where the Labour Party stood a chance of winning and where their help would have the most impact. For those who did want to travel, Momentum created 'Calling for Corbyn', which allowed people to call voters from their own phone. The effect was to make it easier for people to participate (Major 2017).

The Jeremy Corbyn campaign in the UK and the Bernie Sanders campaign in the US pioneered the use of 'peer-to-peer' texting. Using dedicated texting programmes, activists are able to contact large numbers of voters. Not only does this allow for low-cost campaigning, it also opens up the possibility of two-way communication. It is true that two-way communication can be, appropriately perhaps, a two-edged sword. Some activists have reported receiving abuse in reply to their campaigning texts. In one instance during a California primary in 2018, on receiving a picture of a voter's 'all sorts of abnormal' -looking genitalia, an activist replied by sending the party's health care plans. This shows both the challenges of peer-to-peer campaigning and the creativity that volunteers can bring to a campaign (Wong 2018).

The lower rungs of party organisations need to follow suit, otherwise the marketing of local politicians can be limited by the skill level and knowledge of volunteers at this level of politics. Stromer-Galley (2014, 135) reported one Obama organiser commenting that: 'We are training them, teaching them how to be effective, showing them what their role is in our strategy to win the election. . . . We're taking people from raw enthusiasm to capable organizers.' The UK Momentum campaigning organisation provides an 'Activist Handbook', containing guidance on door-knocking, persuasive conversations (including a brief introduction to Aristotelian rhetoric), key policy talking points and a guide to the Labour Party's internal workings (Momentum 2017).

Reeves (2013) explored how political marketing is viewed at the local constituency party level among the UK Conservatives and found that there was partial awareness of the scope of political marketing on aspects such as data management and targeting; and there were people involved at the lower levels with marketing skills, but they needed further training to maximise their potential contribution to the political context. Systems such as Merlin also need to be given to the local levels, otherwise party organisations are left to rely on commercial data, whereas they could be collecting their own data from the constituency to add into the central party system to make the party's targeting more effective.

Although there is a lot of attention on the use of the internet to attract voter support, it is also an effective channel for internal marketing to volunteers. Stromer-Galley (2014, 128) notes 'the power of digital media to help bring super-supporters into the campaign and unleash their enthusiasm strategically to their social networks'. Lees-Marshment and Pettitt (2014, 12) quote Matt Carter, who was involved in the 2005 UK Labour campaign, as noting how the party utilised the internet in 2005: 'not only to convey a message, but to try and mobilise the membership, to try and give them a unique way of understanding where could they help, how could they play a part, what their role could be'. The Obama campaign's MyBo packaged all the functionality of a traditional campaign headquarters into a palm-sized device (Germany 2013, 88), connecting supporters to local political events, voter registration information, and polling locations.

Lilleker and Jackson (2013) analysed the websites and linked online presences of six parties (Conservative, Labour, Liberal Democrat, Green, UK Independence Party and British National Party) that stood across the UK at the 2010 general election and found that party supporters and activists were a key target market. Parties are using their websites to attract supporters and increase their activity and donations. All of the six parties encouraged visitors to the site to get involved, such as through sharing videos and pages, donating, volunteering for the campaign and promoting the party via social networks. After the UK Conservative Party's unexpected loss of their majority in 2017, despite huge polling leads at the beginning of the campaign, it was reported that the party was going to create a network of Momentum-style social action groups and thus quadruple the staff engaged in social media campaigns (Wheeler 2017).

Communicating with volunteers

As well as making it easy to get involved, it is important that volunteers feel wanted and valued. As Lebel (1999, 141) notes, internal communication is extremely important to help volunteers feel recognised and part of the overall campaign because they are at the lower end of the campaign hierarchy and do not often get access to the candidate.

Obama used marketing communications to mobilise his grass-roots during his bid for the Democratic presidential nomination. Bryant (2008) notes how the campaign, built on the themes of hope, action and change, was good at translating such values into simple slogans such as 'Change we can believe in' and 'Yes, we can'. They spoke 'positively to the subconscious in a way that would make NLP (neuro-linguistic programming) practitioners proud.' E-communication was also effective, and run by users themselves instead of the political elites. The *Yes We Can* viral video created by Will.i.am and cYclops achieved nearly six million hits on YouTube. The CEO of cYclops and executive producer of the video recalled that as soon as it went viral 'we got calls from all sorts of groups saying they wanted to do their version of the *Yes We Can* and so we decided to create an online community for this kind of content' (quoted in Byrant 2008). A website (www.hopeactchange.com) was created and became a social community for Obama user-generated content – a sort of pro-Obama YouTube.

Lilleker and Jackson's (2013) analysis of the UK parties at the 2010 general election found that the Conservatives, Lib Dems and British National Party created online communities of supporters, which helped to give them a space to discuss politics and create a feeling of a network – although overall websites were mostly used to get things the party wanted rather than allow open debate or control of the campaign. However, it is also possible to manage dissent without reducing the openness of parties' volunteer social media platforms. MyBo was at one point used by volunteers to organise against Obama's stance on the Foreign Intelligence Surveillance Act (FISA). The FISA protest group became the largest on MyBo. Instead of closing down the group, the Obama campaign issued a statement welcoming open dialogue, and thus, 'rather than shutting down the MyBo group or urging them to move elsewhere, the campaign rhetorically embraced the dissent' (Stromer-Galley 2014, 128).

The nature and style of communications techniques selected should match the requirements of each of the identified segments so as to inform, persuade and encourage continued support and involvement. Cogburn and Espinoza-Vasquez (2011, 201) noted how the 2008 Obama campaign website utilised social media tools alongside a database of details about volunteers which enabled the campaign to provide targeted messages to 'narrow constituencies and slices of their activist base'.

Viewing volunteers as part-time political marketers

Volunteers can be an asset in marketing. As Schneider and Ferie (2015, 84–5) point out, members 'not only can sanction the strategic decisions of party management but also help ensure electoral success by communicating directly with potential voters'. Political parties have moved from seeing volunteers as foot soldiers – to be directed without consideration of their needs – to realising that creating organisational structures and opportunities to suit volunteers can significantly increase their effectiveness. Van Aelst *et al.* (2012) argue that parties should consider volunteers as part-time marketers as they provide useful sources of local market intelligence and help market the party at a local level – for free. They argue that party members know and can communicate public opinion and preferences from mass to elite level so they can provide the party with a cheap form of market research. Their research on Dutch party members found that members are more similar to voters than we might think – on several issues, members had almost identical opinions and ideological positions to voters – and members thus help connect the party to society at large. Indeed, when Obama's strategist David Axelrod advised the UK Labour Party in the lead up to the 2015 general election, he said: 'it is not people like me who win elections, it is people like you. Every day people across the country organizing, rallying, fighting' (Axelrod 2014).

Furthermore, supporters who are open about their political affiliation and willing to spread the word can act as volunteer marketers for the party. Polling does suggest that some supporters are very unwilling to openly admit their support for a party, or at least would be embarrassed to do so (Dahlgreen 2018). Nevertheless, those supporters who are proud of their links with their party can be a significant asset. Staff in the US Democrats certainly took this view; Lees-Marshment (2011, 18) noted that trainer Parag Mehta would tell volunteers: 'come back to me and tell me what are you hearing? What are you seeing? When you knock on your neighbour's door and you have a conversation, are they frustrated? What issues are they upset about? Because we can sit here all day long and have all the polling and research . . . but nothing is more powerful than half a million neighbour-hood leaders who talk to 50 of their neighbours four times over the next 14 months and who come back and tell me what they heard.'

Ubertaccio's (2012, 189) research on the US Republicans explains how the party uti-lised volunteers to carry out direct face-to-face marketing which helps to both recruit and retain volunteers, providing them with solidary benefits and continual opportu-nities for political action. The Republicans built an effective volunteer structure to enable supporters to work in their local areas, utilising existing networks to communi-cate with voters over time and get involved in GOTV at election time. President George W. Bush's key advisor Karl Rove worked with the Republican National Committee (RNC) to create the '72-Hour Task Force', which implemented the '72-Hour Project' designed to increase the number of Republican voters by using personal campaign teams to contact GOP-leaning voters within 72 hours of the polls opening on elec-tion day. Ubertaccio (2012, 181) noted how the task force 'drew heavily on network marketing techniques to create a new organisational level of activism, the grass-roots network, complete with "upline" and "downline" participants, who could more effec-tively reach prospective voters and increase turnout'. Similarly, as the Practitioner Perspective 5.1 suggested, the success for the US Democrats under Dean – and then utilised by Obama once he became the nominated candidate – came through creating volunteer-centred structures. Instead of asking people to go along to where the party needed them, they utilised online methods to enable volunteers to help the party in the way that suited them.

Lees-Marshment and Pettitt (2014) interviewed professional party managers working in the central offices of political parties to find out how they had tried to incentivise vol-unteer activists in a way that helped them win elections – thus merging principles of providing avenues for participation, which is good for democracy, with the pragmatism of needing to win. They found that party staff created solidary incentives – incentives derived from the pleasure of being involved in politics – to mobilise volunteers, and that by involving volunteers more they could increase their activity and retention. As well as the usual internal meetings, they noted that online forums have also opened up new ways for parties to enable internal debate. They quote from an interview with Cyrus Khron, who was e-marketing director for the US Republicans leading up to the 2008 election, who discussed how the party had created a website 'where anybody, regardless of party affili-ation could create an account and tell us what they thought the Republican Party should represent, and we had over 13,000 comments and 180,000 people visit the site over the course of a month' (Lees-Marshment and Pettitt 2014, 10). The party 'incorporated those entries into the platform document', even including specific comments from individuals – the first time it had ever done so – 'in such a way that somebody from South Dakota makes a comment about wind energy, and that shows up in the energy section of the platform, and instead of reading the party's decisions, actually read Americans' thoughts on it'. While final policy decisions remain in the hands of the party leadership, such initiatives enhanced the link between internal party discussions and the manifesto, involving volun-teers in a meaningful way.

Lees-Marshment and Pettitt (2014) also noted how Democratic National Committee (DNC) staffer Parag Mehta discussed the changing attitude of the Democrats in 2004–2008 to seeing volunteers not just as foot soldiers but as potential leaders: 'for so many years the Democratic Party has taken them for granted and used them for electioneering, but then not used them for leadership. There has been no promotion system within the

Democratic Party', but to be effective – as well as democratic – party organisations need to 'empower people at the local level to make their own decisions, train correctly, to have the resources they need to get the job done'. So they gave activists access to the national voter file. Not only was this good in terms of sharing information within the party, it was pragmatically beneficial because the volunteers could then help to ensure the data was regularly updated. Lees-Marshment and Pettitt also quote Republican Political Director Rich Beeson, who explained how the RNC also ran training for volunteers on campaign management, campaign finance and campaign field schools so volunteers knew how to go door to door, run a survey and enter the data into voter vault, something also evident in the Momentum guide mentioned above.

Volunteers can also be enlisted to help create and communicate the party's message. Party staff can explain that campaign messages and positions are for voters not yet converted, and are necessary to win power to achieve more principled aims. Thus, Mehta would acknowledge any disquiet more ideologically led volunteers might have with repositioning of branding changes, but explain how their perspective was very different as an activist and hardcore Democrat to those of voters at large. He would say, 'these messages were not crafted for you. We already have you. We love you, we appreciate you, we're going to get your vote, we thank God for your vote. But these messages are not being crafted for you; these messages are being crafted for that small, narrow group of voters who are truly independent.' It doesn't mean the 'founding cornerstone principles of the party are different' but just 'how we talk about it'. That might seem superficial, but that is the reality of political communication which the party has to fit in with 'because if you want to do all the good things we talked about, you have to win the election first' (interview in Lees-Marshment and Pettitt 2014). Lees-Marshment and Pettitt thus put forward a framework for increasing volunteer involvement (see Table 5.3).

Volunteers can also be involved in government; after winning power in 2008, President Barack Obama and the Democrats sought to turn their organisation for campaign

Table 5.3 Lees-Marshment and Pettitt's framework for volunteer activism through inclusive party organisations

To build an inclusive and electorally effective party organisation		
Enlist activists in creating the party's message	**Create activist centred campaign structures**	**Encourage activists through training and leadership**
– Develop opportunities to discuss and influence policy – Make the argument for power to achieve principles – Separate core party values from campaign communication – Inform them about public opinion – Report back success in achieving principles in power	– Let volunteers help in the way that suits them – Make it easy as possible to work for the party – Develop a more open culture, open to new ways of involving volunteers	– Trust the volunteers with data and resources – Give them leadership positions – Train them as you would staff

Source: Lees-Marshment and Pettitt (2014)

volunteers into a permanent structure, Organising for America (OFA), and ask for the public's help in campaigning for policies in government, which continued into and beyond the 2012 election. OFA retained and recruited new volunteers, getting them to help lobby their representatives to get the President's policies passed and take part in action days. Figure 5.1 has an example of an email sent to encourage people to get involved after the 2012 election.

The relationship between politicians and volunteers is changing just as it is between politicians and voters. Lees-Marshment (2013) discussed how politicians and parties have sought to work with volunteers to a greater extent, and put forward the idea of a political partnership model for political organisation. In a political partnership model, parties build permanently volunteer-oriented organisations, develop engagement to suit the user and view volunteers as a partner in the campaign (see Figure 5.2).

Organising for America's email to involve volunteers in government

---

From: Barack Obama [info@barackobama.com]
Sent: 31 July 2013 04:21
To: XXXX
Subject: I'm asking you

Friend –

There is only so much I can do on my own.

The special interests know it, and they're counting on you to be silent on gun violence and climate change. They hope you're not paying attention to creating jobs or fixing our broken immigration system.

And they plan to make the loudest noise when your members of Congress come home for August recess.

I'm counting on you to be just as vocal – to make sure the agenda that Americans voted for last year is front and center.

Say you'll do at least one thing as part of OFA's Action August in your community, no matter where you live.

I know it's easy to get frustrated by the pace of progress.

But it's not a reason to sit back and do nothing – our system only works if you play your part.

If you don't let your representatives know where you stand in August, we risk losing an important battle on your home turf.

So I'm asking you to speak up – commit to do at least one thing in your community during Action August:

    http://my.barackobama.com/Commit-to-Action-August

Thanks,

Barack

Figure 5.1 Organising for America's email to involve volunteers in government

Source: Barack Obama Campaign for the presidency

Co-create	Co-campaign	Co-communicate	Co-consider
• Use creative and deliberative market research methods to get the public to co-create solutions with political elites	• Train and empower volunteers in parties and campaigns to take leadership and initiative	• Engage in long-term interactive and dialogic communication	• Consider public input into decision making and justify final decisions by political leaders to show public input has been reflected on

Figure 5.2 Lees-Marshment's Political Partnership Model

Source: Lees-Marshment 2013

Creating unity

In political marketing, it is important to consider the multiple markets a party has to appeal to: 'a particular organization [. . .] does not just have to consider the ultimate buyers of the product, but also all the stakeholders [. . .] involved in the making and delivering of the product' (Pettitt 2012, 138). The UK Conservatives were held back in 1997–2005 because of their older, white, middle-class membership being unreflective of society, a problem which has arguably continued to hamper the party's appeal, especially among younger voters (Helm and Savage 2017). Smith (2009, 215–6) argues that party members convey the personality of a political brand; thus, if there is disunity or internal criticism of a rebranding or market-oriented strategy, political marketing will be undermined and conflicting messages are sent to voters (Lees-Marshment 2001; Smith and French 2009, 213; Pettitt 2016). Changing the product or brand is not as straightforward for a party leader or chairperson, who has considerably less autonomy than most chief executives leading a business. As most party leaders are elected by a range of people from the party, their position is actually dependent on those below them.

Parties have to try to increase acceptance among internal supporters for new products, and, given that volunteers tend to have a greater ideological or emotive attachment to the party, this can make it harder for them to accept new ways of operating. This is reflected in Case Study 5.1 of the New Zealand Labour Party by Heather du Plessis-Allan. This shows how efforts to focus on the market can run up against resistance from stakeholders such as party members and other supporters such as trade unions. As Lloyd (2005) noted, part of the product is investment; people who have been members of a party for years and have gone out and trod the streets to campaign on its behalf have an obvious investment. A party leader intent on making a party or campaign market-focused risks encountering resistance from stakeholders. The UK Labour Party is a clear example of this, as internal debates raged about which direction the party should take, where fierce disagreements over the party's direction have long been a source of considerable damage to the party's image (Pettitt 2016). As Wring (2005), who analysed the emergence and development of marketing in the party in relation to internal debate and ideological considerations, noted, over the course of the 20th century Labour held three approaches to electioneering up until Blair's victory in 1997:

1   **The educationalist approach:** campaigning was about converting people to their cause through informing them.
2   **The persuasional school of thought:** using campaigning to create an emotional response and change public opinion so it supported the party perspective.
3   **Market research socialism:** more concerned with responding to public opinion than reshaping it, introduced by the leader Neil Kinnock 1987–1992 and then taken to a new level by Tony Blair 1994–1997.

The third approach, which is more in line with a market-orientation, challenged many long-standing beliefs in the party. Wring (2005, 116) cited a delegate who spoke out at the 1992 Annual Conference saying: 'we have allowed ourselves to be marketed by paid image-makers, but . . . we should beware of the paid image-maker. These are people, mainly middle-class graduates, who have learned their socialism from market research and opinion polls.' Tension in the party between doing what was believed to be right and winning elections continued through until Tony Blair's victory in 1997 and beyond.

Leadership, party culture and party unity are important factors in the success or failure of implementation. Gouliamos *et al.* (2013, 4) argue that campaign culture should be studied in relation to political marketing for it involves 'deep connections through shared histories and reciprocal experiences' and understandings and commitments which might impact on the effectiveness of campaigning. It can influence access to resources, knowledge and competency; as well as the propensity to learn from each campaign.

A stage of implementation or management is therefore needed in the political marketing process because political parties will not necessarily accept change, however important to win an election. As one senior UK Labour Party donor commented, 'managing the expectations and priorities of 500,000 people with disparate views would be a daunting task for anyone, whether in business or politics' (Craig 2018). Campaign teams also need to be unified. The Bush-Cheney 2004 team was, as one Republican staffer commented, made up of 'a lot of us that had been together for years. So it was one group . . . and we had one goal and that was to re-elect the President. Nothing else was more important to that' (Lees-Marshment 2011, 120). There are of course a wide range of stakeholders parties need to consider as well as volunteers, including elected politicians, office holders and candidates (see Dean and Croft 2001, 1206). Stakeholders can exert influence over different activities and decisions the party carries out; they also vary in how active or passive they are, and how much influence they have over political marketing.

One classic example of trying to renew after a devastating rejection of a party's product is the UK Conservatives from 1997 onwards. After losing power in 1997, their new leader, William Hague, set about reforming the party and making it market-oriented again. Lees-Marshment (2009) discussed how Hague, a former management consultant, reorganised the party, tried to recruit new members and a broader range of candidates, conducted market intelligence both formally and informally, and developed early policy priorities in response to public opinion. The party began to pursue a public services strategy in response to market intelligence, begun in major speeches made by Hague and Deputy Leader Peter Lilley in April 1999 and focusing on improving state provision of public services rather than looking to the market and simply reducing taxes. The plan was, then, to produce policy themes showing the more caring side of Conservatives. Guarantees to voters were launched in late 1999 which focused on areas of prime importance, responded to the results from market intelligence and attracted positive press coverage when first launched. However, Hague met with sustained internal resistance to the changes. Archie Norman, a successful businessman, became chief executive, opened up a central office and reassigned staff, meeting internal opposition. The party suffered from a number of defections or resignations. Speeches on the new policy direction away from Thatcherism were criticised internally as repudiating Thatcher's free-market legacy and stimulated a very negative reaction from the parliamentary party. Furthermore, membership and public support failed to increase – in fact, both went down – and senior party figures joined in the critique of what Hague was trying to do. The leadership ended up scaling back on the changes, withdrawing new policies and guarantees, and abandoning the market-oriented strategy in favour of getting the core vote out. As the Conservative politician Kenneth Clarke later commented, 'from about half-way through the parliament we stopped trying to broaden our appeal, we narrowed it' (quoted in Lees-Marshment 2009). Hague's two successors did little to renew the market-orientation efforts. Only with David Cameron's leadership win in 2005 did attempts at changing the Conservative Party continue by trying to 'decontaminate the Conservative brand' (Watt and Wintour 2008). Lees-Marshment and Pettitt (2010) note how he appealed to external markets by creating initial new policy positions on the environment, discussing protecting and safeguarding the NHS, and conveying a different persona via photo opportunities in Darfur and social action days with MPs. However, like Hague, Cameron also faced serious internal opposition, with one defecting MP saying:

> 'They use pollsters to tell us what to tell the voters. Politics to them is about politicians like them. It is a game, a game of spin, position. First under Tony Blair, then under Gordon Brown, now David Cameron.'
>
> (McTague 2014)

While Cameron did manage to return the party to power – first in a coalition, later as a single-party majority government – he ultimately failed to bring the party with him on the issue of the EU, which led to his downfall. This shows with painful clarity that just because leaders want to adopt and implement a market-orientation, it does not mean that it will be successful – they have to get support from the majority within the party.

Achieving a market-orientation arguably takes some time, especially if it necessitates major changes in values and beliefs. It is also unlikely that the leadership will achieve 100 per cent party unity or complete acceptance of a market-orientation, but it would aim for a majority of support for the new behaviour. Marketing management literature suggests a number of guidelines for how to make the process easier (see Box 5.2).

Box 5.2 Guidelines for implementing a market-orientation from marketing management literature

1 Create a feeling that everybody in the party can contribute to making it market-oriented and successful.
2 Acknowledge that the party may already be doing many things that would be classed as marketing activities.
3 Encourage all members of the organisation to suggest ideas as to how the party might respond more effectively to voters.

4 Create a system that enables all forms of market intelligence to be disseminated as widely as possible through the organisation.

5 Present market intelligence reports from professionals, especially in the form of statistics, in a way that everyone in the party can understand.

6 Appoint a marketing executive (or equivalent) to handle market intelligence from within the party and from professional research firms.

7 This executive should meet various groups within the party to learn what they think about the party and voters: first, explaining his or her job position and the nature of marketing and its uses and then encouraging open discussion, inviting ideas for change within the party.

8 The importance of views other than those of the majority of the electorate and the party's history should be acknowledged.

9 Those within the party who support the idea of being market-oriented should be promoted to encourage market-oriented behaviour.

10 Emphasise that becoming market-oriented is the means to achieve the party's goal; it is not the goal in itself.

Source: Lees-Marshment (2001)

Another aid to easing implementation is to consider the internal market *before* completing plans for changing the product. The Lees-Marshment (2001) MOP model argues that parties should carry out internal reaction analysis, taking into account a party's ideology and history to ensure that some product aspects suit the traditional supporter market and MPs as well as new target markets; and Ormrod (2005) notes the need to consider stakeholders and members with an internal and external orientation.

Knuckey and Lees-Marshment (2005) analysed the US presidential campaign of George W. Bush in 2000, which had reached out to new target markets, including middle-class and Hispanic voters, with policies on health care and childhood education – nontraditional Republican issues. During the primaries, he adjusted his behaviour to suit internal criticism, to ensure he would win the nomination. He tried to increase his own conservative credentials and temporarily replaced the 'Compassionate Conservative' slogan with 'A reformer with results' and stressed traditional conservative Republican themes, emphasising his belief in limited government. Once he had secured the party nomination, he moved back towards the centre and focused on issues that opinion polls showed to be of paramount concern for most Americans in the 2000 election – education, social security and health care – but alongside traditional Republican themes such as tax cuts, smaller government and a stronger military. As Medvic (2006, 23) noted, Bush's emphasis on school choice, as well as local control and accountability, fitted Republican ideology but also appealed to swing voters.

Bendle and Nastasoiu (2014) provide the first in-depth analysis of political marketing in primary elections. They note that the US primaries present obstacles to candidates by requiring them to meet the demands of their internal markets, whose views are generally divergent to, and more ideological than, the external market – or voters in the general election. Candidate strategies to manage this internal/external market clash differ, but, despite the importance of the primaries, the general election is the ultimate market. Strong candidates can resolve the internal/external market dilemma by focusing on supporters' desire to stop the other party, while weaker candidates need to convey what only they personally can offer. Otherwise candidates who are successful in getting their party's nomination will find it difficult to reposition after a primary.

Meeting the needs of both internal and external markets is not always easy, however. As with all political strategies, successful implementation can depend on timing, the nature of the competition and how long a party has been out of power. Balancing demands between the two markets is difficult. Hughes and Dann (2010, 88) studied the case of Labor leader Kevin Rudd in Australia in 2007 and observed that 'the ALP remained divided between the desire to become more market-driven and desire to remain faithful to the original ideologies of the party: although a combination of both could represent a more comprehensive market-oriented strategy'. In 2007, Kevin Rudd's leadership of the ALP suggested that the party wanted to become more market-focused to achieve electorate success but without severing traditional ties with the unions. Seventy per cent of the front bench candidates had strong union or party official backgrounds (Ibid). However, the compromise created in election year soon gave way to factional debate when Rudd's opinion polls started to decline in 2010, stimulating a leadership challenge by the deputy Julia Gillard who then led Labor to re-election later that year, only to be replaced by Rudd when she suffered a similar fate in the polls in 2013.

As was discussed above in the UK, upon becoming leader of the Conservatives, David Cameron attempted to reform the party. In doing so he had to appeal to both internal and external markets. Cameron sought to appeal to internal markets by discussing social responsibility; a blend of traditional Conservatism, discussing responsibility, and social, emphasising concern about the nature of society. He declared:

> What I say to traditional Conservatives is that we have lost three elections in a row, we have to modernise and change to reflect changes to British society . . . [but] . . . look at the centrality of what I am saying: social responsibility, parental responsibility – that the state doesn't have all the answers . . . this is a profoundly *Conservative message.*

He also continued support for some traditional policies such as government support for marriage. In the April 2007 party election broadcast, Cameron was seen meeting and talking to a variety of people, and not just listening, but sometimes saying no to what the participants wanted, suggesting a degree of leadership alongside responsiveness. Lees-Marshment *et al.*'s (2010, 289) comparative study concluded that being market-oriented need not mean abandoning internal supporters but that party leaders need to carefully balance potentially quite different demands from different markets. Considering the internal market in product design is not just important to maintain party unity, it may also be essential to the long-term success of political marketing in government.

Relationship marketing within political parties and campaigns

Relationship marketing involves volunteers in creating the new product or marketing design. Party organisational research tells us that volunteers need to be incentivised, so political marketing needs to find ways to include volunteers in product design. Pettitt (2012) argues that relationship marketing concepts offer political marketers ways to nourish relationships with a party's internal market. Integrating understanding from Katz and Mair's (1993) ideas of the three faces of political parties – the public office (party politicians in government), the party on the ground (volunteers) and the party in central office (paid party staff) – Pettitt argues that these three faces mean parties have to consider three distinct internal markets for a political party. These are distinct from external markets which obviously include voters and other stakeholders. He argues that parties can adopt a range of strategies in response to these markets (see Box 5.3).

Box 5.3 Pettitt's strategies for involving volunteers in creating the party product

1   **Offer material incentives.**

  - Paying volunteers.
  - *Problem*: problematic as it is too expensive and fails to motivate political loyalty and attachment.

2   **A base strategy of offering purposive incentives.**

  - Giving internal stakeholders what they want, or purposive incentives, so determining the product to suit internal views not external voters.
  - *Problem*: this can lead a party to lose elections.

3   **Become an empty vessel of glittering generality.**

  - Appeal to purposive incentives in a vague sense with an empty product which appeals to a wide range of people who can project their own ideas on it.
  - Utilise virtue terms such as New Labour.
  - *Problem*: it can lead to disappointment as policy detail delivers something people did not want or expect.

4   **Dignified/empty democracy.**

  - Offer solidary incentives where volunteers get to feel involved in creating the product, whilst still considering external market opinion when making the final decisions.
  - *Problem*: activists will notice where their views are not reflected in the party's product.

5   **Effective or real consultation and democracy.**

  - Offer volunteers real democratic consultation and joint creation of the political product, so that volunteers will support and campaign for the product.
  - *Problem*: what volunteers want is not what voters want; and the realities of government require faster decisions than consultation allows.

Source: Adapted from Pettitt (2012)

Pettitt (2012) acknowledges that there are pros and cons to each approach; thus, practitioners need to weigh up which benefits are most valuable and which problems they can most easily cope with.

Levenshus (2010) argues that Obama's grass-roots campaign in 2008 was grounded in relationship management theory, seeking to create positive relationships.

Drawing on interviews with three of Obama's campaign staff members, media articles and the Obama for America website (www.barackobama.com), he noted how the campaign was designed with a master online strategy and localised plans which stimulated grass-roots activity. New media strategists worked closely with field organisers and were always thinking about the relationships that happened on the ground; and paid organisers worked with volunteer coordinators on local Obama social networking groups sites to monitor and participate in conversations, rather than implement a unilateral, centralised plan. Their approach to the grass-roots was to argue that they had the power to influence the outcome of the campaign; a 'you-centred approach', with the phrase 'Because it's about you' appearing at the top of the Action page. Levenshus (2010, 326) argued that 'Obama campaign managers highly valued the campaign's relationships with the grass-roots', and thus forging a positive relationship between the campaign and volunteers was very important and seen as mutually beneficial. They sought to do so in several ways (see Box 5.4). The focus on the contributions made by individual activists is widespread, as shown below:

> As a Labour member, you'll be a key part of the team helping us fight to form the next Labour Government.
>
> (UK Labour Party 2018b)

> The members are the backbone of the party. As a member you can make a difference.
>
> (The Danish Social Demokrats 2018)

Box 5.4 Levenshus's principles of relationship building with volunteers – from the 2008 Obama campaign

1 **Resources for relationships:** campaign managers ensured resources were in place to build relationships with the online grassroots.
2 **Openness and adaptability:** willingness to change in response to volunteers' comments, room for them to share their thoughts including disagreement in places.
3 **Volunteer empowerment:** a you-centred approach and online tools that gave volunteers the power to organise and take action themselves, so they felt like part of the team along with paid employees.
4 **Sharing volunteer best practice:** campaign staff listened to conversations and shared any useful information emerging from the most active groups with others; promoting the most effective ideas.

Source: Adapted from Levenshus (2010, 327–30)

Levenshus (2010, 331 and 333) thus concluded that 'campaign managers used the internet strategically to create conversation' and 'to empower, dialogue with, and build mutually beneficial relationships with publics'. This meant the campaign lost some control, so befitting Pettitt's last principle of effective or real consultation and democracy, at least in terms of input into the campaign.

Fundraising

Fundraising is an important activity that generates resources to fund political marketing activities. As with voters and volunteers, campaigns and parties need to understand donor behaviour. Political marketing research (e.g. Steen 1999, 161–4 and Bannon 2005a) suggests that several factors increase donations, including:

- affection for the candidate;
- agreement with the candidate's stance on issues or policy;
- the candidate's power to influence legislation;
- relation of donation to outcomes;
- benefits offered to the donor, such as greater access to the candidate; and
- social and enjoyable fundraising events.

Various communication tools can be used in fundraising, including direct mail, telemarketing, events and the internet. There are many examples of using direct marketing to gain donations. Response rates are often extremely low, but when used in fundraising the donations gained can still outweigh the cost to make it worthwhile. Sherman (1999, 366) cites an example from the Bill Clinton presidency after his popularity dived:

> In an effort to get increased support, the firm of Malchow, Adams and Hussey was selected to handle the Democrat's direct marketing fund-raising effort. In 1995 . . . a closed-face envelope with a picture of the White House was sent to 600,000 individuals on Democratic National Committee lists. The message stressed that President Clinton said the recipient was a friend and that he or she was wanted as part of the steering committee. It was a soft call for money, with no explicit call for money until the PS at the end of the letter . . . it pulled in $3.5 million.

Direct emails were used heavily in the 2008 US presidential bid by Barack Obama to encourage donations and volunteering to help with campaigning. Anyone who signed up as a supporter or interested party on the Obama site received emails regularly that asked for both support and donations. Often the attention-seeking element of direct marketing was utilised well, with recipients asked to donate by a certain time to allow Barack to stop fundraising for one day, or before some other deadline, in emails written from Michelle Obama as well as the candidate himself. This technique was also used in 2012 (see Figure 5.3). Ron Paul's supporters also used what was referred to as 'money-bombs'. This involved encouraging supporters to flood the campaign with donations on a specific symbolic date (e.g. the anniversary of the Boston Tea Party in 1773). Not only did this generate significant sums, it also garnered useful media attention (Stromer-Galley 2014, 112).

In 2008, Obama made an unusual decision to forgo public funding to get donations from individuals via social media instead. Cogburn and Espinoza-Vasquez (2011, 200 and 203–4) and Marland (2012b, 168) note how Obama succeeded in obtaining nearly $750 million for his presidential campaign by applying marketing concepts including:

- Donating was made as easy as possible, and the website had a simple but prominent 'donate' button and donation checkout integrated into online advertising. Indeed, most political parties have a 'donate' button featured prominently on their home page.
- Communication via email and YouTube videos was direct, personalised and delivered before or after a key event, connecting the recipient to the candidate and campaign.

Fundraising email appeals in Obama's 2012 presidential campaign

---

From: Barack Obama [democraticparty@democrats.org][1]
Sent: Thursday, November 01, 2012 11:54 AM
To: [Name]
Subject: How this ends:

[Name] –

We got outraised pretty badly in the first half of this past month by Mitt Romney and the Republicans, giving them a $45 million edge on us.

We don't know what kind of impact it will have in the final days of a tight race, but we still have time to fight back and make sure it will not be a decisive factor in this election.

[Name], I need you to make a donation of $5 or more to close the gap and finish strong. http://my.democrats.org/page/m/4052bf04/5eb3dc8/19ceacab/74b41b34/2963130561/VEsH/

I know I've asked a lot to you.

No matter how this ends, on Election Night I'll get up stage and thank you for all the time and effort and hard-earned dollars you've put into this. But I also want to be able to tell our country that our hard work paid off, and that we will continue moving forward for four more years.

Please donate $5 or more today:

https://my.democrats.org/November<http://my.democrats.org/page/m/4052bf04/5eb3dc8/19ceacab/74b41ac8/2963130561/VEsE

Barack

Figure 5.3 Fundraising email appeals in Obama's 2012 presidential campaign
Source: Democratic Party

- Special offers were made, such as if they donate *x* amount they would get something from the campaign merchandise.
- Targeted search engine advertisements were placed via paid keywords.
- Celebrities such as Oprah Winfrey were utilised in blogs and speeches.
- Fundraising strategies responded to market research via data from online donors, those attending events and those who entered contests to win campaign merchandise.

Marland (2012b, 170) also notes how, in the 2010 congressional elections, Organizing for America encouraged supporters to create their own fundraising page and identify a fundraising goal; and a thermometer would show how much progress they had made towards achieving this. They were asked to enter friends' email addresses and the campaign then sent them an email saying:

> *President Obama and I are committed to changing the political process by growing an organization founded on a broad base of support from ordinary Americans. This organization is about putting the people's interests ahead of the special interests, but to do that, Barack needs help from people like you and me. I've set my own personal fundraising goal for the organization, which you can see in the thermometer to the right. Will you click the thermometer to make a donation and help me reach my goal?*

Marland (2012b, 173–4) also cited an example of using online marketing to fundraise money to campaign for policy in government, whereby the Democratic Party organised a competition to vote on the best citizen-created, 30-second videos supporting health insurance policy reform; once the top 20 were selected they asked visitors to the website http:// www.BarackObama.com to donate so they could be aired to the general public. The argument made by Organising for America was:

> *Help put the final ad on the air. In the next few days, we'll be using the winning video as the basis for a new television ad that will air across the country – and you can help, by ensuring we have the resources to make the biggest impact. With only weeks to go before the final vote on health insurance reform, we need to make sure Congress hears this grassroots message. Can you help get this message out, just when it's most critical? Please donate today, using the form on the right.*

Fundraising appeals are well researched and tested; Johnson (2013, 17) notes how the 2012 Obama campaign used constant testing of email messages seeking donations, halting poor-performing email requests and resending those that performed well. Candidate fundraising also draws on the efforts by political parties – the Obama 2012 re-election campaign was able to draw on efforts by the DNC: the Obama Victory Fund, established in April 2011, sought large donations from individual donors for both the Obama campaign and the Democratic Party. Funds were then given out to battleground states in 2012 (Corrado 2013, 65–6).

Managing political marketing staff and resources

Practitioner Perspective 5.2 on the importance of long-term resourcing in winning elections

This is what I generally think about not just the RNC but also the campaign in general, the Romney campaign: I think in the year and a half that we had, I think we did a great job. Unfortunately, I think the other side did a great job for four years . . . Ultimately where this is going to lead is that we have to have a massive operation that is very granular, that is in communities across America for a very long time . . . This idea that we tear down every three years and build up for a one-year monster campaign – I just don't see that being the future. I think the future is a much broader operation for a long period of time.

Reince Priebus, RNC Chairman, 2012

Source: National Review interview quoted in Haberman (2012)

The organisation and staff involved in political marketing may be a less visible part of politics, but it is an important one nonetheless as they help form and run long-term organisations necessary for political marketing, as Practitioner Perspective 5.2 suggests. Marland's (2012a, 71) analysis of political marketing in the 1993 and 2006 Canadian federal elections led him to conclude that good organisation is essential for effective political marketing: 'when campaign units operate with military-like meticulousness, regularly interact, and stick to a plan with a developed product offering, they are more likely to experience marketing success than when they are disjointed, isolated, and impulsive'.

Party staff play an important part in implementing political marketing strategies and tactics. Mills (2012) argues that, although party officials do not attract as much attention as consultants or top political advisors, they play key roles in many areas of political marketing. Mills analysed work by three Australian party officials and concludes that they played significant role in a range of marketing activities including gathering market intelligence, designing the product (policy and leadership), building and using long- and short-term campaign resources, and post-campaign product delivery. Party officials can be highly effective political marketers.

As Practitioner Perspective 5.2 suggests, party organisational structures need to be maintained over the long term. Lynch *et al.* (2006) argue that a resource-based view (RBV) suggests parties need to maintain strong resources, such as leadership, staff, supporters, organisation, knowledge and management. If a party develops superior performance on these aspects over the long term, it can help it outperform rivals – and so ensure it has a strong basis from which to strategise and secure re-election. Parties in government often neglect their party organisation, focusing too much on daily government business, and then turn to consider re-election only to find their party organisation is in tatters, making it harder to rebuild. Wiser parties will ensure the organisation is considered a valuable resource that can help them stay in power. O'Cass (2009) also argues that parties need to develop long-term skills within their organisation including information, knowledge and skills among their staff and volunteers.

The Democratic Party's organisational changes under the chairmanship of Howard Dean could be considered an RBV-building activity. Lees-Marshment (2011, 106) noted how DNC staffer Parag Mehta explained that Dean's intention was to build 'a permanent infrastructure so that we didn't just keep rebuilding the party every two years'. The 50-state strategy wasn't just for the 2008 election but was done with the goal of building a more permanent organisation structure regardless of election time or whether a state was part of the top target list. Mehta worked with the state parties to build a team of constant organisers to maintain the Democratic Party so that when there was an election there was already a machine in place. Without this, the party had to rebuild a structure at each election which would just disappear, and this meant that the party was not talking to the voters during the two years in between. This approach, to value the maintenance of resources over the long term, helped Obama win in 2008, as Mehta explained:

> When Barack became the nominee of our party he had all the resources and all the infrastructure to execute a massive political machine. The elements in that machine were A – the field organisers that we had hired, funded, and trained, and put to work for three years in their states, and they knew their states backwards and forwards, and they knew their districts well, they knew their constituents, they knew the ground, they knew the turf . . . And B – we built a national voter file, which the Democratic Party has never had in a presidential election . . . that had every single registered voter in all 50 states in one place, and we were able to turn that over to Barack Obama for free . . . he had a really extensive network built in before he even became the nominee.

Central versus local versus volunteer control

One pragmatic issue that arises is that, as technology offers candidates greater ability to reach supporters, it reduces control because opponents as well as supporters can use it to make their case. This can dilute the overall brand, give fuel to a rumour, or it can be helpful. Cogburn and Espinoza-Vasquez (2011, 204) noted how email campaigns by Obama's opponents sometimes went viral via YouTube, but its influence was – fortunately for the Obama team – limited as it had to compete with spoofs of the opposition on comedy shows also spread by his supporters via social media. Volunteer-led/fluid campaign organisations might cause difficulties; Johnson (2012, 213) talked of how a more fluid model which encourages citizen input and involvement – while it is democratically desirable to have more people participating in a campaign – can make a campaign chaotic and also over-responsive to the whims and wishes of the moment instead of concentrating on a consistent, long-term strategy, or make it seem like the campaign has a thousand messages and no clear message at all. Likewise, a lack of central coordination can waste the enthusiasm of supporters, resulting in a loss of impact (Stromer-Galley 2014, 114).

Turcotte and Raynauld's (2014) analysis of the Tea Party movement suggested that political mobilisation, engagement and organising may become more bottom-up, led by volunteers on the ground rather than an organisation's central office. This could make it harder for parties and candidates to control their brand and communication. For example, while the obvious threat of the Tea Party was to the Democrats and Obama, it is also potentially a threat to the Republican Party as it makes maintaining a clear brand very hard. The Tea Party may have made it very hard for a moderate, energetic, new market-oriented leader of the Republicans to build support from independents in future and so damaged the Republican chances of recovery also.

Nevertheless, too much centralised control can prevent individual politicians being able to respond to their local political market. In countries with party-based systems, such as the UK, local MPs and candidates are traditionally more restricted as campaigns are national and party-based. Marland (2009) noted how Canadian constituency campaigns act like local franchises, implementing the centrally driven market-oriented strategy created by the party. Candidates are expected to promote the party leader, the label, the manifesto, the key messages, the overall brand – regardless of local electors' viewpoints. Thus, Marland argued that these political franchisees 'are more concerned with getting hamburgers ready for a Saturday morning rush than they are with changing recipes' in order to win elections. However, research by Lilleker and Negrine (2002 and 2003) and Lilleker (2005 and 2006) suggests that candidates are increasingly running local marketing campaigns, having realised the negative consequences of too much central control. In some constituencies, local voters are particularly important and influential on the vote. And in the US, where party organisations are looser, Steger (1999, 663 and 667) notes how candidates employ their own staff and consultants and have freedom from party control to tailor their positions and issues to suit their market. Incumbents get an informal feel for their market through 'direct interactive communication with their constituents to gain first-hand information about their concerns, complaints, and preferences'. The power in the organisation of political marketing has to be carefully balanced to maximise effectiveness on all sides.

The dangers that supporters bring

While supporters can certainly have a massive positive impact on a campaign, if organised well, they also bring risks. Ron Paul's supporters in 2007 were certainly enthusiastic, but they also garnered his campaign negative coverage: 'they developed a reputation of being spammers. Thus, the enthusiasm, though well intentioned, created negative publicity for Paul, and further fuelled the sense that Paul was a marginal candidate' (Stromer-Galley

2014, 129). Another example is the dangers of peer-to-peer texting. One volunteer was reported as using abusive language about a rival candidate in their communication with voters (Wong 2018). In 2015, when Labour was selecting their candidate for Mayor of London, the campaign of Tessa Jowell was damaged after a volunteer suggested her rival, and eventual London mayor, Sadiq Khan, would be a liability because of being a Muslim (Watt 2015). In 2017, the UK Conservative supporting campaign group Activate ran into problems when some of its members exchanged messages in a WhatsApp group about gassing chavs [young working-class people], or using them in medical experiments instead of animals, and joking about 'shooting peasants' (Ferguson 2017). Also in 2017, the United Kingdom Independence Party earned negative coverage when one of their activists was filmed on CCTV urinating against an elderly woman's house (Boyle 2017). These examples are no doubt relatively rare, but they do show how, while volunteers have to be allowed to campaign without minute-by-minute supervision, human weaknesses mean that any campaign would be advised to have processes in place if volunteers publicly embarrass themselves and the party.

Internal political marketing in the workplace

There are an increasing range of jobs related to internal political marketing as parties professionalise, such as top-level roles like campaign managers and party presidents, but also outreach staff, local organisers, field directors and organisers, and fundraising managers. These jobs draw on skills such as people management, coordination, organisation and inter-personal communication. Mills (2014)'s book *The Professionals* conveyed how Australia National campaign directors have over time been transformed from fulfilling an administrative role to more strategic and influential campaign managers. Specific examples of internal marketing jobs include the British Labour Party hiring 'community' organisers, whose role include training 'Labour members, community leaders, activists and elected officials in the methods of community organising and leadership'. Likewise, the British Conservative Party launched a Campaign Manager Programme in 2017. Part of the campaign managers' role is 'supporting our local candidates' and building 'groups of dedicated volunteers in every constituency'. In the US, the Democrats also advertised for Organizers. Again, the job is heavily focused on internal marketing, with a key part of the job being to 'recruit, train and retrain volunteers'. Another example is the Australian Green Party, where part of the role as Campaigner included the need to 'develop and manage a volunteer leadership team: Build a central team of volunteers to support with all elements of the central campaign'.

Summary

Internal marketing is an important part of political marketing. It is crucial to create volunteer-friendly organisational structures in response to research about volunteer needs, trying to involve volunteers in the product design enough so that they accept proposed changes, to ensure that fundraising attempts reflect understanding of donor behaviour, and to make sure campaign and party organisational structures are well staffed and resourced to support political marketing activities. Without effective internal political marketing, good products can get blocked and volunteers will do less or resign, and in the long term this can undermine support for the party. Fundraising and resource management is also an important part of internal marketing that impacts on what parties, campaigns and candidates can do. Box 5.5 offers a guide to doing internal political marketing in practice. Internal marketing is subtle, behind the scenes and does not often yield quick results. However, if it is done well the product will be supported by committed and enthusiastic members and volunteers, and the next stage of communication and campaigning, which will be discussed in the next two chapters, is made much easier.

Box 5.5 Best practice guide to internal political marketing

1   Understand that internal political marketing is important; ineffective internal marketing can derail all other political marketing efforts.

2   Research and respond to the demands, expectations, needs and behaviour of the internal market of volunteers, supporters, donors and members.

3   Create volunteer-centred structures, accepting that volunteers can't always do what you want when you want and instead enable them to get involved in ways that suit them.

4   Help them help you even more: offer volunteers support and training, assign tasks and promote according to skills, and give volunteers leadership positions and access to data.

5   Use e-marketing and internal marketing principles to create online forums for supporters to discuss and get involved in the campaign/party, creating solidary incentives and stimulating participation.

6   Where volunteers are more representative of voters, engage them as part-time marketers, to both provide useful market intelligence and campaign on behalf of the party, and build long-term relationships that outlast the campaigns – and governments – of political candidates and leaders.

7   Use direct marketing to encourage party sympathisers to be involved in a party, designing e-marketing to enable them to campaign for the party.

8   Target online fundraising messages to suit the audience to make them more effective, and aim fundraising at active and satisfied volunteers.

9   Adapt both the concept and mechanics of donor marketing to suit the volunteer and donor cultures and regulatory frameworks within the political system.

10   Train both party staff and volunteers in political marketing to increase their effectiveness.

11   Maintain organisation in all areas/at all levels to ensure a long-term infrastructure is there when needed.

12   Utilise ideology and internal views to create distinctive positions but also to win.

13   Set limits: let volunteers be involved in policy discussion, strategy and the campaign, and let them influence it – but within constraints.

14   Be prepared for volunteers to mess up and embarrass the party; have robust processes in place for responding to negative fallout.

15   Thank them for their efforts.

16   Make the argument about the need for power to achieve moral goals.

17   Use effective internal communication to explain policy decisions and progress, especially in government.

18   Get a balance between unity of the brand at central/local level and enough room for local adaptation.

''

Discussion points

1　Why are members or volunteers important to parties and candidates?
2　Discuss Granik's three main motivations for volunteering for parties or campaigns – social, enhancement and understanding – and discuss how effective *x* party is at meeting these needs and what they need to do to improve their organisation in this respect.
3　What advantages may come from conducting research and then redeveloping what is on offer to members or supporters?
4　Consider which party you support, either at the moment or at the last election, whether as a party member or voter. Discuss which of Bannon's (2005b) types applies: married, the family, true love, kissing cousins, open marriage, tart syndrome, one-night stands, a trapped lover, married for money or the forced partner.
5　List all the ways in which marketing can be applied to volunteers and decide which are most important and why, drawing on the examples here and any personal experience of volunteering.
6　Examine the websites of several political parties and discuss the extent to which they seem to be following Lilleker and Jackson's (2013) suggestion that the internet can be used to manage relationships with volunteers.
7　Do you think it is true that volunteers can be seen as part-time marketers? What are the arguments for and against this?
8　Discuss whether you think internal marketing can be carried out in government through initiatives like Organizing for America.
9　Why should party leaders and strategists bother to worry about creating unity in political marketing?
10　What internal barriers might a leader trying to implement a market-oriented strategy encounter, and what can they do to overcome them?
11　Is it the leader's fault if the internal market blocks their attempt to re-market their party, or is it just bad luck and a matter of timing that they couldn't have done better to create unity?
12　What processes can be put in place to avoid/respond to PR embarrassment caused by volunteers?
13　How should staff and resources best be organised to help political marketing be effective?

Assessment questions

Essay/Exam

1　Discuss ways in which parties and campaigns can create volunteer-friendly organisations, utilising theory and empirical examples.
2　How effectively do parties utilise the internet to attract and retain volunteers, as suggested by Lilleker and Jackson (2013).
3　Academics such as Van Aelst, Ubertaccio and Lees-Marshment and Pettitt argue that parties should see volunteers as part-time marketers. To what extent do you think this is possible?
4　What are the most effective ways to recruit and retain volunteers?
5　How can internal marketing be used by parties and leaders in government to help them achieve policy implementation?

6   Why is creating unity important in political marketing, and what strategies have parties used to achieve this and with what effect?

7   Why is internal culture important to internal political marketing?

8   Identify cases where the internal market blocked political marketing, such as the Australian Labor Party under Rudd and Gillard, UK Labour under Kinnock/Blair and UK Conservatives under William Hague. To what extent did the leaders follow the guidelines for creating unity, and what might they have done better?

9   Discuss the use of marketing in fundraising, using theory and empirical examples.

10 Discuss the nature and importance of party staff and resources in political marketing.

Applied

1   Synthesise theories on how to create a volunteer-friendly organisation (using Granik, Lebel, Lees-Marshment and Pettitt, etc.) and assess a party or campaign against them, making recommendations for improvement.

2   Assess the membership or supporter network (or a sample of it) from a local party organisation, branch, association or network, in terms of how they fall into each of Bannon's (2005b) relationship typologies (married, the family, true love, kissing cousins, open marriage, tart syndrome, one-night stands, a trapped lover, married for money or the forced partner) and the implications for the party's strength of support.

3   Assess a party or campaign against Lebel's (1999) principles for managing volunteers and make recommendations for how they might improve.

4   Drawing on theoretical and empirical research, critique the effectiveness of party or campaign websites as a means to attract and retain volunteers/members, and make recommendations for how they might improve their use of online volunteer marketing.

5   Assess the extent to which a political party, group or campaign considers volunteers to be part-time marketers (Van Aelst *et al.* 2012) and how effectively they allow this resource to be utilised, making suggestions for improvement if appropriate.

6   Apply Lees-Marshment and Pettitt's framework for volunteer activism through inclusive party organisations to *x* party, assessing the extent to which they are doing this, and create a plan for future development.

7   Conduct a critical assessment of the effectiveness of Organizing for America in helping President Obama in government in aspects such as policy implementation.

8   Assess a party or campaign against Lees-Marshment's (2013) Political Partnership Model, identifying strengths and weaknesses and making recommendations for how they could perform better in future.

9   Think of a party that has recently won power after using political marketing, such as becoming market-oriented or creating a research-driven brand. How effectively did they maintain unity within their party?

10 Assess the internal marketing strategies employed by party leaders and whether they followed suggestions in previous research for creating unity, and make recommendations for how future party leaders might be more successful.

11 Outline and explain Pettitt's strategies for involving volunteers in creating the party product, noting both the costs and benefits of each strategy. Assess which strategy *x* party seems to have taken in relation to its volunteers. Recommend whether they should continue to change this, based on consideration of the party goals, context, and the potential costs and benefits of each strategy in relation to them.

12 Critique a campaign website against Levenshus's (2010) principles of relationship building with volunteers.

13 Evaluate the websites of two or three parties in terms of their appeal to potential volunteers.

Case study

Case Study 5.1 Who calls the shots? How centralising power improved NZ Labour's success at the 2017 election

By Heather du Plessis-Allan (journalist/The University of Auckland)

Weeks before the 2017 general election, Labour changed its leader and reversed its fortunes. With the transition from Andrew Little to Jacinda Ardern, Labour immediately rose in the polls and went on to form government following the election. This indicates that, under Ardern, the party became better aligned with voter preferences, making it more market-oriented (Lees-Marshment 2001). The leadership change was only possible because of a temporary shift in power in the party – with power moving away from the membership – leading to the conclusion that centralisation of power is crucial to a party's ability to implement market-orientation.

Literature is divided on how important centralisation is to a party's ability to become market-oriented, with some scholars arguing members must be given some semblance of power in order to obtain their buy-in (Rudd 2005). The strongest argument for centralisation is that members may be driven by ideology, which can get in the way of a party's ability to make the pragmatic changes that better appeal to the wider group of voters (Lees-Marshment and Quayle 2001).

This case study uses the Lees-Marshment framework to measure Labour's market-orientation (Lees-Marshment 2001), utilising Pedersen's framework to measure the party's centralisation (Pedersen 2010), with 'decentralisation' defined as membership involvement in party processes.

Leadership

Labour's leadership change to Ardern on 1 August 2017 immediately led to greater market-orientation, because the new product better aligned with voter preferences. Market intelligence ahead of the leadership change had indicated this was with the case, with Jacinda Ardern consistently out-polling then-leader Andrew Little in preferred prime minister rankings. A market-oriented party should have considered the market intelligence and acted on it (Lees-Marshment 2001.

However, the party could not change leaders before August because of the way power was decentralised to members. Under Labour's Constitution, party leaders are elected through an electoral college vote, in which unions, membership and caucus all vote for the party leader. Unions are given 20 per cent of the vote, membership 40 per cent and caucus 40 per cent. This is how Little won the leadership. He was not caucus' first choice, but he won because of his popularity with unions and members. Little proved unpopular with the public, though, never rising above 20 per cent in preferred prime minister polls.

However, in the three months before the election, the Constitution centralised power to caucus, allowing it to unilaterally choose the leader. It was during this period of greater centralisation that Ardern was elected. She immediately proved more popular with the public, lifting her personal polling as well as Labour's polling within a week of her election.

Ardern was clearly better aligned with voter preferences, indicating that Labour was better market-oriented under her leadership. It is clear that greater centralisation allowed the party to increase its market-orientation in this area.

Candidate selection

Another aspect of centralisation to consider is that candidate selection in Labour was a decentralised process, frustrating attempts by former leader Andrew Little to become market-oriented.

Labour members hold the power to recommend and select party candidates. Even though party leaders have some power – in that they rank the candidates and thus have some ability to determine the chances each list candidate has of winning a seat in parliament – party members clearly have powers of persuasion over even that process. This hampered Labour's ability to market-orient.

In a bid to better market-orient by increasing support among target voters, Little persuaded former radio host and Māori Party candidate Willie Jackson to defect to Labour. In return, Little promised Jackson a top-ten ranking in the party. However, this process was frustrated by members once the news of Jackson's defection became public. Members, including former and current MPs, openly expressed dissatisfaction at Jackson's candidacy. Despite lobbying by Little, party leadership ranked Jackson at 21, saying they were unable to ignore membership sentiment.

This is an example of decentralisation frustrating Little's ability to market-orient by targeting Māori voters with a high-profile Māori candidate ranked high up the party's list. Had he held the power to rank candidates without member involvement, it can be assumed that Jackson would have succeeded in winning a top-ten ranking.

Policy formation

The policy formation process within Labour also provides an interesting example of the need for leadership buy-in to the principles of market-orientation (Kohli and Jaworski 1990). While the process of policy-making in Labour is decentralised, leadership does retain some power, which led to a decision that negatively affected the market-orientation of Labour.

Constitutionally, members hold the power to propose and vote on policy, which is then included in a document called the Policy Platform. Once the document is written, power appears to re-centralise somewhat, with leaders able to adjust policies and prioritise which policies to highlight at an election, as long as those decisions abide by the document.

Ardern used this re-centralised power to adjust the party's tax policy. Once in leadership, she made a 'captain's call' to introduce the recommendations of a tax working group much earlier than Little had intended. Ardern announced that the recommendations would be enacted before the 2020 election. This was an example of centralised power in action.

The reaction to Ardern's announcement was negative, with opinion polls indicating public dissatisfaction. Ardern then reversed her plan based on this market intelligence.

This is an example of how centralised power can hamper the market-orientation of a party, unless a leader is completely committed to the principles of market-orientation. Ardern based her decision on principle, not market intelligence, according to the Labour Party President Nigel Haworth. However, for market-orientation to succeed, decisions must be informed by market intelligence (Lees-Marshment 2001).

Lessons for political marketing and scholarship

Labour's experience in the lead up to the 2017 election illustrates how centralisation of power can help a party to adopt a market-orientation. A party must remove membership involvement in the shaping of the product – including leadership, candidate selection and policy details – and instead make changes according to market intelligence. Allowing membership to make product-shaping decisions only frustrates the market-orientation process, given that members will more likely make decisions based on ideology rather than voter preferences. Finally, it is crucial that a leader buys in to the entire process of market-orientation if it is to succeed.

References

Kohli, Ajay K. and Bernard J. Jaworski (1990). 'Market Orientation: The Construct, Research Propositions, and Managerial Implications'. *Journal of Marketing,* 54, no. 2 (1990): 1–18.

Lees-Marshment, Jennifer (2001). *Political Marketing and British Political Parties: The Party's Just Begun.* Manchester, UK: Manchester University Press.

Lees-Marshment, Jennifer and Stuart Quayle (2001). 'Empowering the Members or Marketing the Party? The Conservative Reforms of 1998'. *The Political Quarterly,* 72, no. 2 (2001): 204–12.

Pedersen, Helene Helboe (2010). 'How Intra-Party Power Relations Affect the Coalition Behaviour of Political Parties'. *Party Politics,* 16, no. 6 (2010): 737–54.

References

Australian Liberal Party (2018). 'Volunteer' webpages for Canberra branch http://canberraliberals.org.au/get-involved/volunteer/, New South Wales https://nsw.liberal.org.au/get-involved/, Queensland www.lnp.org.au/join/ (accessed 8 June 2018).

Axelrod, David (2014). 'Welcoming David Axelrod to the Labour Party'. *UK Labour Party* YouTube video, published 18 April 2014. www.youtube.com/watch?v=eNLG7xaYf64 (accessed 14 June 2018).

Bannon, Declan (2004). 'Marketing segmentation and political marketing'. Paper presented to the UK Political Studies Association, University of Lincoln, 4–8 April 2004.

Bannon, Declan (2005a). 'Internal marketing and political marketing'. UK PSA conference paper, Leeds, 7 April 2005.

Bannon, Declan (2005b). 'Relationship marketing and the political process'. *Journal of Political Marketing,* 4(2/3): 73–90.

Bendle, Neil and Mihaela-Alina Nastasoiu (2014). 'Primary elections and US political marketing'. In Jennifer Lees-Marshment, Brian Conley and Kenneth Cosgrove (eds) *Political Marketing in the US.* New York: Routledge, 85–111.

Boyle, Darren (2017). 'UKIP canvasser "is caught urinating on an elderly great grandmother's home before trying to force his way inside while handing out Paul Nuttall leaflets"'. *The Daily Mail,* 19 February 2017. www.dailymail.co.uk/news/article-4239850/Ukip-tweets-pictures-Bolton-Stoke-campaign.html.

Bryant, Illana (2008). 'An inside look at Obama's grassroots marketing'. *Adweek,* 12 March 2008. www.adweek.com/brand-marketing/inside-look-obamas-grassroots-marketing-95208/.

Cogburn, Derrick L. and Fatima K. Espinoza-Vasquez (2011). 'From networked nominee to networked nation: examining the impact of Web 2.0 and social media on political participation and civic engagement in the 2008 Obama campaign'. *Journal of Political Marketing,* 10(1/2): 189–213.

Corrado, Anthony (2013). 'The money race: a new era of unlimited funding?' In Dennis W. Johnson (ed.) *Campaigning for President 2012: Strategy and Tactics.* New York: Routledge, 59–80.

Craig, Kevin (2018). 'Labour Doesn't have a Leadership Problem – It Has A Membership Problem'. *Huffington Post,* 15 May 2018. www.huffingtonpost.co.uk/entry/labour-membership_uk_5afaa778e4b0200bcab891d1?guccounter=1.

Dahlgreen, Will (2015). 'The stigma factor: UKIP vote most embarrassing, Labour least'. YouGov, 18 April 2015. https://yougov.co.uk/news/2015/04/18/public-most-embarrassed-vote-ukip-most-proud-vote-/ (accessed 14 June 2018).

Danish Social Demokrats (2018). Website of the Social Democratic Party of Denmark. www.socialdemokratiet.dk/da/bliv-medlem/ (accessed 20 June 2018).

Dean, Dianne and Robin Croft (2001). 'Friends and relations: long-term approaches to political campaigning'. *European Journal of Marketing*, 35(11/12): 1197–216.

Ferguson, Kate (2017). 'New Tory campaign group Activate apologises after some of its members joked about gassing chavs in a series of "sickening" WhatsApp messages'. *The Daily Mail*, 30 August 2017. www.dailymail.co.uk/news/article-4837690/Activate-apologises-members-suggest-gassing-chavs.html.

Fisher, Justin, Edward Fieldhouse and David Cutts (2014). 'Members Are Not the Only Fruit: Volunteer Activity in British Political Parties at the 2010 General Election'. *The British Journal of Politics and International Relations*, 16, 75–95.

Foster, Émilie and Patrick Lemieux (2012). 'Selling a cause: Political marketing and interest groups'. In Alex Marland, Thierry Giasson and Jennifer Lees-Marshment (eds) *Political Marketing in Canada*. Vancouver: UBC, 156–71.

Germany, Julie (2013). 'Advances in campaign technology'. In Dennis W. Johnson (ed.) *Campaigning for President 2012: Strategy and Tactics*. New York: Routledge, 81–91.

Gouliamos, Kōstas, Antonis Theocharous and Bruce Newman (2013). 'Introduction: political marketing: strategic "campaign culture"'. In Kōstas Gouliamos, Antonis Theocharous and Bruce Newman (eds) *Political Marketing Strategic 'Campaign Culture'*. London: Routledge, 1–11.

Granik, Sue (2005a). 'Internal consumers – what makes your party members join your election effort?' Political Marketing Group Conference, London, 24–25 February 2005.

Granik, Sue (2005b). 'Membership benefits, membership action: why incentives for activism are what members want'. In Walter W. Wymer, Jr. and Jennifer Lees-Marshment (eds) *Current Issues in Political Marketing*. Binghamton, NY: Haworth Press, 65–90.

Haberman, Maggie (2012). 'Priebus: we did the best we could in the time we had'. *Burns & Haberman* blog post, 12 December 2012.

Hancox, Dan (2017). '"There is no unwinnable seat now": How Labour revolutionised its doorstep game'. *The Guardian*, 13 June 2017.

Helm, Tony and Michael Savage (2017). 'Jolt for Tories as poll suggests under-45s switching to Labour'. *The Observer*, 20 September 2017. www.theguardian.com/politics/2017/sep/30/poll-conservatives-jeremy-corbyn-young-people.

Hooghe, Marc and Ann-Kristin Kölln (2018). 'Types of party affiliation and the multi-speed party: What kind of party support is functionally equivalent to party membership?' *Party Politics*, first Published 17 August 2018. https://doi.org/10.1177/1354068818794220.

Hughes, Andrew and Stephen Dann (2010). 'Australian political marketing: substance backed by style'. In Jennifer Lees-Marshment, Jesper Strömbäck and Chris Rudd (eds) *Global Political Marketing*. London: Routledge, 82–95.

Johnson, Dennis W. (2012). 'Campaigning in the twenty-first century: change and continuity in American political marketing'. In Jennifer Lees-Marshment (ed.) *The Routledge Handbook of Political Marketing*. London and New York: Routledge, 205–17.

Johnson, Dennis W. (2013). 'The election of 2012'. In Dennis W. Johnson (ed.) *Campaigning for President 2012: Strategy and Tactics*. New York: Routledge, 1–22.

Katz, Richard S. and Peter Mair (1993). 'The evolution of party organizations in Europe: the three faces of party organization'. *The American Review of Politics*, 14(4): 455–77.

Knuckey, Jonathan and Jennifer Lees-Marshment (2005). 'American political marketing: George W. Bush and the Republican Party'. In Darren Lilleker and Jennifer Lees-Marshment (eds) *Political Marketing: A Comparative Perspective*. Manchester, UK: Manchester University Press, 39–58.

Lebel, Gregory G. (1999). 'Managing volunteers: time has changed – or have they?' In Bruce Newman (ed.) *Handbook of Political Marketing*. Thousand Oaks, CA: Sage, 129–42.

Lees-Marshment, Jennifer (2001). *Political Marketing and British Political Parties: The Party's Just Begun*. Manchester, UK: Manchester University Press.

Lees-Marshment, Jennifer (2008). *Political Marketing and British Political Parties: The Party's Just Begun*, 2nd revised edition. Manchester, UK: Manchester University Press.

Lees-Marshment, Jennifer (2009). 'Case study 6.2 Examples of internal blockage to market-oriented strategy: the UK Conservatives, 1997–2001'. In Jennifer Lees-Marshment (ed.) *Political Marketing: Principles and Applications*. London and New York: Routledge, 154–55.

Lees-Marshment, Jennifer (2011). *The Political Marketing Game*. Houndmills, UK and New York: Palgrave Macmillan.

Lees-Marshment, Jennifer (2013). 'Political marketing and governance: moving towards the political partnership model of organisation'. In Emmanuelle Avril and Christine Zumello (eds) *New Technology, Organisational Change and Governance*. Basingstoke, UK: Palgrave Macmillan, 218–34.

Lees-Marshment, Jennifer and Robin Pettitt (2010). 'UK political marketing: a question of leadership?' In Jennifer Lees-Marshment, Jesper Strömbäck and Chris Rudd (eds) *Global Political Marketing*. London: Routledge, 218–34.

Lees-Marshment, J. and R. Pettitt (2014). 'Mobilising Volunteer Activists in Political Parties: The view from central office'. *Contemporary Politics*, 20(2): 246–60.

Lees-Marshment, Jennifer and Stuart Quayle (2001). 'Empowering the members or marketing the party? The Conservative reforms of 1998'. *The Political Quarterly*, 72(2): 204–12.

Lees-Marshment, Jennifer, Jesper Strömbäck and Chris Rudd (eds) (2010). *Global Political Marketing*. London: Routledge.

Levenshus, Abbey (2010). 'Online relationship management in a presidential campaign: a case study of the Obama campaign's management of its internet-integrated grassroots effort'. *Journal of Public Relations Research*, 22(3): 313–35.

Lilleker, Darren G. (2005). 'Local campaign management: winning votes or wasting resources?' *Journal of Marketing Management*, 21(9/10): 979–1003.

Lilleker, Darren G. (2006). 'Local political marketing: political marketing as public service'. In Darren Lilleker, Nigel Jackson and Richard Scullion (eds) *The Marketing of Political Parties*. Manchester, UK: Manchester University Press, 206–30.

Lilleker, Darren G. and Nigel A. Jackson (2013). 'Reaching inward not outward: marketing via the internet at the UK 2010 general election'. *Journal of Political Marketing*, 12(2–3): 244–61.

Lilleker, Darren and Ralph Negrine (2002). 'Marketing techniques and political campaigns: the limitations for the marketing of British political parties'. Paper presented to the UK PSA, Manchester, 7–9 April 2002.

Lilleker, Darren and Ralph Negrine (2003). 'Not big brand names but corner shops: marketing politics to a disengaged electorate'. *The Journal of Political Marketing*, 2(1): 55–76.

Lloyd, Jenny (2005). 'Marketing politics . . . saving democracy'. In Adrian Sargeant and Walter Wymer (eds) *The Routledge Companion to Nonprofit Marketing*. New York: Routledge, 317–36.

Lynch, Richard, Paul Baines and John Egan (2006). 'Long-term performance of political parties: towards a competitive resource-based perspective'. *Journal of Political Marketing*, 5(3): 71–92.

Major, Kirsty (2017). 'Momentum are in the middle of building their next secret weapon – and the Tories don't stand a chance'. *The Independent*, 13 July 2017. www.independent.co.uk/voices/momentum-labour-apps-tories-dont-stand-a-chance-a7839526.html.

Marland, Alex (2009). 'Case study 7.6 Canadian constituency campaigns'. In Jennifer Lees-Marshment *Political Marketing: Principles and Applications*. London and New York: Routledge, 190–2.

Marland, Alex (2012a). 'Amateurs versus professionals: The 1993 and 2006 Canadian federal elections'. In Alex Marland, Thierry Giasson and Jennifer Lees-Marshment (eds) *Political Marketing in Canada*. Vancouver: UBC, 59–75.

Marland, Alex (2012b). 'Yes we can (fundraise): the ethics of marketing in political fundraising'. In Jennifer Lees-Marshment (ed.) *The Routledge Handbook of Political Marketing*. London and New York: Routledge, 164–76.

McTague, Tom (2014). '"Cameron is not serious about real change to the EU": Tory MP defects to UKIP with stinging attack on Prime Minister – as Farage warns more may follow'. *The Daily Mail*, 28 August 2014. www.dailymail.co.uk/news/article-2736598/Tory-MP-Douglas-Carswell-defects-UKIP-resigns-Parliament-spark-crunch-Essex-byelection.html.

Medvic, Stephen K. (2006). 'Understanding campaign strategy "deliberate priming" and the role of professional political consultants'. *Journal of Political Marketing*, 5(1/2): 11–32.

Mills, Stephen (2012). 'The party official as political marketer: the Australian experience'. In Jennifer Lees-Marshment (ed.) *The Routledge Handbook of Political Marketing*. London and New York: Routledge, 190–202.

Mills, S. (2014). *The Professionals: Strategy, Money & the Rise of the Political Campaigner in Australia*. Collingwood, VIC: Black Inc.

O'Cass, Aron (2009). 'A resource-based view of the political party and value creation for the voter-citizen: an integrated framework for political marketing'. *Marketing Theory*, 9(2): 189–208.

Ormrod, Robert P. (2005). 'A conceptual model of political market orientation'. In Walter Wymer and Jennifer Lees-Marshment (eds) *Current Issues in Political Marketing*. Binghamton, NY: Haworth Press, 47–64.

People's Action Party (2016). 'Honouring Our Party Activists' YouTube video, published 4 December 2016. www.youtube.com/watch?v=njEqcvLVfTk (accessed 8 June 2018).

Pettitt, Robin T. (2012). 'Internal Party Political Relationship Marketing: encouraging activism amongst local party members'. In Jennifer Lees-Marshment (ed.) *The Routledge Handbook of Political Marketing*. London and New York: Routledge, 137–50.

Pettitt, Robin T. (2014). *Contemporary Party Politics*. Basingstoke, UK: Palgrave.

Pettitt, Robin (2016). 'The "how" of election manifestos in the British Labour Party: A source of ongoing controversy'. *Party Politics*, 24(3): 289–95.

Reeves, Peter (2013). 'Local political marketing in the context of the Conservative Party'. *Journal of Nonprofit & Public Sector Marketing*, 25(2): 127–63.

Rogers, Ben (2005). 'From membership to management? The future of political parties as democratic organisations'. *Parliamentary Affairs*, 58(3): 600–10.

Rudd, Chris (2005). 'Marketing the message or the messenger?' In Darren Lilleker and J. Lees-Marshment (eds) *Political Marketing: A Comparative Perspective*. Manchester, UK: Manchester University Press, 79–96.

Schneider, Helmut and Frederik Ferie (2015). 'How to manage a Party Brand: Empirical Perspectives on Electoral Probability and Internal Conflict'. *Journal of Political Marketing*, 14, 64–95.

Sherman, Elaine (1999). 'Direct marketing: how does it work for political campaigns?' In Bruce Newman (ed.) *The Handbook of Political Marketing*. Thousand Oaks, CA: Sage, 365–88.

Simpson, Dick and Betty O'Shaughnessy (2016). *Winning Elections in the 21st Century*. Lawrence, University Press of Kansas.

Smith, Gareth (2009). 'Conceptualizing and testing brand personality in British politics'. *Journal of Political Marketing*, 8(3): 209–32.

Smith, Gareth and Alan French (2009). 'The political brand: a consumer perspective'. *Marketing Theory*, 9(2): 209–26.

Spiller, Lisa and Jeff Bergner (2014). 'Database political marketing in campaigning and government'. In Jennifer Lees-Marshment, Brian Conley and Kenneth Cosgrove (eds) *Political Marketing in the US*. New York: Routledge.

Steen, Jennifer (1999). 'Money doesn't grow on trees: fund-raising in American political campaigns'. In Bruce I. Newman (ed.) *Handbook of Political Marketing*. Thousand Oaks, CA: Sage, 159–76.

Steger, Wayne (1999). 'The permanent campaign: marketing from the hill'. In Bruce Newman (ed.) *Handbook of Political Marketing*. Thousand Oaks, CA: Sage, 661–86.

Stromer-Galley, Jennifer (2014). *Presidential Campaigning in the Internet Age*. Oxford: Oxford University Press.

Turcotte, André and Vincent Raynauld (2014). 'Boutique populism: the emergence of the Tea Party movement in the age of digital politics'. In Jennifer Lees-Marshment, Brian Conley and Kenneth Cosgrove (eds) *Political Marketing in the US*. New York: Routledge.

Ubertaccio, Peter N. (2012). 'Political parties and direct marketing: connecting voters and candidates more effectively'. In Jennifer Lees-Marshment (ed.) *The Routledge Handbook of Political Marketing*. London and New York: Routledge, 177–89.

UK Labour Party (2018a). 'Why Join the Labour Party'. YouTube video, uploaded 30 May 2018. www.youtube.com/watch?v=fQShQsqRbz8 (accessed 8 June 2018).

UK Labour Party (2018b). 'Why Join the Labour Party'. UK Labour Party website. https://labour.org.uk/members/why-join-labour/ (accessed 20 June 2018).

Van Aelst, Peter, Joop van Holsteyn and Ruud Koole (2012). 'Party members as part-time marketers: using relationship marketing to demonstrate the importance of rank-and-file party members in election campaigns'. In Jennifer Lees-Marshment (ed.) *The Routledge Handbook of Political Marketing*. London and New York: Routledge, 151–63.

Watt, Joseph (2015). 'Tessa Jowell apologises after volunteer claims Sadiq Khan would be "liability" as Mayor because he's Muslim'. *Evening Standard*, 3 September 2015. www.standard.co.uk/news/politics/tessa-jowell-apologises-after-volunteer-claims-sadiq-khan-would-be-liability-as-mayor-because-hes-a2926446.html.

Watt, Nicholas and Patrick Wintour (2008). 'Our next prime minister?' *The Guardian*, 16 July 2008. www.theguardian.com/politics/2008/jul/16/davidcameron.conservatives.

Wheeler, Caroline (2017). 'Sound the retweet: Tories to launch digital war on Labour'. *The Times*, 2 July 2017. www.thetimes.co.uk/edition/news/sound-the-retweet-tories-to-launch-digital-war-on-labour-px8tdtjf8.

Wong, Julia Carrie (2018). 'Campaign volunteers hit with obscene images after sending texts'. *The Guardian*, 19 June 2018. www.theguardian.com/technology/2018/jun/19/campaign-volunteers-texting-voters-unsolicited-pictures-messages.

Wring, Dominic (2005). *The Politics of Marketing the Labour Party*. Houndmills, UK: Palgrave Macmillan.

6 Broadcast political marketing communication

by Vincent Raynauld and Jennifer Lees-Marshment

Practitioner Perspective 6.1 on the need for strategic communication in campaigns and government

You have to map everything . . . the essence of a campaign is to make sure that every single possibility is talked about, thought about, so that when you're in a crisis situation you can go back to the plan and stick to the plan.
Mark Textor, political strategist in Australia, NZ and the UK, 2012

Strategic communication is . . . never done in the moment, because most people aren't listening . . . Most people are going about their business . . . They're taking their kids to school, they're taking their mum to hospital, they're going to work . . . which is why you have to keep communicating the same things again and again and again.
Alastair Campbell, Press Secretary to UK Prime Minister Tony Blair, 2013

Our job is to get, is to drop the bucket further down the well than anybody else, to understand what are those really deep-seated underlying fears, concerns. It's no good fighting an election campaign on the facts because actually it's all about emotion, it's all about emotion.
Mark Thurnbull, Cambridge Analytica Political Global Managing Director, filmed secretly in 2018

You want a great product, you want things that resonate with people and make them dance.
Brad Parscale, 2016 Trump Campaign Digital Media Director and 2020 Trump Campaign Manager

Sources: Lees-Marshment (2011); Campbell (2013); *Channel 4 News* (2018); CBS (2018).

In an era of permanent campaigning, political organisations and politicians rely heavily on broadcast marketing communications to achieve wide-ranging objectives in a cost-effective way in and out of elections (Campbell and Lee 2016; Green and Gerber 2015; Elder 2016). These objectives include improving a government's reputation, launching and strengthening a brand, conceptualising and rolling out messaging strategies targeting narrow audiences, countering opponents' negative attacks, educating voters, placing and keeping an issue on the public agenda, and building and broadening public support for a politician or policy. Politicians turn to marketing research – which encompasses tools and techniques including survey research, focus groups and advanced statistical analysis – to better identify, analyse and understand who they should communicate with, when, on what topic and how, when introducing and selling political products (Temple 2013). Communication can be broadcast, one way – so simply what goes from the political organisation or figure to the public – or two-way through interactive communication between receiver and producer to form a relationship. This chapter takes a deep dive into broadcast communication. It explores:

- Marketing communication of candidates.
- Campaign communication including research-led campaign communication, market-oriented advertising, insights marketing, guerrilla marketing and celebrity marketing.
- Communication tools including GOTV, direct marketing, targeted communication and mobile/virtual marketing.
- Selling policy.
- Communicating change.
- Crisis management.
- Integrated marketing communications.
- Political marketing communications in the workplace.

Marketing communication of candidates

Political marketing research (PMR) has explored several aspects of leader communication, including the need to make an emotional, human connection as well as the importance of nonverbal image. Candidates' ability to forge an emotional connection with voters proved crucial during the 2000 US presidential contest (Newman 2001). Republican hopeful George W. Bush leveraged his natural characteristics to connect with the public, conveying positivity and likeability. Al Gore – his democratic opponent – showed a more serious commitment to specific voters' concerns by talking about issues, but this lacked emotion. The 2016 US Republican primaries were not different. They were marked by Donald Trump developing a strong emotional bond with members of the working class: 'Middle America'. He did so by crafting often polarising messages rooted in his long-established – and to some degree authentic – personal brand (e.g. high-profile businessperson, reality television personality) (Tracey 2017). Conversely, Jeb Bush's deep misunderstanding of the contemporary mediascape coupled with his misreading of the 'electorate that wasn't amenable to establishment candidates' prevented him from connecting meaningfully with primary voters (Berger 2016, 96).

Schweiger and Aadami (1999) note how non-verbal images (NVI) marketing research can be used to understand what makes up a political image and measure responses from voters using a range of pictures representing different characteristics, both positive and negative. Table 6.1 sets out both positive and negative image attributes that candidates can attract.

PMR can help identify potential challenges and enable communication to be devised to address them. One of them is how to market gender in political contexts where there are 'gendered political opportunity structures' (O'Brien 2015, 1022): whether to target branding and communication to female voters and what gendered leadership characteristics to promote. Busby's (2014) analysis of female conservative candidates notes how the 'Mama Grizzly' brand was designed to appeal to specific market segments, including women generally, women suffering economically and women who were socially conservative. The Mama

Table 6.1 Schweiger and Aadami's political candidate positive and negative image attributes

Dimension	Positive attribute	Negative attribute
Honesty	Honest Credible A man/woman of his/her word Transparent Reliable	Entangled in scandals Secretive
Quality	Possesses knowledge and experience Educated Capable	Lacks knowledge of how to manage a government Lacks other skills such as business knowledge or international experience
Strength	Strong Winner Carries his/her point Dynamic Successful	Weak Loser Seems to lack a backbone or the determination to get things done

Source: Adapted from Schweiger and Aadami (1999, 361)

Grizzly brand was not successful in attracting women voters – most prominent Mama Grizzly candidates received more votes from male voters than female voters. Busby argues this was because while women voters desire masculine traits associated to leadership, they also want female political candidates to show emotional and behavioural traits, so the socially conservative, aggressive Mama Grizzly brand was not as effective as had been hoped. During the 2016 US presidential contest, democratic candidate Hillary Clinton leveraged gender when campaigning against Donald Trump. She frequently highlighted her gender in her personal branding as well as referred to women's issues when pushing back against some of Trump's statements and actions. In doing so, she sought to reach out to, mobilise, and drum up and maintain support among moderate women (Elder 2018). Interestingly, Hillary Clinton often downplayed her gender in her public persona and messaging when running for office during previous decades as she sought to establish herself as a tough leader compared to male opponents (Stromer-Galley 2014).

Campaign communication

Campaign communication taking place within the official election campaign period is more focused. It includes research-led communication, market-oriented advertising, insights marketing and guerrilla marketing.

Research-led campaign communication

Market research is particularly important for campaign communication. As noted by Rademacher and Tuchfarber (1999, 202), polling serves specific functions at different stages of a campaign. In the early stages, it identifies what messages should be sent and to whom. During later stages, it measures the effectiveness of different messages to inform any necessary changes. Braun and Matušková (2009) explored how market intelligence and strategy informed campaigning and changed the direction of the 2006 Czech elections. A year before the election, the Czech Social Democratic Party (CSSD) trailed the Civic

Democratic Party (ODS) in public opinion polls by more than 2 per cent. Marketing consultants from the US firm Penn, Schoen and Berland Associates changed this trend by being the first campaign to use market research. They ran focus groups with swing voters followed by a quantitative benchmark poll to assess the position and support for all the parties among different voter blocks, issue importance, and reaction to potential messages and policy offerings. The findings helped to reshape the campaign's goals and develop the strategy, message and tactical tools to achieve those goals. Ultimately, the CSSD tripled its support among voters, even though ODS eventually won the election (Braun and Matušková 2009).

While much attention has been paid to election advertisements, we need to consider dynamics of marketing behind the scenes. Ridout's (2014) analysis of US adverts demonstrates how market research is fundamental to the creation of effective ads: the message and medium is designed to appeal to and suit targets derived from segmentation to maximise resource effectiveness. The ads are also tested before launch to ensure they will achieve their goals. Ridout correctly predicted that ads would be increasingly subject to testing through experimental and analytic marketing research before release. As mentioned in the chapter on political market research, recent developments in big data-driven market research have provided political organisations and politicians with even greater insights – often in real time – into the public's preferences, interests and objectives. Specifically, they have access to large, frequently updated political databases (e.g. CIMS in Canada, Mosaic in the UK, Feedback in Australia) comprising detailed information about individual members of the public (Green and Gerber 2015; McKelvey and Piebiak 2016). Donald Trump's presidential campaign in 2016 spent approximately US$6 million on data services from the UK-based firm Cambridge Analytica (Center for Responsive Politics 2017). This organisation leveraged large datasets to provide Trump and his team with a granular understanding of the US political market, ultimately helping them develop compelling messaging and voter outreach operations focused on specific policy matters (e.g. economy, immigration) (Conley 2018). For example, in some cases the Trump campaign created and circulated between 35,000 and 45,000 iterations of the same Facebook advert in order to reach out to and connect with narrow slices of the audience in ways tailored to their preferences, interests and goals (BBC 2017). Hughes (2018) also explores market-driven advertising.

Furthermore, research can inform communication to get people out to vote. Today's complex media environment – especially with the hyper fragmentation of audiences with the popularisation of social media – has rendered targeted outreach especially effective (Elder and Phillips 2017; Kruikemeier *et al.* 2016). Many studies echo this point. They show that political messages sent through channels that are untargeted or impersonal tend to be ineffective (Panagopoulos and Ha 2015; Green and Gerber 2015). This reiterates our assertion above that political marketing techniques tend to be used in an overlapping fashion that creates a more potent end product. In this case, market research gains power when used in conjunction with other tools like advertising. Conversely, stand-alone advertising is not worth as much. When combined with research and segmentation of the market into target groups and when it fits political organisations' and candidates' overall brand and product messages, it can be most effective.

Market-oriented advertising

Market research data and strategic concepts can be leveraged to develop adverts supporting the product. Robinson's (2006) theory of market-oriented advertising applies market-oriented principles to advertising (see Table 6.2).

Robinson (2010) analysed the New Zealand election campaigns in 1999, 2002 and 2005. She concluded that parties demonstrating strong voter orientation in their political advertisements were most successful. Effective adverts demonstrated an affinity for their target voter groups by showing images of voters and the party leader interacting with them and also used words of togetherness. Less effective advertising only conveyed responsiveness to core supporters. Also of interest is a case study by Thomas J. Seeman, which is based on Robinson's model for identifying a party's market-orientation through the consideration of political adverts (Seeman 2014). He explores how Green Party of Aotearoa New Zealand adverts in 2011 identified target audiences, conveyed responsiveness to voter needs and maintained relationships with core supporters. Specifically, the ads broadened the base of support of the party by targeting an 'ethnically diverse range of people, including groups not normally associated with the Greens, such as business people in suits and parents with children' (Seeman 2014, 194). They showed their market-orientation by demonstrating clearly that their policy offerings were developed in response to voters' preferences and needs. They also indicated that the party kept its promises, thus showcasing a strong commitment to its core supporters. Ultimately, the Green Party of Aotearoa New Zealand enjoyed increased electoral success (see also Robinson 2018).

Insights marketing

Another use of research in communication is insights marketing, where communication is tailored to people's deepest values, hopes and fears. Cambridge Analytica's recent work

Table 6.2 Robinson's criteria for market-oriented political adverts

Market orientation	Observable form
Voter orientation	
• Target voters identified	• Images of target audience and environment featured
• Sense and response to voter needs	• Images of party and/or leader interaction with target voters including images of listening and words of togetherness
• Maintenance of relationships with core voters	• Evocation of party history and myth; acknowledgement of shared characters, themes and stories • Images or words of care for core supporters • Text and wording recognizable to core supporters • Kept policy promises
• Offer in exchange for party vote	• Party vote requested and policy and leadership offered in exchange
Competitor orientation	
• Behaves according to their strategic market position (market leader, challenger, follower, niche party)	• Competition identified and targeted in messages • Policy appropriated from smaller niche parties • Concern to increase market share demonstrated • Openness to coalition arrangements demonstrated • Concern to increase market share demonstrated • Niche parties remain true to original raison d'être

Source: Adapted from Robinson (2006)

for the Leave campaign during the Brexit referendum, Donald Trump's 2016 US presidential run and other campaigns internationally constitute a good example. In a 2018 undercover video by UK's *Channel 4 News*, Cambridge Analytica Political Global's managing director, Mark Thurnbull, argued that the 'two fundamental human drivers when it comes to taking information onboard effectively are hopes and fears and many of those are unspoken and even unconscious' (LeTourneau 2018; *Channel 4 News* 2018). By gaining an in-depth understanding of individual voters' psychological profiles, Cambridge Analytica helped craft emotion-driven messaging on key political and policy matters that catered to current and prospective supporters' deepest hopes and fears, while also potentially demoralising and suppressing some of its opponents (LeTourneau 2018).

Guerrilla marketing

Guerrilla marketing is communication that gets attention by being unexpected and novel. An example is the Australian Labor campaign of 2007, where volunteers wore T-shirts with 'Kevin07' on them, drawing attention to the new leader, Kevin Rudd, who went on to win the election and become prime minister. Kevin 07 was just the name of the campaign website, but it became a moniker for the fresh new product being offered by Labor in 2007. A more recent example is Donald Trump's successful presidential run in 2016. Many of his supporters bought and wore bright red trucker's hats with the slogan 'Make American Great Again' emblazoned in white lettering that were sold by his campaign and other vendors. These hats, which have become a polarising symbol in US political culture, were worn by individuals across America who endorsed Trump's anti-elite message and supported his political and policy views and objectives.

Celebrity marketing

According to Elteren (2013), 'Politics has become a product of a culture obsessed by celebrities'. Several scholars (e.g. Becker 2013; Marland and Lalancette 2014; Mishra and Mishra 2014) echo that point and explore how celebrity endorsement can be an important tool of political marketing. It helps attract attention in a cluttered media environment where political players are competing to attract and retain the attention of, connect with, and influence the attitude and behaviour of increasingly fragmented publics (Lalancette and Raynauld 2017). Celebrities appeal to target markets, including those whom political elites find it hard to connect with, including young, disaffected and floating voters. This can help political organisations and candidates get attention for their brand and help with their fundraising operations. Celebrity endorsement is widely used in US politics: 600+ external celebrities supported Obama and over 200 endorsed Romney during the 2012 presidential election. It is also used in a targeted way by groups supportive to a candidate: YouTube videos endorsing Obama were posted by the National Jewish Democratic Council, featuring a combination of internal and external celebrities, including Broadway star Barbara Streisand.

This approach to political marketing has been facilitated in the last decade by the growing traction of identity-centric social media channels (Ridge-Newman and Mitchell 2016). In Canada, Justin Trudeau turned to his personal Instagram account to engage in celebrity marketing during the first year following his election in October 2015. On top of leveraging his own celebrity status by showing glimpses of his personal life (e.g. family events) as well as his activities as prime minister, his Instagram feed often included pictures of him interacting with nationally and internationally renowned cultural, political, sports and media celebrities, including the UK's Prince Harry and British physicist Stephen Hawkins. (Lalancette and Raynauld 2017). As noted by Marland and Lalancette (2014), this approach can yield positive dividends if these celebrities are liked by the public (see also: Lalancette and Raynauld 2017).

Celebrities can also be used to attack opponents. Of note is Hollywood legend Clint Eastwood speaking to an empty chair at the 2012 Republican National Convention in a critique of Obama, which received significant media coverage. There are potential hazards which researchers and strategists should be aware of in terms of compatibility with brand. Among them include ensuring that celebrities – who have their own commercial brands, of course – fit with and support the political product, adding, not reducing, credibility and appeal.

Communication tools

Political marketing communication tools can make a difference where competition is even and the election is close. They include Get Out the Vote (GOTV) efforts, direct marketing, targeted communication and mobile/virtual marketing.

GOTV

Get Out the Vote operations are now an integral component of election campaigns, using segmentation and voter profiling to turn support into votes on election day. If the election results seem a foregone conclusion, voters might not bother to turn out; or if core supporters are dissatisfied with how a party has changed or governed, they might protest by withholding their vote. Ross (2008) notes that voter identification should be started early by political parties and candidates to identify and firm up existing support. Campaigns should also reach out to areas or communities that may not universally support them as research can identify pockets of potential supporters in even the most hostile areas.

Using volunteers through networking marketing is another important form of GOTV. In 2004, Republicans used mixed motivators to get people out with not just the right message but also the right person: 'a volunteer knocking on their door or a volunteer calling them and saying *"Hey, I live in your neighbourhood, I just want to make sure you're going to go vote"'*. Over the last five years, developments in mobile media technologies have furthered the reach and efficiency of these operations (see also the 'mobile/virtual marketing' sub-section in this chapter). Volunteer canvassers can turn to mobile device apps and use their GPS functionalities to locate potential supporters in order to meet with them face-to-face or share a campaign message, as well as learn and record their views, attitudes, and political engagement preferences and goals (e.g. donating money, attending rallies) ahead of contacts during current or future campaigns (Reeves 2013).

Parties also try to move voters between different GOTV universes in order to expand and strengthen their base of support. Republican Rick Beeson explained that the US Republican Party broke voters down:

> into a GOTV universe, which is people we know are going to vote for us or have a high propensity of voting for us. Then we have persuasion universe. That's a group of people that we need to talk to . . . We want . . . them to get a significant number of persuasion contacts . . . understanding that once they got a certain number of percentage contacts you could move them.
>
> (Lees-Marshment 2011, 22)

Table 6.3 Green and Gerber's advice as to what to do and what to avoid with GOTV

What to do	What to avoid
• Make voters feel wanted at the polls, as if inviting them to a social occasion, using a personal invitation, if not an unscripted phone call	• Simple messages reminding people to vote when election day is near, even if the pre-recorded voices are those of famous or credible people
• Connect with voters' previous voting or expressions of interest in voting	• Information-rich messages about the election such as voter guides
• Remind them that whether they vote or not will be on record as, if others seem to be watching, people seem to be more willing to get out and vote	• Telling people why they should vote for a particular candidate or cause; partisan driven GOTV does not enhance effectiveness

Source: Summarised from Green and Gerber (2004, 137)

Green and Gerber (2004, 137) present a practical guide to GOTV, utilising scientific evidence about what is most cost effective through an experimental research method and advise what to do, how to do it and what to avoid (see Table 6.3). They note that voting is a social act shaped in part by voters' immediate social environments.

Over the last decade, the popularisation of social media among publics in several national contexts has intensified dynamics of networking and, to some degree, crowd-sourced marketing for GOTV. For example, the social networking platform Facebook allows its users 'to digitally canvass their friends, tagging them in status updates that contain voting reminders' (Haenschen 2016, 546). According to Haenschen (2016), this peer-to-peer approach to GOTV can increase voter turnout, especially among younger and ethnically diverse individuals who tend to be heavy social media users.

However, GOTV has limitations. Green and Gerber's research suggests that partisan GOTV is ineffective (see Table 6.3). Johnson (2013, 16) also notes that both US presidential candidates received fewer votes in 2012 than in 2008. Despite billions of dollars spent on GOTV drives, only 57.5 per cent of the eligible adult population voted in 2012. It is also heavily reliant on technology, and the new Republican system Project Orca, adopted in 2012, crashed throughout election day.

Direct marketing

Practitioner Perspective 6.2 on ensuring online communication is direct

My 'top tip' would have to be: understand what platform(s) the people you want to reach are using, and communicate with them through those sites. People's attention is so spread between different online and offline channels (TV, radio, print, news websites, Twitter, Facebook, LinkedIn, Tumblr, YouTube, etc.) that it's important to know where those people most likely to be open to your party are, and with limited resources it's important to be able to identify and market to the channel which most influentially communicates with them.

Gavin Middleton, former staffer with the New Zealand ACT Party

Source: a top tip supplied by email in 2013

Direct marketing is a common part of marketing communications. It includes any other form of communication sent directly to members of the public, personalised in ways to get them to act quickly (e.g. direct mail, internet ads). As Practitioner Perspective 6.2 suggests, it responds to the recipient's behaviour and is used to increase support, recruit new and mobilise existing volunteers, fundraise or GOTV. It uses segmentation data, and sample forms are heavily tested to maximise effectiveness and resources. Direct mail was the original form of direct marketing. The UK Conservative Party used this approach between 1997 and 2001 to boost and widen its membership and profile existing members. It also bought membership lists of wine clubs, garden centres, and rugby or cricket clubs who had a similar outlook for a recruitment drive (Lees-Marshment 2008). In the 2005 UK election, Labour produced direct mail and DVDs for particular candidates in key seats. Direct telemarketing is often used by parties and candidates using call centres for a range of activities (e.g. voter persuasion and identification, volunteer recruitment, GOTV efforts). As discussed in Chapter 5 on internal political marketing, direct marketing can also be used for fundraising.

More recent forms include text messages to mobile phones, email blasts and adverts through pop-up web ads. E-forms of direct marketing offer the same potential to reach individuals directly but more cheaply. The Conservatives direct email campaign during the 2015 general election campaign in the UK constitutes a good example. They often sent emails 'from a party bigwig like Boris Johnson or Cameron' that were 'personalized with recipients' names' and that featured '[p]unchy and intriguing subject headings' to generate interest (Ridge-Newman and Mitchell 2016, 104). In other words, they were tailor-made to the recipient in terms of appeal and content. Still, traditional door-knocking remains valuable. Ales Kudrnác (2014) explores how a local candidate in Slovakia – I. Rončák – utilised direct face-to-face marketing by knocking on everyone's door, which helped him to gain informal market intelligence about the voting public and gain a better understanding of their preferences and objectives. He followed up his visits with partly handwritten, personalised letters to two groups of recipients. The first group consisted of 'people who were not reached at home, thus he wrote that he had been there but he had not been able to meet them' (Kudrnác 2014, 197); he attached his manifesto to the letters sent to this category of recipients. The second group comprised 'people he met and from whom he had had a positive feeling; in the letter he thanked them for meeting them and encouraged them to come to the elections' (Kudrnác 2014, 197). More broadly, it shows that it is possible to win a campaign when using active face-to-face campaigning with a very limited budget.

Direct marketing has weaknesses. For example, each new innovation is copied by competitors and so loses its competitiveness. Also, the public becomes immune to the methodology, which needs to be periodically revisited and improved. Finally, the communication is only as good as the data and assumptions of the list it derives its recipients from or the overall context of the political product. Loewen and Rubenson (2011) conducted an experiment to test the use of direct mail to communicate controversial policy positions in co-operation with the Michael Ignatieff campaign 2006 for the leadership of the Liberal Party of Canada. Their findings suggested that the impact of direct mail on voters was actually negative. Indeed, receiving direct mail from the Ignatieff campaign even moved Ignatieff down in the preference rankings of some delegates. Thus, the ability for leaders to use persuasive communication to gain support for unpopular arguments is limited. Lowen and Rubenson (2011, 59) explain that Ignatieff's positions on foreign policy, the constitution and fiscal federalism were well outside the mainstream of the party he was seeking to lead. In other words, communicating something supporters did not want would only harm him.

Targeted communication

Practitioner Perspective 6.3 on the importance of micro-targeted communications

Micro-targeting allows you to scare people easier. But on the positive side, micro-targeting allows you to get better information to relevant people.

Interview with Vincent Harries, former advisor to politicians such as Rand Paul in the United States and Benjamin Netanyahu in Israel, in 2017

Mobile text messages, unlike email, are rarely spam filtered and have a much higher read-rate. This makes a personal text message to voters much more effective than email, and if collected alongside other personal information, can be targeted towards different market segments with issue-specific information.

Interview with Stephen Quain, political campaign manager in the United States, in 2010

Source: Interview by Dafydd Phillips for the publication *Communication Director*; Brainmates (2010)

As shown in Practitioner Perspective 6.3, trying to communicate the same thing to everyone is less effective than targeted messages. Segmentation can help parties and candidates identify which voter groups to target communication to. Back in 1979, the UK Conservatives segmented the market and focused communication efforts accordingly (see Table 6.4). The New Zealand National Party's billboards in 2008 were clearly aimed at both core and new segments (see Table 6.5). Case study 6.1 by Filippo Trevisan and Robert Rodriguez-Donoso illustrates the importance of targeted communication.

Targeting can be used by smaller and new parties as well as older established ones. McGough (2005) illustrated how the Irish party Sinn Féin segmented the market into six

Table 6.4 Targeted communication by the UK Conservatives in 1979

Target markets	Examples of communication geared to suit the target markets
Skilled working class (C2)	Saatchi and Saatchi created posters with slogans which included the infamous Labour isn't working and Britain's better off with the Conservatives. One newspaper advert was entitled 'Why every trade unionist should consider voting Conservative' and appealed to traditional Labour supporters.
Women	Campaign adverts were placed in women's magazines.
First-time voters	Adverts were run in the cinema to attract support from first-time voters.
Party faithful	Thatcher's speeches appealed to traditional Conservative voters.

Table 6.5 New Zealand National's targeted billboards in 2008

Billboard wording	Target market
1 in 5 school leaders doesn't pass NCEA We'll smarten up the system	Traditional supporters and families/parents
Get them into training Not into trouble. National's youth guarantee	Traditional supporters and families/parents
Make our neighbourhoods safer Tougher bail, sentencing and parole laws	Traditional supporters South Auckland voters
Wave goodbye to higher taxes Not your loved ones	Higher earners
More doctors + more nurses = less bureaucrats	Public sector professionals

Source: Lees-Marshment (2010, 75)

different targets in 2002 (e.g. North – nationalist Catholics, North – Catholic community, Alliance and soft Ulster Unionist supporters, Republic of Ireland voters, Ogra Sinn Féin, Irish-American/international support), understanding their different demands and adopting a different strategy for each one, where appropriate.

Analytic and experimental marketing can help test the effectiveness of communication on different target markets before it is widely released. During the 2012 US presidential election, Obama discovered unlikely ways to reach appropriate targets such as cheaper advertising slots with lower audiences but consisting of viewers more open to voting for Obama and thus more receptive to the campaign communication (Johnson 2013, 17). Germany (2013, 81) notes how both the Obama and Romney campaigns combined masses of data in real time about Americans' consumer patterns, online browsing and voting behaviour. Such high technology was connected to traditional grass-roots contact as well as run through new mobile communication forms. Approximately four years later, the Trump campaign conducted micro-targeted voter appeal and engagement operations on wide-range digital media platforms. Baldwin-Philippi (2017, 629) took interest in its email outreach and noted that 'throughout the summer the Trump campaign was neither targeting nor testing its e-mails'. However, as the campaign progressed and '[a]s the number ramped up, we cannot be sure whether there was both testing and targeting going on, but at the very least, targeted messages were being deployed' (Baldwin-Philippi 2017, 629).

Communication can also be targeted at specific socio-demographic groups. During the 2008 Obama campaign, some of the traditional communication targeted women voters. O'Leary (2009) notes how the issue of equal pay was highlighted through references to Lilly Ledbetter, an Alabama grandmother who sued her former employer after discovering her male counterparts were paid more, via a range of media outlets. Communication in the 2010 UK election was placed in media outlets with high female readership, including *The Sun* newspaper and *Take a Break* magazine. They quote a Labour strategist, Douglas Alexander, for recalling how the party targeted women under 40, homeowners with children living in a small city or town in the Midlands, working part- or full-time, most likely in retail. More broadly, Harmer and Wring (2013) note how US and UK politicians have targeted women using labels such as 'soccer mums', 'school gate mums' and 'sandwich mothers'.

Targeted communication is not fail-proof. Hersh and Schaffner (2013) explore how 'big data' is used to devise targeted campaign communication. They conducted experiments with the public to test responses to fictional candidates for Congress in experimental conditions. They found that targeted appeals are not always effective and can backfire if the data is built on incorrect information about voters' group affiliations; thus, they can lead to misassumptions and mistargeting. Their experiments also suggested that voters do not tend to support candidates who pander to their group identities. More broadly, targeted communication has to fit the overall strategy and brand.

Mobile/virtual marketing

Mobile/virtual marketing communications provides a cost-effective alternative to traditional campaigning. The 2008 Obama campaign succeeded in part because it integrated mobile technology with grass-roots activity. Specifically, it utilised mobile marketing in the form of text messages and tweets to target the 18–29 age group (Cook 2010). Mobile marketing can help field organisers identify volunteers they could recruit into action. It can offer the potential for timely and targeted communication, and can help build positive relationships between voters and politicians. Germany (2013, 85–6) notes how the 2012 US presidential election campaign was marked by a substantial growth in digital – or mobile – advertising. Communication was sent to individuals' mobile phones, including when voters watched non-mobile television. Such digital advertising could be targeted using internet-user profiling. More recently, Ridge-Newman and Mitchell (2016) point out that internet and mobile apps have become a standard component of the UK Conservative Party's public outreach toolkit. Mylona (2008) argues that mobile marketing could add to the public sphere if it integrated interactivity and dialogue to allow voters and politicians to exchange ideas.

Selling policy

Political marketing communication is also used to sell policy. Governments can draw on public funds to create government advertising, leveraging research to find ways to effectively communicate their positions to build public awareness and support. This is especially important as governments need to generate 'easy-to-understand', digestible messages to unpack policy offers that can be complex and comprise 'obscure detail[s]' (Marland 2016, 287).

One example of this dynamic is the UK Conservative government's attempt to sell privatisation of British Telecom and British Gas, previously public utilities, to raise capital and create greater efficiency in the 1980s. Allington *et al.* (1999, 637) discuss how understanding of the desires of the market was used to sell what was once a 'radical political idea' to both businesses and voters. Initially, the Telecom proposal faced opposition from the Labour Party, the unions and the media. In order to gain support, communication was aimed at the general public, many members of which had never been shareholders, with appeals to individual needs and desires, showing how the public could gain from buying shares. Advertising was also emotive in nature, with positive depictions of the UK including the white cliffs of Dover. It was very successful, and all shares were sold easily. Goot (1999) details a similar marketing exercise by Australian Prime Minister John Howard when selling off the publicly owned phone company Telstra.

Government advertising is controversial because it blurs the line between publicly funded information campaigns for the benefit of society and communication in the interest of the party in power (Young 2005). Studies have shown big increases in government spending on advertising in the year preceding an election in the UK and Australia, including advertising to support a policy before it has been legislated. An information leaflet produced in June 2004 by a member of staff at the Politics and Public Administration Section, Information and Research Services in the Australian federal parliament in Canberra notes how, at one level, government advertising has an important democratic function. The public has a right to be informed about programmes funded with their taxes. However, Young (2005) notes that the Liberal government led by John Howard used at least $20 million of taxpayers' money to create ads to build support for its planned industrial relations changes before the legislation had even been seen, let alone passed, by parliament.

Gelders and Ihlen (2010) discuss how, when politicians try out ideas in the public sphere, it can be awkward for civil servants because of the potential to be seen as partisan, which is against their professional principles. Nevertheless, the government needs to build relationships with the public to test ideas to see whether the public is willing to accept a policy change or if it needs fine-tuning. In some cases, advertising is the only way for government to get unpopular policies through in certain policy areas, including climate change. When the Labor-Rudd government in Australia proposed a mining tax, they had to face millions of dollars spent by the mining industry to lobby against it before it had become legislation.

Another form of government advertising is social marketing, which has 'a value of preventive policy' (Picazo-Vela *et al.* 2016) and aims at using government advertising to change behaviours in the interests of society (see McKenzie-Mohr and Smith 1999; Kotler and Roberto 2002). Among them are reducing drink-driving, smoking, child abuse or domestic violence, and increasing the use of sun cream to prevent skin cancer. Understanding the consumer first is important to the success of campaigns, but they take a long time to have any impact. More recent high-profile campaigns with long-term goals – which feature patterns of celebrity marketing – include chef Jamie Oliver's campaign to promote healthy eating at schools. Also of note is governments' increasing uses of social media to engage in social marketing. An example of interest is the Ministry of Health of the state of Puebla in Mexico launching the programme *Puebla Sana* in March 2012. The programme was part of a much larger policy initiative seeking to improve public health. In the context of this programme, the government turned to various social media platforms to promote development and public health (Picazo-Vela *et al.* 2016).

Marketing communications is therefore an important tool of government to change public opinion. Allington *et al.* (1999, 635–6) point out that 'marketing, when employed in conjunction with other communication methods, has the power to change things and even to change the world order'. However, that doesn't mean it can simply persuade voters to support something they are completely against. Instead, research is used to identify commonalities between voter views and aspirations and elite policy positions. It could also be argued that privatisation met a need of the public: it generated significant resources to be used elsewhere, made previous public utilities more efficient and therefore enabled the public to pay less for better services, and so met demand rather than worked against it, even if that demand was latent and not directly voiced. To some degree, it could be seen as a form of consumer research in the context of the planning of a policy, which is an area of practice requiring more research (Aspara and Tikkanen 2017).

Corner and Randall (2011) conclude that social marketing has limitations when it comes to altering public behaviour on climate change and that environmental education and supporting citizenship might be more effective instead because they engage people at a deeper level. There are many barriers to broadcast communication. For instance, the information source rarely communicates directly with the receiver. The public receives multiple communications from multiple senders in a usually mass-mediated 'noisy cocktail' (Lloyd 2009). As Temple (2010, 268) notes, 'voters' perceptions and understanding of politics in general are also largely derived through the filters of the media'. Savigny and Temple (2010, 1053) argue that while in business communication might be more controllable, 'in politics things are different'. The media's role is to act as a critic and watchdog of government and political elites. In other words, 'politicians cannot simply present "messages" about their product which are directly relayed to the public' (Savigny and Temple 2010, 1054).

The limited impact of government communications to the marketing of war also illustrates this constraint. Fletcher *et al.* (2009) discuss how the Canadian government launched an information campaign about the war in Afghanistan to boost support for the country's involvement in late 2006. It drew on focus groups which explored levels of understanding and beliefs about the mission and Afghanistan, and factors driving support for or opposition to it. Government communication focused on facts and information to present its case, but had limited effect. The research suggests that Canadians do not just receive government information passively, but instead process it according to their individual predispositions. Another weakness in the government's communication was that it failed to connect emotionally. Similarly, the use of careful communication by the then UK Prime Minister Tony Blair to increase support for his foreign policy was limited in its effectiveness. Holland (2012) argues that Tony Blair used highly strategic discourse to achieve support from target voters for his foreign policy. Communication was carefully crafted to resonate with target markets, with discourse connecting with the cultural make-up of Middle England with references to the UK's moral and pragmatic leadership role in foreign policy within the context of globalisation.

Communicating change

Practitioner Perspective 6.4　on the slowness of communicating change

Everything is very slow. People have very strong opinions of the politicians they know, very strong impressions of the parties . . . and it's pretty hard to shift those impressions.

Roger Mortimore, MORI polling company UK, interview
in Lees-Marshment (2011)

If you've got a big job – and the Conservative party has done a really big job to change perception or to win a general election – that's going to be a three- or four-year project. You can't come in shortly before the election and expect to win for them.

Damian Collins, M&C Saatchi UK Managing Director,
interview in Lees-Marshment (2011)

Communicating change in a product or politician that has already been designed or has a long history is very hard as the public already has existing images and perceptions of the brand or position. If a political product changes, it can take a long time for the public to perceive such a change. Communication needs to be linked to actual behaviour to be convincing and authentic. In the UK, when David Cameron took over leadership of the Conservative Party after the 2005 election, significant and sustained communication strategies were put in place to convey a new image of the party in response to market intelligence about what the public wanted from the party. Communication included photo opportunities of Cameron cycling to work, visiting Darfur in Africa, planting trees on a social action day, visiting a Norwegian glacier and meeting Nelson Mandela, all of which helped to convey a new strategy of focusing on environmentalism, the poor and world affairs. The party also adopted a new party symbol, a green tree and blue sky, used the slogan 'Vote Blue, Get Green' in local elections and redeveloped the party website with fresh blue-green colours, using pictures that convey a more mainstream Britain (Lees-Marshment and Pettitt 2010). This approach of communicating change has also been used in other national contexts. During the 2013 general elections in Pakistan, the party Tehreek-e-Insaf portrayed itself as an agent of political change 'by appointing new candidates, a powerful electoral campaign was run to enforce the old age adage that the Pakistani public should not re-elect the already tested candidates' (Yousaf 2016, 146).

Lees-Marshment (2011, 136–7) interviewed practitioners about the best way to communicate change. They suggested that a completely fresh style is one way to do it. Neil Lawrence, Kevin Rudd's creative strategist in the 2007 Australian election, recalled that the 'campaign gave a very, very fresh view of the Labor Party. We started by redesigning the entire livery for the Labor Party, which was old-fashioned . . . the style of our advertising was quite upbeat, it was positive.' Unconventional forms of communication also help attract attention to change. When asked what made John Ansell's 2005 billboards for the New Zealand National Party so successful, the leader Don Brash replied: 'well, they were very unconventional . . . National Party billboards are blue, and you would never see Labour Party billboards with me on it either, but here was National putting half the billboard in red and a photograph of Helen Clark' (quoted in Lees-Marshment 2011).

Crisis management

> ### Practitioner Perspective 6.5 on the pervasiveness and importance of crisis management in government
>
> *Most of my time is spent with day-to-day crisis management . . . We're not permanently in crisis. But dealing with all the issues that arise on a day-to-day basis. I'm surprised on a day-to-day basis . . . You know there's no accounting for the conduct of individuals.*
> > Oliver Dowden, David Cameron's Deputy Chief of Staff who oversees domestic policy, 2012
>
> *You've got to face up to what you've done . . . when we apologise, and we're sincere about it, then people will be willing to give you a second chance . . . in that whole process you've got to try and protect a reputation and a brand. It's like a chess game.*
> > Judy Smith, crisis management advisor, 2012
>
> Sources: Rocky Mountain PBS (2012); Comedy Central (2012)

Crisis management is needed in campaigning and government. Garrett's (2014) discussion of crisis management in US campaigns highlights how crisis can threaten political marketing strategies and, in some cases, lead to the transformation of existing practices (Stephenson 2013). For example, changes to campaign finances can create a crisis and require the strategy and resource allocation to be changed. A cascade of failures can ensue and potentially cause the campaign's demise. In the heat of a campaign, it is difficult to make appropriate strategic choices, and candidates may be prone to reverting to more tactical, day-to-day political marketing which can be less successful. More resources need to be invested in predicting and preparing for potential crises and risks that might occur in future campaigns (see also Garrett 2009).

Crisis is an inevitable – and, in some cases, diverting – part of being in government. Foley (2009, 500) notes how the former UK Prime Minister Gordon Brown

> became embroiled in a succession of crises that touched upon practically every aspect of social life. Severe political and administrative difficulties became compounded with slumps in the government's public and professional standings, which in turn fused with electoral shocks, political scandals and allegations of chronic deficiencies in the organizational integrity of central government.

This was partly due to the near collapse of the global financial system and associated economic downturn, but crisis happens in every government. As Practitioner Perspective 6.5 indicates, it is important that politicians get a grip of any crisis to try to limit potential damage from it. Foley argues that Brown's crisis management was ineffective because it failed to convey governing competence and stay in control of events; which of course damaged his leadership image.

Crisis management is partly about managing expectations. As Coombs (2011) explains, if stakeholders believe there is a crisis because expectations have been violated, then it will become a crisis, whether or not the government sees it as such. Foley (2009) argues that political leaders try to influence how a crisis is perceived by the public and those within government itself. They need to try to define the crisis themselves and offer reassurance that they understand and will act on the problem so that the public trusts their competence to manage it. Coombs (2011) argues that crises are events that have the potential to seriously damage political reputations, and that emotions such as fear, anger, uncertainty and sadness play a key role in crisis. It is obviously harder to frame a crisis that develops quickly, not least as the public expects government to react quickly – and that is not always easy in situations such as earthquakes and tsunamis. Part of crisis management is acknowledging whether there is a problem, assigning blame and deciding whether to change behaviour in response. Coombs notes how, when Congressman Gary Condit was found to have had an affair with an intern who was later found murdered, he might have been re-elected if he had admitted and apologised, and thus apology is a key tool of political crisis management (see also Boin 2005).

Integrated marketing communications

Integrated marketing communications (IMC) seeks to combine and coordinate different communications concepts into one campaign. Building on work by Reeves (2013, 127), it can be argued that IMC rests on principles of 'consistency', 'orchestration', 'clarity', 'simplicity' and 'synergy' that are guiding the conceptualisation, production and rolling out of 'messages transmitted via internal and external communication tools'. During the

2000 US presidential contest, both Democrats and Republicans combined targeting to market segments and direct and indirect marketing to mobilise voters – or get them out to vote, noting that more than $10 million was spent trying to motivate Latino voters in the election (Barreto *et al.* 2011). Parties created unique political adverts in Spanish, and there were 3,000 airings of such ads in states which had significant Latino populations. They also ran GOTV campaigns using door-to-door, mail and telephone forms of direct marketing in Latino communities. Their analysis concluded that messages that are both direct and targeted are more effective: 'the strengths and weaknesses of the different elements are used to offset one another' (Barreto *et al.* 2011, 310).

IMC uses a range of communications tools, mediums and strategies to achieve a common goal; overall, the public or recipients of the communication then receive multiple messages which, as a whole, convey the same, unified message. Papagiannidis *et al.* (2012, 305) conclude that for the web to be used to its full potential in politics, there is the need 'for integrated political marketing communications that leverage the web for its strengths and using it as a complementary tactic in the candidates' political marketing arsenal'. Similarly, Seidman (2010, 23) argues that all communication must be connected effectively. The visual logo 'communicated and reinforced his brand'; the colour, imagery, typography, lighting, slogans and positive tone all fitted with the brand as being inspirational, unifying, moderate, cool and charismatic (Seidman 2010, 23).

In the conclusion to *Political Marketing in the US*, the editors note how research demonstrated that each component of marketing was limited by each other, with different marketing tools interacting with and influencing each other's success (Lees-Marshment *et al.* 2014), suggesting there is now a move towards integrated political marketing overall.

Political marketing communications in the workplace

The steady intensification, professionalisation, and digitisation of political communication, mobilisation, and organising over the last three decades have led to an enhanced role for broadcast marketing communications in political processes in and out of elections (Grusell and Nord 2016). Politicians and political organisations (e.g. political parties, advocacy groups), as well as local, regional and national governments, are increasingly looking for and hiring individuals with marketing-related expertise, including branding, advertising and market research. These hires are also fulfilling growingly large – and, in some cases, key – responsibilities. Of note is the appointment of Brad Parscale as campaign manager for Donald Trump's 2020 re-election campaign in the United States. Parscale, who was born in Kansas in 1976, served as Trump's digital media director during the 2016 presidential contest. As the campaign unfolded, his responsibilities grew to include 'advertising, data collection and fundraising' (Ducharme 2018). Prior to joining the Trump campaign, Parscale founded a San Antonio-based marketing firm that provided advice to different businesses. In other words, he had limited political experience as most of his work was done in the commercial world.

As noted in this chapter, the expansion and diversification of the contemporary mediascape – both online and offline – coupled with the hyper fragmentation of publics have led to growing employment opportunities in the field of political marketing. In fact, in a non-stop political campaigning environment that is increasingly competitive, individuals with highly specialised political marketing skills are sought out to design and carry out political messaging and GOTV operations catering to the increasingly narrow interests, preferences and objectives of small slices of the public. Of particular interest is the growing need for marketing specialists in the field of digital and social media-based politicking (see Ryoo and Bendle 2017). As the social mediascape is expanding, diversifying, and becoming a go-to channel for public political information acquisition and engagement, politicians are increasingly present in this arena to reach out to, connect with, and influence the attitudes and patterns of behaviour of members of the public. Marketing professionals with wide-ranging specialties, including polling, data analytics, message targeting and personal branding, are needed to plan out campaigns – during and outside of elections – that are adapted to the distinct structural and function properties of social media platforms, including Instagram, Twitter and Facebook. In other words, this sector of political marketing activity is likely to experience a steady growth over the next decade.

In the case of Donald Trump's 2016 US presidential election, digital marketing specialists worked on several projects that were instrumental in devising and coordinating its voter outreach and engagement efforts. Pollsters, coders and data specialists worked on 'Project Alamo', a massive database comprising information on approximately '220 million Americans and contained approximately 4,000 to 5,000 individual data points about the online and offline life of each person' (Winston 2016). This database was leveraged by branding and messaging professionals to gain insights into narrow segments of the audience and craft engaging and persuasive messages. For instance, they rolled out Facebook ads located in side-bars and embedded in personal news feeds that targeted 'demographics and other Facebook-created interest categories, as well as 'dark posts (nonpublic posts that the campaign can make visible to whomever it wants) and promoted posts' (Baldwin-Philippi 2017, 630).

This dynamic is not limited to the United States. During the 2017 UK general election, the Labour Party invested heavily in digital marketing, which ultimately helped them gain 21 seats. For example, marketing specialists developed and launched the online message targeting tool 'Promote' that allowed the production and distribution of tailored policy messages designed to reach individual voters. In Canada, social media has become a pivotal component of Justin Trudeau's approach to political branding, as discussed by Lalancette and Raynauld (2017). From a broader perspective, it can be argued the demand for political marketers globally is likely to increase, especially with the on-going growth and further development of the digital political mediascape. New specialties in the field of marketing could also emerge over the next decades with the transformation of existing mass communication platforms and the emergence of new ones, as well as with the shifting and narrowing political expectations and goals of the public at large.

Summary

This chapter explored how political marketing communication can be used to communicate information about political leaders, in a campaign, to increase support in particular segments of the public, and to sell policy and political change, as well as to manage crises in a context of non-stop campaigning, in and out of elections. Communication involves utilising many other aspects of marketing including strategy and market analysis, to make the communication effective and suitable for the receiver. It needs to be well researched, fit with the strategy and brand, and be believable. Principles of effective broadcast communications are laid out in Box 6.1 in the best practice guide.

It should be noted that recent political developments over the last five years have raised profound ethical questions related to dynamics of broadcast political marketing communication. Among them include uses of big data for voter profiling as well as voter psychological targeting through social media and other digital platforms (see González 2017; Matz *et al.* 2017). From a broader perspective, several authors' recent work, including Marland (2016), have taken interest in the effects of broadcast political marketing on different facets of the democratic process. In Democratic Debate 6.1, Miloš Gregor addresses some of these questions by examining some aspects of the ethical compass guiding political consultants' work. However, work remains in order to better identify, characterise, and understand the different ethical considerations in broadcast political marketing communication in and out of elections, especially in an era of increased broadcast political marketing activity in the digital mediascape.

The next chapter looks at more interactive and relational forms of marketing communication in politics.

Box 6.1 Best practice guide to broadcast political marketing communication

1 Plan out time to think strategically about communication and campaigning in and out of elections.
2 Know and stick to your strategy during all phases of the broadcast political marketing cycle; don't get bogged down in daily news cycle/social media chatter/planet politics/following the pack.
3 Identify, conceptualise, and communicate clearly one clear central vision reflecting the candidate's personality as well as favouring the establishment and strengthening of an emotional connection with people over time.
4 Ensure non-verbal images convey honesty, credibility, knowledge, experience, strength and energy. Don't forget that 'images often supersede words', especially in a highly competitive media environment where 'they can have greater visibility and garner much more attention and scrutiny than in the past' (Lalancette and Raynauld 2017, 3).
5 Don't convey 'the common touch' at the neglect of leadership and governing skills; both are important.
6 Engage in multifaceted PMR, including more traditional forms of market research as well as large, frequently updated large political databases, more commonly known as big data, to gain a granular understanding of individuals' personal attitudes and behaviour.
7 Devise communication taking into account the findings of PMR (see point 6).
8 Use guerrilla marketing to generate awareness and excitement for a new leader, policy, brand or position. Use unconventional, fresh or new styles, colours, labels, hinges or logos to convey change, and start early.
9 Use celebrity marketing to help raise funds and draw attention to often specific aspects of products, but do so carefully, making sure the celebrity profile matches the brand and position of the candidate.
10 Make communication market-oriented so that it targets specific slices of the electorate, shows the party leader responding to their needs, evokes party history to connect with core voters and conveys appropriate co-operation with the competition. While core supporters are important, reaching new markets is valuable as it can help broaden the base of support.

11 Use dark (nonpublic) and promoted ads on the internet in order to reach out to individual members of the public in more individualised ways and appeal to their core preferences, interests and objectives.

12 To get the vote out, employ face-to-face and web-based networked approaches to connect and engage with members of the public repeatedly and over a long period of time. Also, adapt the communication as much as possible to individuals' narrow interests and objectives.

13 Design communication to suit the receiver's behaviour in terms of when, where, what and how.

14 Target communication in terms of medium and message, but avoid conflicting messages that could please certain markets but alienate others.

15 Pre-test communication using experimental and analytic marketing.

16 Identify initial brand strengths and ensure that campaign activities build upon, protect and strengthen these.

17 Define yourself before the competition defines you, and if attacked rebut immediately.

18 Leverage market research and social marketing to create effective government advertising to counter anti-legislative campaigns and promote positive public behaviour in areas such as healthy eating, exercise and drink-driving.

19 Plan communication linked with behaviour and events over a long period to change an established reputation.

20 During a moment of crisis, acknowledge the problem and offer immediate action to remedy it, and constantly reassure the public by demonstrating that you are in control.

21 Create an integrated communications plan tying all forms of political communications together.

Discussion points

1 To what extent are political leaders effective at fostering an emotional connection with voters?

2 Pick several current or former political leaders and rate their non-verbal communication against Schweiger and Aadami's (1999) political candidate positive and negative image attributes of honesty, quality and strength. Who performs the best and why?

3 How does market research – especially with the rise and growing traction of big data over the last decade – inform campaign communication?

4 Think through the effects of big data research on politicians' and political organisations' approaches to campaigning. How do you think it impacts the design and rolling out of messaging and mobilisation operations?

5 Think of recent or well-known political adverts. To what extent do they follow Robinson's (2006) criteria for market-oriented political adverts?

6 Does insights marketing in politics constitute a threat to democracy? Could it be beneficial to the reengagement of the public in the political process?

7 Think of recent examples of guerrilla political communication. Create a plan for future guerrilla communication to help a candidate or party leader gain traction for a new idea, policy, position, brand or leadership.

8 What is the main goal of GOTV? How effective do you think it is? How are social media redefining dynamics of GOTV?

9   What are the pros and cons of direct marketing in politics?

10   Identify examples of where politicians and parties have targeted their communication, and discuss how effective it was.

11   How is big data changing dynamics of targeted communication, especially with the on-going development and growing traction of social media as tools for political information and engagement?

12   Discuss the nature and effectiveness of targeted communication to reach women voters in recent elections.

13   Debate whether political marketing communications might help politicians sell policies that are right for the country but might otherwise be rejected by the political market.

14   How does social marketing differ from government advertising? How effective do you think it is in changing society's behaviour, such as reducing drink-driving? Is it a worthwhile use of government funds?

15   As social marketing can be used by politicians and political organisations in power to bolster their support, do you think its uses should be guided by a clear ethical framework?

16   Think of crises faced in recent campaigns and government. How well did politicians handle them, and what might they have done better?

Assessment questions

Essay/exam

1   Identify and critique how marketing communications have been used to forge a positive image for political organisations, leaders and candidates.

2   Discuss theories and empirical examples of campaign communication devised in relation to market research.

3   Identify examples of guerrilla political communication and discuss how effective it is.

4   How is GOTV used in politics – especially with the popularisation of social media – and with what impact?

5   Review and critique the effectiveness of direct marketing in politics.

6   Identify and critique targeted communication by recent political leaders and campaigns.

7   Discuss the potential and limitations of government advertising to increase support for governments' policies and work.

8   Outline the difference between government advertising and social marketing, utilising theory and empirical examples.

9   Review the effectiveness of social marketing by governments in changing public behaviour, using both examples and theory.

10   Review recent attempts by governments to use marketing communications to increase war efforts support. Draw conclusions about the potential and limitations to the marketing of war.

11   Discuss the importance and effectiveness of crisis management in politics.

Applied

1   Assess the non-verbal communication of a candidate or leader against Schweiger and Aadami's (1999) political candidate positive and negative image attributes of honesty,

quality and strength. Draw conclusions as to how effective their image is, and how they might improve it.

2 Evaluate political adverts at the last election against Robinson's (2006) criteria for market-oriented political adverts, noting strengths and weaknesses. Discuss the degree to which the degree of market-orientation found in the ads related to the election outcome.

3 Assess GOTV's uses and effectiveness among recent political campaigns. Create a plan for a future GOTV campaign for a candidate, campaign or party that takes into account the latest development in the political mediascape, both online and offline.

4 Drawing on previous research into partisan GOTV, create a plan for the Electoral Commission to use GOTV to increase turnout regardless of individuals' past voting records.

5 Assess uses of direct marketing in all its forms – mail, email, mobile text, web ad – in a recent election campaign, reviewing its nature and effectiveness to achieve goals such as increase donations, support and volunteer activity. Make recommendations on how it could be improved at the next election.

6 Evaluate uses of targeted communication at the last national/federal/presidential election and how effective they were. Create a plan for improved targeting at the next election.

7 Create a plan for a minor party to engage in targeted communication at the next election, drawing on examples of other parties' targeted communication and an analysis of the party's goals and potential segments.

8 Identify and critique the use of communication to target women voters in the 2017 UK election and 2016 US presidential election. Following this analysis, create a plan for how parties might target women more effectively in the future.

9 Critique the effectiveness of recent government advertising to sell a proposed policy or new programme in terms of how it utilised marketing or followed principles noted in Allington *et al.* (1999).

10 Create a plan for a government to design effective advertising for a proposed policy, utilising a range of marketing concepts and tools.

11 Evaluate the effectiveness of communication by the Labor government and mining companies in Australia for the proposed mining tax in terms of the way it used marketing communications principles. From this, draw generic lessons for the appropriate and effective use of public money for government advertising, given the arguments for the need for climate change policies in Australia.

12 Create a list of principles to market war, drawing on previous successes and failures such as the attempts by UK, US and Canadian governments to gain support for the wars in Afghanistan and Syria. These principles must take account the changed nature of political marketing, particularly the decline in deference towards political leaders and increased availability and diversity of political communication.

13 Review uses of crisis management by recent governments such as George W. Bush's response to Hurricane Katrina in 2005, Trump's handling of the aftermath of Hurricane Maria in Puerto Rico in 2017, and Justin Trudeau's response to the political crisis following the G7 summit in Charlevoix, Québec in 2018. Critique their effectiveness and, from this, draw lessons for future governments.

14 Create an integrated marketing communications plan for a political figure or organisation for the next 12 months or for the next election. It must utilise a range of marketing communications concepts and draw on theory, other empirical cases, and a critique of the political figure's or organisation's past behaviour, ensuring that the different types of communication are integrated together effectively.

Case study

Case study 6.1 Targeting neglected voter groups online: The 2016 Hillary Clinton campaign and Americans with disabilities

By Filippo Trevisan and Robert Rodriguez-Donoso (American University)

Effective voter segmentation plays an increasingly important role in elections. Early segmentation attempts used basic demographic information such as age, gender, race and class to identify potentially responsive publics. Despite promising results, these targeting efforts were inherently limited by the broad nature of these categories (Baines *et al.* 2005). More recently, campaigns have increasingly preferred to bypass 'first-order' segmentation, based on categories such as age and gender, and instead focus on groups drawn from second-order information such as media habits and lifestyle (Davidson and Binstock 2011). Digital media have significantly expanded opportunities to identify and reach out to potentially supportive voters on the basis of more sophisticated and unconventional variables. Specifically, online media have opened up opportunities for campaigns to engage with groups that in the past were neglected despite representing important reservoirs of votes.

One such neglected but potentially influential group is people with disabilities. In 2016, estimates prepared from US Census Bureau data indicated that in the United States approximately 35.4 million people with disabilities were eligible to vote. To put this number into perspective, it is useful to note that the Pew Research Center estimated that, in 2016, US Black and Latino voters, two groups that have played an especially important role in the marketing strategies of Democratic politicians, totalled 27.4 million and 27.3 million, respectively. This characterises people with disabilities as a potentially powerful group that campaigns should consider targeting through specific messages. Moreover, this group is of interest to all candidates given that, contrary to public belief that often stereotypes voters with disabilities as Democratic voters, they identify in similar proportions with both the major parties (Schur and Adya 2013).

Online campaigning provides new opportunities to reach this group as a fast-growing number of Americans with disabilities are online. In 2017, 70 per cent of Americans with disabilities aged 18–64 owned a smartphone and over two thirds had in-home broadband (Anderson and Perrin 2017). Disabled Americans are politically active online, and disability rights advocacy has become increasingly digitalised in recent years (Trevisan 2016). Barack Obama was the first US presidential candidate to pioneer targeted online engagement with voters with disabilities. Both the 2008 and 2012 Obama campaigns created groups for 'Citizens with Disabilities for Obama' on their online portals. These were part of an innovative segmentation strategy that aimed to mobilise several groups based on their specific interests, ideals or identity such as African Americans, environmentalists and LGBT people.

Following in Obama's footsteps, the 2016 Clinton campaign also sought to target the disability community. While the Clinton campaign did not implement specific interest- or identity-based online voter groups, it developed an unprecedented amount of dedicated online content about disabilities. The campaign's website included sections on disability rights, mental health, autism, Alzheimer's disease, support for those caring for disabled family members, and the issues faced by disabled veterans. Each of these topics was also covered in the campaign's sister website – 'The Briefing' – which was set up to resemble a news site and illustrated Clinton's policy agenda in great detail through statements and 'factsheets' from the campaign. These pages included primarily written text with a limited amount of professionally shot video. Following a controversial and widely reported episode during a 2015 campaign rally in which Donald Trump mocked a reporter with a disability, the Clinton campaign ramped up its efforts towards this group. Disability rights advocate Anastasia Somoza was a prominent speaker at the Democratic National Convention, and Clinton herself gave a landmark speech on disability issues just a few weeks before election day.

We carried out focus groups with voters with a wide range of disabilities during and shortly after the election to explore their reaction to this targeting effort from the Clinton campaign. Virtually all the participants agreed that online campaigning had the potential to make election information more accessible and relevant for voters with disabilities. Participants particularly praised Google and YouTube, which they said helped them to overcome some of the limitations of traditional media, especially television. For example, one participant said that YouTube is 'really good for people who have learning disabilities or ADD, ADHD. 'Cause you can stop and go back and watch the same part over and over and over again until you understand it.' These comments supported Clinton's choice to invest in online communications to target voters with disabilities. Participants spontaneously acknowledged the efforts of the Clinton campaign in this area, showing awareness and commenting positively on Clinton's decision to put disability issues forward in her campaign.

At the same time, however, participants also criticized this campaign for communicating disability-specific content ineffectively. As one participant put it, 'Hillary's platform [on disability issues] was excellent. [. . .] You could tell that they really researched it. [. . .] but it was only her written platform. [. . .] they should've disbursed her ideas and [made them more] easily digestible' (Sylvia, 52). Thus, participants tended to agree that Clinton's text-based content was difficult to access for many voters with disabilities, failed to capitalise on the advantages of online communications for persons with disabilities, and, finally, was not memorable.

Lessons for political marketing

Several political marketing lessons can be drawn from this case. First, online campaigning widely broadens the scope of voter segmentation efforts, enabling candidates to target traditionally neglected groups. Some of these, such as people with disabilities, are very sizeable publics that make it worth investing in this kind of political strategy. The fact that focus group participants noted Clinton's efforts to engage with the disability community suggests that initiating this innovative type of segmentation can raise the profile of a candidate with that group. In light of this, and given what voters with disabilities said about how they used Google to identify specific disability-related election information, search engine optimisation represents a particularly effective channel to push targeted content.

Nevertheless, this case also showed that voter segmentation becomes even more difficult when the targets are groups that typically have been overlooked. This requires a specific understanding and sensitivities to the targeted group. Putting together dedicated content is only the first step in this process. Campaigns need to consider not only technical accessibility standards but also how the ways in which specialised content is 'packaged' caters to the needs of those for whom it is intended. For example, Clinton's text-based briefings were 'technically' accessible but nonetheless difficult to engage with for voters with disabilities. Campaigns should be mindful of the benefits of providing targeted information in a range of formats and engage with the communities of interest to explore the suitability of each format. Finally, references to Clinton's message for voters with disabilities not being memorable remind campaigns that seek to target neglected groups not to forget about the basic tenets of message development and aim for content that is both meaningful and easily remembered by their primary targets.

References

Anderson, Monica and Andrew Perrin (2017). 'Disabled Americans Are Less Likely to Use Technology'. Pew Research Center, 7 April 2017. www.pewresearch.org/fact-tank/2017/04/07/disabled-americans-are-less-likely-to-use-technology/.

Baines, Paul, Robert Worcester, David Jarrett and Roger Mortimore (2005). 'Product Attribute-Based Voter Segmentation and Resource Advantage Theory'. *Journal of Marketing Management*, 21(9–10): 1079–115.

Davidson, Scott and Robert Binstock (2011). 'Political Marketing and Segmentation in Ageing Democracies'. In J. Lees-Marshment (ed.) *Routledge Handbook of Political Marketing*. London: Routledge, 20–33.

Schur, Lisa and Meera Adya (2013). 'Sidelined or Mainstreamed? Political Participation and Attitudes of People with Disabilities in the United States'. *Social Science Quarterly*, 94(3): 811–39.

Trevisan, Filippo (2016). *Disability Rights Advocacy Online: Voice, Empowerment and Global Connectivity*. New York: Routledge.

Democratic Debate 6.1 Political consultants' ethics of conviction

By Miloš Gregor (Masaryk University)

The question of morality and ethics is nothing new to politics and political science, nor is it new for political marketing. In political marketing, the question of morality and ethics is usually connected to specific tools or strategies used in campaigns, such as negative advertising (Banker 1992), or how ethical it is to apply marketing principles in an environment as sensitive as democratic states (O'Shaughnessy 2002). This level of discussion leads to academic justification, but has few ties to the practical aspects of the craft. No matter what the conclusions of our papers and research are, there are still political consultants who offer their services to candidates running for the office. But what is moral and what is immoral in campaigning? What ethical questions do the consultants have to answer for themselves?

How to approach ethics in political consulting

There are many approaches and definitions dealing with the question of moral or immoral behaviour in politics and answering what is ethical and what is not. There are basically two sets of ethical virtues defined by Max Weber, which can also be used to examine the decision political consultants make about whether to join a campaign or not – the ethic of *conviction* and the ethic of *responsibility* (Weber 1976). Of course, according to the ethic of responsibility, on the one hand, an action is given meaning only as a cause of an effect, that is, only in terms of its causal relationship to the field the consultant is involved in. An ethical question is thereby reduced to a question of technically correct procedure – i.e. whether a political strategy has been well implemented, the communication mix has been set effectively, or the campaign schedule has been adequate. The consultant feels responsibility only for the instruments and results he or she is directly responsible for. According to the ethic of conviction, on the other hand, a consultant should be able to choose autonomously not only the means, but also the end. In this perspective, professionals participating in a campaign should be aware of a politician's intentions. These two kinds of reasoning represent categorically distinct modes of rationality, and while the ethic of responsibility has been normally taken into account, the ethic of conviction is rarely publicly mentioned.

The absence of discussion on the ethic of conviction can be a problem, as Western democratic societies seem to be changing and the normative requirements placed on candidates are not so clear. Almost nobody expected the results of either the United Kingdom referendum on leaving the European Union (Brexit) or the 2016 presidential election in the United States. And while the results of the 2017 parliamentary elections in the Czech Republic are hardly imaginable in a democratic country, nevertheless that is what happened. For political consultants it may have become a big task to consider connecting their names with these campaigns.

Considerable campaigns

In the first referendum on United Kingdom membership of the then European Community, held on 5 July 1975, 67 per cent of voters opted to stay in the European Community. Forty-one years later, on 23 June 2016, the UK held another referendum and almost 52 per cent of the electorate voted to leave the European Union. The Vote Leave campaign won in England and Wales; only in Scotland, Northern Ireland and London did the campaign fail to surpass 50 per cent (Goodwin and Heath 2016). The stakes in the referendum were high: to be part of European commonwealth, or to stand alone? And besides the political views and arguments, there were many lies in the campaign that were discovered just a few days after the referendum. One of the most visible slogans and arguments said the EU costs the UK over £350 million every week, and even the main representatives of the Vote Leave campaign admitted this figure was exaggerated. But in such close voting results, it becomes a question of how many people voted to leave because of this argument? And political consultants helped to spread this false argument. They helped people believe the message.

Donald J. Trump has been accused of grubby behaviour, previously unimaginable for a United States president. Trump was seen as a showman rather than as a serious candidate when he introduced his intention to run in the 2016 US presidential election. During his campaign in 2016, 15 women claimed to have been sexually assaulted by him; we have witnessed insults, allegations of lies and accusations of financial improprieties surrounding Trump. Ties between Trump's campaign and Russia and Russian interference in the election have been investigated by the FBI even a year after the election. And the result is in sight. We can hardly claim that Trump's consultants were aware of everything during the campaign; however, many questions and doubts arose long before the elections. At the very least, Trump's inappropriate behaviour towards women was publicly known. And still, his consultants kept doing their job to help win the elections.

The ANO Movement was a part of the coalition government in the Czech Republic before the 2017 parliamentary elections. In spite of this, ANO continued their anti-establishment populist rhetoric. Even more surprising is the combination of its anti-corruption rhetoric while its leader Andrej Babiš was accused of EU funds fraud by both the Czech national investigator and the European Anti-Fraud Office (OLAF) at the time of the election. Despite these facts, ANO was able to get almost 30 per cent of votes and win the elections by a landslide. The simplified story behind this achievement is the successful narrative of the campaign describing Babiš in a way voters wanted to see him – as a successful businessman fighting against corruption. Scandals were then perceived as merely part of rival campaigns. And this was possible because of detailed knowledge of voters' attitudes, needs and preferences, as well as the professional communication strategy set by ANO's experts.

Summary

All of these campaigns had problematic aspects that should have probably been considered as obstacles on the way to victory. And still, all of them were successful, largely thanks to political consultants and the great job they did. This chapter does not have the ambition to analyse the moral maxims of campaigns or voter decisions. The goal of the above-mentioned thoughts, rather, is to cultivate an examination of political consultants in order to raise awareness of the ethical issues associated with campaigning for politicians who have a complicated history and/or personality. Although all of the above-mentioned campaigns were legal, we still encounter scandals in almost every election. It is almost impossible for political consultants to avoid them. Regardless, it is up to every consultant to consider whether he or she can be responsible for the success of such a candidate, whether the politician is a threat for democracy or not.

References

Banker, Steve (1992). 'The Ethics of Political Marketing Practices, The Rhetorical Perspective'. *Journal of Business Ethics*, 11(11): 843–8.

Goodwin, Matthew J. and Oliver Heath (2016). 'The 2016 Referendum, Brexit and the Left Behind: An Aggregate-level Analysis of the Result'. *The Political Quarterly*, 87(3): 323–32.

Henneberg, Stephan (2004). 'The Views of an Advocatus Dei: Political Marketing and Its Critics'. *Journal of Public Affairs*, 4(3): 225–43.

O'Shaughnessy, Nicholas J. (2002). 'Toward an Ethical Framework for Political Marketing'. *Psychology & Marketing*, 19(12): 1079–94.

Weber, Max (1976). *Roscher and Knies: The Logical Problems of Historical Economics*. New York: Free Press, 304.

References

Allington, Nigel, Philip Morgan and Nicholas O'Shaughnessy (1999). 'How marketing changed the world. The political marketing of an idea: a case study of privatization'. In Bruce Newman (ed). *The Handbook of Political Marketing*. Thousand Oaks, CA: Sage, 627–12.

Aspara, Jaakko, and Henrikki Tikkanen (2017). 'Why do public policy-makers ignore marketing and consumer research? A case study of policy-making for alcohol advertising'. *Consumption Markets & Culture*, 20(1): 12–34.

Baldwin-Philippi, Jessica (2017). 'The myths of data-driven campaigning'. *Political Communication*, 34(4): 627–33.

Barreto, Matt A., Jennifer Merolla and Victoria Defrancesco Soto (2011). 'Multiple dimensions of mobilization: the effect of direct contact and political ads on Latino turnout in the 2000 presidential election'. *Journal of Political Marketing*, 10(4): 303–27.

BBC (2017). 'The digital guru who helped Donald Trump to the presidency'. *BBC News*, 13 August 2017. www.bbc.com/news/av/magazine-40852227/the-digital-guru-who-helped-donald-trump-to-the-presidency.

Becker, Amy B. (2013). 'Star power? Advocacy, receptivity, and viewpoints on celebrity involvement in issue politics'. *Atlantic Journal of Communication*, 21(1): 1–16.

Berger, Arthur Asa (2016). 'Marketing the President: political marketing'. In Arthur A. Berger, *Marketing and American Consumer Culture*. Cham, Switzerland: Palgrave Macmillan, 93–100.

Boin, Arjen (ed.) (2005). *The Politics of Crisis Management: Public Leadership Under Pressure*. Cambridge: Cambridge University Press.

Brainmates (2010). '5 Minutes with Stephen Quain, US political campaign manager'. Brainmates blog post. https://brainmates.com.au/general/5-minutes-with-stephen-quain-us-political-campaign-manager/ (accessed 1 September 2018).

Braun, Alexander and Anna Matušková (2009). 'Case study 7.2 Czech Republic: Social Democrats strike back'. In Jennifer Lees-Marshment *Political Marketing: Principles and Applications*. London and New York: Routledge, 181–3.

Busby, Robert (2014). 'Mama Grizzlies: Republican female candidates and the political marketing dilemma'. In Jennifer Lees-Marshment, Brian Conley and Kenneth Cosgrove (eds) *Political Marketing in the US*. New York: Routledge, 202–19.

Campbell, Alastair (2013). 'Alastair Campbell in Conversation: Politics, the People and the Press'. Public Conversation with Steve Richards. The British Library YouTube video, 17 May 2013. www.youtube.com/watch?v=_Gu4ZEMOB78.

Campbell, Vincent and Benjamin Lee (2016). 'Party branding: A case study of online political posters'. In Darren Lilleker and Mark Pack (eds) *Political Marketing and the 2015 UK General Election*. London: Palgrave Macmillan, 49–65.

CBS (2018). 'Who is Brad Parscale?' *60 Minutes*, air date 27 February 2018. www.cbs.com/shows/60_minutes/video/elHhrLFmOS2ZYFqRG68KQPAu0_aUKPKC/who-is-brad-parscale-/ (accessed 1 September 2018).

Center for Responsive Politics (2017). 'Expenditures Breakdown, Donald Trump, 2016 cycle'. OpenSecrets.org. www.opensecrets.org/pres16/expenditures?id=n00023864 (accessed 1 September 2018).

Channel 4 News (2018). 'Cambridge Analytica uncovered: Secret filming reveals election tricks'. *Channel 4 News YouTube video*, published 19 March 2018. www.youtube.com/watch?time_continue=1&v=mpbeOCKZFfQ (accessed 1 September 2018).

Comedy Central (2012). Broadcast, *The Daily Show*. www.thedailyshow.com/watch/thu-april-19–2012/judy-smith (accessed 19 April 2012).

Conley, Brian (2018). 'Thinking what he says: Market research and the making of Donald Trump's 2016 presidential campaign'. In Jamie Gillies (ed.) *Political Marketing in the 2016 US Presidential Election*. Cham, Switzerland: Palgrave Macmillan, 29–48.

Cook, Catherine (2010). 'Mobile marketing and political activities'. *International Journal of Mobile Marketing*, 5(1): 154–63.

Coombs, W. Timothy (2011). 'Political public relations and crisis communication'. In Jesper Strömbäck and Spiro Kiousis (eds) *Political Public Relations: Principles and Applications*. New York: Routledge, 213–34.

Corner, Adam and Alex Randall (2011). 'Selling climate change? The limitations of social marketing as a strategy for climate change public engagement'. *Global Environmental Change*, 21(3): 1005–14.

Ducharme, Jamie (2018). 'What to know about Brad Parscale, Donald Trump's 2020 campaign manager'. *Time*, 27 February 2018. http://time.com/5177627/brad-parscale-donald-trump-campaign-manager/ (accessed 1 September 2018).

Elder, Edward (2016). 'Market-Oriented Governing Leaders' Communication: John Key and Barack Obama'. *Journal of Nonprofit & Public Sector Marketing*, 28(1): 5–21.

Elder, Edward (2018). 'The Clinton campaign: Appeals to moderate swing voters through anti-Trump targeted communication'. In Jamie Gillies (ed.) *Political Marketing in the 2016 US Presidential Election*. Cham, Switzerland: Palgrave Macmillan, 81–95.

Elder, Edward and Justin B. Phillips (2017). 'Appeals to the Hispanic demographic: Targeting through Facebook autoplay videos by the Clinton campaign during the 2015/2016 presidential primaries'. *Journal of Political Marketing*, 16(3/4): 319–42.

Elteren, Mel (2013). 'Celebrity culture, performative politics, and the spectacle of "democracy" in America'. *The Journal of American Culture*, 36(4): 263–83.

Fletcher, Joseph F., Heather Bastedo and Jennifer Hoce (2009). 'Losing heart: declining support and the political marketing of the Afghanistan mission'. *Canadian Journal of Political Science*, 42(4): 911–37.

Foley, Michael (2009). 'Gordon Brown and the role of compounded crisis in the pathology of leadership decline'. *British Politics*, 4(4): 498–513.

Garrett, R. Sam (2009). *Campaign Crises: Detours on the Road to Congress*. Boulder, CO: Lynne Rienner.

Garrett, R. Sam (2014). 'Crisis-management, marketing, and money in US campaigns'. In Jennifer Lees-Marshment, Brian Conley and Kenneth Cosgrove (eds) *Political Marketing in the US*. New York: Routledge.

Gelders, Dave and Øyvind Ihlen (2010). 'Government communication about potential policies: public relations, propaganda or both?' *Public Relations Review*, 36(1): 59–62.

Germany, Julie (2013). 'Advances in campaign technology'. In Dennis W. Johnson (ed.) *Campaigning for President 2012: Strategy and Tactics*. New York: Routledge, 81–91.

González, Roberto J. (2017). 'Hacking the citizenry?: Personality profiling, "big data" and the election of Donald Trump'. *Anthropology Today*, 33(3): 9–12.

Goot, Murray (1999). 'Public opinion, privatization and the electoral politics of Telstra'. *Australian Journal of Politics and History*, 45(2): 214–38.

Green, Donald P. and Alan S. Gerber (2004). *Get Out the Vote! How to Increase Voter Turnout*, 1st edition. Washington: Brookings Institution Press.

Green, Donald P. and Alan S. Gerber (2015). *Get Out the Vote: How to Increase Voter Turnout*, 3rd edition. Washington: Brookings Institution Press.

Grusell, Marie and Lars Nord (2016). 'Setting the trend or changing the game? Professionalization and digitalization of election campaigns in Sweden'. *Journal of Political Marketing*. doi: 10.1080/15377857.2016.1228555.

Haenschen, Katherine (2016). 'Social pressure on social media: Using Facebook status updates to increase voter turnout'. *Journal of Communication*, 66(4): 542–63.

Harmer, Emily and Dominic Wring (2013). 'Julie and the Cybermums: marketing and women voters in the UK 2010 general election'. *Journal of Political Marketing*, 12(2/3): 262–73.

Hersh, Eitan D. and Brian F. Schaffner (2013). 'Targeted campaign appeals and the value of ambiguity'. *Journal of Politics*, 75(2): 520–34.

Holland, Jack (2012). 'Blair's war on terror: selling intervention to Middle England'. *The British Journal of Politics and International Relations*, 14(1): 74–95.

Hughes, Andrew (2018). *Market Driven Political Advertising: Social, Digital and Mobile Marketing*. Basingstoke, UK: Palgrave.

Johnson, Dennis W. (2013). 'The election of 2012'. In Dennis W. Johnson (ed.) *Campaigning for President 2012: Strategy and Tactics*. New York: Routledge, 1–22.

Kotler, Philip and Eduardo L. Roberto (2002). *Social Marketing: Strategies for Changing Public Behavior*. New York: Free Press.

Kruikemeier, Sanne, Minem Sezgin and Sophie C. Boerman (2016). 'Political microtargeting: Relationship between personalized advertising on Facebook and voters' responses'. *Cyberpsychology, Behavior, and Social Networking*, 19(6): 367–72.

Kudrnác, Ales (2014). 'Case study 6.3 Door-to-door canvassing in local elections: case study of Ružomberok, Slovakia 2010'. In Jennifer Lees-Marshment (ed.) *Political Marketing: Principles and applications*, 2nd edition. New York: Routledge, 195–7.

Lalancette, Mireille and Vincent Raynauld (2017). 'The power of political image: Justin Trudeau, Instagram, and celebrity politics'. *American Behavioral Scientist*. doi: 10.177/0002764217744838.

Lees-Marshment, Jennifer (2008). *Political Marketing and British Political Parties: The Party's Just Begun*, 2nd revised edition. Manchester, UK: Manchester University Press.

Lees-Marshment, Jennifer (2010). 'New Zealand political marketing: marketing communication rather than the product?' In Jennifer Lees-Marshment, Jesper Strömbäck and Chris Rudd (eds) *Global Political Marketing*. London: Routledge, 65–81.

Lees-Marshment, Jennifer (2011). *The Political Marketing Game*. Houndmills, UK and New York: Palgrave Macmillan.

Lees-Marshment, Jennifer, Brian Conley and Kenneth Cosgrove (eds) (2014). *Political Marketing in the US*. New York: Routledge.

Lees-Marshment, Jennifer and Robin T. Pettitt (2010). 'UK political marketing: a question of leadership?' In Jennifer Lees-Marshment, Jesper Strömbäck and Chris Rudd (eds) *Global Political Marketing*. London: Routledge, 113–27.

LeTourneau, Nancy (2018). 'Why was Cambridge Analytica so interested in tapping into our fears? *Washington Monthly*, 21 March 2018. https://washingtonmonthly.com/2018/03/21/why-was-cambridge-analytica-so-interested-in-tapping-into-our-fears/ (accessed 1 September 2018).

Lloyd, Jenny (2009). 'Keeping both the baby and the bathwater: scoping a new model of political marketing communication.' *International Review on Public and Nonprofit Marketing*, 6(2): 119–35.

Loewen, Peter John and Daniel Rubenson (2011). 'For want of a nail: negative persuasion in a party leadership race'. *Party Politics*, 17(1): 45–65.

Marland, Alex (2016). *Brand Command: Canadian Politics and Democracy in the Age of Message Control*. Vancouver: UBC Press.

Marland, Alex and Mireille Lalancette (2014). 'Access Hollywood: celebrity endorsements in American politics'. In Jennifer Lees-Marshment, Brian Conley and Kenneth Cosgrove (eds) *Political Marketing in the US*. New York: Routledge.

Matz, Sibylle C., Michael Kosinski, Gideon Nave and David J. Stillwell (2017). 'Psychological targeting as an effective approach to digital mass persuasion. *Proceedings of the National Academy of Sciences*. doi: 10.1073/pnas.1710966114.

McGough, Sean (2005). 'Political marketing in Irish politics: the case of Sinn Féin'. In Darren G. Lilleker and Jennifer Lees-Marshment (eds) *Political Marketing: A Comparative Perspective*. Manchester, UK: Manchester University Press, 97–113.

McKelvey, Fenwick and Jill Piebiak (2016). 'Porting the political campaign: The NationBuilder platform and the global flows of political technology'. *New Media & Society*, 20(3): 901–18.

McKenzie-Mohr, Doug and William Smith (1999). *Fostering Sustainable Behavior: An Introduction to Community-Based Social Marketing*. Gabriola Island, BC: New Society Publishers.

Mishra, Anubhav A. and Abhinav Mishra (2014). 'National vs. local celebrity endorsement and politics'. *International Journal of Politics, Culture, and Society*, 27(4): 409–25.

Mylona, Ifigeneia (2008). 'SMS in everyday political marketing in Greece'. *Journal of Political Marketing*, 7(3): 278–94.

Newman, Bruce I. (2001). 'An assessment of the 2000 US presidential election: A set of political marketing guidelines'. *Journal of Public Affairs*, 1(3): 210–16.

O'Brien, Diana Z. (2015). 'Rising to the top: Gender, political performance, and party leadership in parliamentary democracies'. *American Journal of Political Science*, 59(4): 1022–39.

O'Leary, Noreen (2009). 'GMMB'. *Mediaweek*, 19(24): AM2.

Panagopoulos, Costas and Shang E. Ha (2015). 'Billboards and turnout: A randomized field experiment'. *Journal of Political Marketing*, 14(4): 391–404.

Papagiannidis, Savvas, Constantinos K. Coursaris and Michael Bourlakis (2012). 'Do websites influence the nature of voting intentions? The case of two national elections in Greece'. *Computers in Human Behavior*, 28(2): 300–7.

Picazo-Vela, Sergio, Marilu Fernandez-Haddad and Luis F. Luna-Reyes (2016). 'Opening the black box: Developing strategies to use social media in government'. *Government Information Quarterly*, 33(4): 693–704.

Rademacher, Eric W. and Alfred J. Tuchfarber (1999). 'Pre-election polling and political campaigns'. In Bruce I. Newman (ed.) *Handbook of Political Marketing*. Thousand Oaks, CA: Sage, 197–222.

Reeves, Peter (2013). 'Local political marketing in the context of the conservative party'. *Journal of Nonprofit & Public Sector Marketing*, 25(2): 127–63.

Ridge-Newman, Anthony and Mary Mitchell (2016). 'Digital political marketing'. In Darren Lilleker and Mark Pack (Eds) *Political Marketing and the 2015 UK General Election*. London: Palgrave Macmillan, 99–116.

Ridout, Travis N. (2014). 'The market research, testing and targeting behind American political advertising'. In Jennifer Lees-Marshment, Brian Conley and Kenneth Cosgrove (eds) *Political Marketing in the US*. New York: Routledge, 220–35.

Robinson, Claire E. (2006). 'Advertising and the market orientation of political parties contesting the 1999 and 2002 New Zealand general election campaigns'. PhD thesis, Massey University, Palmerston North, New Zealand.

Robinson, Claire (2010). 'Political advertising and the demonstration of market orientation'. *European Journal of Marketing*, 44(3/4): 451–9.

Robinson, Claire (2018). 'Chapter 6: Minor Party Campaign Advertising: A Market-Oriented assessment'. In J. Lees-Marshment (ed.) *Political marketing and management in the 2017 New Zealand election*. Basingstoke, UK: Palgrave Macmillan, 85–98.

Ross, Jim (2008). Excerpts from: www.completecampaigns.com/article.asp?articleid=27, origi-nally posted on CompleteCampaigns.com and written by Alex Gorman (accessed 4 March 2008). Now accessible as 'Give Your Volunteers the Tools they Need' blog post, 25 September 2014, http://aristotle.com/blog/2014/09/give-your-volunteers-the-tools-they-need/?articleid=27 (accessed February 2018).

Ryoo, Joseph and Neil Bendle (2017). 'Understanding the social media strategies of US primary candidates'. *Journal of Political Marketing*, 16(3/4): 244–66.

Savigny, Heather and Mick Temple (2010). 'Political marketing models: the curious incident of the dog that doesn't bark'. *Political Studies*, 58(5): 1049–64.

Schweiger, Gunter and Michaela Aadami (1999). 'The nonverbal image of politicians and political parties'. In Bruce Newman (ed.) *The Handbook of Political Marketing*. Thousand Oaks, CA: Sage, 347–64.

Seeman, Thomas J. (2014). 'Case study 6.2 Rivers, kids, and jobs: market-orientated advertising from the Green Party of Aotearoa New Zealand'. In Jennifer Lees-Marshment (ed.) *Political Marketing: Principles and Applications*, 2nd edition. New York: Routledge, 194–5.

Seidman, Steven A. (2010). 'Barack Obama's 2008 campaign for the US presidency and visual design'. *Journal of Visual Literacy*, 29(1): 1–27.

Stephenson, Paul (2013). 'Solidarity as political strategy'. *Public Management Review*, 15(3): 402–15.

Stromer-Galley, Jennifer (2014). *Presidential Campaigning in the Internet Age*. Oxford, UK: Oxford University Press.

Temple, Mick (2010). 'Political marketing, party behaviour and political science'. In Jennifer Lees-Marshment, Jesper Strömbäck and Chris Rudd (eds) *Global Political Marketing*. London: Routledge, 263–77.

Temple, Mick (2013). 'The media and the message'. *Journal of Political Marketing*, 12(2/3): 147–65.

Tracey, Sean (2017). 'Trust, Trump, and the turnout: A marketer's point of view'. *American Behavioral Scientist*, 61(5): 526–32.

Winston, Joel (2016). 'How the Trump campaign built an identity database and used Facebook ads to win the election'. *Medium*, 18 November 2016. https://medium.com/startup-grind/how-the-trump-campaign-built-an-identity-database-and-used-facebook-ads-to-win-the-election-4ff7d2 4269ac#.xpwe08w8b (accessed 12 June 2018).

Rocky Mountain PBS (2012). *World Denver Talks,* broadcast 28 September 2018.

Young, Sally (2005). 'Government advertising cost us dearly'. *The Age,* 30 August 2005. www.theage.com.au/news/opinion/sally-young/2005/08/29/1125302509121.html (accessed 10 April 2008).

Yousaf, Salman (2016). 'Political marketing in Pakistan: Exaggerated promises, delusive claims, marketable development projects and change advocacy'. *Journal of Public Affairs*, 16(2): 140–55.

7 Relational political marketing communication

by Edward Elder and Jennifer Lees-Marshment

Political marketing communication has developed beyond simply selling a product, with a greater strategic focus on relationship building between politicians and the public. These more interactive forms of political communication hold the potential to lift the public from passive consumers to active participants in the communication process, enhancing the public sphere. Web 2.0 and social networking developments have changed communication from a means for elites to sell the public their product to get into office to an opportunity for the public to provide input and feedback before, during and after a politician designs their political product, gets into power and delivers. This chapter examines:

- E-marketing including principles of effective e-marketing, two-way and user-generated relational e-marketing, participatory e-marketing, and e-marketing by challengers and social movements.
- Public relations.
- Interactive and responsive leadership communication.
- Voter responsibility communication.
- Reputation management.
- Political marketing relational communications in the workplace.

E-marketing

E-marketing is communication via digital devices such as mobile phones and the internet that integrates understanding from market research and other marketing concepts. Jackson (2005, 95, 159; 2006) argues that effective e-marketing combines direct marketing and relationship marketing concepts over the long term, rather than just being used in short-term sales campaigning and one-off transactions. In a study of 14 candidates from the 2010 UK general election, one candidate noted that '[e]mail was a bit better at getting to people . . . but I did not start the emails early enough to build up a big database' (Jackson 2013). Individual politicians can use websites and email as an inexpensive and easy means to contact their constituents in a targeted manner to put out unmediated communication over which they have greater control because they can speak directly to constituents. It is also a source of market intelligence to help MPs better represent their constituents, develop their political campaigns and policy stances, and build credibility and a delivery record for re-election.

Principles of effective e-marketing

Jackson (2005) suggests four criteria for effective e-marketing, as seen in Box 7.1.

Box 7.1 Jackson's principles for effective e-marketing in politics

1   E-political marketing is regularly used outside an election campaign.
2   Communication is tailored to the requirements of the receiver.
3   Communication is two-way and not just one-way.
4   It builds 'networks' between an MP and the constituents.

Source: Jackson (2005, 95)

Small's (2012) study of the extent to which Canadian parties' use of Facebook met relationship marketing criteria shows similar findings. Small adapted Jackson's 2006 principles, as seen in Table 7.1.

Small applied this to Canadian political parties in 2010 and found that the first criterion of continual updating was only met by the Liberals. Facebook was rarely used for recruitment by the Canadian parties, with only the Liberals and the Greens featuring a 'take action' tab with links to activities including donating, becoming a member and signing up for an e-newsletter. Small (2012, 203) notes that Facebook's how-to guide for politicians states it 'is a culture of conversations, giving politicians and political campaigns/organisations a huge opportunity to get immediate feedback on various issues'. Comments were allowed on all Facebook pages of the Canadian parties, but they were not interactive – the political elites did not respond to comments made by the public. Only three pages operated a discussion board. The Liberals were the most open to interactivity, offering discussion boards and allowing friends to post their own content on the party page. Thus, the overall pattern was mixed in terms of following a relationship marketing strategy; some did, some did not.

Table 7.1 Small's relationship marketing criteria for Facebook

Continuous	Updated at regular intervals	Yes/No
Value	Information not easily available elsewhere	Yes/No
	Information of relevance to non-members	Yes/No
Recruitment	Membership	Yes/No
	Donations	Yes/No
	Volunteer	Yes/No
	E-newsletter sign-up	Yes/No
	Events	Yes/No
Interactivity	Feedback (Like or Comment)	Yes/No
	Wall post	Yes/No
	Discussion board	Yes/No

Source: Small (2012, 199)

Online communication by individual politicians has been less effective (see Jackson *et al.* 2012). Such principles seem not to have filtered down the different levels of the political system as yet, or perhaps the infrastructure in terms of volunteers, staff, and data collection and analysis is not easy and cheap enough for all levels of politics to use it. Jackson's study of UK politicians' websites found they failed to meet these principles, as did Papagiannidis *et al.*'s (2012) analysis of political candidates' websites in Greece. Jackson's (2013) more recent research found that the internet was still seen as a secondary tool at the local level, as opposed to more traditional forms of direct marketing such as door-knocking and leafleting, during the 2010 UK general election. Websites were more often than not used as another form of one-way communication. Twitter was experimented with. However, candidates seemingly did not believe it offered enough of a direct line to their particular constituents, with one incumbent suggesting only about 5 per cent of her followers actually came from her electorate. Facebook was only used as a marginal tool, with at least two candidates having their accounts run by a friend.

In the United States, Williams and Gulati's (2014) analysis of congressional-level online communication concluded that politicians failed to realise – or at least to operationalise – the potential to build long-term relationships. E-marketing was not being used permanently to build relationships, or interactively, or to build social networks. While some candidates and staff recognised the need to use social media more strategically, most needed to integrate marketing principles within their online communication, such as conducting market intelligence with feedback to the campaign and segmenting the market to target campaign messages to specific groups.

Two-way and user-generated relational e-marketing

As Small's (2012) research highlights, effective e-marketing should utilise interactive and two-way communication, especially through social media. Numerous studies have found a correlation between such communication and political gains. In terms of public relationship building, Painter (2015) found that not only did people who were exposed to the 2012 US presidential candidates' Facebook pages report greater gains in their connection to the candidates than those exposed to their campaigns' websites, but those who engaged (i.e. liking, sharing, commenting) with the candidates' Facebook pages reported even greater gains than those who just observed the posts.

In terms of electoral success, LaMarre and Suzuki-Lambrecht (2013) found in their examination of House of Representative candidates' use of Twitter during the 2010 US mid-term elections that effective Twitter use stems from stakeholder engagement rather than using the platform as another way to release communication, stating that 'the key to Twitter's effectiveness in an election campaign lies in developing large, engaged audiences . . . Namely, developing audience involvement through the list and dialogic functions will likely produce more significant results than simply sending messages via Twitter.' Similar results were found by Kruikemeier (2014), who, in looking at Twitter use in the 2010 Dutch national elections, notes that the level of interactively in a candidate's Twitter use had 'a significant positive impact on the number of preferential votes a candidate receives: candidates that use a more direct way of communicating received more support than those who did not'.

US President Donald Trump's use of Twitter during the 2016 election campaign is a prime example of this working effectively. Zeitzoff (2017) notes that Trump has likely been defined by his use of social media more than any other political leader. And, when comparing the messages of Trump and Clinton through their websites and Twitter, Lee and Lim (2016) found that Trump was far more interactive by the public on Twitter than Clinton. While Clinton's communication was more traditional, controlled and consistent, Trump frequently utilised user-generated content in the form of retweets and replies. Such communication by Trump, where citizens communicate the message that is then promoted by politicians, can appeal to the public by increasing the message's perceived credibility – since it is coming from a third party.

Lilleker (2015) notes that, while political parties in the UK had tried to control the public narrative surrounding their brand in 2008, by the 2010 election campaign they had started to adapt to a more interactive approach. Labour's online communication strategy, for example, included a heavy focus on 'a series of co-produced supportive messages that involve party activists'. This included promoting the hashtags #changewesee, which encouraged supporters to tweet comments with pictures highlighting how the decisions made by the Labour government had resulted in progress for their community, as well as #Labourdoorstep, which promoted on-the-ground canvassing. The user-generated content was then fed directly onto the party's website.

In other words, practitioners should make sure they build interactivity into their digital communication strategies and avoid the less effective one-way communication strategies that are based on the premise of narrative control. But while new media platforms allow for less publicly passive and more interactive communication strategies, political elites have rarely utilised citizen-generated content outside of that which is in line with their own narrative (Miller 2013). Lilleker (2015) argues that political parties in the UK tried to control what user-generated messages were visible to the public through their online platforms in 2008, two years before next election, with little follow-up communication from the parties. User content on parties' websites and social media was often filtered, only showing positive comments, and with little follow-up interaction from party staff or politicians.

Participatory e-marketing

Practitioner Perspective 7.1 on creating volunteer-friendly and online forms of field experience

When you walk into a field office, you have many opportunities . . . You can knock on doors, and they'll have these stats there for you . . . 'here's how you compare to the rest of them'. But it's all very offline . . . so what we set out to do was create that offline field experience online.

Harper Reed, CTO for Barack Obama's 2012 re-election campaign, 2013

I didn't care where . . . what time . . . how you organised, as long as I could track it. . . [so we built] a piece of software that tracked all this and allowed you to match your friends on Facebook with our lists, and we said . . . 'so-and-so is a friend of yours, we think he's unregistered [or undecided], why don't you go get him to register [or be decided]?'

Jim Messina, Obama 2012 Campaign Manager, 2013

Source: Balz (2013)

As Turcotte and Raynauld (2014) suggest, e-marketing can be combined with other aspects of political marketing – such as segmentation, targeting and internal marketing – to create powerful volunteer support-building mechanisms on key political issues, which might be used by parties, interest groups or movements. Thus, e-marketing helps to reinforce existing relationships, and is effective within the long-term context. Indeed, one of the reasons such communication appeals to millennials and the next generation of young voters is that it gives them the opportunity to be active and involved, on their own terms, in a way that suits them.

In 2006, for example, the Democratic National Committee placed its data online for volunteers to access, so they could run canvassing operations, organise meetings and oversee telemarketing themselves. Stirland (2008) notes that it enabled the same old-fashioned organising to be carried out, but with the use of fewer resources. Thus, when Barack Obama became the Democratic presidential nominee, he had the machine already in place to build on, which he used to further recruit volunteers. The campaign's online mechanisms made it easy for volunteers to get involved with the campaign, applying principles from internal marketing and mixing online with old-fashioned field activity (Harfoush 2009). Cogburn and Espinoza-Vasquez (2011) identified how they asked for volunteers' contact details during rallies, then sorted this information geographically, working with their regional coordinators to communicate directly with them after the event to get them more involved. The Obama team also created web-facilitates, hosted meetings, and organised peer-to-peer political campaigning and public education as well as raised donations. Jackson *et al.* (2012, 293) found that the campaign 'adopted key innovations, where my.barackobama.com (MyBo) created literally thousands of participatory opportunities.' Jackson and Lilleker (2014) note that, while the McCain 2008 and Romney 2012 campaigns used online communication to sell their product instead of involving voters in its creation and dissemination, the Obama campaign in both 2008 and 2012 sought to move volunteers up the political loyalty ladder – from being passively engaged to active community members and evangelists. It also helped maintain and enhance the president's relationship with his supporters, demonstrating the importance of relationship marketing.

Likewise, Lilleker (2015) argues that the purist form of interactivity between the parties and the public during the 2010 UK general election was seen in party-centred online community websites such as Labournet, LibDemAct and MyConservatives. Like the Obama campaign's social network, these websites gave supporters a hub to 'interact, create, and join campaigns and upload content in the form of links, campaigning material, profile pictures, and personal information'. Lilleker argues that not only does this allow activists to feel closer to the political brand they are supporting but it also helps demonstrate the party brand as an assessable political community, 'which provides that sense of self-reference and belonging actually and symbolically'. This might have democratic positives by increasing deliberation within political communication and democratic engagement in participation, though it is not without practical problems as it reduces elite control.

E-marketing by challengers and social movements

The ability for political challengers and social movements to effectively use e-marketing as a communication tool has been more mixed. In their examination of House of Representative candidates' use of Twitter during the 2010 US mid-term elections,

LaMarre and Suzuki-Lambrecht (2013) found that incumbents were much more likely to use platforms such as Twitter than their challengers. Thanks to their better name ID, media penetration and resources, incumbents generally had a higher number of followers and enjoyed a higher average number of appearances on followers' lists, 'challenging the assumption that social media level the playing field between known insiders and unknown outsiders'. Similarly, when studying public activity on the 2012 US presidential candidates' Facebook pages, Painter (2015) found that greater gains in their connection to the candidates were found with people interacting with Obama's posts than those interacting with Romney's. As Painter notes, 'Considering that the Obama campaign devoted significantly greater resources to their online strategies than the Romney campaign, this finding is not surprising'.

When interviewing candidates from the 2010 UK general election, Jackson (2013) found that resources and how well the party did in the electorate in the previous election played a major role in the sophistication of campaigns 'in terms of use of segmentation, prior research and more extensive use of direct communications over a longer time both before and during the campaign'. Jackson also notes that in some cases challengers have other obligations, such as day jobs, which limits the amount of time, and thus the amount for sophisticated campaigning, they can do.

Conversely, Zeitzoff (2017) argues that non-incumbents can use e-marketing, such as communication through blogs and influential online users, to get their message out indirectly through traditional media outlets. Zeitzoff argues that:

> especially during conflicts or contentious events, challengers are able to get their side of the story out to the public by seeding it in blogs and social media that are then picked up by mainstream domestic and international media . . . This mechanism is particularly relevant to protestors and challengers in autocratic regimes, where social media provides an alternative outlet to closed off media outlets.

Furthermore, Turcotte and Raynauld's (2014) work on the use of Twitter by the populist Tea Party shows how online communication may be used to enable political movements to engage in marketed messages among the grass-roots. More recently, the organisers of the Women's March protests across the US used social media to promote the protests, resulting in a collective attendance of somewhere between 3.2 million and 5.2 million people during the first set of marches in January 2017. The organisers also used this engagement to build a database of email addresses in an effect to recruit members for follow-up activity and to identify women to run for political office (Zeitzoff 2017).

Movements can use social media to generate highly targeted, emotive communication among individuals at the grass-roots level and to build up grass-roots support. Social media enables and encourages followers to communicate between themselves to build up a movement, instead of relying on one charismatic leader: a hyper-decentralised network of individuals and organisations. Other movements may use e-marketing in this way to bring attention to, and increase support for, neglected issues among the general public and elites – such as the Me Too movement utilising the Twitter hashtag #metoo to raise awareness of the history and prevalence of sexual harassment and assault in many workplaces; interest groups advocating gay marriage and wanting to raise awareness of child trafficking; or increasing public support for policy measures such as emissions trading schemes and carbon taxes to halt climate change.

Public relations

Public relations (PR) is the initiation of a series of communication events designed to build and maintain a positive relationship between a political organisation/figure and its/their stakeholders. It is carried out over the long term, involves multiple events, and is not confined to an election campaign or a single piece of communication, such as advertising. As Strömbäck and Kiousis (2011, 1–2) note, although the academic study of political PR is relatively new, the practice is old, going back as far as 64 BCE, through the American Revolution and to the work of Edward Bernays in the mid-20th century. However, most literature on PR is about the corporate sector, so their book sought to outline the nature of the field and the practice of political PR.

Strömbäck and Kiousis (2011, 4) review definitions of PR and note that there are several key characteristics running through such definitions, and thus PR is about:

- the management of communication between an organisation and its publics (or stakeholders);
- the relationships between an organisation and its publics, which should be mutually beneficial; and
- the management of the reputation of an organisation.

Political PR goes beyond media management and encompasses interactive, ongoing communication to develop long-term relationships. In their studies of variables affecting the relationship between citizens and political parties during the 2008 US presidential election campaign and the following debate over health care reform, Seltzer and Zhang (2011a; 2011b) found that perceptions of engaging in two-way symmetrical communication (where the organisation shows a willingness to listen and substantively respond to key stakeholders) with one's political party had a significant impact on perceptions of their relationship with said party, much more so than interpersonal communication (one-off face-to-face, telephone) communication or mediated communication (television, radio). They therefore argue that, although mediated and interpersonal communication may help with short-term maintenance of the relationship between citizens and a political organisation leading up to an election, utilising two-way symmetrical communication with voters over the long term will help lay the groundwork for maintaining a healthy relationship between the two groups by facilitating better understanding and agreement around issues of mutual concern.

Political PR is therefore defined as 'the management process by which an organisation or individual actor for political purposes, through purposeful communication and action,

Table 7.2 Ledingham and Bruning's five dimensions of an organisation-public relationship

Dimension	Operationalised by the organisation:
Trust	doing what it says it will do.
Openness	sharing their plans for the future with the public.
Involvement	being involved in the welfare of the community.
Investment	investing in the welfare of the community.
Commitment	being committed to the welfare of the community.

Source: Adapted from Ledingham (2003, 185)

seeks to influence and to establish, build, and maintain beneficial relationships and reputations with its key publics to help support its mission and achieve its goals' (Strömbäck and Kiousis 2011, 8). Because PR should be mutually beneficial, it is about organisations and their publics understanding each other's interests and reducing the conflict between them; and thus, Ledingham and Bruning (1998) argue, there are five key dimensions to an effective PR relationship: trust, openness, involvement, investment and commitment (see Table 7.2).

There are a range of different publics, which can be segmented in a number of different ways. Hong *et al.* (2012), when looking at how to segment the public for effective communication to improve public participation and trust, outline two board publics that need to be communicated to differently in order to build participation and trust:

- *Underserved inactive majority*, who have a lower level of trust in government, and, thus, the goal is to encourage more participation and build greater trust between the government and them. This group generally needs to be reached through more traditional mass media platforms as they are likely to engage in passive information processing and less likely to actively search for information.
- *Satisfied active public*, who have a higher average level of trust in government, and, thus, the goal there is more focus on maintaining participation and trust. This group needs to be engaged with more often, in a timely manner, and more often through new media platforms, such as websites and online forums, that allow for more active and two-way communication.

Lieber and Golan (2011, 56) divide the public more on the basis of the nature of the public such as:

- *Non-publics*: those that don't face any similar problem; or if they do, they don't recognise it or organise to do anything about it.
- *Latent publics*: those that face the same problem but do not recognise it or do anything about it.
- *Aware publics: those that* have the problem and are aware of it, but fail to act on it.
- *Active publics*: those who have the problem, recognise it and seek to do something about it.

Marketers therefore need to identify and monitor the behaviour of different segments of the public in order to decide how to use PR to build beneficial relationships with them. Jackson (2012, 271) notes that it is not about promoting a specific political product but building and maintaining positive relationships with key audiences through dialogue, consideration of the receiver of communication and reputation management. There are several aspects to PR which Jackson explores through identifying the different schools of thought in the literature, as seen in Box 7.2.

Box 7.2 Jackson's political PR approaches

1   **Relations with publics** – focuses on using research to identify the best message to send to the right audience.
2   **Grunigian** – strategic two-way communication based on feedback to build positive relationships.

3 **Hype** – seeks to make a noise through publicity for short-term benefit.

4 **Persuasion** – seeks to change opinions and behaviours through promotion campaigns.

5 **Relational** – develops influential relationships through issue and crisis management to ensure a positive long-term reputation.

6 **Reputation management** – similar to relational except includes other activities such as lobbying and aims to shape public opinion and organisational image.

7 **Relations in publics** – use of issues management and internal communications to develop a public sphere to debate free-flowing information.

8 **Community building** – creating a sense of a community through two-way communication, issues management and community affairs.

Source: Adapted from Jackson (2012, 273–4)

The pragmatic and democratic implications of these vary; some are closer to more conventional views of PR as short-term persuasion, whereas others are more about fostering true dialogue, debate and free information, and, through this, positive long-term relationships. Parties, candidates and governments may choose different approaches at different times – reputation management may be more useful for governments than opposition parties, for example. Jackson (2012) applied these concepts to candidates standing for 12 seats in Devon, a region in south-west England, but found that there was very little evidence of the more relational or community building types of PR, with greater focus on persuasion but also reputation management, while less indication of hype forms of PR.

Political PR includes a range of tools such as information subsidies, agenda building and message framing. Information subsidies make it easy or low cost for people to get access to information. Lieber and Golan (2011, 60) discuss how the Obama presidency used social media to make information about the health care bill easy to access; given it was available 24/7 it helped ensure anyone could access information whenever they liked and thus help create a consensus towards supporting the legislation.

Message framing tries to influence how an issue, event or situation is perceived among elites as well as the public. Hallahan (2011) notes how linguist George Lakoff trained the US Democrats to use certain words, narratives and metaphors to convey the desired story over the long term; and after worldwide international talks, world leaders will speak in public to convey their interpretation of events. Governments can also frame attributes, such as a rising number of homeowners being a good sign for the economy; or they can frame the size of a risk. Framing can also influence perceptions of responsibility such as whether the public should blame a political leader for a bad situation. Hallahan (2011) points out how, when there was a big oil spill in the Gulf of Mexico in 2010, framing was used so that BP was to blame, not President Obama, although there was critique that the US government should have regulated the industry more heavily and enacted greater attacks on BP with regard to fixing the leak.

However, Strömbäck and Kiousis (2011, 18–19) argue that the political environment is more contentious and may present challenges to this more positive form of PR. In their investigation of the role of relationships, authenticity and genuineness in public relations messaging, Sweetser and Tedesco (2014) argued that political-public relations is 'still a very traditional form of public relations'. They note that tactics such as controlling the message and shaping the media environment, as well as the importance of information subsidies such as speeches, are still relevant and effective. Sweetser and Tedesco also note that partisanship still plays a major role in the perception of candidates, more so than the assessment of personal qualities such as authenticity and genuineness, and that external communication can have a major impact on candidate perceptions.

Furthermore, it does not always succeed. Waymer (2013) notes that while the US government, as a democratic institution, should provide a prime example of relationship management, polls suggest almost nine of ten Americans distrust the government to do the right thing. Indeed, Tedesco (2011, 84) discusses US presidents' ability to influence the media agenda and notes that, despite the central position of the president in political discourse, their scope to control the agenda is constrained; even after the September 11th terrorist attack in 2001, President George W. Bush did not demonstrate agenda building capacity. Such capacity depends on the president's approval ratings and personality, and the issue, among other factors. Similarly, Eshbaugh-Soha (2011) notes how the US president utilises a communications office, press office and office of public liaison in order to engage in political PR. Such extensive staff enables strategic and planned communication to reach out to different publics and respond to public expectations. This helps the president manage public expectations, convey the work the president does and build support for policies. However, the evidence suggests the ability of such staff to influence the agenda has been limited and recommends that presidential PR needs to become more targeted to narrow groups.

Additionally, the practice of political PR is often very limited and narrow in scope. Xifra (2010) notes that political PR is also not just about media management or a set of techniques, despite practitioners they interviewed in Spain claiming so, thus indicating that one barrier to effective political PR is the limited understanding of party staff involved in communications. Baines (2011, 116) observes that the UK Labour government 1997–2010 was criticised for engaging in more persuasive forms of PR to influence its image through symbols rather than substantive behaviour.

Interactive and responsive leadership communication

Lloyd's (2012) analysis of communication in the 2010 UK general election concludes that voters thought there were more opportunities for two-way communication with politicians through platforms such as Twitter, telephone, email and talk radio. With these opportunities now available, political leadership communication needs to be interactive and convey responsiveness more effectively to show they have listened, reflected and acted on dialogue with the public in a meaningful way.

Robinson (2012) argues that it is important that political communication explicitly shows leaders interacting with voters, including waving and making physical contact such as shaking hands and hugging. Robinson advises that, for example, images of leaders in small groups suggests they can relate more widely to and care for others. Furthermore, Robinson's research suggests that other visual communication – such as facial expressions and hand gestures, camera shot type (i.e. use of close-up shots), the clothes the leader wears, and the setting – can also influences how close the viewer feels to the leader. She cites the example of UK Conservative leader David Cameron in the 2010 election without a tie, in a middle-class family backyard, talking directly to camera. Such communication is designed to suggest a politician is honest, friendly and trustworthy – all in an effort to seem more 'in touch' with the public.

But assuming office introduces political leaders to a whole new set of social, political and logistical constraints not present in opposition (Ormrod 2006), and such constraints can hurt a governing leader's ability to maintain the image of being 'in touch' with their public (Lees-Marshment 2009). Recent research suggests that governing leaders do not have to blindly follow public opinion to be perceived as being in touch, as long as their communication suggests they are talking with the public, rather than at them. Such practices also allow governing leaders to show strong, decisive and honest leadership (Scammell 2007). Elder (2016), therefore, puts forward a model for how to convey a market-orientation once a leader is in power (see Table 7.3).

Elder argues that political leaders need to adopt more reflective forms of communication, such as communicating respectful acknowledgement of public concerns and criticism. But governing leaders need to do this while also communicating their leadership and authenticity, which has historically been difficult for governing leaders to balance. Former New Zealand Prime Minister John Key's communication around increasing the national rate of Goods and Services Tax (GST) in 2010 provides an example. On this issue, Key would often explicitly outline the arguments against raising GST expressed by detractors, often with the caveat that he understood why people had those concerns. After acknowledging and addressing these concerns, Key would make his argument for the change in policy, despite these concerns and criticisms. Most importantly, Key's ability

Table 7.3 Elder's Contemporary Governing Leaders' Communication Model

Elder's Contemporary Governing Leaders' Communication Model		
Quality	**Goal**	**Common ways to communicate**
Responsiveness	**Communicate the governing leader is listening to the public**	*Verbal* ➤ *Start frequent communication early on in the decision making process* ➤ *Maintain rhetoric encouraging public feedback and debate* ➤ *Retell ordinary peoples' stories* *Visual* ➤ *Visual evidence of the leader with members of the public*
	Communicate respectful acknowledgement of public concerns and criticism	*Respectfully explain* ➤ *What the public are concerned about* ➤ *Why they have this concern* ➤ *Why the governing leader disagrees* *Other verbal* ➤ *Communicate potential solutions to public concerns*
	Communicate an emotional bond between the governing leader and the public	*Verbal* ➤ *Suggest togetherness, affinity or an understanding of the public* ➤ *Communicate end goals and aspirations that resonate with the public* ➤ *Show reflection on hard yet necessary decisions*

(continued)

Table 7.3 (continued)

Elder's Contemporary Governing Leaders' Communication Model

Quality	Goal	Common ways to communicate
Leadership	**Communicate leadership strength**	*Verbal* ➢ *Communicate personal conviction* ➢ *Strong and authoritative tone of voice* ➢ *Use language cues associated with determination and strength* ➢ *Not attacking the Opposition* *Visual* ➢ *Squared shoulders* ➢ *Dark formal clothing* ➢ *Strong facial expressions* ➢ *Firm hand gestures* ➢ *In front of group/ focal point of imagery*
	Communicate leadership com petence	*Verbal* ➢ *Communicate delivery, the reasoning behind and the benefits of the decision* ➢ *Suggest relationship with members of other political parties, branches of government and stakeholder groups* ➢ *Discuss other potential options* *Visual* ➢ *Imagery of leader working constructively with other political elites*
Credibility	**Communicate honesty**	*Verbal* ➢ *Be open, honest, and encouraging of media and public questioning* ➢ *Communicate challenges to delivery* *Communicate drawbacks of decisions* *Visual* ➢ *Maintain reasonable eye contact* ➢ *Lean forward*
	Communicate authenticity and relatability	*Verbal* ➢ *Communicate non-political personality* ➢ *Speak with a cadence that does not sound scripted* *Visual* ➢ *Open arms and hand gestures* ➢ *Lighter coloured, less formal clothing* ➢ *Smile*

to promote his authenticity through subtle cues, such as his less formal choice of language and the use of close-up camera shots to simulate closeness, helped him gain the public trust needed to make policies that were not necessarily in line with public opinion. In other words, even if the public did not agree with Key's decision, they believed he was doing it for the right reasons – to achieve the goals they shared.

Elder (2018) notes that Bill English, John Key's successor, had tried to present a more personable public image through imagery of himself as a family man during the 2017 New Zealand general election. But English was less responsive when the concerns and hardships of the public were brought to his attention – instead focusing heavily on his role as the architect behind New Zealand's post-2008 recession recovery through statistics–heavy policy language. In essence, English followed a more traditional communication strategy, which highlighted the positives while disregarding or ignoring the negatives. Conversely, English's Labour Party opponent in that campaign, Jacinda Ardern, had tried to mitigate questions around her leadership strength and competence through communication, but struggled due to her party's reversal on a key policy – seemingly due to attacks from Key and National. While Labour had experienced a surge of momentum under Ardern's leadership, Ardern was hurt by her lack of a long-established leadership image. That said, Ardern took advantage of the fact that she was not in government. While English tried to downplay the concerns and hardships the public voiced, Ardern acknowledged them, and used them to present an aspirational view of the future under her leadership. Furthermore, through consistent subtle visual and verbal cues, Ardern was able to let her natural personability promote her authenticity for her.

Trust, authenticity and credibility are vital to the long-term relationship between politicians and the public. If the public do not believe that the messenger has credibility, they are unlikely to believe the message (Van Zuydam and Hendriks 2018). In contemporary politics, where the public expect more dialogue-driven communication, trust, authenticity and credibility can effectively be built through communication that is less micro-managed and highlights a politician's non-political personality. Sweetser and Tedesco (2014) note that, while communication plays an important role in the relationship between political parties and the public, this connection is more effectively maintained when politicians' messages are voiced in a way that is reminiscent of the way citizens talk to their friends, rather than through the use of traditional political communication. For example, Lee and Lim (2016) note that while Trump's communication during the 2016 presidential campaign was undisciplined and inconsistent across platforms, his communication style of was often framed as authentic, even if not always honest.

Practitioner Perspective 7.2 on authenticity on trust

I think the coin of the realm today is authenticity. And I value my communications staff, but I tell all of my colleagues that they should be sending less of their communications through their policy communications staff. That, ultimately, it gets sort of whitewashed to the point that it's not you any longer . . . We have to be authentic, we have to be real. I make mistakes on Twitter, I do. There are a lot of times where I send something out that I regret. But people know that it's ultimately me. In the end, my constituency in Connecticut, I think, will excuse me for maybe not being 100% aligned with their issues if they know that what I'm doing comes from my heart and my gut.

Chris Murphy, Democratic Senator for Connecticut

Source: Favreau et al. (2017)

Again, social media plays a major role in the growing importance and effectiveness of such communication. In looking at Twitter use in the 2010 Dutch national elections, Kruikemeier (2014) notes that the platform encourages political elites to utilise more personalised communication, allowing greater focus on politicians' private lives, as well as on their emotions and feelings. Unlike traditional mass media platforms, where professionalised political communication is surrounded by professionalised communication in other forms (i.e. adverts for soap), more personalised forms of communication need to be used in order to fit with the more personalised content that inhabits social media, such as status updates and photos from friends. Take the example of Beto O'Rourke's first advert as the Democratic candidate in the Texas senate election race in 2018 (O'Rourke 2018). The Twitter post for the advert itself promotes it as 'filmed using an iPhone and was created entirely with live stream footage from our travels to all 254 counties of Texas'. The advert, predominately featuring low-quality footage (and sound) of O'Rourke interacting with members of the public, has received over 71,000 likes, 34,000 shares and 2,100 comments as of August 2018. On the other hand, if political communication on these platforms resembles the professional communication seen in newspapers, news soundbites and television commercials, it will likely look unnatural, overly planned and out of place – hindering its ability to establish or maintain a connection between the politician and the public.

Furthermore, Lilleker (2015) notes how the communication of politicians' non-political personalities can help make their personal brand more distinctive from the brand of their party. During the 2010 UK general election, for example, certain politicians effectively used posts on these platforms – and discussions with people engaging with their posts – to communicate things such as their interest in books, music and films, and their sporting activities. Thus, Lilleker notes, '[social media] enables [politicians] to stress who they are as a person, an element of branding not really available to political parties. MPs are able to provide the vividness and telepresence central to true interactivity and crucial for maximizing the positive impressions visitors may take away'.

The context surrounding the issue the leader is communicating about should also determine how communication conveying responsiveness, leadership and credibility is balanced. This includes the public persona/brand of the governing leader, and the salience and type of issue being discussed, as well has how much control the government has over the communication process. Importantly, timing should play a role in which aspect of a governing leader's qualities should be emphasised the most when making a decision on a salient issue, as outlined in Figure 7.1.

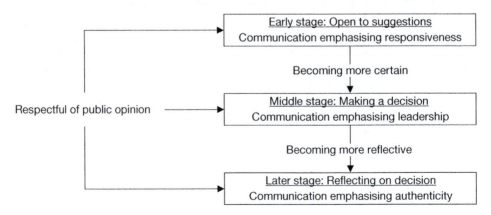

Figure 7.1 The change in governing leaders' communication of decisions over time

Source: based on Elder (2016), 127

In government, communicating leadership is important as politicians cannot simply research the market and offer voters what they want. George W. Bush, for example, ran in both 2000 and 2004 on a platform that included Social Security reform as a policy offering, yet never managed to implement it. Modern political leadership thus calls for a more modern form of communication. More hierarchical and authoritative forms of leadership communication such as: 'I am the leader, I need to follow my conviction' no longer prove effective. Leaders need to find new forms of communication to convey the realities and challenges that leadership in government necessitates. Obama's mini-documentary called *The Road We've Travelled* did this by discussing the difficulties of being president; it helped remind voters so their judgement on his performance could be conducted within the right context. This is also important for delivery marketing, which will be discussed in the next chapter.

Voter responsibility communication

As outlined in the first chapter, there has been a move from transaction-based campaigning to transformational campaigning, whereby voters are called to action to get involved in campaigning and government. Obama used the word 'we' – *Yes WE can* – in his 2008 campaign, but also in his 2012 re-election campaign, where he said: 'If there's even one thing we can do – even one life we can save – we have an obligation to try'. When calling for volunteers to get involved again in 2012, a series of ads were launched saying 'Are you in?', and supporters talked about how Obama could not do it all himself, despite the fact that he was president; it was up to his supporters to take the lead to win re-election. Similarly, he issued an advert during the election called *Young Americans are Greater Together* that discussed the achievements of Obama's first administration which they themselves should be proud of. Johnson (2012, 211) notes that campaigns are becoming open-sourced in that volunteers are getting involved in campaign design and implementation, and this holds the potential for voters to feel they are participating in the campaign. They can share their ideas online with candidates, talk with others, share their experiences and feel a sense of ownership.

Reputation management

Reputation is the overall assessment the public might make of all the information they receive about a politician or political organisation – a wide range of sources including imagery, party origins, its policies, speeches, advertising, media commentary and personal discussions (see Davies and Mian 2010, 345). Van Zuydam and Hendriks (2018) argue that to gain or maintain a reputation for competence, caring and trustworthiness through communication, political leaders need to be able to:

- Reroute critique that might damage their reputation by providing counter-evidence and by staying away from the language that resembles the critique itself.
- Show initiative when answering questions to make sure the answers given connect to the underlying frames and values of the leader's coherent narrative and vision. In doing so, leaders can show they understand what is going on, why, and what needs to be done to address problems.
- Communicate clarity by using less formal 'political' language and through concrete and relatable examples, thus allowing them to clarify their views and make them more tangible for the public.

In their examination of the Dutch parliamentary election campaign of 2010, Van Zuydam and Hendriks note how the leader of the People's Party for Freedom and Democracy, Mark Rutte, was able to transform his image from a 'collegiate boy and eternal bachelor . . . to being considered the next prime minister: a smart, well-informed debater who would take care of individual citizens' (economic) concerns'. Part of this change in reputation over the course of the campaign came from his ability to avoid reaffirming critique by repeating the language of the critique, such as the accusation that he was turning his back on the weak. When challenged, Rutte instead rerouted the critique from who would pay the price for any pain measures needed during the economic crisis to who needs to be protected. Furthermore, Rutte proactively answered questions from journalists in a well-informed way that all connected to his underlying theme of a 'responsible society'. Importantly, while Labour Party Leader Job Cohen used vague, abstract language, seemingly without knowledge of the consequences of his proposals, Rutte utilised shorter sentences, palatable language and concrete examples to illustrate his awareness of the consequences of his proposals.

Government itself needs to use marketing communication to manage its reputation over the long term. Whereas crisis communication, discussed in the previous chapter, is very focused and short term, reputation management is, like PR, about efforts to support the brand's image over the long term. Once a politician is in power, they are held more responsible for what happens and what goes wrong. Managing problems is, therefore, even more important as they can damage the overall image of credibility of a government, which relates to delivery and trust.

In government, consultants work to maintain a leader's image, even where scandals and failures of policy occur. The same management of a politician's personal characteristics in a campaign for office can occur in power. Newman (1999, 88) observes how Bill Clinton's advisors dealt with a number of scandals during his presidency 'by carefully crafting an image of himself as leader in charge and almost above the rumour mongering of the media about his sex life'. He focused on what was important and, amazingly, he did not lose public support, despite continual criticism from the opposition.

Practitioner Perspective 7.3 on handling scandals in government

It told people [Bill Clinton's] still working on the business of the government . . . Sam Donaldson would ask him some latest question about Ken Star and he would say 'Sam, I know you've got a job to do, it's your job to ask that question. Here's my job, it's to make sure these children have access to good affordable healthcare. And that's what I'm going to focus on. So you focus on what you want.' . . . It was exactly the kind of message that had sustained him in his campaigns when he had scandals. But then also, it's what voters wanted to know.

Paul Begala, counsellor to the President 1997–1999

Source: *Conversations with Bill Kristol* (2015)

Davies and Mian (2010, 345) discuss the reputation of UK parties in 2001 and 2005, and note how the Liberal Democrat Party's reputation was of being moderate and informal, and the Conservatives' chic, more ruthless, quite macho and less agreeable relative to their other scores. Labour was seen as more competent and enterprising in 2001. In party systems such as the UK's, the reputation of the party is affected by that of the leader, and vice versa; they are separate but linked.

As discussed in previous chapters, communication was used to try to restore Tony Blair's relationship with voters in 2004–2005 because it had been damaged as he became increasingly dismissive of public input and argued he was the leader and knew best what was right for the country. Communication enacted for the reconnection strategy sought to change the way Blair spoke and appeared to listen to voters; he was therefore pictured receiving strong public criticism, and when he spoke he acknowledged public concern with his decisions and showed respect for those who opposed him, and he used phrases such as 'working in partnership with the public'. This reconnection strategy helped to rehabilitate Blair's overall image. Scammell's (2008) research identified that Labour improved its opinion poll rating over the campaign, increasing its lead over the Conservatives as the best party to deal with the issues of the economy, health and education; and Blair improved his advantage over the opposition leader Michael Howard. It increased the female vote by 8 per cent. After winning the 2005 election, Mr Blair said outside Number 10: 'I have listened and I have learned. And I have a very clear idea of what the British people now expect from this government for a third term'.

Political marketing relational communications in the workplace

There are at least four common job roles related to relation and interactive political marketing communication: communication advisors, digital advisors, public/community engagement officers, and government relations. The skills needed in these jobs include time management and organisational skills (including flexibility and adaptability), with the ability to multi-task, juggle projects and work to strict deadlines. This is due to the fact that such jobs are often not based on a strict 9-to-5 work structure, but rather project oriented. Further details on each type are below. This shows that many of the tasks involved in these jobs overlap, so those wishing to get into this area of work should aim to develop a broad set of skills.

Communications advisors

Being a communications advisor to a political party, campaign, government department, NGO or non-profit involves offering advice and assistance to the communications manager in the planning and delivering of communication on projects and programmes across the organisation in order to achieve their goals. Such projects and programmes often include developing and executing engagement best practices to connect stakeholders and the general public with the organisation, in terms of logistical communication, reputation management, and relationship building and maintenance. These roles also often include identifying potential public relations risks and assisting in addressing them. The desired knowledge and experience for communications advisors jobs include writing and editing skills – as well as the ability to make complex subjects clear and palatable – knowledge of communications and engagement tools, and experience building relationships with external stakeholders as well as with internal staff. It is also often desirable for communications advisors to be fluent in digital technology given the increasing amount of politically oriented communication (and communication more broadly) that is done online.

Digital advisors

Being a digital advisor to a political party, campaign, government department, NGO or non-profit involves providing advice and assistance in the development of broader online strategies and narratives to achieve the organisation's goals. In particular, this work often includes developing and editing content with the goal of provoking action from the receiver – such as donating, fundraising, canvassing, spreading the word – as well as deepening engagement with key stakeholders and the public on a range of issues. Internally, this job also often includes assisting staff who are less technically proficient with tech-related issues, as well as helping in the development and maintenance of databases and segmentation to ensure the right communication is delivered to the right stakeholders and publics. The knowledge and experience required for digital advisors jobs includes having a broad understanding of digital capabilities and the digital environment they are to be utilised in (i.e. understanding of online usability). Such jobs also often require technical proficiency in areas such as web design and web and media editing, and data analytics, as well as the ability to use certain types of online tools such as customer relationship management technologies. Like communications advisors, these jobs also often require good written communication skills, especially how to effectively write for online content (which is different than writing for print), as well as relationship management with internal and external stakeholders.

Public/community engagement officer

One job relating more specifically to the public relations side of political marketing is that of a public or community engagement officer. The main task in these jobs is often to establish and maintain effective relationships with stakeholders to promote, support, and integrate community and stakeholder involvement into governance and/or decision making. A big part of these roles also has a relational market intelligence aspect to it, as it involves making sure key stakeholders' opinions are collected and taken into consideration when the organisation makes a decision. These roles also often involve the planning, developing and implementation of strategies, programmes, policies, procedures and protocols to help facilitate said involvement. Jobs adverts in this area often ask for applicants with great listening skills, as well as both written and verbal communication. Since public or community engagement officer roles can involve collaborating on field data, the ability to analyse data and come up with solutions to potential problems is also preferred. Thus, being able to utilise marketing principles to create a successful plan, coordinate with other organisations and generally have the ability to build and maintain relationships with people at different levels of the organisation/government and with the public is key.

Government relations

A somewhat similar job is in government relations. Here, rather than focusing on politicians developing a relationship with the public, stakeholders develop a relationship with politicians to achieve an organisation's end goals. This involves supporting clients in managing communications with government, including talking with government staff and politicians about their organisation's or client's interests as well as relaying information back to the organisation/client and their respective stakeholders. Jobs in this area also involve attending meetings briefings and hearings on behalf of clients, assisting in event planning and management, researching policy issues relating to the organisation's subject/issue area, and identifying possible funding opportunities. As 'Jen', the Director of Federal Government Affairs for Land O'Lakes Inc, commented, 'Most days I'm rarely in my office. I'm very reliant on my Blackberry and I am advocating directly for our members' (Land O'Lakes Inc 2012). Skills required include the ability to develop and maintain interpersonal relationships with numerous clients, stakeholders and political staff. These jobs also require excellent written, editing and speaking skills, as well as quantitative and qualitative analytical skills.

Summary

This chapter has explored more relational forms of political marketing communication, including e-marketing, public relations and reputation management by political leaders, political parties and governments. This type of communication involves a longer-term commitment and seeks to build and maintain positive relationships between politicians and the public. It is also more interactive, as it enables the public to communicate with the politician and can be used to stimulate face-to-face communication and volunteer participation. A best practice guide to relational forms of political marketing communication is given in Box 7.3.

Box 7.3 Best practice guide to relational political marketing communication

1　Treat the public as active participants rather than passive consumers in the communication process.
2　Understand that using new technology is not in itself as important as using it in the right way and connecting it to an effective and strategic brand.
3　Utilise e-marketing over the long term, not just during election campaigns, to build relationships that seem more authentic and less transactional.
4　Treat e-marketing as a primary communication avenue, rather than a supplementary or secondary avenue to the broader traditional communication strategy.
5　Utilise two-way and user-generated online communication tools to help make the public, and particularly supporters, feel involved and listened to.
6　Utilise e-marketing to build and reinforce existing relationships with supporters, allowing interaction and stimulating volunteer involvement.
7　Allow space for supporters to build relationships among themselves to further promote the feeling of acceptance and involvement.
8　Create a PR strategy to suit the nature of the organisation's or political figures' publics (non, latent, aware and active).
9　In government, choose the PR strategy to suit the goals – while listening and responding to feedback helps to build positive relationships, if the goal is to implement chosen policies, persuasive and hype approaches are more suitable to help maintain support and avoid crisis.
10　Utilise media platforms that allow two-way dialogue-driven communication as a form of relationship building, leadership image definition and as a form of market research.
11　Politicians need to be visually shown interacting with the public to seem relatable and in touch.

---

12 Leaders in power need to use responsive communication that conveys responsiveness, leadership and authenticity.
13 On social media, utilise less polished production values to reflect the content surrounding it.
14 Utilise less formal political language to make content palatable.

66
99
Discussion points

1 Discuss examples of e-marketing that you have seen recently, or in recent elections, and how they relate to or deviate from some of the prescriptive criteria noted.
2 Discuss the potential advantages and disadvantages of newer forms of e-marketing for non-incumbents (challengers) and how the disadvantages might be overcome.
3 What is political PR and how can it help create positive relationships between the government and the people?
4 Identify the non-publics, latent publics, aware publics and active publics for a party or politician.
5 Discuss the potential and limitations for political PR to help create and maintain a positive reputation for politicians and governments.
6 What is interactive political communication? Think of some examples from recent elections.
7 Discuss how politicians benefit, when it comes to decision making, from having established long-term credibility and public trust through communication.
8 Discus examples where you have seen a politician's communication on an issue or decision change over time. What changed about their communication? Why do you think it changed?
9 Discuss examples of communication you have seen shared online. What aspects of relationship marketing might have motivated people to share them?
10 Discuss whether voter responsibility communication will expand in the coming years.
11 Discuss examples of democratic and undemocratic relational and interactive political marketing communication in practice. What impacts could these examples have on public engagement in politics or political decision making?
12 Has trust in political institutions increased? If so, can this in some way be attributed to relational political marketing communication? If not, why hasn't relational political marketing communication helped?

Assessment questions

Essay/exam

1 What are the principles of effective e-marketing, and to what extent do parties and candidates follow these in their online communication?
2 Discuss why less formal and more personalised communication has become more important in 21st-century political-public relationship management.

3   Define the nature of political PR and explore how politicians and governments have sought to use it to achieve more positive relationships with their publics.
4   Explain why political PR is not about promoting a product but building positive relationships, using theory and empirical examples to support your answer.
5   Explain and illustrate Jackson's different political PR approaches.
6   Note the three broader qualities leaders need to convey to the public to promote their market-orientation in government and why different qualities are more important to communicate at different times.
7   Discuss the potential and limitations for political leaders to use interactive communication.
8   Discuss and critique the ways in which reputation management has been used to promote or restore a leader's image in office.

Applied

1   Apply Jackson's relationship marketing email criteria to the use of email by elected representatives, and discuss how effectively they are using email, making recommendations for improvement and further development.
2   Assess a party's or a politician's Facebook page against the relationship marketing criteria by Small (2012), and make recommendations for future development.
3   Use Ledingham and Bruning's five dimensions of an organisation-public relationship to evaluate a current government's ability to develop a relationship with voters.
4   Identify the publics that a political leader or government needs to build a positive relationship using Lieber and Golan's (2011) explanation, and critique how they have used political PR to reach each one, making suggestions for improvement.
5   Assess which of Jackson's political PR approaches a government uses, with what impact and, therefore, which seems to be the most effective.
6   Critique the range of political PR activities used by a recent or current government and make suggestions for how they might improve their strategy in future.
7   Devise a PR plan for a local politician, using guidelines and ideas from the cases presented in this textbook.
8   Apply Elder's Contemporary Governing Leaders' Communication Model to the verbal and visual communication of a governing leader in their second or third term in office.

Case study

Case study 7.1 Communicating contemporary market-oriented governing leadership: Justin Trudeau 2015–2017

By Danielle Parshotam (University of Auckland) and Edward Elder (University of Auckland)

Background

During the 2015 Canadian federal election, Liberal Party Leader Justin Trudeau experienced international accolade for his progressive policies and authentic image (Mandel 2015). With an election platform committed to offering 'real change' and a dedication to engaging and listening to his constituents, Trudeau was elected the 23rd Prime Minister of Canada following a nine-year Conservative Party reign. After assuming office in November 2015, however, Trudeau and the new Liberal Government had to urgently address a lagging economy (Armstrong 2016) and deal with a new set of logistical challenges that were not present during his time in opposition or through the campaign. This case study examines the extent to which Trudeau in his first year in office followed the Contemporary Governing Leaders' Communication Model, outlined earlier in this chapter, in relation to his verbal communication in 27 media texts on Canada's lagging economy.

Case study

Responsiveness

In addition to his continual willingness to listen to the public in order to make the most effective and responsible policy decisions, Trudeau's use of inclusive language to suggest togetherness and unity showed an understanding of, and respect for, public dissent towards globalisation as a driver of economic growth. This can be seen in Trudeau's communication during a CTV interview when he addressed the issue of globalisation and its effects on Canadian communities (Trudeau 2016c). Trudeau explicitly stated that his government was 'very much focused on . . . recognising [the] anxiety' Canadians felt about the 'high level of indebtedness', trade and lack of job opportunities. Furthermore, Trudeau took the time to explain why he thought differently, and reassured voters that his government was focused on acting for those most pressured by trade. This was done with civility and respect for opposing opinions.

Trudeau's communication, however, did not suggest a high level of truly reflective thinking. While Trudeau empathised with those who were struggling to afford childcare, retain their jobs or save enough for retirement, he did not take responsibility for such pressures as these were consequences created by the previous Conservative Government.

Leadership

Trudeau promoted leadership strength and competence through his communication of the Liberal Government's economic plan to put more money in the pockets of middle-class Canadians and invest in communities. His reasoning behind his policy decisions was clearly mapped out, noting that 'putting a little more money in the pockets [of Canadians] is money that gets spent, it gets invested . . . in a way that will help the entire economy' (Trudeau 2016a). When Trudeau would explain the new Canada Child Benefit, he would typically state that this would allow families to 'spend on childcare, on groceries and school supplies, on whatever [is] needed in a tangible way to help with the high cost of raising kids' (Trudeau 2016a). Similarly, investing in communities allowed for the development of public transit, social infrastructure and green infrastructure, which 'means better opportunities for future generations' (Trudeau 2015b).

Trudeau was also successful at using small but frequent verbal indicators that demonstrated leadership strength. He would often state that he was 'working very hard' to ensure Canadians had a better future, or that he was 'absolutely focused on growing the economy that gives everyone opportunities'. Trudeau would also emphasise his 'commitment' to investing in communities, creating jobs and empowering young Canadians. In such communication, Trudeau would highlight his investment in getting results based on what he as a 'responsible leader' thought was best for Canada, rather than his 'personal feelings' (Trudeau 2016b). Accordingly, Trudeau implied he had strong personal conviction and was determined to get results.

Authenticity

In addition to being open and encouraging of media and public questions, Trudeau continually communicated the challenges he faced with growing the economy as prime minister. Two prime examples were maintaining jobs in provinces that rely heavily on natural resources in the face of rising oil prices and responding to the housing crisis. For example, he stated that, 'anything we do for Vancouver and maybe for Toronto . . . would possibly create unintended consequences on the housing market in places that aren't facing the same issue', and so picking the right mechanisms to address the issue was a complicated exercise (Trudeau 2016b). Rather than ignoring the fact that challenges existed, Trudeau openly communicated the difficulty in deciding upon responsible approaches. He reassured voters that instead of implementing a quick fix which could produce further 'unintended consequences', his government was working to solve the root problem.

Notably, Trudeau rarely emphasised a relatable image when he discussed Canada's economic issues. This could be because of Trudeau's fortunate upbringing and lack of experienced hardships faced by a sluggish economy, but this is not to say that he never communicated his non-political personality. Trudeau often spoke about what pushed him into politics, his time as a schoolteacher and the importance of his family. He was particularly effective in relating to young people and communicating the reasons behind his decision to appoint himself as the Minister of Youth. The connection between this and his economic policies, however, was seldom made.

Lessons for political marketing

This case study highlights the importance of maintaining and promoting market-oriented qualities in government. Trudeau's communication in government, for the most part, highlighted his market-oriented qualities, and positively correlated with the polling figures regarding his performance and leadership qualities at the time. This case study also reinforces the importance of context and how the Contemporary Governing Leaders' Communication Model is seen in practice. For example, Trudeau's lack of demonstrated reflective thinking could be due to this form of communication coming so early in his tenure as prime minister. Sufficient time is needed between a decision being made and the governing leader being reflective about it. Additional evidence for the importance of context is Trudeau's lack of relatable communication when it came to the economy. While this may seem surprising given Trudeau's empathetic reputation, his fortunate upbringing and non-political personality may have distanced him from those facing economic hardships and concerns. If this study were to broaden and examine Trudeau's communication in government, it is likely that we would see the promotion of a more relatable image, especially around social issues. Given Canada's economic situation at the time, however, emphasising strong leadership was arguably required to minimise voter anxiety.

References

Armstrong, J. (2016). *'Cost of living, economy among most important issues in upcoming election, says new poll'*. *Global News*, updated 21 January 2016. http://globalnews.ca/news/2138142/cost-ofliving-economy-among-most-important-issues-in-upcoming-election-says-new-poll/.

Mandel, C. (2015). *'Justin Trudeau's fight for the top'*. *Canada's National Observer*, 25 August 2015. www.nationalobserver.com/2015/08/25/news/justin-trudeaus-fight-top.

Trudeau, J. (2016a). '*A speech and conversation with Canadian Prime Minister Justin Trudeau*'. Centre for American Progress YouTube video, 11 March 2016. www.youtube.com/watch?v=BgUTOr4pduU.

Trudeau, J. (2016b). '*One-on-one with Prime Minister Justin Trudeau*'. *CTV Morning Live Interview*, 17 June 2016. www.ctvnews.ca/video?clipId=893936.

Trudeau, J. (2016c). '*Powerplay: Ask the Prime Minister, part two*'. *CTV News*, interviewed by D. Martin, 14 September 2016. www.ctvnews.ca/video?clipId=951126.

Democratic Debate 7.1 The varied implications of relational political marketing communication

By Edward Elder (University of Auckland)

There are some democratic questions that need to be asked when thinking about the fact that there is a greater strategic focus on longer-term relationship building between political actors and the public through strategic communication. Some of the potential positive outcomes of the prescriptions noted in this chapter may seem obvious.

For one, if political actors do utilise and encourage the two-way functions of new media platform, this can increase deliberation, public participation and democratic engagement in the political process. This could be especially beneficial for younger generations, who have been less politically active than older generations but are also most likely to use these new media platforms (Smith and Anderson 2018). Beto O'Rourke, the Democratic candidate in the Texas senate election race in 2018, utilised relationship e-marketing communication to help collect small-dollar donations and get people involved in his campaign without political action committees (PACs) financed by well-off donors. Not only did this play into O'Rourke's political brand of 'no PACs, just people' and allow him to outraise his opponent from April to June 2018 by more than double (US$10.4 million compared to $4.6 million, at an average of $33 per donation), but, as O'Rourke himself noted, 'I never want you to have to wonder whether I'm voting for you or the special interests. It will be you each and every single time' (O'Rourke 2018). So not only could such communication help get more people involved in the political process, it may also indirectly elevate the disproportionate monetary pressure certain interest groups can place on politicians' decision making that impact society as a whole.

Furthermore, if we look at political decision making from a 'trustee' perspective – where politicians are elected to do what they think is right on behalf of citizens – the building of trust between politicians and the public through such communication may also give politicians more room to do what they believe is right in the longer term, rather than what is politically popular in the short term. As noted by Elder (2016), politicians do not necessarily have to do what the public want to be seen as 'in touch'. If politicians use relational strategic communication that highlights that they have listened to the public, the public are less likely to penalise them for making decisions they do not agree with.

If used ethically, the personalisation of the candidates through social media specifically and through political-public relations more broadly – designed to foster trust between political elites and the public – may also have longer-term democratic benefits in terms of democracy at its most fundamental level. Trust in politicians in many Western democracies has declined in the 21st century, and this is arguably having a negative impact on voter turnout (Grönlund and Setälä 2007). As a newer generation of more social-media literate politicians starts to become the norm, this personalisation of political communication and relationship building may help remedy this lack of trust in politicians through humanisation, and thus help remedy declining voter turnout.

However, political actors have not always used the advantages of these platforms in ways that may seem healthy for democracy. The growing personalisation of politics has not only started with the introduction of relational marketing communication or new media technologies. The same drawbacks from the personalisation of politics more broadly could apply here, too. Namely, with a greater focus on the personality of politicians, less focus is placed on issues.

Furthermore, while political engagement with user-generated content may help members of the public feel more included in the democratic process, it lacks the checks and balances placed on communication by political professionals. This could have several democratic implications. Notably, given that this user-generated content is being communicated through political elites' social media pages or peer-to-peer through political parties' other online forums, they may be given more credibility than they warrant. This also leaves politicians with the opportunity to potentially promote messages with an easy 'out' if the information presented turns out to be wrong ('fake news'), or from an undesirable source. Take Iowa congressman, Steve King, for example. After retweeting a post from the account of a Holocaust denier about young Italians opposing mass immigration, King suggested, 'It's the message, not the messenger [that is important]'. King also refused to apologise or take down the tweet, noting that 'then it'd be like I'm admitting that I did something, now I'm sorry about it. I'm not sorry. I'm human' (Raju 2018).

Finally, Toledano and McKie's (2013) book on PR and nation branding discusses how public relations has been used in public diplomacy to try to build a more positive perception of countries such as Israel, but potentially unethically. They note that in a strongly nationalistic climate, public relations can too easily be used as a form of government propaganda. For example, they note that the early and heavy emphasis on solidarity, exclusiveness and unity in the public relations communication of the Israeli Government, as well as the blurring of the lines between Israel's journalists and politicians, promoted uncritical support of the national institutions and government. In other words, as Toledano and McKie note, if used nefariously, public relations can inhibit the development of open liberal democracy, tolerance of dissident voices and respect of individual human rights.

In essence, the democratic implications of relational political marketing communication depend very much on how it is used by political elites.

References

Elder, Edward (2016). *Marketing leadership in government: communicating responsiveness, leadership and credibility*. London: Palgrave Macmillan.

Grönlund, Kimmo and Maija Setälä (2007). 'Political Trust, Satisfaction and Voter Turnout.' Comparative European Politics, 5(4): 400–22.

O'Rourke, Beto (2018). 'No PACs – just people'. *Facebook* video. www.facebook.com/betoorourke/videos/no-pacs-just-people/10100791008250181/ (accessed July 2018).

Painter, David. L. (2015). 'Online political public relations and trust: Source and interactivity effects in the 2012 U.S. presidential campaign'. Public Relations Review, 41(5): 801–8.

Raju, Manu (2018). 'Steve King says retweet of Nazi sympathizer's message was unintentional, won't delete tweet'. *CNN*, 27 June 2018. https://edition.cnn.com/2018/06/26/politics/steve-king-retweet-nazi-sympathizer/index.html.

Smith, Aaron and Monica Anderson (2018). 'Social Media Use in 2018.' Pew Research Center, 1 March 2018. www.pewinternet.org/2018/03/01/social-media-use-in-2018/.

Toledano, Margalit and David McKie (2013). *Public Relations and Nation Building*. London: Routledge.

References

Baines, Paul (2011). 'Political public relations and election campaigning'. In Jesper Strömbäck and Spiro Kiousis (eds) *Political Public Relations: Principles and Applications*. New York: Routledge, 115–37.

Balz, Dan (2013). 'How the Obama campaign won the race for voter data'. *The Washington Post online*, 29 July 2013. www.washingtonpost.com/politics/how-the-obama-campaign-won-the-race-for-voter-data/2013/07/28/ad32c7b4-ee4e-11e2-a1f9-ea873b7e0424_story.html.

Cogburn, Derrick L. and Fatima K. Espinoza-Vasquez (2011). 'From networked nominee to networked nation: examining the impact of Web 2.0 and social media on political participation and civic engagement in the 2008 Obama campaign'. *Journal of Political Marketing*, 10(1/2): 189–213.

Conversations with Bill Kristol (2015). 'Paul Begala on Bill Clinton and the Clinton White House'. *YouTube video, published 15 March 2015*. www.youtube.com/watch?v=7OwuqRkHaK4 (accessed 20 May 2018).

Davies, Gary and Takir Mian (2010). 'The reputation of the party leader and of the party being led'. *European Journal of Marketing*, 44(3–4): 331–50.

Elder, Edward, (2016). *Marketing leadership in government: communicating responsiveness, leadership and credibility*. London: Palgrave Macmillan.

Elder, Edward (2018). 'Communicating Market-Oriented Leadership in Power and Opposition'. In Jennifer Lees-Marshment (ed.) *Political marketing and management in the 2017 New Zealand election*. London: Palgrave Macmillan, 99–116.

Eshbaugh-Soha, Matthew (2011). 'Presidential public relations'. In Jesper Strömbäck and Spiro Kiousis (eds) *Political Public Relations: Principles and Applications*. New York: Routledge, 95–114.

Favreau, Jon, Jon Lovett and Tommy Veitor (2017). 'Some Kind of Decline'. *Pod Save America* podcast, 5 June 2017. https://crooked.com/podcast/some-kind-of-decline/ (accessed 20 May 2018).

Hallahan, Kirk (2011). 'Political public relations and strategic framing'. In Jesper Strömbäck and Spiro Kiousis (eds) *Political Public Relations: Principles and Applications*. New York: Routledge, 177–212.

Harfoush, Rahaf (2009). *Yes We Did; An inside look at how social media built the Obama brand*. Berkeley, CA: New Riders.

Hong, Hyehyun., Hyojung Park, Youngah Lee and Jongmin Park (2012). 'Public Segmentation and Government–Public Relationship Building: A Cluster Analysis of Publics in the United States and 19 European Countries'. *Journal of Public Relations Research*, 24, 37–68.

Jackson, Nigel (2005). 'Vote winner or a nuisance: email and elected politicians' relationship with their constituents'. In Walter W. Wymer, Jr. and Jennifer Lees-Marshment (eds) *Current Issues in Political Marketing*. Binghamton, NY: Haworth Press, 91–108.

Jackson, Nigel (2006). 'Banking online: the use of the internet by political parties to build relationships with voters'. In Darren G. Lilleker, Nigel Jackson and Richard Scullion (eds) *The Marketing of Political Parties*. Manchester, UK: Manchester University Press, 157–84.

Jackson, Nigel A. (2012). 'Underused campaigning tools: political public relations'. In Jennifer Lees-Marshment (ed.) *The Routledge Handbook of Political Marketing*. London and New York: Routledge, 271–85.

Jackson, Nigel. (2013). 'General election marketing – selling a can of beans, building a favours bank or managing an event?' *Journal of Public Affairs*, 13(3): 251–9.

Jackson, Nigel and Darren G. Lilleker (2014). 'Brand management and relationship marketing in online environments'. In Jennifer Lees-Marshment, Brian Conley and Kenneth Cosgrove (eds) *Political Marketing in the US*. New York: Routledge, 165–84.

Jackson, Nigel A., Darren G. Lilleker and Eva Schweitzer (2012). 'Political marketing in an online election environment: short-term sales or long-term relationships?' In Jennifer Lees-Marshment (ed.) *The Routledge Handbook of Political Marketing*. London and New York: Routledge, 286–300.

Johnson, Dennis W. (2012). 'Campaigning in the twenty-first century: change and continuity in American political marketing'. In Jennifer Lees-Marshment (ed.) *The Routledge Handbook of Political Marketing*. London and New York: Routledge, 205–17.

Kruikemeier, Sanne (2014). 'How political candidates use Twitter and the impact on votes'. *Computers in Human Behavior*, 34, 131–9.

LaMarre, Heather L. and Yoshikazu Suzuki-Lambrecht (2013). 'Tweeting democracy? Examining Twitter as an online public relations strategy for congressional campaigns'. *Public Relations Review*, 39(4): 360–8.

Land O'Lakes Inc (2012). 'Meet Jen: Government Relations'. *YouTube* video, 25 January 2012. www.youtube.com/watch?v=PpYrFbIebiU (accessed 29 May 2018).

Ledingham, John A. (2003). 'Explicating relationship management as a general theory of public relations'. *Journal of Public Relations Research*, 15, 181–98.

Ledingham, John A. and Stephen D. Bruning (1998). 'Relationship management in public relations: Dimensions of an organization–public relationship'. *Public Relations Review*, 24, 55–65.

Lees-Marshment, Jennifer (2009). 'Marketing after the election: the potential and limitations of maintaining a market orientation in government'. *Canadian Journal of Communication*, 34(2): 205–27.

Lee, Jayeon and Young-shin Lim (2016). 'Gendered campaign tweets: The cases of Hillary Clinton and Donald Trump.' *Public Relations Review*, 42(5): 849–55.

Lieber, Paul S. and Guy J. Golan (2011). 'Political public relations, news management, and agenda indexing'. In Jesper Strömbäck and Spiro Kiousis (eds) *Political Public Relations: Principles and Applications*. New York: Routledge, 54–74.

Lilleker, Darren G. (2015). 'Interactivity and Branding: Public Political Communication as a Marketing Tool.' *Journal of Political Marketing*, 14(1/2): 111–28.

Lloyd, Jenny (2012). 'Something old, something new? Modelling political communication in the 2010 UK general election'. In Jennifer Lees-Marshment (ed.) *The Routledge Handbook of Political Marketing*. London and New York: Routledge, 243–56.

Miller, William J. (2013). 'We Can't All Be Obama: The Use of New Media in Modern Political Campaigns'. *Journal of Political Marketing*, 12(4): 326–47.

Newman, Bruce I. (1999). *The Mass Marketing of Politics*. Thousand Oaks, CA: Sage.

O'Rourke, Beto. (2018). 'Just launched our first ad. Entitled "Showing Up," it's filmed using an iPhone and was created entirely with live stream footage from our travels to all 254 counties of Texas. Watch and RT to share.' Twitter post, 27 July 2018, 1:01am NZST. https://twitter.com/BetoORourke/status/1022466953288593409.

Ormrod, Robert. P. (2006). 'A critique of the Lees-Marshment Market-Oriented Party model'. *Politics*, 26(2): 110–88.

Painter, David L. (2015). 'Online political public relations and trust: Source and interactivity effects in the 2012 U.S. presidential campaign'. *Public Relations Review*, 41(5): 801–8.

Papagiannidis, Savvas, Constantinos K. Coursaris and Michael Bourlakis (2012). 'Do websites influence the nature of voting intentions? The case of two national elections in Greece'. *Computers in Human Behavior*, 28(2): 300–7.

Robinson, Claire (2012). 'Interacting leaders'. In Jennifer Lees-Marshment (ed.) *The Routledge Handbook of Political Marketing*. London and New York: Routledge, 257–70.

Scammell, Margaret (2007). 'Political brands and consumer citizens: the rebranding of Tony Blair'. *The ANNALS of the American Academy of Political and Social Science*, 611(176): 176–92.

Scammell, Margaret (2008). 'Brand Blair: marketing politics in the consumer age'. In D. Lilleker and R. Scullion (eds) *Voters or Consumers: Imagining the Contemporary Electorate*. Newcastle, UK: Cambridge Scholars Publishing, 97–113.

Seltzer, Trent and Weiwu Zhang (2011a). 'Toward a model of political organization–public relationships: Antecedent and cultivation strategy influence on citizens' relationships with political parties'. *Journal of Public Relations Research*, 23(1): 24–45.

Seltzer, Trent and Weiwu Zhang, (2011b). 'Debating healthcare reform: How political parties' issue-specific communication influences citizens' perceptions of organization–public relationships'. *Journalism and Mass Communication Quarterly*, 88(4): 753–70.

Small, Tamara (2012). 'Are we friends yet? Online relationship marketing by political parties'. In Alex Marland, Thierry Giasson and Jennifer Lees-Marshment (eds) *Political Marketing in Canada*. Vancouver: UBC, 193–208.

Stirland, Sarah Lai (2008). 'Inside Obama's surging net-roots campaign'. In *Wired*, 3 March 2008. Excerpts available at www.wired.com/politics/law/news/2008/03/obama_tools (accessed 1 April 2008).

Strömbäck, Jesper and Spiro Kiousis (2011). 'Political public relations: defining and mapping an emergent field'. In Jesper Strömbäck and Spiro Kiousis (eds) *Political Public Relations: Principles and Applications*. New York: Routledge, 1–32.

Sweetser, Kaye D. and John C. Tedesco (2014). 'Effects of Bipartisanship Messaging and Candidate Exposure on the Political Organization–Public Relationship'. *American Behavioral Scientist*, 58(6): 776–93.

Tedesco, John C. (2011). 'Political public relations and agenda building'. In Jesper Strömbäck and Spiro Kiousis (eds) *Political Public Relations: Principles and Applications*. New York: Routledge, 75–94.

Toledano, Margalit and David McKie (2013). *Public Relations and Nation Building*. London: Routledge.

Turcotte, André and Vincent Raynauld (2014). 'Boutique populism: the emergence of the Tea Party movement in the age of digital politics'. In Jennifer Lees-Marshment, Brian Conley and Kenneth Cosgrove (eds) *Political Marketing in the US*. New York: Routledge, 61–84.

Van Zuydam, Sabine and Frank Hendriks (2018). 'Credibility Enacted: Understanding the Meaning of Credible Political Leadership in the Dutch Parliamentary Election Campaign of 2010'. *Journal of Political Marketing*, 17(3): 258–81.

Waymer, Damion (2013). 'Democracy and government public relations: Expanding the scope of "Relationship" in public relations research'. *Public Relations Review*, 39(4): 320–31.

Williams, Christine B. and Girish J. 'Jeff' Gulati (2014). 'Relationship marketing in social media practice: perspectives, limitations and potential'. In Jennifer Lees-Marshment, Brian Conley and Kenneth Cosgrove (eds) *Political Marketing in the US*. New York: Routledge, 185–201.

Xifra, Jordi (2010). 'Linkages between public relations models and communication managers' roles in Spanish political parties'. *Journal of Political Marketing*, 9(3): 167–85.

Zeitzoff, Thomas (2017). 'How Social Media Is Changing Conflict'. *Journal of Conflict Resolution*, 61(9): 1970–91.

8 Political delivery marketing

by Jennifer Lees-Marshment

Practitioner Perspective 8.1 on the importance of delivery

Perceived economic management and delivery competence is almost like a qualification parties need to have to be in the game to win an election.

Neale Jones, NZ Labour's Chief of Staff in 2017, interviewed in Lees-Marshment (2018b)

When I talk to opposition politicians one of the measures I now have in my head about whether they are really serious about running this country is whether they are already thinking about how to do delivery.

Michael Barber, first Head of UK Delivery Unit, interviewed in Lees-Marshment (2011)

It's important to keep the language of delivery in the mindset of the politicians and their staff.

Ben Keneally, Australian NSW Premier's Delivery unit, interviewed in Lees-Marshment (2011)

Political marketing is most commonly associated with efforts to win an election, but if a politician wins power they need to deliver if they want to implement promised changes and maintain public support. As the quote from New Zealand practitioner Neale Jones in Practitioner Perspective 8.1 suggests, delivery is the qualification parties need to have in order to be in the game to win elections (Lees-Marshment 2018b). All of the market research and strategy conducted to help create policies that voters want is vital, but so is convincing voters the candidate or party can deliver them.

Once elected, delivery is crucial. Citizens want to see tangible political outcomes. Every time I teach delivery in my class on political marketing at the University of Auckland, I show a billboard the UK Conservatives used against New Labour in the 2000 election which has a picture of a pregnant Tony Blair on it with the words 'Time to Deliver' (see *The Telegraph* n.d.). It is highly amusing, and gets a laugh every time, but it has a serious message. The ultimate goal of political marketing – indeed, of politics itself – is to deliver a new product and policy progress in power. The New Zealand National Party even adopted the slogan *Delivering for New Zealanders* for the 2017 election. Elected governments need to become, as Anna Esselment suggests in Democratic Debate 8.1, a 'devotee of delivery'.

However, delivery marketing is not easy in practice. This chapter discusses:

- Delivery challenges, including the constraints of government and public perceptions of delivery.
- Pre-election delivery, including using pledges, connecting expectations to outcomes, reassuring voters about the potential costs and benefits of proposed policies, building a reputation for managing delivery and communicating delivery challenges.
- Making delivery happen in power, including delivery relationships, delivery units, delivery by minority governments and implementing policy.
- Managing problems in delivery.
- Communicating progress and success, including using good visuals, delivering quick wins, showing progress if not completion, conveying the benefits of policies, giving voters credit for delivery, individualising delivery, reminding voters of achievements and harvesting a reputation for delivery, communicating delivery in coalition governments, and communicating mayoral and individual politicians' delivery.
- Political delivery marketing in the workplace.

Delivery challenges

> ### Practitioner Perspective 8.2 on the challenges of delivery in government
>
> *Somebody put out the concept of a hundred-day plan . . . But things change. There has to be flexibility . . . it's massive. And every agency is, like, bigger than any company. So you know, I really just see the bigness of it all, but also the responsibility . . . the human life that's involved in some of the decisions . . . in business, you don't necessarily need heart, whereas here, almost everything affects people.*
>
> President of the United States, Donald Trump (2017)
>
> *Since time immemorial – certainly since the institutions of democracy in the 20th century – governments make commitments, get elected, and then struggle to deliver on their promises.*
>
> Delivery consultant Michael Barber (Wells 2016)

The constraints of government

In government, politicians are thwarted by unpredictable issues such as war and economic recession that constrain their ability to deliver their political product as designed before the election. As Johnson (2013, 3–4) notes, on winning power in 2008:

> President Obama inherited a financial and economic mess from his predecessor, an auto industry about to collapse, and layoffs and job cutbacks reminiscent of the 1930s . . . January 20, 2009, Barack Obama was sworn in as the forty-fifth president of the United States; that month 839,000 Americans had lost their jobs.

While in government there are more resources, with the bureaucracy now employed to help the politician or party work in office, these need managing. Delivering the political product involves a whole range of organisations, departments and units. Praprotnik (2017)'s analysis of Austria noted how the involvement of extra-governmental actors, such as local government, in the policymaking process impacted on parties' abilities to fulfil their promises. But even just internally within Parliament or Congress, the legislative process itself can thwart election promises being converted into action. The fight to pass and retain Obama's health care legislation, leading to a government shutdown in 2013, was an obvious recent example of this, and Rehr (2013, 25) notes how Obama's challenges in his first term included changing the Washington culture, handling an aggressive ideological media, justifying economic policies that seemed to have little impact on the economy, and managing the increase in Republican politicians after the poor performance of Democrats in the 2010 midterms. Politicians also have to work with the civil service to develop and implement policies and legislation and are subject to input from a range of stakeholders including lobbyists who try to influence its detail. As Practitioner Perspective 8.2 indicates, the pressures and demands are intense.

Political consumer perception of delivery

Practitioner Perspective 8.3 on the difficulties getting credit from voters for delivery

The media deliberately obstruct the link between government and hospitals/NHS [and when government has delivered] they don't credit the government for it.

> Alastair Campbell, Press Secretary to UK Prime Minister Tony Blair,
> interviewed in Lees-Marshment (2011)

[In] campaign training one of the skits we used to show is that snippet from The Life of Brian, you know 'What did the Romans ever do for us? Apart from roads, sanitation, and education, and law and order . . . what have they done for us lately?'. . . that's the challenge of government . . . It's always, what have you done for us lately?

> Eric Roozendaal, Australian campaign manager and politician,
> interviewed in Lees-Marshment (2011)

Another challenge is that it is hard to get credit from voters for delivery. Political consumers may not always evaluate politicians' delivery objectively, fairly or clearly. By the end of Obama's first term, the President was, as Johnson (2013, 1 and 3) puts it, 'the beleaguered president': despite his success in passing the $831 billion stimulus bill and national health care (Obamacare), neither attracted public approval, and on election day voters approved Obama's performance by just 2.8 per cent over those who disapproved. Michael Barber (2007, 369–71), who headed the first UK Delivery Unit, explains that 'citizens have to see and feel the difference and expectations need to be managed'. Even if they have positive experiences, they do not give politicians credit for it.

Part of the problem is the media. Temple (2010, 268) notes how the media play a key role in interpreting government success. The media see their role as being to report problems rather than carry success stories. As the Practitioner Perspective 8.3 by Blair's former press secretary Alastair Campbell conveys, this forms a big barrier to getting credit for delivery. Temple (2010, 269) notes how while the media are generally neutral towards commercial products, politics is different:

> No one shouts at the television their hatred of Heinz baked beans and their commitment to Crosse & Blackwell's alternative product . . . Politicians and political parties have a much tougher and fundamentally different ride in the media . . . the representatives and messages of political parties are subject to intense scrutiny and criticism.

Demand is also insatiable: even when voters do give credit for successful delivery, they then want more. In his last party conference speech as UK Prime Minister in 2006, Tony Blair noted:

> I spoke to a woman the other day, a part-time worker, complaining about the amount of her tax credit. I said: Hold on a minute: before 1997, there were no tax credits, not for working families, not for any families; child benefit was frozen; maternity pay half what it is; maternity leave likewise and paternity leave didn't exist at all. And no minimum wage, no full-time rights for part-time workers, in fact nothing. 'So what?', she said 'that's why we elected you. Now go and sort out my tax credit.'

Campaign managers use the Monty Python clip '*What have the Romans ever done for us?*' when training practitioners to get over the point that voters always want more. This is in part how we keep progressing as a society, but it presents continued challenges for government. Delivery marketing is therefore needed to try to manage expectations and communicate success once in power as well as pre-election.

Pre-election delivery

The first aspect to marketing in government is to consider delivery before the election. Political marketing is not just about promising what voters want but ensuring the product is achievable, and one way to convey this is to make specific pledges.

Making precise promises or pledges

Politicians and parties have developed a range of ways to convince the public they are capable of delivering and to manage expectations. One tool is pledges, contracts or guarantees. One of the earliest examples of this was the 1994 midterm Contract with America put forward by the House Republicans in the US. The contract attracted considerable votes but also created a mandate which the party used to dominate Congress for the rest of Bill Clinton's time as president.

Tony Blair's Labour Party in the UK issued a contract and credit-card-sized pledges, both to get into government in 1997 and then when in power in 2001 and 2005 (see Table 8.1). However, the preciseness of the pledges deteriorated over the three terms. They changed from outputs (what government would achieve) to inputs (what government would put into the system), which are easier to control than outputs. They also changed to generalised, rhetorical pledges which were very vague on the front side, with flexible measurements on the back such as 'mortgages as low as possible', which thus failed to be as effective in managing expectations.

Table 8.1 Blair's New Labour Party credit card pledges 1997–2005

1997 Pledges	2001 Pledges	2005 Pledges
1 We will cut class sizes to 30 or under for five-, six- and seven-year-olds by using money saved from the assisted places scheme. 2 We will introduce a fast-track punishment scheme for persistent young offenders by halving the time from arrest to sentencing. 3 We will cut NHS waiting lists by treating an extra 100,000 patients as a first step by releasing £100 million saved from NHS red tape. 4 We will get 250,000 under-25-year-olds off benefit and into work by using money from a windfall levy on the privatised utilities. 5 We will set tough rules for government spending and borrowing and ensure low inflation and strengthen the economy so that interest rates are as low as possible to make all families better off.	1 Mortgages as low as possible, low inflation and sound public finances. 2 Ten thousand extra teachers and higher standards in secondary schools. 3 Twenty thousand extra nurses and 10,000 extra doctors in a reformed NHS. 4 Six thousand extra recruits to raise police numbers to their highest-ever level. 5 Pensioners' winter fuel payment retained, minimum wage rising to £4.20.	1 Your family better off. 2 Your child achieving more. 3 Your children with the best start. 4 Your family treated better and faster. 5 Your community safer. 6 Your country's borders protected.

Nevertheless, pledges and contracts have been copied around the world: Helen Clark adopted them for the New Zealand Labour Party in 1999. Unlike Blair, she retained their more specific nature over time in government, and in 2005 the pledges promised no interest on student loans, a final date for treaty claims, an increase in the rates rebate, KiwiSaver, 250 extra community police, more cataract and major joint operations, and 5,000 more modern apprenticeships.

The use of contracts raises broader issues such as trust – an aspect governments care about deeply, because trust is essential to maintaining a positive relationship with voters in the long term. Steen (2009) explored the use of contracts in Danish politics by the Liberal Prime Minister Anders Fogh Rasmussen, who, like Clark, copied delivery concepts from Tony Blair, noting how important it was to deliver promises otherwise politicians risk losing voter trust. He created a Partnership with the People: six specific pledges under slogans such as 'You know, we will make it happen': 1.5 mia. dkr extra to hospitals; 500 mio. dkr extra for homecare; one-year flexible maternity leave; a firm and fair immigration policy; a consequential judicial policy; and a tax freeze. The party won power in the 2001 election, but also scored higher on perceptions of trust. Steen reports how surveys demonstrated that confidence in Danish politicians improved 13 per cent from 1999 to 2005. When pledges, contracts or guarantees are implemented effectively they help to focus voters' and politicians' minds on what is most important. Politicians are saying, 'At the very least, we will get these few things done'.

Connecting expectations to outcomes

Practitioner Perspective 8.4 on setting out clear promises that can be linked with outcomes

In order for delivery to be a political asset, the electorate needs to understand what your promises are and they need to have expectations of what those outcomes are . . . they have to be clear enough so that the voter links the outcome with the expectation or the promise. We were able to say 'We came to power, we promised five big things, and we have delivered five big things.'

Patrick Muttart, Deputy Chief of Staff to Canadian Prime Minister
Stephen Harper, interviewed in Lees-Marshment (2011)

You have to tell them the impact . . . people don't really want to know the details, they just want to know you've got a plan of action . . . how it's going to change their day-to-day lives.

Frank Luntz, US communications expert and political
strategist (PolicyExchangeUK 2012)

As Practitioner Perspective 8.4 suggests, if delivery promises are clear and then achieved once in power, it helps governments to manage expectations and get credit for those achievements. A Canadian consultant, Leslie Noble, noted that Ontario Premier Mike Harris said in his campaign, 'look, we'll give you a money-back-guarantee. If I don't do this, I'm going to resign' (interview in Lees-Marshment 2011, 170–1). All the candidates actually signed a pledge and stuck to it, so when it came to re-election the number-one characteristic was that Harris did what he said he'd do, which 'was a great brand characteristic to have' and gained public support.

Delivery measures can, however, create problematic pressures in government. As Australian consultant Robert Griggs noted, specific promises made in Australian NSW Premier Bob Carr's campaign in 1995 made government difficult. They said they would 'halve the waiting list within eighteen months or Bob would make Andrew resign. We essentially did it, but it blew the budget out, lasted about three months before the waiting lists went skewed again' (interview quoted in Lees-Marshment 2011, 150). The implications for governance and policy are discussed further in Democratic Debate 8.1 at the end of this chapter.

Reassuring voters about the potential costs and benefits of proposed policies

Not all policies are popular with every voter, of course, and political marketers increasingly need to find ways to communicate the benefits of proposed policies. Conveying why a policy to increase taxes is beneficial is challenging. In the branding chapter, we noted how Needham's model included discussion of the need to be credible and reassuring. In the 2015 Canadian election, Liberal Party leader Justin Trudeau attempted to reassure voters that a proposed tax increase was fair, noting on Facebook that the average income of Canada's wealthiest 1 per cent had grown by 77 per cent in the last 30 years, and thus he was just asking them to 'pay a little bit more, to help Canadians who need it most'. The Liberals also released an ad titled '*Fairness for the Middle Class*' (Liberal Party of Canada 2015), which said their plan 'starts by making sure you have more money to help your family' and detailed the Canada Child Benefit and how they would lower taxes for those less well-off while Trudeau proposed creating a new top tax bracket which would mean 'the wealthiest Canadians will pay a bit little more but that also means a fairer chance for the middle class to make ends meet and to help our economy grow'.

Building a reputation for managing delivery

Elder (2018, 101) explored how leaders in the 2017 New Zealand election campaign attempted to convey delivery competency: 'like sitting governing leaders, opposition leaders need to convey their ability to govern in order to win elections, as perceived competence is so important, not least to delivery.' In the 2017 New Zealand election, Labour were aware of their perceived weaknesses on delivery: as one practitioner noted, potential voters 'just believed in their heart of hearts, despite any evidence, that Labour would, if they got a chance to run the country, just spend all the money, blow the budget, and drive us into recession. And it was a deeply held belief' (interview quoted in Lees-Marshment 2018a, 59). The party therefore released a fully costed alternative budget, set budget responsibility rules, created a fiscal plan and a 100-day plan outlining specific policies they would quickly deliver. Similarly, Donald Trump set a 100-day mark for delivery with declaring a bold set of 28 promises to fulfil in 100 days in his *Contract with the American Voter* (Trump 2016).

Communicating delivery challenges

Political leaders already in office have also integrated communication of delivery challenges into their campaigns. For example, when seeking re-election in 2012, President Obama released a mini-documentary *The Road We've Travelled* (Obama 2012), which detailed the global financial crisis and other complex issues Barack Obama was faced with upon winning office. Similarly, the Canadian Conservatives tried to convey the challenges of government and Stephen Harper's strong experience in managing them in a 2015 campaign ad titled '*Proven Leadership*' (Conservative Party of Canada 2015), which discussed the unexpected and unpopular decisions prime ministers have to make.

Making delivery happen in power

Delivery relationships

Actually delivering requires politicians to engage in careful negotiation and relationships with a range of stakeholders connected to government. One of the most well-known cases of failed delivery was health care by Bill Clinton, whose package was blocked when it went through Congress despite it being a visible part of the product he offered to voters and won election for. Esselment (2012b, 133) argues that the Canadian Conservatives achieved success in 2006–2008 because they gave the bureaucracy clear instructions on what policies to prioritise and the Privy Council Office (PCO) helped the government fulfil its commitments. Kevin Lynch, an experienced public servant, headed the PCO and drove implementation from there. Similarly, New Zealand government staffer Grant Robertson recalled how talking to civil servants about the product promises works (interview quoted in Lees-Marshment 2011, 176):

One thing we did do after the 2005 election is that I actually sat down with the Prime Minister's departmental officials, the bureaucrats and we actually went through the manifesto and said what are we going to be able to do to implement these things.

Delivery units

Establishing units in government that focus on delivery is a trend that started in 2001 when, after winning his second term, Tony Blair established the Prime Minister's Delivery Unit (PMDU) at the centre of government. The PMDU monitored the implementation of prioritised policies such as health, education, crime and transport and tried to help ensure that the government met its targets. It helped drive implementation, improving relationships between government departments (Esselment 2012a, 304–5). Australia copied this idea, creating a Cabinet Implementation Unit (CIU) at the centre of government in October 2003. As Peter Hamburger (2006) of the Department of the Prime Minister and Cabinet wrote:

> It is no longer enough for those advocating major policy to have a good idea . . . the Government demands that we think through our ideas and how they are going to be implemented.

The Australian NSW state government also created a delivery unit under Premier Morris Iemma. Ben Keneally headed it and argued that Iemma did this to improve service delivery and achieve 'delivering measurable change and performance' (interview quoted in Lees-Marshment 2011, 169). Having the leaders' support helps to make such units effective as it links administrative progress with electoral goals. The Queensland government also created an implementation unit in March 2004. Esselment (2012a, 306) observed how the delivery unit model has also been adapted to the US including the state of Maryland and the city of Los Angeles:

> delivery units can thus keep a majority government focused, even in its second or third mandate, and can assist coalition partners by doggedly pursuing the implementation of its agreed-upon agenda, thereby minimizing conflict between the parties and contributing to a productive government partnership.

Canadian Prime Minister Justin Trudeau became, as Anna Esselment puts it in Democratic Debate 8.1, a 'delivery devotee' since being elected in 2015. As Hannah Lobb's Case Study 8.1 explains, Trudeau brought Michael Barber to Canada to advise them and appointed Matthew Mendelsohn as Deputy Secretary to the Cabinet to lead a Results and Delivery Unit (Government of Canada 2016). The government issued a mandate letter tracker which focuses on 12 top priorities identified by the government and described in the mandate letters sent from the Prime Minister to each Cabinet Minister (Government of Canada 2017).

Delivery by minority governments

Delivering in a minority government is harder because the product design is compromised during coalition formation before governing even begins, and the major party lacks majority control of the legislature. In 2010, Julia Gillard secured re-election as Australian Prime Minister but only through breaking her promise not to implement a tax on carbon in order to secure support from the Greens and Independents to form a government. Such tangible breaking of a promise scarred her leadership. Nevertheless, minority governments can succeed in delivery. Esselment (2012a) analysed the Conservative minority under Stephen Harper's first term (2006–2008) in Canada. The Conservatives had campaigned on five clear priorities for delivery in power:

1   Reduction in the goods and services tax (GST) – from 7 per cent to 5 per cent.
2   Childcare allowance for families with children aged five and under.
3   Stronger government accountability measures.
4   Criminal justice reform.
5   Patient wait times guarantee.

Harper was relatively untested and unknown, and thus focused on quick delivery of some of these promises to establish legitimacy. The GST reduction and childcare allowance were passed in the first budget and took effect in July 2006. The government passed the Federal Accountability Act to deal with the Liberal scandal and addressed a general concern with government accountability in December 2006, delivering three major policy items within the first year of government. The last two promises were more difficult. The justice reforms got delayed through the parliamentary committee system, so the government responded by creating the Tackling Violent Crime Act, framing it as 'for or against' crime in Canada, and it was passed in early 2008. However, the patient waiting times guarantee was never fully delivered, and the government adapted it to make it more flexible and then declared success. Nevertheless, overall the image was of a government that delivered, and it won re-election as a minority government in 2008.

While delivering is more difficult in a minority government, it is possible. Esselment (2012a, 309) argues that this may in part be psychological:

> delivery takes on heightened importance since the government is at the mercy of parliament; a vote of no confidence is a continuing threat and, should the governing party be thrust into an early election, a record of some achievements is critical to a new campaign.

She suggests key principles to achieve delivery (see Box 8.1).

Box 8.1   Esselment's model for successful political marketing delivery

1   Create a separate 'delivery unit' to drive implementation.
2   Focus on delivering a few campaign promises almost immediately for 'quick wins' to create an early record of achievement.
3   Work with opposition parties to get legislation through parliament.
4   Build relationships with those who will affect delivery – staff in government departments, opposition parties and lower levels of government such as provinces, states or devolved parliaments.
5   Communicate delivery of policy promises with memorable events and photo opportunities.
6   Repackage and reframe promises if needed to make it unpopular to oppose them.
7   Continue market research while in government to monitor public perception of delivery progress.

Source: Adapted from Esselment (2012a, 311)

Implementing policy

Delivery management doesn't just stop with the passing of legislation. Even after Obama succeeded in passing his health care plan, his staff engaged in another stage of delivery marketing to ensure the policy is implemented in the sense that the public actually take out the new health insurance on offer (see Klein and Kliff 2013).

Managing problems in delivery

Practitioner Perspective 8.5 on managing failures in delivery

Use a three-step approach to communicate that you have:

1   *Recognised and spotted the problems straight away.*
2   *That you're doing something about it.*
3   *That you're doing something about it to make sure it doesn't happen again.*

Eammon Fitzpatrick, former media advisor and consultant,
interviewed in 2008

Number one is that people need someone to blame. Someone to hold accountable. And you don't spend that much time on it, but you've got to talk about why it happened. Number two is they expect the solutions and they don't expect political rhetoric . . . tell them what you're going to do.

Frank Luntz, US communications expert and political
strategist, 2012

Source: Lees-Marshment (2011); PolicyExchangeUK (2012)

Failure in delivery causes concern for politicians and strategists as it threatens the chances of re-election. It is impossible to ensure that 100 per cent success will be achieved. As those in Practitioner Perspective 8.5 argue, it is best to be honest about failures. Esselment (2012b, 129) discusses how the Canadian Conservatives under Harper handled failure to keep their promise not to tax income trusts – a specific pledge in their campaign. In 2006, Finance Minister Jim Flaherty reversed this decision, arguing that businesses had increasingly used income trusts as a way to avoid paying corporate taxes. Instead of pretending or ignoring it, they addressed it directly and visibly, facing up to the fact that they were breaking a promise and trying to explain why and leaving the public to decide whether to trust them again. The Department of Finance also released information about how the financial circumstances had changed since the election.

In a similar way, New Zealand Prime Minister John Key did the same with New Zealand National's decision to increase GST, which they had also promised not to. However, Key went one step further: he introduced the idea into the public sphere, discussing the pros and cons in various media to test public response to the idea before deciding to go ahead with it (see Elder 2016a; 2016b).

Communicating delivery progress and success

Practitioner Perspective 8.6 on communicating delivery	

Delivering results is as much about telling the people you've delivered as and how they interpret what you tell them as it is about actually delivering them.

Robin Maclachlan, Summa Strategies (2016)

It is important that politicians or governments communicate that they have delivered. In his delivery manual, Barber (2007) outlined the need for delivery reports, setting targets, consideration of delivery chains, an assessment framework and sample presentations to the media. But there are many other tools, including using good visuals, delivering quick wins, showing progress if not completion, conveying the benefits of policies, giving voters credit for delivery, individualising delivery, reminding voters of achievements and harvesting a reputation for delivery.

Good visuals

Communication about product delivery needs clear visuals. One of the best examples is how the Canadian Conservatives under Stephen Harper placed a bright blue '5%' GST sticker onto a cash register in a retail store – a strong visual that can stay in people's minds (Esselment 2012b, 135).

Delivering quick wins

Esselment (2012a/b) argues that new governments need to secure 'quick wins', a few delivery successes after coming to power, to gain voters' trust to then work on promises that take longer. Lobb's Case Study 8.1 details how Trudeau implemented over 50 promises in its first year including tax cuts for the middle class and the Canada Child Benefit. A year into his first term, Trudeau issued an advert titled '*27 Promises Kept*', which mentioned achievements such as a gender-balanced Cabinet, New Canada Child Benefit, lowered taxes for the middle classes and higher taxes for the wealthiest 1 per cent (Liberal Party of Canada 2016).

Similarly, the Labour Government in New Zealand elected in 2017 under Jacinda Ardern focused on delivering its 100-day plan including policies such as fee-free study for the first year of university, setting up a tax working group and beginning Kiwibuild to address the housing crisis. Ardern also completed a Facebook live event while on parental leave to talk about the launching of their new families package (Ardern 2018).

US President Donald Trump's election in 2016 broke many pre-election delivery theories, given his top promises such as building a wall between the US and Mexico border were not easily achievable in practice. Once in office, Trump resorted to signing executive orders to suggest action to his supporters. While such events offer 'delivery symbolism' they do not equate to making a real difference on the ground to voters' daily lives. It remains to be seen if this will convince sceptical voters that key policies have actually been delivered. In government, Trump also downplayed his contract to deliver 28 promises in 100 days as 'just an artificial barrier' and said that the public should not hold him accountable to this in judging his success because 'things change. There has to be flexibility . . . much of the foundation's been laid. Things came up.' This undermines any future delivery promises.

Showing progress if not completion

One way for new governments to communicate delivery is to convey work in progress even if it is not complete. A few years into his first term, President Obama was pictured amid building infrastructure projects, seeking to convey that progress was being made on the recovery, even if it was not yet complete. Governments try to show what progress has been made while conceding there is more to do – thus encouraging voters to give them credit for what had been successful but reason to vote them in again to do more. Lees-Marshment (2012, 184) notes how, when seeking re-election in 2011, the New Zealand National Government adopted the slogan *Building a brighter future*, which tied in with their aspirational, brighter-future theme when first elected in 2008 but argued delivery was in process – it was being built, on the way. Billboards talked of *Rebuilding Christchurch, Staying strong on crime* and *Building better public services*. This helped their argument to voters to give them a second term to complete the process.

Conveying the benefits of policies

As Elder (2016a; 2016b) notes, political leaders need to convey the benefits of policy decisions. US President Barack Obama also targeted his communication of delivery benefits around the Recovery Act, such as to save and create jobs or being globally competitive. However, such communication should avoid simply selling – Elder notes how President Obama spoke in a salesperson-like manner to a town hall audience about the benefits of health care reform, adding 'there are so many good things about this I might have forgotten one' (2016b, 13). If they can get the communication right, however, and convince the public that they are effective at delivering on their goals, this can generate trust that the governing leader will achieve future delivery. This also helps to justify leadership decisions. Former New Zealand Prime Minister John Key, who succeeded in remaining in power for nearly three terms, communicated the range of benefits for the public of proposed tax changes including increased GST. As the proposal to increase GST broke a previous election promise, he introduced the idea carefully into the public sphere, discussing the pros and cons and justifying it in the economic context. For example, he linked the proposal to public frustrations with limited progress on improving living standards within the context of the global recession and how they had done as much as they could. Arguably this approach worked: Key's public standing increased between October 2008 when elected and October 2010, with a media poll showing an increase from 38 per cent thinking he was more honest than other politicians to 67 per cent; and from 55 to 70 per cent thinking he had sound judgement.

Giving voters credit for delivery

In the UK, the Labour government gave credit to voters for helping achieve change when seeking re-election in 2001, with adverts picturing ordinary voters with slogans such as,

'I did it. I created new jobs for a million people.' In the 2012 election, Obama issued an ad called '*Young Americans are Greater Together*', which listed achievements including ending combat operations in Iraq, getting rid of the 'Don't ask don't tell' military policy on homosexuality, comprehensive health becoming a reality and Wall Street being reformed, and then the President said, 'All that is thanks to you.'

Individualising delivery

Lees-Marshment (2011, 181–3) identified how practitioners increasingly try to individualise delivery success and impact. The UK Conservatives under David Cameron pictured the leader sitting in people's houses bought using the government's *Help to Buy* scheme to convey the personal impact of the policy. But delivery can also be individualised much more precisely than that. Practitioners argue that people don't live in the 'state on average': they live in, and experience services, in specific locations. Governments need to convey what has been achieved more individually. UK Labour's 2005 online manifesto had a personalised section where you could type in your address, your age, your family status and your working status. You would get the benefits that you and your local community would have seen: *x* number of more police on the beat, more teachers in your local schools, more doctors and nurses, etc.

New Zealand practitioner Simon Pleasants, who worked in Labour Prime Minister Helen Clark's office, noted how they collected and supplied local data on national developments to go to local MPs to use. For example, if they had administrative articles about school funding or early childhood education grants being given out, this would normally be announced by the minister but not get any interest in local media (interview quoted in Lees-Marshment 2011, 183):

> the *Gisborne Herald's* not going to be interested in that. The *Manukau Courier* isn't going to have interest in that at all . . . so, what I [do] would be to follow the local stats, numbers . . . and make up a whole lot of local media releases and fit those out to the local MPs.

Similarly, once back in power the Labour Party under Jacinda Ardern created an app for people to use to identify how much they were better off under the new government's policies after they had been in power for ten months.

Reminding voters of achievements and harvesting a reputation for delivery

Reminding voters of achievements is an important aspect of delivery communication. Conley's (2014) analysis noted how Obama issued a series of adverts leading up to his re-election in 2012 called '*Keeping his word*' on issues such as hate crime legislation, credit card reform, extending unemployment insurance, early childhood education, making college affordable, lowering the cost of Medicare prescriptions, equality for LGBT Americans, health coverage for young Americans and creating manufacturing jobs. New Zealand National's ads in 2017 reminded voters of achievements such as having built four new hospitals and having given 800,000 children under 13 free GP visits. Once a reputation has been built up for delivery in power, parties can utilise this in future elections. Elder (2016b, 106) notes how in the 2017 New Zealand election the National Party's communication focused on a message that they had delivered, but there was more they could do, discussing delivery directly in their *'Clear choice'* television commercial, as seen below:

> First, we got New Zealand back in the black. Then we got hundreds of thousands more Kiwis working. Now our economy is growing strongly, and we have a chance to do more for you and solve some of our greatest long-term challenges . . . Vote for the team that's delivering.
>
> (New Zealand National Party 2017)

> The National Party also campaigned on the track record of their leader, Bill English, for getting them through the global financial crisis when Minister of Finance, calling him a 'rock'.
>
> (Lees-Marshment 2018a)

Communicating delivery in coalition

Communicating delivery in coalition is difficult for both major and minor partners. Major parties have to take care to ensure their minor partners can be seen to deliver significant change to be re-elected and continue to support them in parliament. Rudd (2005) notes how the New Zealand Labour Party tried to ensure it gave credit for delivery of certain policies to its junior coalition partner, the Alliance, during 1999–2002, such as the establishment of the 'People's Bank' as a subsidiary of New Zealand Post.

However, it does not always work out to be an advantage to take part in a coalition for the junior partner. The UK Liberal Democrats issued a party political broadcast in September 2012 noting their achievements in coalition government with the Conservatives after being elected in May 2010, such as the scrapping of identity cards and the shutting down of the national identity database, the removal of income tax for low earners, cutting of emissions and extra funding for poor children at school. Nevertheless, key elements of their brand – such as changing the electoral system to proportional representation – were not successfully delivered after they lost a referendum to implement a system different to the one they themselves wanted. Their overall competency for delivery was then further threatened by having to compromise to fit in with Conservative policies such as those on student fees and loans.

Communicating mayoral and individual politicians' delivery

Individual politicians can also communicate their own delivery. In the US, Steger (1999, 668–9) observed that, given the decentralised structure which means they act individually, elected officials in Congress are able to claim credit for a number of activities in their state, such as:

- fixing funding formulas to the benefit of their market;
- pressurising bureaucrats who decide who qualifies for funding;
- securing tax breaks for their constituents;
- opposing potentially damaging regulatory legislation; and
- helping the public with problems with government and agencies, and fighting for benefits and grants.

Similarly, Lilleker (2006, 212–4) argues that, at a local level, an incumbent candidate's success in delivery in terms of the service they have provided for their constituents can affect the outcome of the election. MPs carry out casework for their constituents, or campaign to attract industry or other funding, such as from the European Union, or create networks between associations; all of which can create a positive reputation for a politician when they face re-election.

For example, one US consultant Lees-Marshment (2011) interviewed noted how an incumbent in a governor's race in Michigan in 2006 found they had to give specific examples, such as noting how the governor had gone to Japan and got ten companies to come and invest money to build a plant in the state; and how Google opened their East Coast place in Michigan, which would employ 1,000 people. When they told those individual stories and they were able to get a lot of traction, then they were able to get people to agree he had achieved something.

Another example in Australia is where a Labor MP, Tanya Plibersek, issued leaflets in the 2010 election with specific statistics related to local areas, such as $150 million to build a new Chris O'Brien Cancer Centre at Royal Price Alfred Hospital in Camperdown, $3 million to support the rebuilding of the Wayside Chapel and $2 million to help redevelop South Sydney Youth Services in Waterloo. Such specific examples help to show action in an area that is more visible to local residents. In the UK, Jim Knight, Labour MP for Dorset South, used communication to weather the unpopularity of the incumbent Blair government in the 2005 general election (Lilleker 2009). Knight conducted local market research through extensive media monitoring to discover the issues of the area. Anything he could deliver a solution to was communicated to voters. For example, he supported local campaigns such as a campaign to reduce deaths on the roads and reported how he had dealt with 5,953 individual pieces of casework solving the problems of local voters. He personalised his campaign, focusing on local delivery, and research on voter perception showed that the MP was overwhelmingly seen as the *'best representative for me and my community'* and the *'candidate who best addressed my concerns'*.

As well as national/federal governments, premiers, governors and mayors also engage in delivery marketing. Maki (2014) explored how mayors in New Zealand and Australia utilised innovative forms of delivery marketing to create 'signature moments'. For example, in July 2011, train passengers travelling to Auckland's Britomart station were greeted with cake from Mayor Len Brown to celebrate a record 10 million train passenger journeys in one year. The large cake was made in the shape of a train, along with an edible marzipan Mayor Brown figurine leading the way in front of a sign saying, 'To be continued', implying his delivery would carry on progressing. Better public transport and increased numbers were part of the Auckland Plan, and this signature moment was an effective way of displaying service delivery. The simple act of sharing slices of cake with citizens at the train station innovatively celebrated and communicated Brown's delivery progress. Similarly, Brisbane Mayor Graham Quirk's election pledge included tackling traffic congestion and improving suburban roads. Thus, when the 500th new bus was completed, Quirk advertised this delivery using large banners printed onto the buses stating: 'We've delivered 500 new buses! More buses, more comfortable, more often'. Emblazoned on the vehicle itself, as these buses drove around Brisbane they provided a constant reminder of Mayor Quirk's marketing in government and communication of delivery. Ryan Mearns also discusses mayoral marketing in Case Study 8.2. Exploring the use of delivery marketing by Auckland mayor Phil Goff, he details how the mayor met the passenger who completed the 100 millionth trip on Auckland's public transport network in a single year, and how, after announcing progress on his commitment to plant one million trees, he conducted media interviews and a promotional video.

Political marketing delivery in the workplace

The emphasis on delivery in modern governments is increasing, and thus jobs in this area will grow. Practitioners working on delivery can have a range of job titles. While Michael Barber was Chief Advisor on Delivery and head of the first delivery unit, Matthew Mendelsohn's role in the Trudeau government is called Deputy Secretary to the Cabinet (Results and Delivery) Privy Council Office, and Ben Keneally was called Executive Director in the NSW Department of Premier and Cabinet. Press secretaries and chiefs of staff also work on delivery, as do directors of finance and policy. In the UK Government, delivery is currently overseen by a unit called the Efficiency and Reform Group (ERG), which works in partnership with HM Treasury and government departments to deliver efficiencies, savings and reforms on behalf of UK taxpayers.

Practitioners working on delivery reflect on pre-election pledges/commitments and revisit them to make sure the strategy to achieve them is okay. They coordinate and encourage achievement of policy implementation within the government, and monitor progress in policies. They also create ideas for communicating progress/achievement to the public – see for example Obama's 'keeping his word' ads in the 2012 election – to try to get the public to give them credit for success and insatiable demand, such as by localising and individualising achievement.

The role includes working with multiple stakeholders – as Mearns notes in Case Study 8.2, the Auckland Mayor's Office has to engage in careful negotiations and relationship building with the organisations controlled by the Council, the Governing Body of Councillors, and key community and business stakeholders.

When interviewed about his role, Mendelsohn (2017) said,

> My role is about ensuring that government is in a good place to deliver on the commitments in the ministers' mandate letters. It's to help ministers and departments overcome obstacles that may arise in terms of delivery. [My role and the unit] is really about doing three simple things. First, it ensures the objectives are clear for new programs or policies. Second, it ensures the delivery plans are clear. Third, it ensures there is an appropriate measurement strategy to see if results are being achieved, if the policy outcomes promised to Canadians are being realized and, if not, how the policy can be re-calibrated or adjusted.

The tasks and skills involved in delivery include monitoring and tracking results, data analysis, outcome analysis including medium- and longer-term outcome measures, aligning the public service and ministers to focus on the same outcomes, establishing accountabilities and metrics, monitoring operational performance and change management, as well as communicating progress – public reporting on results, data and evidence. As Mendelsohn (2017) explained, they need 'the public service to have big data analytical skills . . . people who can visualize data and processes and have the ability to communicate that visually through infographics and other means' as well as 'crowd sourcing, open-source policy-making, and stakeholder engagement activities'. For further insight, see Barber's (2007; 2011) books.

Summary

Delivery is an increasingly important part of political marketing as we move towards greater focus on the change that politicians achieve. It starts with ensuring that pre-election promises are costed and achievable and clear, to help convey that politicians are ready to govern and manage expectations. Once in power, politicians need to overcome constraints of government and build good relationships with the bureaucracy to get legislation passed and make delivery happen. Any failures need to be carefully managed, and success has to be communicated at individual levels to get traction with the public. Box 8.2 offers an overall guide to effective delivery marketing in practice.

Delivery management and marketing is an area of practice that will grow in the future. Effective delivery marketing helps to create trust and convey leadership competence. Whiteley *et al.* (2016, 234)'s analysis of British governments concluded that if the public feels the government is delivering policy then they will trust it even if they do not agree with all the decisions made. Similarly, Elder (2016) makes clear how important it is to communicate the benefits of policy decisions to maintain voters' perception that the leader is competent. Getting delivery right is important to create space for policy leadership in power.

Nevertheless, delivery marketing raises democratic issues. Anna Esselment explores the wider consequences in Democratic Debate 8.1, including how delivery marketing can encourage cynicism among the public, because it encourages parties to prioritise four to five policy areas in campaigns, and then in government not all delivery issues can be easily 'tracked' and it can take several years if not decades to deliver effective solutions for more complex policy areas. However, Michael Barber defends delivery as being part of, not counter to, leadership. He argues that:

> People 'need a leader they trust, an agenda they believe in, ideology they identify with . . . but behind all great politicians, all inspiring leaders, is somebody working it through and actually delivering it . . . [politicians] really do mean their promises. They might struggle to implement them, but they believe them when they make them. They're not just bribes.'
>
> (Barber 2015)

There are many potential ethical implications of all aspects of political marketing, and the next and final chapter explores these as well as summarising key lessons from the textbook.

Box 8.2 Best practice guide to political marketing delivery

Think about delivery before you fight the election and use pre-election delivery tools:

1 Create key pledges or priorities to build credibility that can be delivered easily once in power, to help build initial support to help mitigate more difficult delivery.
2 Connect expectations to outcomes.
3 Reassure voters about the potential costs and benefits of proposed policies.
4 Build a reputation for managing delivery.
5 Communicate delivery challenges.

To make delivery happen once in power:

6   Sit down with bureaucrats after the election and go through promises and priorities.
7   Facilitate networks, relationships and conversations to prevent fallouts, stepping on people's toes and so forth and get legislation delivered.
8   Create delivery units to help success.
9   Create the will of those doing the delivery to succeed: give examples of progress and success, don't blame them publicly, ensure tasks and goals are clear, and work with – not against – them.

Communicate delivery progress and success:

10   Use good visuals with symbolic as well as specific delivery images.
11   Deliver quick wins – e.g. 100-day plans.
12   Show progress if not completion.
13   Convey the benefits of policies.
14   Give voters credit for delivery.
15   Individualise delivery – localise central government stories and statistics.
16   Remind voters of achievements and harvest a reputation for delivery.

Manage problems in delivery:

17   Be honest about problems or failures in delivery.
18   Propose a solution to the failures.

In coalition/partnership:

19   Make sure all parties can show some delivery.

At mayoral/governor level:

20   Use all the same techniques as well as guerrilla or signature communication moments to focus attention on delivery.

" Discussion points

1   Why is delivery marketing in government difficult?
2   How have recent politicians sought to manage expectations for delivery before getting elected? How effective do you think these are?
3   In what ways did Donald Trump's 2016 election campaign go against delivery marketing theory? What consequences has this had for his government?
4   How effective do you think pledges, contracts and guarantees are in making the product seem more deliverable and managing expectations?
5   What factors do political leaders have to bear in mind when trying to make delivery happen once elected?
6   To what extent do you think the current government has followed Esselment's model for successful political marketing delivery?

7 How effectively to you think politicians manage failures in delivery?
8 Drawing on Anna Esselment's Democratic Debate, discuss whether delivery marketing is good or bad for democracy.

Assessment questions

Essay/exam

1 How effective do you think current governments are at communicating their delivery progress? What do they need to improve on, and how might they do this?
2 How successfully have leaders in power communicated delivery?
3 Have you seen examples where your local politician has tried to communicate delivery? How have they done it – did they individualise results, show progress – and how effective did it seem to you?
4 Discuss the difficulties and potential solutions to marketing delivery in government.
5 Discuss the different relationships and stakeholders involved in making delivery happen in power, using both theory and empirical examples.
6 'Delivery units can thus keep a majority government focused and can assist coalition partners by doggedly pursuing the implementation of its agreed-upon agenda, thereby minimizing conflict between the parties and contributing to a productive government partnership.' To what extent do you think Esselment is correct that organisational units help governments deliver?
7 Critique the way that governments have communicated delivery progress and success using literature and empirical examples.
8 In what ways have governments and politicians sought to communicate delivery progress and success, and how effective is this?
9 To what extent do you think over-ambitious promises like building a border wall can be delivered symbolically through alternative immigration policies or executive orders?

Applied

1 Assess the pre-election delivery marketing of a major party and how effective it was at managing expectations and helping get credit once promises were delivered, and from this draw guidelines for the future.
2 Critique a current leader's management of stakeholder relationships in the delivery of a key policy (e.g. Obamacare, Trump's travel ban) in light of recommendations from existing research on that and other cases of successful and failed delivery, and draw up generic lessons from this for future governments' delivery management.
3 Assess the delivery marketing of a current government against Esselment's model for successful political marketing delivery, and suggest how they might improve in future.
4 Critique governments' management of failures to deliver or when they renege on promises and, from this as well as existing literature, identify principles of effective delivery problem management.
5 Compare and contrast the effectiveness of delivery communication of progress and success by different governments. Drawing on this and academic research, devise lessons for future governments about how to communicate progress and success.

6   Analyse five different incumbent politicians' communication of delivery success during an election campaign, discussing whether it follows guidelines in the literature or shows any new trends, and provide guidelines from this for future communication of delivery success.

7   Discuss whether delivery, motivated by other aspects contributing to the political marketing framework, can negatively impact what we consider to be good governance, as Esselment suggests in Democratic Debate 8.1.

Case studies

Case study 8.1 The importance of communicating delivery: A case study of Justin Trudeau's government

By Hannah Lobb (University of Auckland)

After running a very successful election campaign, Justin Trudeau was elected Prime Minister of Canada in November 2015. This case study analyses the Trudeau government's delivery progress and communication halfway through its term in office. It illustrates the importance for leaders to follow through on election promises and communicate delivery successes in order to retain support.

The Trudeau government has been delivery focused from the beginning

Trudeau took office in Canada immediately following Stephen Harper, whose government is recognised as exemplary in terms of delivery. In general, there is an increasing pressure on leaders to deliver during their time in office, but following Harper, Trudeau had even more expectant eyes upon him.

Trudeau's Liberal Party, therefore, established itself as delivery focused very early on. The party's campaign slogan 'Real Change' made evident their commitment to delivering promises and implementing policies to positively change the lives of Canadians.

Upon entering office, the Prime Minister then took steps to ensure that his government would stay focused on delivering promises. Most significantly, Trudeau brought Michael Barber in as a delivery consultant. Barber is known as a delivery guru, as he successfully led UK Prime Minister Tony Blair's delivery unit between 2001 and 2005. In addition to hiring Barber, the Trudeau government also hired Matthew Mendelsohn to keep a constant eye on their delivery progress.

Experts agree that having teams dedicated solely to delivery is essential for governments who want to appear credible to their voters and retain support throughout their term in office (Esselment 2012). It is easy for the government to get distracted by daily tasks and issues management, so it is imperative that delivery is made a priority.

Trudeau demonstrated his commitment to delivery early on, by bringing Barber and Mendelsohn on board. It is evident two years on that this commitment has proved effective in terms of policy wins.

The government experienced a successful first year in office

The Trudeau government was able to fulfil more campaign pledges in the first year than any other Canadian government. These 'quick wins' are incredibly valuable in terms of political marketing best practice, as they help to earn the government credibility early on and can be relied upon in the event of a surprise election (Esselment 2012).

Among the 54 promises that the Trudeau government managed to implement in its first year were a number of substantial policies that could constitute 'real change'. Reaffirming one of his major campaign promises to 'grow the middle class', Trudeau managed to introduce tax cuts for the middle class and implement the Canada Child Benefit, which is a policy designed to improve the lives of struggling families.

Unfortunately, the Prime Minister has not yet benefited from his delivery successes, because he has yet to communicate them effectively.

Despite quick wins, Trudeau lost support during his first year

In June 2017, polls showed that Trudeau was still the most popular leader in Canada, but his approval ratings had fallen during his first year in office (Grenier 2017). During this period, the popularity of the Liberal Party had also fallen (Grenier 2017).

These results suggest that despite the government being delivery focused and following through on their campaign promises, the public has not yet registered Trudeau and his government's delivery achievements.

Similar to many other contemporary governments, there is a feeling among the Canadian public and academic community that the government is not working effectively. This emphasises the need for the government to focus on the communication of delivery in addition to passing policies.

The Trudeau government has fallen victim to a service delivery gap

Two years into his term in office, Trudeau is suffering from a service delivery gap. A gap occurs between performance and perception when a government has delivered on promises in their priority areas but the public does not feel as if this is the case (Lees-Marshment 2011).

The government's priorities upon entering office were:

1   Growing the middle class.
2   Stronger diversity.
3   International engagement that makes a difference in the world.
4   Improved relationships with, and outcomes for, Indigenous peoples.

Despite passing the two policies for the middle class mentioned earlier, as well as many others that fall into these four priority areas, the Trudeau government is not currently perceived as effective.

Political marketing research has shown that leaders must communicate their delivery successes effectively if they wish to retain or increase support in return for their kept promises. Leaders not only need to communicate progress to the public as soon as possible, they also need to show how their new policies are going to make a difference (Conley 2014).

In terms of best practice, a good strategy for communicating delivery is focusing on local benefits and telling personal stories of how policies have affected real people (Lees-Marshment 2011). Trudeau's government has an opportunity to improve in this area.

Lessons for political marketing scholarship and practice

Political marketing scholarship has shown that delivery-focused governments are successful in retaining public support throughout their time in office. For this reason, new governments, including Trudeau's, continue to make use of delivery teams and delivery experts in the hope of retaining public support and earning re-election.

The Trudeau government emphasised its commitment to becoming a delivery-focused government early on in the campaign and followed some aspects of best delivery practice, including bringing experts on board and achieving quick wins.

Unfortunately, Trudeau's government has not as yet proved as effective as other delivery-led governments, as the Prime Minister and the Liberal Party have both lost support during their time in office. This emphasises the need for governments not only to deliver but also to communicate their achievements meaningfully.

Trudeau's government emphasises the need for governments to show the public how their lives have changed positively as a result of policy successes, in order to earn public support.

Further Reading

Conley, Brian (2014). 'Does Obama care?: assessing the delivery of health reform in the United States'. In Jennifer Lees-Marshment, Brian Conley and Kenneth Cosgrove (eds) *Political Marketing in the US*. New York: Routledge, 272–88.

Esselment, Anna (2012). 'Delivering in Government and Getting Results in Minorities and Coalitions'. In Jennifer Lees-Marshment (ed.) *Routledge Handbook of Political Marketing*. New York: Routledge, 303–15.

Grenier, Éric (2017). 'Justin Trudeau's approval ratings down since last summer recess: polls'. *CBC News*, 26 June 2017. www.cbc.ca/news/politics/grenier-trudeau-approval-1.4173056.

Lees-Marshment, Jennifer (2011). *The Political Marketing Game*. London: Palgrave-Macmillan.

Case Study 8.2 Delivering as the Mayor of Auckland: Phil Goff's first year

By Ryan Mearns (University of Auckland)

Phil Goff's campaign positioned him to be Mayor of Auckland based a mix of policy proposals with widespread support, a reputation as a competent Cabinet Minister in the previous Labour government, and as a voice of experience. Goff's political positioning was based on his ability to deliver, which makes his alignment with the literature on political delivery marketing during his first year worth consideration.

During the election campaign in 2016, the Goff campaign set out pre-delivery expectations

Esselment and Lees-Marshment argue policy promises should be both 'realistic' and 'achievable' in order for voters to consider the product deliverable (Esselment 2012; Lees-Marshment 2014). A realistic but unachievable election promise is outside of the resources available of the Mayor's Office and requires actors outside the Mayor's Office's control.

An unrealistic but achievable election promise is within the resources of the Mayor's Office to deliver but may take longer than the mayor's term to complete.

The policies that the mayor's campaign promised were for the most part achievable, clear and realistic, with some exceptions. An analysis of the mayor's policies on his campaign website indicate 47 promises that should be in the process of being completed during his three-year mayoral term. Of the mayor's promises, 32 promises were realistic and achievable, 11 were realistic but unachievable and 4 were unrealistic but achievable (Goff 2016). A range of promises were unrealistic because they require actions from actors that are outside the control of Auckland Council, such the introduction of a 10-cent levy on plastic bags, which would require legislation from central government. A clear example of an achievable and realistic environmental policy that can be delivered by Council is the planting of one million trees, as Auckland Council has land available and partner organisations which can provide the seedlings and plant the trees.

As Mayor of Auckland, Goff begun the process of delivering from day one

The mayor does not have the power to unilaterally deliver on all of their election pledges. To do so requires the Mayor's Office to engage in careful negotiations and relationship building with the organisations controlled by Auckland Council, the Governing Body of Councillors, and key community and business stakeholders.

The mayor has the power to set the agenda through their office's communications resources, and the fact that they control the organisation of Council policy committees and who is selected to chair these committees. The mayor still relies, however, on being able to gain a majority of 11 votes on the Governing Body to pass resolutions, including budgets. This adds complexity to the process of delivery. An example of the Mayor's Office organisational self-awareness was the establishment of a so called 'kitchen cabinet' of the committee chairs and deputies of the three most important committees.

The Mayor's Office began the process of creating a delivery unit with the appointment of David Wood as the Director of Finance and Policy in the Mayor's Office. The Director of Finance and Policy directs the formation of the mayor's budget. Bringing a former senior Treasury official to oversee the priorities of the Mayor's Office would indicate the Mayor's Office has moved towards the 'deliverology' approach of Barber and is in line with the literature on political marketing delivery (Barber 2007).

So far, the Mayor's Office has achieved a range of quick wins that have established momentum and generated visible results. An example of the Mayor's Office taking steps to build an important relationship that will support delivery and ensure greater accountability between the mayor and a Council Controlled Organisation was the appointment of Sir Michael Cullen, the former Finance Minister who served with Goff in the previous Labour government, to be on the board of Auckland Transport.

For voters to see their expectations met, the Mayor's Office must communicate the progress and successes of policy initiatives at every stage

Political delivery communication should ideally be a mix of showing progress, if not completion, showing that the mayor is working together with other stakeholders, individualising delivery and generating what Barber calls 'signature moments' to demonstrate delivery (Barber 2007).

The passing of the 2017–2018 Annual Budget was a good chance to communicate policy progress of the Mayor's agenda. As part of the Annual Budget process, the mayor had an issue attracting support for a new accommodation levy after pressure came from the Tourism Lobby. News articles framed the policy as 'Goff's Bed Tax' (Maude 2017). There was a lack of clarity about how it would be delivered and what was its purpose. By finding a middle ground and halving the accommodation levy, the mayor was successful in attaining the votes for it to pass. This demonstrates that the mayor is getting the credit for the budget, but focuses more on the controversy over it, rather than what it means for the budget in terms of the $13 million revenue the accommodation levy would generate.

The mayor used signature moments to be seen engaging with the public and demonstrating delivery. The mayor met the passenger who completed the 100 millionth trip on Auckland's public transport network in a single year for the first time. Another example of a signature moment was the mayor's announcement of how he was delivering on his one million trees commitment. The mayor's announcement of the progress on the policy was at a local nursery and was supported by media interviews and a promotional video on the Auckland Council Facebook page. This illustrates a clear alignment with the political delivery marketing theory and execution.

Lessons for political marketing scholarship and practice

The case shows that delivering as Mayor of Auckland can be a challenge, but specific lessons can be drawn from Phil Goff's first year, including:

- Political delivery marketing literature provides insights not just for central government, but also ones that can be applied to local government and vice-versa.
- Both in the pre-delivery phase and when in power, policy which is within the clear control of a Mayor's Office should be prioritised in communication.
- For realistic but unachievable election promises, a Mayor's Office should make sure to communicate the limitations of delivery to ensure voters don't punish them in the next election for not fully delivering.
- For unrealistic but achievable election promises, a more interim goal should be sought.
- The structure of local government committees can be used to increase accountability for political delivery from independent political representatives.
- A small-scale delivery unit that is accountable to policy areas within a Mayor's Office can help to provide impetus for delivery.
- Relationships are important, and appointing former colleagues that are both qualified and have shown previous ability to deliver will aid policy delivery.
- To avoid issues with industry groups' opposition to proposals, a strategy should be developed in coordination with industry to strengthen the arguments for a policy initiative being put into action.
- Signature moments and quick wins help to add peaks to delivery communication that demonstrate progress and momentum.

References

Barber, Michael (2007). *Introduction to Deliver*. London: Politicos.

Esselment, Anna (2012). 'Market Orientation in a Minority Government: The Challenges of Product Delivery'. In Alex Marland, Thierry Giasson and Jennifer Lees-Marshment (eds) *Political Marketing in Canada*. Vancouver: UBC, 123–38.

Goff, Phil (2016). 'Policies'. Phil Goff For Mayor website. www.forabetterauckland.org.nz/policies (accessed 4 June 2017).

Lees-Marshment, Jennifer (2014). 'Political Delivery Marketing'. In *Political Marketing: Principles and Applications*. New York: Routledge, 224–46.

Maude, Simon (2017). 'Auckland Mayor Goff's "Bed Tax" Passes 10–7'. *Stuff*, 1 June 2017. www.stuff.co.nz/business/93238804/auckland-mayor-goffs-bed-tax-gets-by-in-tight-vote.

Democratic Debate 8.1 Canada's Liberal Government as delivery devotees

By Anna Esselment (University of Waterloo)

Delivering on promises is a significant stage of the political marketing framework. Parties present their ideas to the electorate, voters make their choices, and newly installed governing parties display energy and enthusiasm with regard to checking off the items in their campaign platform. Before long, of course, the achingly slow churn of the machinery of government has either indefinitely delayed the implementation of election promises or triggered their abandonment altogether. Governments can find it exceedingly difficult to focus on delivering priority outcomes by the end of a four-year mandate. As we have seen in this chapter, devoting resources to a dedicated 'delivery' or 'implementation' unit at the centre of government can help keep a governing party on track to uphold their pledges. Delivery encourages governments to think hard about what they want to achieve, how they will go about meeting those goals, and how to measure whether or not their promises are ultimately met.

Canadian Liberal Prime Minister Justin Trudeau is a devotee of delivery. Elected in the fall of 2015, his government moved swiftly to set up a 'Results and Delivery' unit within the Privy Council Office (PCO). The unit itself staffs 40 public servants and has three subdivisions: data integration, impact and innovation, and results and delivery. Within its first year of governing, the Liberal Cabinet had been briefed three times by Michael Barber himself on the key aspects of 'deliverology' (Barber *et al.* 2010); as a result (and in addition to the PCO unit), many government departments have also designated an official responsible for results and delivery, as well as a data officer who analyses and tracks the pertinent metrics.

The emphasis on delivering results to the public has commendable features. When done well, a focus on delivery demands transparency from government. The Trudeau government was the first federal government in Canada to publicly publish mandate letters to ministers (Government of Canada 2015). A mandate letter is written from the Prime Minister to a Cabinet Minister, outlining the policy issues that should be prioritised within the minister's department. They are helpful in many respects, not least of which is the reminder to new ministers, in particular, of where they should concentrate departmental resources. But these are documents that have traditionally been kept private between the Prime Minister's Office and the individual Ministers of the Crown. The Liberal government decided that, in the interest of openness, all Canadians should know what each minister has been asked to deliver, and posted each letter on the Prime Minister's website for Canadians to review.

Knowing the directives to each department is one thing, but tracing the progress on the key commitments is entirely another, and doing so is the linchpin of the delivery model. Consequently, in November 2017 the government went further and began publicly reporting on headway towards fulfilling their promises. A new website called the 'Mandate Letter Tracker' (Government of Canada 2017) was created, and interested Canadians could check in on how the Liberals were doing and, by extension, hold the Government accountable. As of late March 2018, the tracker indicated that of the 364 commitments made by the Liberals, 80 had been fully met, 232 were underway, and others were either underway but facing challenges, not being pursued, completely modified, or were considered 'on-going commitments'. From their computers, Canadians can click on the different priorities of the government and read the explanations for why commitments were completed, in progress or deserted. Tracking mechanisms means delivery is on display, and this can spark conversations among citizens, students, academics, journalists and others about what the government is doing about certain matters of public policy, how they are going about effecting change in their identified priority areas, and where they are falling short. In some areas, the degree to which delivery is complete (or not) has a material impact on the lives of citizens. If the government is lagging on improved housing and services for Indigenous peoples, for example, future outcomes for those young people remain at risk. When high-speed broadband coverage does not materialise, residents in rural areas are cut off from sources of information that could be helpful in any number of ways, including online job searches. The transparency and accountability emphasised through the lens of delivery opens government more fully to its citizens; when opportunities arise, such as town hall meetings held by the Prime Minister, Canadians can ask some hard questions about policy outcomes.

At the same time, the emphasis on delivery can also have negative implications. When parties make promises and do not deliver, cynicism among the public may increase. If citizens question the sincerity of their leaders, or the capacity of their political institutions to implement changes to public policy, that scepticism can transform into lower levels of political participation and trust in government, which is problematic for the democratic experiment. Emphasis on results also tends to oversimplify the complexities involved in governing, which is to the detriment of citizens and their representatives alike. Not all problems or issues can be easily 'tracked', and sometimes small progress in a policy area can have a positive impact on affected communities, even though a bold 'commitment upheld' label on a website is not suitable. As a result, governing parties often choose outcomes that are rather vague, precisely because delivery success can be defined rather loosely. Promising a 'crackdown on tax evaders', as Justin Trudeau's government has done, leaves a lot of room for interpretation when it comes to delivery and results. The same is true where governments are embedded in federal arrangements. There could be a number of policy areas where the federal government has promised improvement, but implementation is dependent on cooperation with provincial or state governments; this creates an obvious complication to delivery.

Scholars have noted that, on average, democratically elected governments in the Western world deliver on 63 per cent of their promises; Canadian governments do slightly better at 68 per cent (Thomson *et al.* 2017). When we consider the popular perception that governments tend to *break* their commitments (Ibid), these rates are quite respectable. This also suggests that a fixation on delivery is more about a governing party's struggle to effectively communicate its achievements to the public than it is about encouraging that particular government to actually follow through on its pledges.

It behoves us to remember that in order to win at delivery most governments only prioritise four or five commitments, and doing so raises democratic concerns. An obsession with delivery in an era of increasingly lower voter turnout means that the only promises *really* worth pursuing in government will be the ones that please certain segments of the electorate – the groups who can be counted on to support the governing party. This can have the effect of isolating citizen out-groups and deepening divisions within the larger citizenry. Furthermore, what happens when delivery in one area becomes so important that it dominates public resources at the risk of budget needs elsewhere? Can delivery, motivated by other aspects contributing to the political marketing framework, negatively impact what we consider to be good governance? These are just some of the considerations that are critical to an examination of delivery through a democratic lens.

Sources

Barber, Michael, Andy Moffit and Paul Kihn (2010). *Deliverology: A field guide for educational leaders*. Thousand Oaks, CA: Corwin.

Government of Canada (2015). Mandate letters. *Office of the Prime Minister*. https://pm.gc.ca/eng/mandate-letters (accessed 12 January 2018).

Government of Canada (2017). Mandate letter tracker. *Privy Council Office*. www.canada.ca/en/privy-council/campaigns/mandate-tracker-results-canadians.html (accessed 1 February 2018).

Thomson, Robert, Terry Royed, Elin Naurin, Joaquín Artés, Rory Costello, Laurenz Ennser Jedenastik, Mark Ferguson, Petia Kostadinova, Catherine Moury, François Pétry and Katrin Praprotnik (2017). 'The fulfillment of parties' election pledges: A comparative study on the impact of power sharing'. *American Journal of Political Science*. doi: 10.1111/ajps.12313.

References

Ardern, Jacinda (2018). Facebook live discussion about the Families Package, 1 July 2018. www.facebook.com/jacindaardern/videos/today-is-the-day-the-families-package-comes-in-couldnt-help-but-share-a-few-thou/10155347263617441/.

Associated Press, The (2017). 'Transcript of AP interview with Trump', 23 April 2017. https://apnews.com/c810d7de280a47e88848b0ac74690c83.

Barber, Michael (2007). *Instruction to Deliver*. London: Politicos.

Barber, Michael (2015). Quoted in '"It doesn't feel credible": the political parties' pledges rated and slated' by Jon Henley. *The Guardian*, 5 April 2015. www.theguardian.com/politics/2015/apr/05/wages-healthcare-schools-taxes-can-parties-deliver-promises.

Barber, Michael, Andy Moffit and Paul Kihn (2011). *Deliverology 101: A Field Guide For Educational Leaders*. Thousand Oaks, CA: Sage.

British Library (2013). 'Alastair Campbell in Conversation: Politics, the People and the Press'. Public Conversation with Steve Richards. *YouTube video*, 17 May 2013. www.youtube.com/watch?v=_Gu4ZEMOB78.

Conley, Brian M. (2014). 'Does Obama care?: assessing the delivery of health reform in the United States'. In Jennifer Lees-Marshment, Brian Conley and Kenneth Cosgrove (eds) *Political Marketing in the US*. New York: Routledge.

Conservative Party of Canada (2015). 'Proven Leadership'. YouTube campaign advert, published 25 May 2015. https://youtu.be/um1pc0ZpW10.

Elder, Edward (2016a). 'Market-Oriented Governing Leaders' Communication: John Key and Barack Obama'. *Journal of Nonprofit & Public Sector Marketing*, 28(1): 5–21.

Elder, Edward (2016b). *Marketing leadership in government: communicating responsiveness, leadership and credibility*. London: Palgrave Macmillan.

Elder, Edward (2018). 'Chapter 7: Communicating Market-Oriented Leadership in power and opposition'. In J. Lees-Marshment (ed.) *Political marketing and management in the 2017 New Zealand election*. Basingstoke, UK: Palgrave Macmillan, 85–100.

Esselment, Anna (2012a). 'Delivering in government and getting results in minorities and coalitions'. In Jennifer Lees-Marshment (ed.) *The Routledge Handbook of Political Marketing*. London and New York: Routledge, 303–15.

Esselment, Anna (2012b). 'Market orientation in a minority government: the challenges of product delivery'. In Alex Marland, Thierry Giasson and Jennifer Lees-Marshment (eds) *Political Marketing in Canada*. Vancouver: UBC, 123–38.

Government of Canada (2016). 'Sir Michael Barber: Results and Delivery Unit: Lessons for Canada'. Canada School of Public Service YouTube video, published 26 May 2016. www.youtube.com/watch?v=JogXHgPXhVs.

Hamburger, Peter (2006). 'The Australian Government Cabinet Implementation Unit'. In *Improving implementation: organisational change and project management*. http://press-files.anu.edu.au/downloads/press/p118751/mobile/ch18.html (accessed 11 April 2008).

Johnson, Dennis W. (2013). 'The election of 2012'. In Dennis W. Johnson (ed.) *Campaigning for President 2012: Strategy and Tactics*. New York: Routledge, 1–22.

Klein, Ezra and Sarah Kliff (2013). 'Obama's last campaign: inside the White House plan to sell Obamacare'. *The Washington Post Wonkblog post*, 17 July 2013. www.washingtonpost.com/blogs/wonkblog/wp/2013/07/17/obamas-last-campaign-inside-the-white-house-plan-to-sell-obamacare/ (accessed 18 July 2013).

Lees-Marshment, Jennifer (2011). *The Political Marketing Game*. Houndmills, UK and New York: Palgrave Macmillan.

Lees-Marshment, Jennifer (2012). 'National and Labour's leadership, branding and delivery in the 2011 New Zealand election'. In Stephen Levine and Jon Johansson (eds) *Kicking the Tyres: The New Zealand General Election and Electoral Referendum of 2011*. Wellington: Victoria University Press, 177–89.

Lees-Marshment, J. (2018a). 'Chapter 4: Messy Marketing in the 2017 New Zealand Election: the incomplete market-orientation of the Labour and National Parties'. In J. Lees-Marshment (ed.) *Political marketing and management in the 2017 New Zealand election*. Basingstoke, UK: Palgrave, 43–66.

Lees-Marshment, J. (2018b). 'Chapter 8: Conclusion: Political marketing and management lessons for research and practice'. In J. Lees-Marshment (ed.) *Political marketing and management in the 2017 New Zealand election*. Basingstoke, UK: Palgrave, 117–38.

Liberal Party of Canada (2015). 'Fairness for the Middle Class'. YouTube campaign advert published 5 May 2015. https://youtu.be/h-wKMJ3zsiA.

Liberal Party of Canada (2016). '27 Promises Kept'. YouTube advert published 4 November 2016. https://youtu.be/OWGV9ORPctQ.

Lilleker, Darren (2006). 'Local political marketing: political marketing as public service'. In D. Lilleker, N. Jackson and R. Scullion (eds) *The Marketing of Political Parties*. Manchester, UK: Manchester University Press, 206–30.

Lilleker, Darren G. (2009). 'Case study 7.5 Local political marketing: connecting UK politicians and voters'. In Jennifer Lees-Marshment *Political Marketing: Principles and Applications*. London and New York: Routledge, 188–9.

Obama, Barack (2012). 'The Road We've Traveled'. Pre-campaign minidocumentary, published 15 March 2012. www.youtube.com/watch?v=2POembdArVo.

Maclachlan, Robin (2016). Comment in CBC programme featured in '"Deliverology" guru schools Trudeau government for 2nd time at cabinet retreat'. *CBC News*, 26 April 2016. www.cbc.ca/news/politics/deliverology-liberal-cabinet-retreat-1.3553024.

Maki, Renisa (2014). 'Case study 8.2 Marketing mayors in government: Graham Quirk and Len Brown's delivery communication'. In Jennifer Lees-Marshment *Political Marketing: Principles and Applications*, 2nd edition. London and New York: Routledge, 243–5.

Mendelsohn, Matthew (2017). 'Meet Canada's "deliveryman"'. *Queens University Gazette*, 16 January 2017. www.queensu.ca/gazette/stories/meet-canadas-deliveryman.

New Zealand National Party (2017). 'Clear Choice'. YouTube election advert, 18 September 2017. www.youtube.com/watch?v=S6fbp8G3mks.

Praprotnik, K. (2017). 'Jurisdiction, time, and money: The role of resources in pledge fulfillment'. *Party Politics*, 23(6): 848–59.

PolicyExchangeUK (2012). 'Frank Luntz interview – Political communication: New lessons from the US'. YouTube video, 26 November 2012. www.youtube.com/watch?v=eYAuvyA216c.

Rehr, David R. (2013). 'The challenges facing Obama'. In Dennis W. Johnson (ed.) *Campaigning for President 2012: Strategy and Tactics*. New York: Routledge, 25–42.

Rudd, Chris (2005). 'Marketing the message or the messenger?' In Darren Lilleker and J. Lees-Marshment (eds) *Political Marketing in Comparative Perspective*. Manchester, UK: Manchester University Press, 79–96.

Steen, Jens Jonatan (2009). 'Case Study 8.3 When politics becomes contractual: a case from Denmark'. In Jennifer Lees-Marshment (ed.) *Political Marketing: Principles and Applications*. London and New York: Routledge, 230–2.

Steger, Wayne (1999). 'The permanent campaign: marketing from the hill'. In Bruce Newman (ed.) *The Handbook of Political Marketing*. Thousand Oaks, CA: Sage, 661–86.

Telegraph, the (n.d.) 'Memorable Conservative, Labour and Liberal Democrat posters from previous election campaigns'. www.telegraph.co.uk/news/picturegalleries/uknews/7582239/Memorable-Conservative-Labour-and-Liberal-Democrat-posters-from-previous-election-campaigns.html?image=14 (accessed 28 August 2018).

Temple, Mick (2010). 'Political marketing, party behaviour and political science'. In Jennifer Lees-Marshment, Jesper Strömbäck and Chris Rudd (eds) *Global Political Marketing*. London: Routledge, 263–77.

Trump, Donald (2016). *Contract with the American Voter*. https://assets.donaldjtrump.com/_landings/contract/O-TRU-102316-Contractv02.pdf (accessed June 2018).

Wells, Paul (2016). 'Meet Sir Michael Barber, the political delivery man'. *Macleans*, 18 February 2016. www.macleans.ca/politics/ottawa/meet-sir-michael-barber-the-political-delivery-man/.

Whiteley, Paul, Harold D. Clarke, David Sanders and Marianne Stewart (2016). 'Why Do Voters Lose Trust in Governments? Public Perceptions of Government Honesty and Trustworthiness in Britain 2000–2013'. *British Journal of Politics & International Relations*, 18(1): 234–54.

9 Conclusion

Political marketing practice and ethics

by Jennifer Lees-Marshment

Political marketing involves strategy, market research, branding, communication and delivery. It is used by all political organisations, including government, parties, campaign teams and NGOs to achieve wide-ranging goals including creating policy change, representing particular groups in society, changing behaviour, increasing participation, winning or being part of government, managing leaders' reputations and maintaining or attracting public support. Political marketing is used to help organisations build positive relationships with their market, which includes stakeholders such as voters, members, donors, staff, lobbyists, groups and the media. This chapter will summarise how political marketing is used in practice and discuss ethical implications.

Political marketing in practice

Political marketing involves researching the market, strategising about how best to respond to it in terms of what decisions to make and which policies to pursue, and organising resources including volunteers, staff and budgets, as well as communicating.

Political marketing practitioners work in strategy, market research, branding, internal organisation, communication and delivery. They work both within and outside political organisations and in neutral and partisan positions. For example, there are directors of strategy, pollsters, data analysts, branding directors, campaign managers, outreach officers and community organisers, communications advisors, advertisers, press secretaries, digital marketers, heads of delivery units and chiefs of staff.

Practitioners take different approaches to the way they use political marketing. They can use it to sell – conducting research to identify how best to persuade the market to support their offerings and actions. Or they can use that research to inform what they do, creating products and brands responding to what the market wants. They can also use relational political marketing such as public relations and careful leadership communication to create long-term positive relationships. And they can involve the market in co-creating the political product.

Similarly, academics are researching different facets of political marketing through wide-ranging methods. The best overarching research philosophy for political marketing that allows for varied methods is pragmatism, because it aims to have a potential practical application by identifying what works. The great strength of political marketing research (PMR) is its applied potential: it can generate guidelines for best practice to improve – not just comment on or critique – the real world.

Strategising in practice

Political marketing strategy is about how political practitioners and organisations formulate plans that address and respond to multiple factors including market demands, stakeholders, competitors and resources to achieve their goals. Strategising includes sales- or market-oriented and populist strategists, targeting, positioning and political branding, the latter of which includes brand equity, brand personality, brand heritage and authenticity, brand delivery, policy branding, nation branding and managing, and decontaminating brands.

Strategies include sales- or market-oriented approaches which influence the overall strategic decisions as to whether politicians and parties should use research to sell the product on offer or design a product the market wants. Sales-oriented parties use market intelligence to identify persuadable voters and design more effective communication to make people want what they offer, whereas market-oriented parties (MOPs) and politicians use market intelligence to identify voter demands and design a product that meets their needs and wants.

For MOPs, marketing is less about persuasion and more about responding to the demands of the market. Barack Obama's 2008 presidential campaign in the US, David Cameron's 2015 campaign in the UK, Justin Trudeau's 2015 federal campaign in Canada and Jacinda Ardern's 2017 campaign in New Zealand provide clear examples of market-oriented strategy (Mullen 2016; Delacourt 2016; Lees-Marshment 2018). But once in government, parties and politicians have to work hard to retain a market-oriented strategy because the pressures, workload and need to show leadership mean politicians lose that sense of being in touch. Practitioners need to use tools to regain a market-orientation such as conducting listening exercises, refreshing the overall team, using non-political communication, acknowledging public concern with unpopular leadership decisions and ensuring there is space to think about product development for the next election. For instance, UK Labour conducted 'The Big Conversation' in 2003 and Canadian PM Justin Trudeau went on a listening tour in 2018.

Political organisations and politicians also respond to external changes when devising their strategy. These responses can include conforming to change, refusing to change, or trying to influence – or getting ahead of – change by being more entrepreneurial. Obama's 2008 campaign sought to transform the playing field by using language, symbols and norms focusing on change (Winther Nielsen 2012). Populist strategies capitalise on discontent to do whatever is needed to win, something which leaders such as Venezuelan leader Hugo Chavez and Austrian Freedom Party's (FPÖ) leader Jörg Haider have followed. More recently, radical right-wing parties have done the same. Marine Le Pen and the National Front in France combined a populist 'ideology' and 'style' along with anti-immigrant policies (Stockemer and Barisione 2017), while Donald Trump turned to simplistic messaging, negative repetition and anti-immigrant policy proposals to appeal to voters dissatisfied with the Obama government and their living standards (Conley 2018).

Targeting involves allocating resources and energy to understanding, responding to and attracting specific segments and micro-targets that are needed to achieve goals, rather than trying to please everyone. This utilises market research to divide the market into different groups – also known as universes (see the chapter on static political marketing communications) – by geographic, demographic and psychographic characteristics. This then informs policy development and enables differentiated communication. For example, the Liberal Party in Canada divided the nation's 388 electoral districts into six types, which varied from 'platinum ridings' which were regarded as 'sure bets', to 'gold' and 'silver' districts where the party had a real chance of picking up seats, to 'bronze' districts that would likely make the party the majority if they made any gains, to 'steel' and 'wood' districts where the party was essentially non-competitive (Delacourt 2016, 299).

Positioning is about ensuring the organisation or politician is placed in an effective position in relation to the competition. There is no point for everyone to go after the same voters and to hold the same policy positions: it is important to devise and maintain differentiation from competitors to stand out, but also to inform the most appropriate strategies. The position should be clear and consistent. Strategy also needs to take account of market position: leaders need to have broad appeal and defend their market share, challengers should focus on new issues and characterise the leader negatively, and nichers aim to serve the needs of a specific market and propose more radical policies. US presidential candidate Donald Trump benefited from adopting the challenger position. He did so by referring to his opponent as 'Crooked Hillary' and championing dissatisfaction with the status quo in 2016. The Canadian Liberal campaign in 2015 used an 'escalator' ad to position Trudeau to the left of both the Conservative and New Democratic Party leader on the issue of deficit spending. Trudeau argued that, unlike the other leaders who would stall growth (and stop the escalator), he had a plan to get the economy (and the escalator) going again by investing in the country (Delacourt 2016, 314).

Political brands are the overall impression the market has of an organisation or practitioner. Brands need to be simple, differentiated, reassuring, aspirational, symbolising better values, and seen as credible and likely to deliver. Canadian Liberal Party Leader Justin Trudeau created a brand for the 2015 election with a *Real Change* slogan. It emphasised aspiration within a value-driven frame of 'better Canada', and Trudeau's discussion of being ready with a plan to deliver built credibility (see Case Study 4.1 by Amber Wharepapa). Similarly, Barack Obama's 2008 brand was simple and reassuring. It was centred around the aspirational rhetoric *Yes We Can* and offered Obama's political and community experience as credibility (Conley 2012, 128; Cosgrove 2012, 109). Party brands need to be developed in response to research but also implemented internally, otherwise they do not help the candidate. Conley (2012) argues that the US Democratic Party struggled to link with the success of the Obama brand. This may have contributed to Hillary Clinton's failed bid to win the presidency in 2018.

Brand equity involves ensuring a party or candidate is viewed as superior to the competition by being the one voters are most aware of, loyal to, perceive highly and have positive associations with. Australian Labor built up a very positive brand around their new leader Kevin Rudd in 2007. It increased their equity, but that equity declined when Rudd failed to deliver on key brand-defining promises, such as action on climate change. This left voters with a severe case of post-purchase dissonance and brand discipline dissolved in government (Downer 2016).

Brand personality is important to political leaders and candidates. Positive personalities have characteristics such as openness and empathy, honesty, energy and charisma, competence and leadership, toughness and strength, and uniqueness. Challengers with high energy and charisma tend to win over incumbents with competence. Charismatic and high-energy outsider Donald Trump beat the insider and highly competent Hillary Clinton in the US 2016 presidential election, and open and charismatic Jacinda Ardern won over the proven competence of incumbent Bill English in the New Zealand 2017 election.

Brand heritage is the long-standing reputation of political parties. Candidate Donald Trump harnessed the Reagan-originated Republican Party brand of a smaller state, lower taxes and a strong America, projecting himself as someone who would restore America's glory. He also integrated his own personality traits and position as an outsider to update it to a change-making brand: *Make America Great Again* (Cosgrove 2018).

Brand authenticity is increasingly important as it can limit the ability of strategists to 'design' the perfect party or candidate brand. Candidates each have their own personality, physical attributes and history, which has to be taken into account. The case where Palin was designed to be a vice-presidential brand that appealed to Walmart-Mom swing voters but was then dressed in designer clothes and later revealed strong traditional core Republican views is a clear illustration of this (Busby 2012, 220). Branding needs to be authentic for voters to believe it.

Policy branding is used by leaders in office to attract public support and in turn influence other stakeholders including politicians, lobbyists and the media. Practitioners devise key phrases to convey the values of policy and overall brand concepts, such as *The New Deal, The Great Society and No Child Left Behind*, that resonate with the public, and common values such as strength, reliability and fairness, and convey wider benefits beyond the specific policy (Barberio and Lowe 2006).

Nation branding is used to help countries attract tourists and business by identifying strengths and weaknesses, and attempting to overcome any historically outdated images. For example, New Zealand suffered from being seen as geographically remote and full of sheep. It was firstly branded as '100 per cent pure', then boosted by connecting the country and the national airline with movies *The Lord of the Rings* and *The Hobbit* to increase tourism, and most recently broadened to include NZ Story with themes such as *Open Hearts, Open Minds and Open Places*.

Re-branding and decontaminating brands is needed as negative images are hard to change. Negative associations from Prime Minister Margaret Thatcher's 1979–1990 government still impacted the UK Conservatives when David Cameron was trying to re-brand the party in 2005. Cameron sought to decontaminate the brand by conceding past mistakes, adopting new policy focuses such as environmentalism and social welfare, and organising communication of community action days to ensure behaviour and communication consistently conveyed the new brand position (see Lees-Marshment and Pettitt 2010; Smith and French 2009).

Researching in practice

Political market research includes polling and surveys, segmenting and profiling the market, data analytics, focus groups, co-creation, informal low-cost political market research and opposition research.

Polling uses quantitative methods to measure opinion and its strength, providing big numbers or surface-level data. Polls are used at different times and for varying purposes, including benchmarking the existing situation at the start of a campaign, delving into particular issues or crises, and tracking progress. Polling is ubiquitous in politics, both public for the media and privately for parties and campaigns.

Segmenting and profiling the market breaks up the heterogeneous, mass electoral market into smaller sections according to geographic, demographic, psychographic and behavioural factors. It helps identify groups that are then targeted in terms of product, message and medium. In the 2004 US presidential election, Republicans divided Michigan voters into 31 political categories such as religious conservative Republicans, tax-cut conservative Republicans and flag-and-family Republicans, anti-terrorism Republicans and harder-to-reach groups such as wageable weak Democrats (Johnson 2007).

Strategists for the Canadian Conservatives in the 2006 and 2008 federal elections identified about 500,000 voters out of the 23 million eligible voters to target to achieve victory, creating swing voter categories (Turcotte 2012, 85).

Data analytics collects and harvests behavioural data from multiple sources, time periods and organisations to produce new understanding and insights to inform strategy and communication. Data is also utilised to build statistical models that predict how voters will behave in response to a range of potential actions and messages from political organisations and politicians. For example, in the 2008 Obama campaign, an analyst identified that, of the hundreds of variables on voters in Wisconsin which the algorithms explored, mass-transit ridership was most influential: those who rode on public transport were most likely to support Obama. The campaign then combined data on the city's bus routes with individuals with high support scores and commissioned the media/advertising agency GMMB to purchase ads on those buses (Issenberg 2012, 11–12).

Focus groups are used to understand current views and desires, potential for change in opinion, and test reactions to proposed policies and communication phrases. For example, the UK Labour Party strategist Phillip Gould used focus groups to understand why the party lost in 1992 despite the unpopularity of the Conservative Government. It identified that Labour was judged by its past, associated with phrases such as Winter of Discontent, union influence, strikes and inflation; that Labour's values were negative, aimed at depriving people of wealth, choice in education and health, and ownership; that the party was seen as hostile to aspiration, wealth and entrepreneurship, and that it was no longer seen as the party of 'ordinary working people', with people saying, 'I've left the Labour Party and the Labour Party has left me' (Gould 1998, 5). This informed the substantial redesign of the party to New Labour, with the new slogan *New Labour*, the new logo known as 'the red rose' and the adoption of more market-oriented centre-ground policies.

Co-creation includes methods such as role play and two-chair work. It is used to involve the consumer in creating solutions to the problem instead of just identifying what they want. The firm Promise used co-creative techniques to understand and find solutions to the disconnection between Blair and UK voters which had grown during Labour's second term. The creative techniques they used not only explored the underlying feelings of voters towards Blair to help understand the problem on a much deeper level than polls would ever identify – because they took the approach of asking the public how to make things better – but also identified a potential solution to Blair's unpopularity. They asked participants to write letters to Blair to express how they felt and used 'two-chair work' to role play Blair as they currently saw him and then how they would like him to be. This informed a reconnection strategy where Blair acknowledged and listened to criticism. This helped improve his public standing (Langmaid 2012).

Opposition research involves researching a candidate's background, both professional and personal, as well as identifying any weaknesses including scandals, unethical behaviour, problematic voting records, tax history, property records, social activities and public comments that may be used by against them in campaigns to inform attack or defence strategy. One notable example is when Obama resigned from the Trinity United Church of Christ in Chicago, which he had been a member of for 20 years, when controversial comments made by the pastor, the Reverend Jeremiah Wright, were widely circulated by the media and threatened to damage his brand for the 2008 election.

Political market research is all about obtaining information to inform other aspects of political marketing. It is resource intensive, but potentially extremely important to ensure strategic decisions and communication are effective.

Organising in practice

Political organising includes understanding volunteer demands, creating volunteer-friendly organisations, creating unity, engaging in relationship marketing and fundraising.

Understanding volunteer demands is important to parties wanting to build strong volunteer and membership bases to help them gain market intelligence and campaign for funds and votes. Research needs to be conducted to understand what volunteers want and need, which can include social – not just political – factors but also flexibility to suit volunteers' busy and varied lives, segmenting volunteers into different types and levels of activity. For example, in 2015 the New Zealand Labour Party issued a survey on Facebook to help people let them know how they would like to get involved; it asked them what skills they might contribute and what activities they would be willing to do in their area as well as online.

Creating volunteer-friendly organisations is about responding to what volunteers want and need and designing organisational structures to suit the volunteer, not just the party or NGO. Organisations should offer multiple ways of engaging with a party and campaign. The aim is to make it as easy as possible for someone to get involved. Training and support are offered to volunteers. Online communication and resources have replaced traditional campaign headquarters. Volunteers also help act as part-time marketers for their party or candidate, gathering informal market intelligence for them. In 2014, the Canadian Liberals conducted a survey exploring their supporters' views on different issues. Between 2004 and 2008, the US Democrats told volunteer neighbourhood leaders to report back on what they were hearing, seeing and what issues were coming up in conversations with neighbours (Lees-Marshment 2011). The Obama campaign's MyBo website gave details on local events, voter information and information on who to target, not only making it easier for volunteers to help but by giving them access to data helping them feel empowered and involved (Lees-Marshment and Pettitt 2014).

Creating unity involves careful internal management of the implications of, and work involved in, the rest of the political marketing activities. Changing the product or brand can create internal discontent as it appears to threaten values, ideology and policies. Efforts to focus on the market can meet resistance from stakeholders, and leaders have to work hard to maintain unity behind any new direction they wish to forge. Tactics include involving stakeholders in discussions about reform, disseminating market research to demonstrate the need for change, holding internal meetings, acknowledging the party's history, and emphasising the ultimate goals of getting into power or advancing key policy goals. The product and brand need to be adjusted to suit the internal market. George W. Bush did so in 2000 to suit internal criticism in the primaries by stressing traditional conservative Republican themes such as limited government (Knuckey and Lees-Marshment 2005). Leaders try to blend new and old views. For example, UK Conservative leader David Cameron sought to appeal to internal markets by discussing social responsibility which blended traditional conservatism focused on self-responsibility with the need to care about society and others.

Engaging in relationship marketing involves volunteers in creating new products and brands, seeking ideas and participation beyond campaigns to the long term and forging a strong relationship that can then support politicians in government and through crisis. During Obama's 2008 campaign, strategists worked closely with paid field organisers to support volunteer coordinators on local Obama social networking groups and help them feel empowered, with the phrase 'Because it's about you' appearing at the top of the Action page. The campaign was open to changing the way it worked in response to volunteers' views. It also gave them tools to take action themselves and promote internal discussion to help share best practice among volunteers in order to forge positive relationships between the campaign and the grass-roots (Levenshus 2010).

Fundraising draws on many aspects of internal political marketing, such as conducting market research to understand donor behaviour, segmenting the potential ways to contribute from small to big donations, pre-testing appeals for funds, enabling volunteers to help fundraise and seeking to form positive relationships with donors. Appeals are connected to tangible outcomes not just in campaigns but in government. The Democratic Party's *Organising for America* utilised online marketing to fundraise money to support Obamacare. It first ran a competition to vote on the best citizen-created video supporting health insurance reform and then asked for donations to air the winning ad (Marland 2012). The New Zealand National Party offered different options for contributing in 2016, linked to tangible outcomes, such as $30 for a billboard or hoarding, $60 for a door-knocking pack and $125 for a paid video ad on Facebook.

Communicating in practice

This includes static communications – selling – which covers research-led and targeted communication and ads to garner support and get the vote out, celebrity marketing, selling policy, communicating change, crisis management, and relational and interactive communications, which includes e-marketing, public relations, leader communication and reputation management. Delivery marketing covers making precise promises or pledges, building a reputation for managing delivery, communicating delivery challenges, delivery units, managing problems in delivery and communicating progress and success using good visuals, delivering quick wins, showing progress if not completion and conveying the benefits of policies.

Research-led communication is about responding to the market in the way political practitioners and organisations communicate, utilising research to identify what it is the market wants and needs. For example, Donald Trump created simplistic, polarising messages which helped to forge an emotional bond with members of the US working class. Communication includes phrases and speeches as well as non-verbal attributes such as clothing and body language. Campaign ads are designed according to research. They help identify a range of views, insights, hopes, fears and perceptions. Big data research profiles prospective voters, which helps with the design of campaign messages and ads. Communication is pre-tested to attain various objectives, including identifying the best phrases to use to sell policies or novel guerrilla-type forms of communications. Online ads are adapted to suit different segments or micro-targets, directly reaching individuals. Research-informed communication is also used to get the vote out at polling time.

The Czech Social Democratic Party (CSSD) tripled its support among voters in the 2006 elections by using research to inform campaign strategy and message, utilising focus groups with swing voters, a quantitative benchmark poll to assess the position and support for all the parties among different voter blocks, issue importance, and reaction to potential messages and policy offerings (Braun and Matušková 2009). Volunteers wearing T-shirts with 'Kevin07' in the 2007 Australian Labor campaign helped to boost the new leader Kevin Rudd's brand, and in 2016 Donald Trump's supporters bought and wore bright red trucker's hats with the slogan *Make American Great Again*. Donald Trump's presidential campaign in 2016 utilised data services from the UK-based firm Cambridge Analytica to provide a granular understanding of the US political market, which they used to develop compelling messaging focused on specific policies, including the economy and immigration. Ads were highly segmented with thousands of versions of the same Facebook advert specifically tailored to connect with slices of the market (Conley 2018; BBC 2017).

Celebrity marketing involves celebrities in campaigns to help politicians capitalise on their following. For example, Justin Trudeau's personal Instagram feed included pictures of him interacting with nationally and internationally renowned cultural, political, sports and media celebrities, including the UK's Prince Harry (Lalancette and Raynauld 2017).

Selling policy is used in advertising to promote specific programmes, policies or behaviours, ostensibly for the public good through social marketing campaigns like 'Don't drink and drive'. It is also utilised in order to help the party in power be re-elected. The UK Conservative government previously used research-driven advertising to see the privatisation of public utilities British Telecom and British Gas, to raise capital and create greater efficiency in the 1980s, appealing to individual needs and desires by showing how the public could gain from buying shares, with emotive advertising such as the White Cliffs of Dover, and more down-to-earth ads featuring ordinary people discussing how they could become shareholders (Allington *et al.* 1999, 637). The Liberal government led by John Howard used at least $20 million of taxpayers' money to create ads in order to build support for its planned industrial relations changes before the legislation had even been seen, let alone passed, by parliament (Young 2005).

Communicating change involves multiple patterns of communication over the long term, especially if it is to convey changes in the brand. David Cameron's re-branding of the Conservative Party after the 2005 election involved sustained communication strategies to convey a new research-informed strategy focusing on environmentalism, the poor and world affairs, such as photo opportunities of Cameron cycling to work, visiting Darfur in Africa, planting trees on a social action day, visiting a Norwegian glacier and meeting Nelson Mandela, as well as a new party symbol with a green tree and blue sky (Lees-Marshment and Pettitt 2010).

Crisis management involves handling unexpected crises and is particularly important in government, which gets hit by daily crises and unforeseen events. It is also conducted in campaigns when crisis can derail the planned strategy, or whenever any major issue or scandal hits a political figure or political organisation. Crisis management involves getting control over the situation, conceding any failure and reassuring the public the matter is being managed effectively.

E-marketing is about utilising online communication. Best practice involves ensuring it includes two-way communication, stimulates engagement and interaction, and builds networks and relationships rather than simply 'selling'. It can be used to increase participation and reinforce relationships rather than just sell a product, and for internal supporters within parties and campaigns. For example, candidates who used Twitter interactively in the 2010 Dutch national elections benefited from a significant positive impact on the number of preferential votes they received (Kruikemeier *et al.* 2016). During the 2010 UK general election, party-centred online community websites such as Labournet, LibDemAct and MyConservatives utilised interactive communication, giving supporters a place to connect, interact and mobilise (Lilleker 2015).

Public relations can be viewed as another form of relationship-building communication. It is designed to activate and utilise publics which are supportive or open to supporting an organisation or practitioner. It involves on-going activities designed to forge positive relationships with key publics through multiple events and communication, rather than single campaigns or events. The New Zealand Greens worked over several elections to put climate change on the agenda, through careful strategising, ad creation and brand building, and in 2017 succeeded in having it adopted as a key focus by the Labour leader Jacinda Ardern and then acted on in government. While they did not reap rewards in voting terms, they activated latent publics with vote compass data revealing strong support for environmental policies (Lees-Marshment 2018).

Leader communication and reputation management is about placing political leaders among voters to show genuine concern for and appreciation of their views, even where they disagree. Communication needs to show them interacting with the public, and listening to them through the body language, even on issues where they are showing leadership. Leaders need to communicate respectful acknowledgement of public concerns and criticism as well as strength and competence to be able to maintain an image of being in touch. They also use language that echoes the way ordinary members of the public talk to teach other, and discuss non-political factors such as their own family and personal interests to come across as more authentic. Reputation management is proactive communication designed to create a reputation for competence, care and trustworthiness that will withstand any crisis. New Zealand Prime Minister John Key's communication around increasing the Goods and Services Tax (GST) in 2010 involved acknowledging critiques, noting the potential benefits to the public and conveying genuine concern through close-up camera shots to simulate connection with the public (Elder 2016). Similarly, the leader of the Dutch People's Party for Freedom and Democracy transformed his image in 2010 from being ill-suited to be a contender for prime minister by re-directing critique from who would pay the price for any pain measures needed during the economic crisis to who needed to be protected, connecting to his core theme of a 'responsible society' and showing awareness of the consequences of his proposals with concrete examples (Van Zuydam and Hendriks 2018).

Pre-election delivery includes a range of activities leading up to an election to convey the ability to deliver. The first is making precise promises or pledges, which, if achieved once in power, can help leaders to manage expectations and get credit for those achievements. Politicians also seek to reassure voters about the potential costs and maximise the benefits of proposed policies. Another method is to build a reputation for managing delivery through releasing fiscal plans and 100-day plans. Incumbent leaders communicate the delivery challenges they have faced and overcome, aiming to capitalise on their delivery record to gain re-election. Tony Blair's UK Labour Party issued credit-card-sized pledges with specific measurable outcomes such as 'we will cut class sizes to 30 or under for five, six and seven-year olds by using money saved from the assisted places scheme' and Helen Clark's New Zealand Labour Party also offered credit-card pledges such as no interest on student loans, 250 extra community police and 5,000 more modern apprenticeships in 2005. In 2015, Canadian Liberal leader Justin Trudeau attempted to reassure voters that a proposed tax increase was fair, noting on Facebook that the average income of Canada's wealthiest 1 per cent had grown by 77 per cent in the last 30 years, and thus he was just asking them to 'pay a little bit more, to help Canadians who need it most'. The Liberals also released an ad titled '*Fairness for the Middle Class*', which detailed the Canada Child Benefit and how they would lower taxes for those less well-off while Trudeau proposed creating a new top tax bracket meaning, according to the ad, that 'the wealthiest Canadians will pay a bit little more but that also means a fairer chance for the middle class to make ends meet and to help our economy grow' (Liberal Party of Canada 2015). The Canadian Conservatives tried to convey Stephen Harper's strong experience in the 2015 ad '*Proven Leadership*', which discussed the unexpected and unpopular decisions prime ministers have to make.

Making delivery happen in power includes forging effective relationships with relevant stakeholders to get legislation through and creating delivery units to drive achievement across government. For example, the UK Labour Government under Blair set up the Prime Minister's Delivery Unit (PMDU) in 2001, Australia created a Cabinet Implementation Unit (CIU) at the centre of government in 2003, and Canadian Prime Minister Justin Trudeau appointed Matthew Mendelsohn as Deputy Secretary to the Cabinet to lead a Results and Delivery Unit in 2015.

Managing problems in delivery involves acknowledging weaknesses and making it clear you are taking action to address them. When the Canadian Conservatives under Harper failed to keep a promise, they addressed it directly, conceding they were breaking a promise but explaining why given challenging and changed financial circumstances since the election (Esselment 2012, 129).

Communicating progress and success can be done through using good visuals that convey achievement effectively, delivering quick wins to build trust, showing progress if not completion of delivery, conveying the benefits of policies – especially at an individual level – and reminding voters of achievements once in power. Examples include Harper's Conservatives placing a bright blue '5%' GST sticker onto a cash register in a retail store – a strong visual that stayed in people's minds (Esselment 2012, 135). The Canadian Liberal Government under Justin Trudeau implemented over 50 promises in its first year, including tax cuts for the middle class and the Canada Child Benefit. It also issued an advert titled '*27 Promises Kept*', showcasing achievements such as gender-balanced Cabinet, new Canada Child Benefit, lowered taxes for the middle classes and higher taxes for the wealthiest 1 per cent. The Labour Government in New Zealand elected in 2017 focused on delivering its 100-day plan, which included policies such as free study for the first year of university, setting up a tax working group and beginning Kiwibuild to address the housing crisis. The New Zealand Labour Government under Helen Clark collected and supplied local data on national developments to go to local MPs to release to local media, breaking high-level ministerial data on school funding or early childhood education grants down into local statistics. Obama issued a series of '*Keeping His Word*' ads during his re-election year (2012). It reminded voters of tangible achievements on issues such as hate crime legislation, credit card reform, extending unemployment insurance, early childhood education, equality for LGBT Americans and health coverage for young Americans.

Overall, political marketing practice is diverse and rich, encompassing the following four core areas: strategising, researching, organising and communication. Box 9.1 summarises the key concepts in political marketing practice.

Box 9.1 Twenty-five core best practice political marketing principles

1   Allow time for creating a strategy early on, but keep adapting it to suit any changes in the environment.
2   Integrate research, understanding of stakeholders, targets, and party history and beliefs into strategy development.
3   Use a range of PMR methods continuously including quantitative polling, surveys, data analytics, profiling, focus groups and co-creation on voters and key stakeholders.

4   Use PMR to understand consumerist voters in terms of what they want, need, hope, fear, and to test how they might behave or react to different products and messages.

5   Try to respond to the market as much as possible, rather than just using marketing to sell your views. Use PMR proactively to create room for leadership on key policy areas.

6   Don't go after everyone: segment the market and focus on micro-targets that will most likely influence outcomes. Adopt differentiated positions from competitors.

7   Develop and maintain an effective political brand that is clear and coherent, differentiated, reassuring; aspirational, symbolic of superior internal values, credible and competent, sincere and trustworthy.

8   Communicate a politician's positive brand personality traits such as openness and empathy, honesty, energy, charisma, competence, leadership, toughness, strength and uniqueness. Challengers should emphasis energy and charisma to connect emotionally.

9   Manage a party's brand equity to ensure the public's awareness of the brand is high, they remain loyal and they hold positive associations of it.

10 Use policy branding to gain public support for key policies to influence stakeholders and ensure legislative success.

11 Decontaminate a negative brand before re-branding through comprehensive behaviour and communication to make the re-brand convincing.

12 Make sure the brand design fits with the politician's own personality, product and behaviour to ensure it comes across as authentic.

13 Research and respond to the demands, expectations, needs and behaviour of the internal market of volunteers, supporters, donors and members. Provide a range of ways for them to be involved and help you achieve your goals.

14 Involve volunteers in collecting market intelligence as well as campaigning.

15 Train and reward volunteers to maintain motivation.

16 Make the argument about the need for power to achieve policy change to ensure unity.

17 Develop communication to suit the market, using research-led and pre-tested advertising in terms of focus, message, medium and style, and heavily targeting online dark ads to suit individual preferences, interests and profile.

18 Attract attention through novel communication and celebrity marketing.

19 Use multiple communication forms, including public relations and reputation management over the long term, to build positive relationships and trust with voters.

20 Use e-marketing to enable two-way and interactive communication, not just selling a position.

21 Leaders need to acknowledge criticism of unpopular decisions to remain in touch with less polished communication forms and less formal language.

22 Use pre-election delivery tools such as pledges, benefit explanations, reassurance about costs, and budgetary plans to build delivery competence.

23 Work with stakeholders and create delivery units to drive delivery in power.

24 Manage problems in delivery by conceding problems and proposing solutions.

25 Communicate delivery progress and success through good visuals, quick wins, showing on-going progress, and conveying the benefits of policies on an individual level with localised stories and statistics. Make sure minor parties in a coalition can claim credit for delivery of key policies.

Marketing deeply permeates elections, parties, campaigns and government. It has profound effects on the way politics works. As has been seen through the democratic debates in previous chapters, the breadth of political marketing practice raises a range of ethical issues which will be debated in the next section.

Political marketing and ethics

The ethical issues from political marketing, and potential rebuttal

As we have seen in this book, political marketing is broad in scope, and impacts on policy, representation, leadership and indeed democracy itself; there is a continual debate among scholars about its impact on democracy. Earlier works such as Lees-Marshment's market-oriented party (2001) argued that the use of research made politicians more responsive to voters, ensuring they were more in touch with voters' key concerns. But the recent success of politicians such as Donald Trump, which has been tied to more problematic use of market research data, encourages new reflection on that conclusion. There has not yet been comprehensive research into the democratic nature of Trump's use of political marketing to offer a full conclusion on that case. Indeed, democratic debates in this book have pointed both to his potentially manipulative use of big data and to his representation of previously ignored voices. The jury is therefore still open when it comes to these cases, but it is clear we need to be aware of both the negative and positive implications political marketing can have so that those who practice political marketing make informed choices as to how they decide to use it. The core issues are summarised in Table 9.1.

Using political marketing unethically

There is no doubt there are legitimate concerns about the importance political marketing places on the value of the voter. Marketing is about designing political products to suit the consumer, after all. But what if the consumer is 'wrong' and leads politicians to make bad decisions for the country? A market-oriented strategy is criticised for putting

Table 9.1 Ethical issues from political marketing: Concerns and rebuttal

	Ethical concerns	**Potential rebuttal**
Policy	Marketing encourages a focus on short-term actions the market wants now, rather than more effective long-term solutions the country needs in the long term.	Market research and strategic communications are used to identify ways to increase public support for less popular but justifiable policy. Government public opinion research can help ensure that policy is effective in achieving its goals.
	Emphasising the need to ensure policies appeal to the market reduces policy innovation.	More creative and deliberative forms of qualitative research are used to explore new policy problems and solutions, and research can help identify the best way to communicate to build support for new policy ideas.

(continued)

Table 9.1 (continued)

	Ethical concerns	**Potential rebuttal**
Leadership	Market research encourages political leaders to listen to public opinion, which is problematic due to lack of information, expertise and objectivity.	Market researchers argue that the public is rational and smart. Research has demonstrated that leaders do not just follow market research; it is just one of many inputs into their decision making.
	Consumerist voters do not judge governments fairly.	Delivery marketing is used to demonstrate achievements.
	Prevents politicians showing leadership on unpopular but socially beneficial policies such as climate change.	Politicians use research to help show their leadership on key issues. Research can be used to identify persuadable segments of the public and develop effective communication. Limitations on leadership are reflective of democracy itself, not political marketing.
Representation	Appealing to the most influential markets gives some people more power than others.	Greater research, segmentation and strategy helps elites understand the diverse needs of different segments and target markets in order to develop policies to suit.
	Marketing can encourage false and inauthentic stereo-typical appeals such as photo opportunities between politicians at cultural events or eating ethnic foods.	The best political marketing will genuinely seek to understand and respond to the needs of different segments in the population.
Citizenship	Treating voters like consumers discourages them to consider ethical, moral and community aspects.	Consumers can consider, and be encouraged to consider, the ethical implications of their choices.
	Marketing politics like a product encourages focus on policies that produce tangible outcomes rather than what actually works.	Delivery marketing helps identify key tangible outcomes and quick wins in a few areas, building trust to enable a focus on more complex policies over the long term.
Participation	As the larger market, voters are more important than members, reducing the value of party participation.	Research and segmentation are used to understand how people want to participate and create more individualised options for involvement.
Authenticity	Research leads candidates to change their policies, presentation and even personality, rendering politics to a false shopping exercise.	Political marketing research argues that all tools and strategies need to be adapted to suit the politician as voters want their candidates to be authentic.

too much emphasis and trust in public opinion. Lane (1991, 47–9) argues that the mass public is generally less interested in politics, less tolerant and more punitive towards disliked groups, less willing to discuss sensitive policies, and less able to weigh the costs of policies supported than political elites. The results of the UK's Brexit referendum and the 2016 US presidential election have given more steam to these arguments in recent years.

Conley (2018, 30–1) argues that 'Trump based his core message and policy positioning on a detailed, research-driven understanding of how specific voters segments targeted by his campaign think and behaved politically.' By itself, this is not new. But what made Trump different according to Conley was his 'bald attempt to formulate policy, and communicate those policies based solely on mimicking what specific voters thought about selected issues, without any effort to interact or shape those opinions' and with total disregard for the implications and repercussions of those policies. Similarly, Paula Keaveney discusses the implications of the Brexit referendum in Democratic Debate 9.1, noting that while it was 'a democratic triumph' in giving voters a direct say on policy design, it has caused much democratic angst among politicians, parties, the government and the public at large. Criticisms have raged on the potential false nature of claims made by both sides of the campaign, where complex decisions and consequences were reduced to over-simplistic and exaggerated arguments, leaving voters feeling hoodwinked. Otto Eibl also raised concerns in Democratic Debate 2.1 about the impact of effective but problematic marketing exaggerations to uninformed voters in politics. Ultimately, though the wider issues are that voters paid the ultimate price of consumer choice, they have to now live with the implications of the choice they were making, even though they were not aware of them when making their decision.

There are also ethical questions over how political market research is both conducted and used. The use of focus groups in politics has been hotly debated in academic literature because of fears about moderator bias, small sample size and over-influence on product decisions. The way focus groups are run can inhibit rather than facilitate the expression of what the market wants. Savigny (2007, 130) argues that in the case of UK Labour in the 1990s, 'Gould also used focus groups as a site to test his own ideas [r]ather than listening and collecting the opinions of the selected public.' Ethical issues will only grow as the use of PMR expands geographically. For instance, Balla (2017) looks at how the Chinese government is trying to address issues such as transparency, feedback, participation and information disclosure through online consultation because even in a non-democratic country, politicians need to listen and demonstrate palpable outcomes. Democratic Debate 3.1 also highlighted the issues with unethical uses of big data.

Political marketing can encourage more focus on short-term solutions – what the market wants for the next electoral period – rather than what is right for the country in the long term. The market-oriented concept of political marketing may conflict with the need for long-term solutions because there is a conflict between immediate consumer wants and the long-term welfare of citizens. Paré and Berger (2008)'s analysis of the Canadian Conservative's adoption of a market-oriented strategy in the leadup to winning the 2006 election suggests the party avoided discussing contentious policy issues. As Paleologos (1997, 1184) argues, a poll-driven society 'ignores creativity. It overlooks new ideas. It prohibits change and true reform.' Marketing can thus prevent politicians from showing leadership.

Furthermore, it treats voters like consumers, ignoring the ethical and moral aspects of citizenship seen as essential to the effective functioning of society. It can also reduce policy innovation and internal participation because it emphasises the need to develop popular policies and suit voters rather than members. Another problem is how market segmentation enables and encourages politicians to target certain groups whose support they need – rather than represent the public as a whole. This renders the vote of some groups worth more than others, which goes against core democratic principles of equal rights to participate in the electoral process (Savigny 2008).

Arthur Beckman considers how political marketing can result in unfair competition in Democratic Debate 9.2 because the marketplace of ideas is distorted by selective targeting and questionable claims in ads, which alter the receiver's autonomous opinion formation and erode democratic principles. Delivery marketing can also oversimplify the complexities involved in governing, and encourage a focus on only a few areas of policy, which limits debate, as Anna Esselment makes clear in Democratic Debate 8.1.

There is also a general sense that political marketing encourages politicians to lose their authenticity. There is no doubt that by informing product development in response to market demands, marketing exacerbates age-old tensions between doing what is right and winning an election. It emphasises the concern that something may be lost in the attempt to respond to the market, or segments of it, to win control of government.

Using political marketing ethically

Many argue that problems with political marketing are just the same as those with democracy itself. As Mortimore and Gill (2010, 259) argue, 'the weakness here is not in the marketing model but in democracy itself: an MOP is no more than the most efficient expression of the democratic will. If there is a danger here, it does not rest in the possibility that parties might become market-oriented but that the will of the voters might cause market-orientation to lead to wrong choices. In other words, democracy is dangerous because the public is not always right; and we knew that already.'

In reality, politicians rarely just follow what the market wants. Mills (2011, 31–2) argues that anyone who really knows how politics works would know that PMR is 'only a small part of the complex mix of factors that drive political decision-making'. Strategy and market research can be – and often are – utilised by politicians to help them show leadership, to identify and better understand potential opposition to a desired change, find a way to explain and justify a vision to navigate around that opposition, and implement it among the constraints that democratic elections and governing present. Lees-Marshment (2015)'s interviews with political market researchers found that their role was much more constrained, with their views being just one of many inputs that politicians consider before making decisions.

Politicians can also use marketing to help them make room for leadership and to help gain support for new policies. Research-informed communication is used to adapt and communicate policy to gain enough support for change. Goot (1999) detailed how the Australian Liberal-National coalition was able to use polling to inform its desire to implement an unpopular policy – selling off the publicly owned phone company Telstra. Pre-decision-making polling suggested the party would lose votes with the privatisation policy. However, market intelligence also suggested two ways to make the proposal more attractive: it showed strong public concern with public debt and the environment. Coalition leader Howard, therefore, announced that funds from such a sale would go towards reducing the public debt and environmental projects. This made the proposal more appealing to voters concerned about the environment. Goot (1999, 215) concludes that market intelligence 'may be just as effective as a means of working out how to galvanise support, neutralise opposition or convert those who might otherwise be reluctant to see things the party's way'. Similarly, Birch and Petry (2012, 350)'s research found that government public opinion research can help ensure that policy is effective in achieving its goals by informing policy design to suit the reality of behaviour and monitoring policy as it is implemented. Marsh and Fawcett (2012) suggest that branding public policy might bring increased attention to public health issues like HIV/AIDS, or help increase public acceptance and make policy easier to implement.

Research can also help connect elites to under-represented groups and understand the diversity of others. Mills (2011, 35) argues that focus groups with soft and undecided voters 'are a highly effective means of bringing forward the views of voters who are mostly outside any political insider communication channel'. Despite many legitimate concerns raised with Trump's presidency, Ken Cosgrove notes in Democratic Debate 4.1 that the campaign gave a voice to an underserved market. Less controversially but still significantly, Binstock and Davidson's (2012) research in segmentation strategies in the retiree or pensioner segment in the US and UK demonstrated that it can be used by elites to better understand a seemingly homogenous group and thus represent voters more effectively as well as make appropriate decisions for a changing society. Similarly, Democratic Debate 3.1 argued that big data can be used to help government policymakers identify, understand and respond to the public's preferences, interests and objectives.

Voters can be seen as a mixture of citizens and consumers, as political consumers who expect a share of responsibility and blame when things go wrong if they appreciate a link between their own choice and the outcome (Scullion 2008). Political marketing can be used to balance immediate consumer demands and leadership judgment. The close outcomes of recent elections and referenda helps to make clear the importance and influence of voting.

As the internal political marketing chapter noted, research is used to segment the volunteer market and create a range of ways for people to get involved in ways that suit them (Lees-Marshment and Pettitt 2014). As Johnson (2012, 209) noted, over 2 million people participated via MyBo in 2008, and they contributed 400,000 blog postings; 35,000 volunteers were recruited, and they held 200,000 offline events. This gave voters a much greater opportunity to participate; not only can marketing help mobilise them, it can enable them to mobilise themselves. Edward Elder also notes in Democratic Debate 7.1 that relationship and interactive communication can increase deliberation, public participation and democratic engagement in the political process. It can help leaders explain and gain support for difficult decisions and less popular policies. In doing so, it can help them build more trust.

Research into the perspective of political practitioners on political marketing and ethics – which was done in part through 100 interviews with practitioners in the UK, US, Canada, NZ and Australia, including former advisors to world leaders – concluded that winning the political marketing game is about using marketing in a way that blends principle and pragmatism (Lees-Marshment 2011). As the UK Labour strategist Phillip Gould explained in reflecting on ten years of marketing the party both in opposition and government:

> It's absolutely crucial to listen in modern politics, but equally important to lead . . . you have to balance flexibility and resolution . . . The art of . . . modern politics is . . . being able to perfectly blend these two together and to make them work.
>
> (interviewed in Lees-Marshment 2011)

This will then enable political leaders to take voters with them as they try to achieve important change in the interests of society, balancing listening with leading, and forging a more positive relationship of partnership between government and the governed. As Scammell (2014, 185) explains so eloquently:

> The argument is not so much that more marketing is needed, but better marketing. Politicians must sell themselves to us. The point is not to lament that they do so; it is to find ways of encouraging more inclusive marketing, more in tune with democratic ideals.

As many of the authors of the democratic debates in this book note, political marketing can be used as a force for good or it can cause significant problems. It hinges on how it is used. As Miloš Gregor cautions in Democratic Debate 6.1, though, political consultants need to have an ethics of responsibility. Box 9.2 outlines best practice principles for using political marketing ethically: we need to debate and expand on this to produce comprehensive guidelines for practice.

Box 9.2 Best practice principles for using political marketing ethically

1   Use a wide range of market research sources, consultants and methods for all stakeholders, not just voters, including encouraging co-creation of solutions, not just demands, future possibilities for change, not just current wants, and discussing new policy problems and solutions, and long-term needs.

2   Use market research proactively for a range of purposes: to identify new market demands and needs, ensure any decision is informed, encourage reflectiveness, confirm the existing position, check a new direction is gaining support, monitor policy implementation against desired outcomes, identify ways to adjust unpopular but justifiable policies to gain support and, make specific changes or wholesale change.

3   Use segmentation to better understand a complex market: to create new groups in the market, identify and understand under-represented or emerging groups in society, to better understand the diverse needs of existing segments and better understand how to tailor internal offerings to volunteers.

4   Use research to create more effective communication in a range of ways. Among them include checking assumptions, pre-testing, identifying ways to build support for a new policy, highlighting the most popular product aspects and the issues people care most about to focus on, inform, persuade and change behaviour.

5   Use branding and positioning to create distinctive, visionary products, creating choice for voters.

6   Adapt political marketing to suit the candidate and party to maintain authenticity.

Summary

As this book demonstrates, political marketing plays a substantial and significant role in democracies around the world. There are a range of tools and concepts that political organisations and practitioners can draw on to practice political marketing effectively. Marketing influences the policies politicians pursue, the opportunities they give to people to be involved in campaigns and party organisations, the staff they employ, the way they communicate, and the way they govern and lead.

Political marketing is a pervasive force in our lives, impacting on representation, policy, participation, citizenship and leadership. While this raises significant ethical issues, ultimately whether the impact on politics is positive or negative depends on how practitioners choose to use it. On one hand, political marketing can be used to stifle debate, prevent innovation, retain elite power and manipulate public views. On the other, political marketing can also be used to listen effectively, consider diverse needs, create more responsive policies and participation avenues, ensure promises are delivered on in government, and achieve important change that helps societal progress.

Political marketing does not remove the need for effective decision making. However, it can help ensure that those making such choices are better informed. Emphasis should therefore be placed on increasing scholarship, training and awareness of political marketing with all its potential implications so that we encourage a more ethical use of marketing in politics, working towards an agreed code of conduct, rather than simply staying on the sidelines lamenting the marketisation of the political and governmental area.

Democratic Debate 9.1 The Brexit Referendum and the limitations of consumer choice in political decisions

Paula Keaveney (Edge Hill University) Keavenep@edgehill.ac.uk

The UK Brexit referendum of 2016 was on one level a democratic triumph. Against concern about some election turnouts (36 per cent at the previous European Election, 66 per cent at the 2015 general election), this vote saw more than 70 per cent of registered voters take part. (Electoral Commission 2016). This is not as high as the over-80-per-cent turnout at the 2014 Scottish Independence Referendum, but it is high nevertheless in UK modern election terms.

It was a democratic triumph, which ever since has been the cause of much democratic angst.

The vote in favour of leaving the UK led to the resignation of then Prime Minister David Cameron, to arguments within the Labour Party about that party's role in the campaign, to arguments between leading Brexiteers about the way forward, and to the beginnings of demonstrations and campaign set ups calling for a second referendum or an Exit from Brexit. At the time of writing, with only months to go until Article 50 Day (article 50 is the clause in the EU rules which those wanting to leave need invoke) polls are showing shifts of opinion and growing support for the so-called People's Vote, or second referendum.

But why is this?

There was a clear binary choice and a clear 52:48 result. No one could have been unaware of the referendum. And the two official campaign sides – 'Britain Stronger in Europe' and 'Vote Leave' – were given air time and public money so that every citizen could hear the messages.

The UK has a long history of Euroscepticism of one sort or another. Even those supporting EU membership would have to admit the problems. The lack of interest in, and enthusiasm for, the EU was maintained by a mainstream press which showed little or no interest in reporting EU news, coupled with a section of the press which loved to promote alleged EU policies which sounded completely absurd. A recurrent example was the rules on straight bananas. As recently as 2017, an audience member on the BBCs *Question Time* programme said she changed her vote because of the 'silly rules' on bananas. (The EU does have rules about fruit, but you can have as many straight or curved bananas as you like.) It is no coincidence that in the 1970s TV sitcom *Yes Minister*, the hapless Jim Hacker becomes prime minister partly on the back of a campaign to protect the British sausage from the evil EU bureaucrats.

So, the UK was always ready to believe extreme-sounding statements about Europe.

In 2016, that meant the environment for political marketing consisted of an audience with not much knowledge, who were ready to believe extreme statements and who saw a real difference between their own country and Europe. At the same time, the country had been living through austerity and there were on-going debates about migration, about the NHS and about the state of public services.

There is much criticism today of the Leave campaign for not spelling out the actions which would be needed after a Leave vote. While it is right to expect contingency planning by the government, it is questionable whether a campaign group, set up purely for the purposes of a contest, has any role post result. At a general election, we expect the party which campaigns and then wins to be able to go on and govern. The democratic issue with a referendum is that the two official campaign bodies existed solely to fight the referendum. So while a political party, mindful that it might have to put its policies into practice, may rein itself in when making campaign statements, there was no reason for Vote Leave or Stronger In to do this. And Vote Leave, along with the unofficial campaign groups who were also allowed to take part, certainly did not rein itself in.

What this in turn means is that to get across a simple message – Vote Leave – marketers get increasingly outspoken and use exaggeration. Complex argument is replaced by increasingly short and simple statements. Of course, both sides did this. But Vote Leave, playing cleverly on the emotional and cultural side of the debate, were able to do this better.

The famous example is the red bus. Red buses have an iconic status in parts of the UK. Here we had the official Vote Leave bus and its message. It could travel to events. It could be on TV behind interviewees. It could be in photo opportunities up and down the country. And its message was simple: 'We sent the EU £350 million pounds a week. Let's fund the NHS instead. Vote Leave.' Of course, it's all a bit more complicated than that. Some of the money comes straight back from the EU. And there is actually no promise there to give any money to the NHS. It all sounds, though, as if all the country's health problems can be solved with a simple vote on one day in 2016.

Since the vote, there has been criticism of broadcasters for allowing this claim, and others like it, to go unchallenged. The placement of the bus, always in shot, has been particularly attacked. Some have said that the need for broadcasters to be unbiased simply led to programmes permitting statements on both sides with little peak-time fact checking.

Since then, also, the use of data-based campaign techniques by companies such as Cambridge Analytica has thrown a focus on targeting. There is of course nothing wrong with targeting. Marketers do it all the time. But whereas in the older days of politics, messages and opinions could be tested in public at large gatherings, precise targeting removes debate. Victorian Prime Minister William Ewart Gladstone would talk to thousands. Debate and discussion were normal. Views could be changed, but after exchanges and arguments. Today targeting is so precise that one person's received message may not be seen by their neighbour, and campaigners know so much about us that it is easier to manipulate fears and dreams.

In the context of Brexit, this leaves many saying they feel conned. They now realise that neither campaign gave them the full story. They now realise that they didn't properly understand the EU or the implications of staying or leaving. And while this has led to increased activism by some, it has led to increased disillusion among others. There were older people who rarely vote who voted in 2016. They were so unused to the practice that they had to ask what to do. I talked to one of them myself on the way to the polling station. This is the group who, some argue, may decide not to try again.

So how do we find a balance? Politics can't work without marketing. Politicians need to find ways of communicating ideas simply and persuading people of those ideas. Where is the point at which the simplicity becomes lying and the persuasion becomes manipulation?

References

Baldwin, Tom (2018). *Ctrl Alt Delete: How Politics and the Media Crashed our Democracy*. London: Hurst and Co.

Electoral Commission UK. (2016) 'Referendum on the UK's membership of the European Union' web page. www.electoralcommission.org.uk/find-information-by-subject/elections-and-referendums/past-elections-and-referendums/eu-referendum.

Farrell, Jason and Paul Goldsmith (2017). *How to Lose a Referendum: The Definitive Story of Why Britain Voted for Brexit*. London: Biteback Publishing.

Jackson, Daniel, Einar Thorsen and Dominic Wring (eds) (2016). *EU Referendum Analysis 2016: Media, Voters and the Campaign*. Political Studies Association, Loughborough University and Bournemouth University. www.referendumanalysis.eu/.

Oliver, Craig (2016). *Unleashing Demons: The Inside Story of Brexit*. London: Hodder and Stoughton.

Scientists for EU (2016). 'Returning Brexit – it doesn't work as advertised'. YouTube video, published 23 September 2016. www.youtube.com/watch?v=sXVVCT4Jcs8.

Democratic Debate 9.2 Political marketing and unfair competition in politics

By Arthur Beckman (TwoPointEnergy/former adjunct at GWU)

Political marketing can be a force for good. When used in an ethical manner, it can inform citizens and promote political participation. As a practice based on social research, it can help political candidates and public officials understand and become more responsive to citizens. At the same time, it can employ empirically tested methods to manipulate citizens, inflame their attitudes and strategically channel their behaviours in unethical ways.

Democracy is fundamentally a competitive process. Even the most egalitarian theories of democracy demand that political power be sanctioned by equitable competition in a 'marketplace of ideas'. But the competitive tactics political actors use often impinge upon the realisation of other democratic norms; in particular, the requirement that citizens should be able to deliberate about politics autonomously – without being driven, in unscrupulous ways, into taking certain actions or forming certain opinions that would not have been taken or formed otherwise (Beckman 2018). Fair competition in politics, as a normative precept of democracy, therefore demands that citizens not be manipulated and thereby denied a reasonable level of autonomy in opinion formation.

Marketing tactics are often said to be 'manipulative'. There is a vital difference, however, between *manipulation* and *persuasion*, the latter of which must surely be part of any deliberative process – another key feature of democratic governance. Manipulation is the use of coercion, deception or ploys that limit available choices, in the attempt to alter another's opinions or decisions, whereas persuasion is generally defined as the attempt to alter another's opinion in a transparent, intellectually honest and coercion-free fashion. When statements made in marketing communications are manipulative, they deny the receiver a true knowledge of his or her choices and, in so doing, violate the receiver's autonomy. They additionally produce a state of unfair competition and violate democratic principles (Beckman 2018; Le Cheminant and Parrish 2011).

In addition to lying and misrepresentation, selective presentation and targeting of political messages, whether factual or not, can constitute deception. But the goal of all marketing communications is to produce desired responses, and in turn, a competitive advantage. And if a candidate has 30 seconds on television to get his or her message across to promote that candidacy, he or she cannot be expected to provide a 'balanced' perspective in that limited amount of time. The candidate/marketer will necessarily engage in a process of strategically including and excluding information and will give priority to reaching certain audiences in preference to others. Marketers are not constrained, as journalists and scholars are, by the need to present pros and cons. Indeed, few marketers could be expected to spend valuable resources explaining the shortcomings of their offerings. Marketers therefore must be expected to omit much vital information when presenting their brands. Accordingly, this kind of activity should not qualify as wilful manipulation of audiences and can instead be properly conceived of as a marketer dealing with a practicality of communication.

On the other hand, selective presentation of information may constitute lying by omission if it produces a factual misrepresentation as opposed to strategic emphasis. For example, the infamous 'Willie Horton' television commercial in support of US President George H. W. Bush's 1988 campaign pilloried his competitor, Democratic Massachusetts governor Michael Dukakis, for having instituted a prison furlough programme in which, it was said, many individuals who were temporarily released from jail committed violent crimes. The spot neglected to note, however, that the programme was created by Dukakis's Republican predecessor, and that such programmes had been implemented widely across the nation by state governments as well as the US federal government (Hall Jamieson 1992). Here, strategic omission was used to make a highly misleading characterisation of a competitor as opposed to selectively emphasising some fact.

The 2016 American presidential election is notable for tactics that greatly exceeded the bounds of spirited, competitive persuasion and ethical standards, with the widespread use of targeted disinformation supporting the Trump presidential campaign. Here, marketing communications containing false and misleading claims were repeatedly delivered to select audiences identified on the basis of demographics, attitudes and behaviour. Absent countervailing information, the heavy consumption of these kinds of communications can overwhelm the ability of individuals to question or refute them – and the ability of individuals to deliberate autonomously about politics (Faris *et al.* 2017; Gosh and Scott 2018).

Of course, no such thing as perfect personal intellectual autonomy could ever exist, and the notion of completely autonomous thought suggests the ability of a mind to develop and exist in a vacuum which is neither possible nor desirable. But being able to reflect upon one's choices with awareness of what has informed those choices, and to be able to choose among ideas without deception, omission of essential facts or force of imposed habit, is an attainable state. Such an ability is likewise necessary to having a polity made up of citizens exercising free choice and not preferentially engineered behaviour.

At the same time, while marketers may vigorously endeavour to alter relatively autonomous opinions and attitudes, no such thing as a flawlessly effective marketing has ever existed. Finally, it must be said that perfectly ethical marketing does not exist. Therefore, the ethics of political marketing must be considered in practical and not strictly abstract terms.

While marketing is a practice that is defined by responsiveness to consumer preferences, it is primarily designed to produce a result that is advantageous to the marketer. Fortunately, consumers are generally aware that advertising presents a biased perspective when marketing communications are clearly identifiable as such. But media content which is made to appear as bona fide news reporting but is in fact well-placed and highly biased public relations material deceives the consumer and, in turn, violates the consumer's autonomy. 'Fake news', which often takes the form of revenue-generating 'sponsored content' on websites or social media posts meant to look like linked news items from reputable sources, has this effect.

To be able to retain a reasonable degree of intellectual autonomy and navigate biases in the presentation of political information, the consumer of political information must be highly aware of marketing processes and the workings of media and public relations – both the ethical and unethical varieties – which are often complex and driven by arcane technologies. They must additionally be possessed of a very sophisticated level of critical thinking skills not generally available to those who have not been educated in marketing communications, media studies and computer science.

References

Beckman, Arthur (2018). 'Political Marketing and Intellectual Autonomy'. *Journal of Political Philosophy*, 26, no. 1 (2018): 24–46.

Faris, Robert M., Hal Roberts, Bruce Etling, Nikki Bourassa, Ethan Zuckerman and Yochai Benkler (2017). 'Partisanship, Propaganda, and Disinformation: Online Media and the 2016 U.S. Presidential Election'. *Berkman Klein Center for Internet & Society Research Paper*.

Ghosh, Dipayan and Ben Scott (2018). *#digitaldeceit: The Technologies Behind Precision Propaganda on the Internet*. Washington, DC: New America.

Hall Jamieson, Kathleen (1992). *Dirty Politics: Deception, Distraction, and Democracy*. New York: Oxford University Press, 15–42.

Le Cheminant, Wayne and John M. Parrish (2011). *Manipulating Democracy: Democratic Theory, Political Psychology, and Mass Media*. New York: Routledge, 4–24.

References

Allington, Nigel, Philip Morgan and Nicholas O'Shaughnessy (1999). 'How marketing changed the world. The political marketing of an idea: a case study of privatization'. In Bruce Newman (ed.) *The Handbook of Political Marketing*. Thousand Oaks, CA: Sage, 627–12.

Balla, Steven J. (2017). 'Is Consultation the "New Normal?": Online Policy-making and Governance Reform in China'. *Journal of Chinese Political Science*, 22, 375–92.

Barberio, Richard P. and Brian M. Lowe (2006). 'Branding: presidential politics and crafted political communications'. Prepared for delivery at the 2006 Annual Meeting of the American Political Science Association, 30 August–3 September 2006.

BBC (2017). 'The digital guru who helped Donald Trump to the presidency'. *BBC News*, 13 August 2017. www.bbc.com/news/av/magazine-40852227/the-digital-guru-who-helped-donald-trump-to-the-presidency.

Binstock, Robert H. and Scott Davidson (2012). 'Political marketing and segmentation in aging democracies'. In Jennifer Lees-Marshment (ed.) *Routledge Handbook of Political Marketing*. London and New York: Routledge, 20–33.

Birch, Lisa and François Petry (2012). 'The use of public opinion research by government: insights from American and Canadian research'. In Jennifer Lees-Marshment (ed.) *Routledge Handbook of Political Marketing*. New York: Routledge, 342–453.

Braun, Alexander and Anna Matušková (2009). 'Case study 7.2 Czech Republic: Social Democrats strike back'. In Jennifer Lees-Marshment (ed.) *Political Marketing: Principles and Applications*. London and New York: Routledge, 181–3.

Busby, Robert (2012). 'Selling Sarah Palin: political marketing and the "Wal-Mart Mom"'. In Jennifer Lees-Marshment (ed.) *Routledge Handbook of Political Marketing*. New York: Routledge, 218–29.

Conley, Brian Matthew (2012). 'The politics of hope: the democratic party and the institutionalization of the Obama brand in the 2010 mid-term elections'. In Jennifer Lees-Marshment (ed.) *Routledge Handbook of Political Marketing*. New York: Routledge, 124–35.

Conley, Brian M. (2018). 'Thinking what he says: Market research and the making of Donald Trump's 2016 presidential election'. In Jamie Gillies (ed.) *Political Marketing in the 2016 U.S. Presidential Election*. New York: Palgrave Macmillan, 29–48.

Cosgrove, Kenneth M. (2012). 'Political branding in the modern age – effective strategies, tools and techniques'. In Jennifer Lees-Marshment (ed.) *Routledge Handbook of Political Marketing*. New York: Routledge, 107–23.

Cosgrove, Kenneth M. (2018). 'Chapter 4: Trump and the Republican Brand Fresh'. In J. Gillies (ed.) *Political Marketing in the 2016 U.S. Presidential Election*. New York: Palgrave Macmillan, 49–64.

Delacourt, Susan (2016). *Shopping for votes: How politicians choose us and we choose them.* Madeira Park: Douglas and McIntyre.

Downer, L. (2016). *Political Branding Strategies: Campaigning and Governing in Australian Politics.* Basingstoke, UK: Palgrave Macmillan.

Elder, Edward (2016). *Marketing leadership in government: communicating responsiveness, leadership and credibility.* London: Palgrave Macmillan.

Esselment, Anna (2012). 'Market orientation in a minority government: the challenges of product delivery'. In Alex Marland, Thierry Giasson and Jennifer Lees-Marshment (eds) *Political Marketing in Canada*. Vancouver: UBC, 123–38.

French, Alan and Gareth Smith (2010). 'Measuring political brand equity: a consumer-oriented approach'. *European Journal of Marketing*, 44(3–1): 460–77.

Goot, Murray (1999). 'Public opinion, privatization and the electoral politics of Telstra'. *Australian Journal of Politics and History*, 45(2): 214–38.

Gould, P. (1998). 'Why Labour Won'. In I. Crewe, B. Gosschalk and J. Bartle (eds) *Political Communications: Why Labour won the 1997 General Election*. London: Frank Cass, 3–11.

Issenberg, Sasha (2012). *The Victory Lab: The Secret Science of Winning Campaigns.* New York: Crown Publishing Group.

Johnson, Dennis W. (2007). *No Place for Amateurs*, 2nd edition. New York: Routledge.

Johnson, Dennis W. (2012). 'Campaigning in the twenty-first century: change and continuity in American political marketing'. In Jennifer Lees-Marshment (ed.) *Routledge Handbook of Political Marketing*. London and New York: Routledge, 205–17.

Knuckey, Jonathan and Jennifer Lees-Marshment (2005). 'American political marketing: George W. Bush and the Republican Party'. In D. G. Lilleker and J. Lees-Marshment (eds) *Political Marketing: A Comparative Perspective*. Manchester, UK: Manchester University Press, 39–58.

Kruikemeier, Sanne, Minem Sezgin and Sophie C. Boerman (2016). 'Political microtargeting: Relationship between personalized advertising on Facebook and voters' responses'. *Cyberpsychology, Behavior, and Social Networking*, 19(6): 367–72.

Lalancette, Mireille and Vincent Raynauld (2017). 'The power of political image: Justin Trudeau, Instagram, and celebrity politics'. *American Behavioral Scientist*. doi: 0002764217744838.

Lane, Robert W. (1991). *The Market Experience*. Cambridge: Cambridge University Press.

Langmaid, Roy (2012). 'Co-creating the future'. In Jennifer Lees-Marshment (ed.) *Routledge Handbook of Political Marketing*. New York: Routledge: 61–76.

Lees-Marshment, Jennifer (2001). *Political Marketing and British Political Parties: The Party's Just Begun*. Manchester, UK: Manchester University Press.

Lees-Marshment, Jennifer (2011). *The Political Marketing Game*. Houndmills, UK and New York: Palgrave Macmillan.

Lees-Marshment, Jennifer (2015). 'The Democratic Contribution of Political Market Researchers'. *Journal of Public Affairs*, 15(1): 1–10.

Lees-Marshment, J. (ed.) (2018). *Political marketing and management in the 2017 New Zealand election*. Basingstoke, UK: Palgrave Macmillan.

Lees-Marshment, Jennifer and Robin Pettitt (2010). 'UK political marketing: a question of leadership?' In Jennifer Lees-Marshment, Jesper Strömbäck and Chris Rudd (eds) *Global Political Marketing*. London: Routledge, 218–34.

Lees-Marshment, Jennifer and Robin Pettitt (2014). 'Mobilising volunteer activists in political parties: the view from central office.' *Contemporary Politics*, 20(2): 246–60.

Levenshus, Abbey (2010). 'Online relationship management in a presidential campaign: a case study of the Obama campaign's management of its internet – integrated grassroots effort'. *Journal of Public Relations Research*, 22(3): 313–35.

Lilleker, Darren G. (2015). 'Interactivity and Branding: Public Political Communication as a Marketing Tool'. *Journal of Political Marketing*, 14(1/2): 111–28.

Marland, Alex (2012). 'Yes we can (fundraise): The ethics of marketing in political fundraising'. In Jennifer Lees-Marshment (ed.) *Routledge Handbook of Political Marketing*. New York: Routledge, 164–76.

Marland, Alex (2014). 'Chapter 4: The Branding of a Prime Minister: Digital information subsidies and the image management of Stephen Harper'. In Alex Marland, Thierry Giasson and Tamara A. Small (eds) *Political communication in Canada: meet the press and tweet the rest*. Vancouver, BC: UBC Press, 55–73.

Marsh, David and Paul Fawcett (2012). 'Branding public policy'. In Jennifer Lees-Marshment (ed.) *Routledge Handbook of Political Marketing*. New York: Routledge, 329–41.

Mills, Stephen (2011). 'Focus groups: myth or reality'. In Alastair Carthew and Simon Winkelmann (eds) *Political Polling in Asia-Pacific*. Singapore: Konrad Adenauer Stiftung, 27–38.

Mortimore, Roger and Mark Gill (2010). 'Implementing and interpreting market orientation in practice: lessons from Britain'. In Jennifer Lees-Marshment, Jesper Strömbäck and Chris Rudd (eds) *Global Political Marketing*. London: Routledge, 249–62.

Mullen, Andrew (2016). 'Election strategies, campaign themes and target voters'. In D. G. Lilleker and M. Pack (eds) *Political Marketing and the 2015 UK General Election*. Basingstoke, UK: Palgrave 11–34.

Paleologos, David A. (1997). 'A pollster on polling'. *American Behavioral Scientist*, 40(8): 1183–9.

Paré, Daniel J. and Flavia Berger (2008). 'Political marketing Canadian style? The Conservative Party and the 2006 federal election'. *Canadian Journal of Communication*, 33(1): 39–63.

Savigny, Heather (2007). 'Focus groups and political marketing: science and democracy as axiomatic?' *British Journal of Politics and International Relations*, 9(1): 122–37.

Savigny, Heather (2008). 'The construction of the political consumer (or politics: what not to consume)'. In Darren G. Lilleker and Richard Scullion (eds) *Voters or Consumers: Imagining the Contemporary Electorate*. Newcastle: Cambridge Scholars Publishing, 35–50.

Scammell, M. (2014). *Consumer Democracy: The Marketing of Politics*. New York: Cambridge University Press.

Scullion, Richard (2008). 'The impact of the market on the character of citizenship, and the consequences of this for political engagement'. In D. Lilleker and R. Scullion (eds) *Voters or Consumers: Imagining the Contemporary Electorate*. Newcastle: Cambridge Scholars Publishing, 51–72.

Smith, Gareth and Alan French (2009). 'The political brand: a consumer perspective'. *Marketing Theory*, 9(2): 209–26.

Stockemer, Daniel and Mauro Barisione (2017). 'The "new" discourse of the Front National under Marine Le Pen: A slight change with a big impact'. *European Journal of Communication*, 32(2): 100–15.

Turcotte, André (2012). 'Under new management: market intelligence and the Conservative resurrection'. In Alex Marland, Thierry Giasson and Jennifer Lees-Marshment (eds) *Political Marketing in Canada*. Vancouver: UBC, 76–90.

Van Zuydam, Sabine and Frank Hendriks (2018). 'Credibility Enacted: Understanding the Meaning of Credible Political Leadership in the Dutch Parliamentary Election Campaign of 2010'. *Journal of Political Marketing*, 17(3): 258–81.

Winther Nielsen, Sigge (2012). 'Three faces of political marketing strategy'. *Journal of Public Affairs*, 12(4): 293–302.

Young, Sally (2005). 'Government advertising costs us dearly'. *The Age,* 30 August 2005. www.theage.com.au/news/opinion/sally-young/2005/08/29/1125302509121.html (accessed 10 April, 2008).

Index